The Dragon Roars Back

The Dragon Roars Back

TRANSFORMATIONAL LEADERS AND DYNAMICS
OF CHINESE FOREIGN POLICY

Suisheng Zhao

STANFORD UNIVERSITY PRESS

STANFORD, CALIFORNIA

STANFORD UNIVERSITY PRESS
Stanford, California

Printed in the United States of America on acid-free, archival-quality paper

Library of Congress Cataloging-in-Publication Data
Names: Zhao, Suisheng, 1954- author.
Title: The dragon roars back : transformational leaders and dynamics of Chinese foreign policy / Suisheng Zhao.
Description: Stanford, California : Stanford University Press, [2023] | Includes bibliographical references and index.
Identifiers: LCCN 2022012282 (print) | LCCN 2022012283 (ebook) | ISBN 9781503630888 (cloth) | ISBN 9781503634145 (paperback) | ISBN 9781503634152 (ebook)
Subjects: LCSH: Political leadership—China. | China—Foreign relations—1949-
Classification: LCC DS777.8 .Z44 2023 (print) | LCC DS777.8 (ebook) | DDC 327.51—dc23/eng/20220622
LC record available at https://lccn.loc.gov/2022012282
LC ebook record available at https://lccn.loc.gov/2022012283

Cover design: Zoe Norvell

Cover illustration: Shutterstock/9comeback

Typeset by Newgen in Adobe Garamond Pro 11/15

Contents

Abbreviations

ADB	Asian Development Bank
ADIZ	air defense identification zone
AIIB	Asian Infrastructure Investment Bank
APEC	Asian Pacific Economic Cooperation
ASEAN	Association of Southeast Asian Nations
BRFIC	Belt and Road Forum for International Cooperation
BRI	Belt and Road Initiative
BRICS	Brazil, Russia, India, China, and South Africa
CCG	Center for China and Globalization
CCP	Chinese Communist Party
CFAC	Central Foreign Affairs Commission
CFAO	Central Foreign Affairs Office
CICIR	China Institutes of Contemporary International Relations
CIIS	China Institute of International Studies
CMC	Central Military Commission
CPD	Central Propaganda Department
CPSU	Communist Party of the Soviet Union
CPVA	Chinese People's Volunteer Army
CSFM	Community of Shared Future for Mankind

DCS	Dual Circulation Strategy
DPRK	Democratic People's Republic of Korea
EAS	East Asia Summit
EEZ	Exclusive Economic Zone
EU	European Union
FALSG	Foreign Affairs Leadership Small Group
G7	Group of Seven
GLF	Great Leap Forward
IAEA	International Atomic Energy Agency
ICAO	International Civil Aviation Organization
IMF	International Monetary Fund
KMT	Kuomintang
LSG	Leadership Small Group
MFA	Ministry of Foreign Affairs
MFERT	Ministry of Foreign Economic Relations and Trade
MFN	Most Favored Nation
MOC	Ministry of Commence
MSS	Ministry of State Security
NATO	North Atlantic Treaty Organization
NDB	New Development Bank
NDRC	National Development and Reform Commission
NPC	National People's Congress
NPT	Nuclear Non-Proliferation Treaty
NSLSG	National Security Leadership Small Group
NTBT	Nuclear Test Ban Treaty
PLA	People's Liberation Army
PLAN	People's Liberation Army Navy
PMRILSG	Protecting Maritime Rights and Interests LSG
PRC	People's Republic of China
PSC	Politburo Standing Committee
RCEP	Regional Comprehensive Economic Partnership
RMB	Renminbi (Chinese currency)
SCO	Shanghai Cooperation Organization
SOE	state-owned enterprises
SSC	State Security Commission

UFWD	United Front Work Department
UN	United Nations
UNCLOS	UN Convention on the Law of Seas
UNHRC	UN Human Rights Council
UNPKO	UN peacekeeping operation
UNSC	United Nations Security Council
WHO	World Health Organization
WTO	World Trade Organization

The Dragon Roars Back

Introduction

Dynamics of Chinese Foreign Policy: Leaders Matter

[handwritten annotation: Dragon roaring back to regain its glory]

[handwritten annotation in right margin: Century of humiliance]

AN EMPIRE STRETCHING BACK TWO MILLENNIA and symbolized as the dragon from the haven, Imperial China began a steady decline and plunged into wars and revolutions after it was defeated by foreign imperialist powers in the nineteenth century. Now the dragon is roaring back toward the center of the world stage to regain the glory it once enjoyed when the Chinese empire incorporated vast areas into its territories. In 1902, British economist John A. Hobson mapped futures for the twentieth century depending on whether China was broken up, subordinated to a foreign power, or asserted itself as a nation-state. Hobson's insights did not catch much attention throughout the twentieth century, when China suffered through foreign invasions and internal upheavals. But his observation has confronted the world of the twenty-first century.[1]

[handwritten annotation in right margin: hub of global supply chains]

In modern world history, no other rising power has ever experienced China's turbulent history in relations with its neighbors and Western powers, achieved its current scale and central role as the biggest trading nation and hub of global supply chains, and been led by a political leader with Xi Jinping's power and sense of mission to restore China to what he believes is its natural position as a world power. When China was weak, it subordinated to others. Now China is strong, and it wants others to subordinate to China, at least on the issues involving what it regards as core national interests, including its sovereignty claims over Taiwan and territories in the East and South China Seas. The ascendance of China has, therefore, not only alarmed policy-makers in many countries but also prompted scholars to understand how China has reemerged to global power and what forces have shaped its international behavior in the past, now, and possible the future.

Understanding Chinese Foreign Policy Dynamics

Structural realism is used most often to correlate China's relative power and its international behavior. Realist scholars have long warned that as China's relative power expands, its ambition expands. A more powerful China inevitably becomes an anti–status quo power in order to redefine its national interests more expansively. A rising China, like any other rising power, has sought to maximize its share of power; become assertive in its territorial disputes with neighbors; and intensify the rivalry with the immovable United States for regional and global dominance. The rise of China, therefore, has upset the balance of power and sparked power realignments. The power transition theory adds that, in a Sino-US power showdown, the distinct absence of cultural and ideological affinity between the two countries could make the conflict violent.[2]

The linear logic is convenient to help understand China's assertive behavior in the recent decade but cannot adequately explain the dramatic foreign policy turns and shifts since the founding of the People's Republic of China (PRC). The PRC was a revolutionary state led by Mao Zedong when China's relative power was seriously constrained. As table I-1 shows, it took six military operations during the period, including the wars with the United States in Korea and Vietnam, clash with the Soviet Union along the Chinese border, and the war with India. Beijing also competed with the Soviet Union for leadership of world revolutionary movements and supported Maoist revolutionary insurgencies around the world. Deng Xiaoping shifted Chinese foreign policy to emphasize reconciliation and cooperation, although China's relative power was not fundamentally changed. He only engaged one military conflict against Vietnam. Jiang Zemin and Hu Jintao continued Deng's moderate policy and promised peaceful development after China was recognized as a rising power. China was involved in three external operations under their watch. Xi Jinping has hardened the rhetoric and taken a tough foreign policy posture, but China has been involved only in one external conflict, with India in 2020.

Table I-1 PRC Involvement in External Operations

	war	opponents	results
The Era of Mao Zedong (1949–1976)	Korean War (1950–1953)	US-led UN forces	ceasefire
	First Taiwan Strait Crisis (1954–1955)	Taiwan and the US	ceasefire
	Second Taiwan Strait Crisis (1958)	Taiwan and the US	ceasefire
	Sino-Indian War (1962)	India	victory
	Vietnam War (1965–1969)	The US and South Vietnam	partial victory
	Sino-Soviet border conflict (1969)	The Soviet Union	ceasefire
The Era of Deng Xiaoping (1978–1991)	Sino-Vietnamese War (1979)	Vietnam	both sides claimed victory
Jiang Zemin's and Hu Jintao's Years (1991–2012)	Third Taiwan strait Crisis (1996)	Taiwan and the US	ceasefire
	Operation Ocean Shield (2009–2016)	Somali Pirates	victory
	Occupation of Scarborough Shoal (2012)	The Philippines	victory
The Era of Xi Jinping (2012–)	Sino-Indian border conflict (2020)	India	ceasefire

Assigning a determinative role to structural forces in the international system,[3] structural realism ignores the complex process through which China's foreign-policy-makers understand international affairs, identify policy objectives, and make policy decisions. While Chinese leaders must weigh China's relative strength and vulnerability, the change in Chinese power cannot have a direct influence on foreign policy until it is acted upon by Chinese leaders through their ideational lens, decision-making process, and perceptions about the desirability and undesirability of international norms and rules that have guided interactions among states.

The regime-type theory is also used often to attribute China's international behavior to its authoritarian system. This theory argues that authoritarian regimes act more aggressively than democracies because they are based on domination and coercion, and there are fewer constraints on what leaders can do. Because they are in a permanent state of aggression against their people and a constant crisis of regime legitimacy, they are more likely to turn to foreign operations to distract public attention. Leadership change does not matter because foreign policy outcomes stem from the rigid structure of the regime.

Only regime change can bring a fundamental change.[4] The regime-type theory is helpful to understand the arbitrary nature of foreign-policy-making in China but cannot explain why Chinese foreign policy moderated immensely after Mao's death while the authoritarian regime remained.

Other theories have been used, although less often, to understand the dynamics of Chinese foreign policy. Institutionalism tries to find the influences of bureaucratic politics, such as the rise of military interests, on Chinese foreign policy. In the attempt to open the black box of domestic politics, institutionalism has a hard time empirically proving the significant influence, if any, of bureaucratic interests on China's international behavior. Constructivism analyzes how Chinese strategic culture, values, and other norms have helped shape the cognitive environment in which leaders make foreign policy, either aggressively or peacefully. But Chinese foreign policy has experienced many turns while the cognitive environment has not changed as much.[5]

Foreign policy change is a multilevel and complex process. But an empirical investigation of the Chinese foreign policy dynamic and the multilevel driving forces that themselves have undergone profound change since the founding of the PRC has been mysteriously lacking. The few works on interaction between internal and external forces have focused on specific policy decisions or relations with certain countries. Most Chinese foreign policy works have narrowly focused on China's bilateral relationships; involvements in certain geographical regions and multilateral institutions; Chinese diplomacy and foreign-policy-making on certain issue areas or during certain periods; and handling of specific challenges ranging from territorial disputes to energy security, economic policy, and other functional aspects of China's international quests.[6]

This book contributes to the literature by conceptualizing and documenting the critical turns, twists, and course shifts of PRC foreign policy shaped by dynamic internal and external forces. Synthesizing and reexamining existing literature and making use of available primary sources—particularly those in Chinese, such as personal memoirs, government documents, and other publications, verified by field research and personal interviews—this book weaves together complex events, processes, and players and provides a historically in-depth, conceptually comprehensive, and up-to-date analysis of foreign policy dynamics in the PRC.

A Leadership-Centered Framework

Painting a transitional picture, this book develops a leadership-centered framework that integrates multilevel variables to explain the PRC's international behavior. It argues that while leaders matter in all political systems, they matter more in totalitarian and authoritarian systems that allow for the propensity of leaders' ambitions. Political leaders in democracies are constrained by electoral cycles, term limits, and public opinions, but leaders in the PRC's one-party system operate relatively unchecked by bureaucracy, opposition forces, and public opinions.[7] The Chinese Communist Party (CCP), as a Leninist party, emphasizes discipline, hierarchy, and the norm of democratic centralism. Although the stage of Chinese foreign policy has become increasingly crowded over the years, one fundamental aspect that remained constant is the concentration of foreign policy power in the hands of the leaders at the apex of the party-state. They possess an almost untrammeled monopoly of power with the ultimate decision-making authority on national security and strategic policies.

The emerging literature on leadership in foreign-policy-making has focused on leaders' cognitive attributes such as personality, bounded rationality, leadership style, and perception and image of the outside world to reveal the incongruities between perceived and real operational environments.[8] The cognition process is important for understanding specific decisions but not adequate to understand foreign policy transformation.[9] Going beyond the effect of personal traits and cognition on specific decisions, this book examines how transformational leaders have not only operated within but also reshaped the large political and institutional environment to define priorities and put policy into practice .

The PRC has been led by five generations of leaders: Mao Zedong, Deng Xiaoping, Jiang Zemin, Hu Jintao, and Xi Jinping, according to the current official count. This count leaves out Hua Guofeng, Hu Yaobang, and Zhao Ziyang, who all held top party-state positions and attempted to change policy direction but failed because they lost power in the jungle of CCP politics. The five leaders who survived have not exercised the same amount of personal power and official authority or made the same level of influence. Mao Zedong, Deng Xiaoping, and Xi Jinping are transformational leaders; each held—or in the case of Xi, currently holds—lifetime tenure in power and set a unique

[handwritten: transactional leaders]

course of foreign policy. Jiang Zemin and Hu Jintao were transactional leaders and stayed on a course set by Deng Xiaoping.

Mao Zedong led revolutionary diplomacy to break through the isolation, containment, and encirclement of the hostile imperialist powers from 1949 to 1978. Deng Xiaoping formulated developmental diplomacy to create a favorable international environment to jump-start economic growth from 1978 to 2012. Xi Jinping has reoriented Chinese foreign policy since 2012 to return China to the position of global centrality. One Chinese scholar characterized Xi's reorientation as "the change from ordinary state diplomacy to big-power diplomacy, from weak-posture diplomacy to strong-posture diplomacy, and from a passive diplomacy to a proactive diplomacy."[10] Amending the PRC constitution in 2018 to abolish the term limit on his presidency for a lifetime tenure in office, Xi Jinping will chart the course of Chinese foreign policy for a long period. These transformational leaders have played a key role to bring about the changes in Chinese foreign policy priorities, defensive or offensive posture, the pattern of engagement with the rest of the world, alignment with the major powers, and relations with its neighbors. In the Chinese official parlance, Mao led China standing up (站起来); Deng made China rich (富起来), and Xi will make China strong (强起来).

The literature of leadership has featured transformational leaders as providing new visions and appealing to followers' higher ideals and moral values. In contrast, transactional leaders focus on policy implementation and rely on the "hard power" resources of carrots and sticks and motivate their followers by the "exchange" of interest.[11] The transformational leaders in the PRC must have new visions and have appealed to higher ideals to inspire followers, but they have relied more on the hard power of arbitrary authorities to ensure compliance. More importantly, they have combined personal power (charisma) and office authority to make their visions prevail. Additionally, they have effectively made political use of ideational forces, tailored bureaucratic institutions, exploited international power distribution, and responded strategically to international norms and rules to become game changers.

Mao Zedong: A Revolutionary Crusader

Mao Zedong believed that the PRC was born in an era of imperialism; the themes of the era were war and revolution because when imperialism existed, war was inevitable and would inevitably lead to revolution.[12] Downplaying

[handwritten left margin: Xi's reorientation of diplomacy/FP]
[handwritten left margin: transformational vs transactional leaders]
[handwritten right margin: transformational leaders]
[handwritten right margin: characterization of transformational leaders]

[handwritten: themes: war & revolution]

traits of transformational leaders

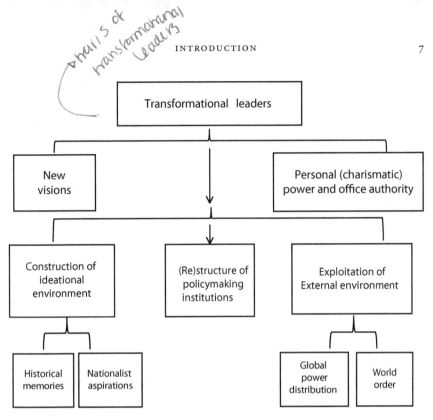

CHART I-I   A Leadership-centered Framework

Mao's FP style

the imperialist powers and nuclear weapons as "paper tigers", Mao was never hesitated to confront hostile foreign powers for the PRC border and regime security.

Demonstrating his exceptional ability during the revolution, Mao established strong charisma as the founder of the PRC. Although he was not immersed in the day-to-day decisions and delegated routine matters to his trusted lieutenant, Premier Zhou Enlai, he was a crusader to stifle all opposition and dissent and did not hesitate to challenge institutional and other constraints, and made critical decisions alone if necessary. Holding power for a lifetime, Mao did not tolerate any comrades daring to challenge his authority and policy and purged them ruthlessly. He even launched the Cultural Revolution to destroy the entire party-state apparatus that, he believed, had come against his policy.

goal of cultural revolution

As elaborated in chapter 1 of this book, Mao's resolve, despite the considerable doubt and opposition from his colleagues, was decisive for Beijing to enter the Korean War in 1950. Mao also dominated China's decision in the Sino-Soviet split. Mao's displeasure over Nikita Khrushchev's denouncement of

Joseph Stalin at the Twentieth Congress of the Communist Party of the Soviet Union (CPSU) in February 1956 sent the first sign of the Sino-Soviet conflict. When the congress opened, Premier Zhou Enlai read a message from Mao that praised the CPSU as created by Vladimir Lenin and reared by Stalin. Ten days later, Khrushchev denounced Stalin. Not only was Moscow's apparent lack of previous consultation with Beijing embarrassing to the Chinese delegation, but Khrushchev's bitter denunciation of Stalin's cult of personality also exasperated Mao, whose rule had many features in common with Stalin's. Mao's private doctor from 1954 to 1976 confirmed that "Khrushchev's speech was a watershed . . . Mao never forgave Khrushchev for attacking Stalin."[13] After the split, Mao personally wrote the open letters of the CCP in the ideological battles against the CPSU.

The Sino-Soviet split put China in a possibly dangerous position of fighting wars with both superpowers. Mao made the strategic decision of alignment with the United States, an outcome of Mao's dramatic personal struggle between promoting the world revolution and rethinking China's security strategy. Aspiring to be the leader of the world revolution against imperialism, Mao made the switch because he was disappointed over the lack of momentum in the world revolution. Chinese-supported insurgencies and military struggles in Third World countries failed to produce appreciable results. The Soviet Union and many communist parties of the world no longer followed Marxism-Leninism. The CCP shouldered the heavy responsibility of promoting and assisting the world revolution, only to witness a single spark did not ignite a prairie fire. Baffled by the US ping-pong team's request to visit China, the Foreign Ministry declined the request on April 3, 1971, claiming "the US leftists and dignitaries have not yet visited China." Premier Zhou could not make his mind and submitted the request to Mao for final approval. Mao pondered his decision for three days and endorsed the Foreign Ministry's decision. After sending the report back to the Foreign Ministry, however, he changed his mind and approved the visit. The "Ping-Pong Diplomacy" opened the Sino-US rapprochement.[14]

Deng Xiaoping: A Pragmatic Strongman

Deng Xiaoping proclaimed peace and development rather than war and revolution as the themes of the era and was determined to avoid war with

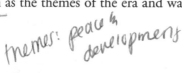

the superpowers. He proposed anti-hegemonism, national reunification, and modernization as China's "three grand historical goals" in his 1980 speech,[15] but he rearranged the order in 1982 to place modernization first and declared, "Our strategy in foreign affairs is to seek a peaceful environment for four modernizations" to recover from the fallout of the Cultural Revolution and rebuild legitimacy for the party.[16] Deng opened China to the outside world to learn from the positive experiences of advanced countries but maintained China's independent position between the two superpowers during the Cold War. Demonstrating the flexibility to adjust course, Deng formulated the low-profile principle to minimize external attention and bide China's time through the shadow of Tiananmen and difficult post–Cold War years.

A veteran communist leader and talented administrator, Deng was a pragmatic strongman and consensus builder receptive to new information; he reacted to practical issues and challenges, respected constraints, and tried to accomplish his goals through a gradual process.[17] He was purged twice by Mao but reemerged as a member of the Politburo Standing Committee (PSC), vice-chairman of the Central Military Commission (CMC), vice-premier, and People's Liberation Army (PLA) chief of staff after Mao's death. Never holding the top party or government positions, he placed his protégés as the party general secretary and premier and became the paramount leader behind them. Deng's authority derived from his personal stature, connections, and breadth of experience.

Suffering during the Cultural Revolution, Deng realized that the lack of effective institutions and checks on arbitrary authority had helped bring about disasters in the Mao years.[18] He started institutionalization of decision-making and leadership politics, including regular party and state decision-institution meetings, and a constitutionally mandated two-term limit for the top leaders and mandatory retirement age for all officials. Deng also promoted collective leadership in which a group of senior leaders jointly made decisions. Retaining the privilege over key national security decisions throughout his reign but delegating power to bureaucrats to make routine decisions, he ratified them if they reached consensus and stepped in if they could not.

Actively involved in building relations with the United States, Japan, and other major countries, Deng took personal charge of the final negotiation on normalizing the diplomatic relationship with the United States because he realized that "all countries that have a good relationship with the United States have become rich."[19] His vision and pragmatism were crucial in the breakthrough. On the most difficult issue, Taiwan, while the United States accepted Deng's three conditions—withdrawal of US military forces from Taiwan; termination of the US-Taiwan Mutual Security Treaty; and severance of diplomatic relations with Taiwan—it could not commit to the ending of arms sale and the termination of the US-Taiwan Mutual Security Treaty on time for normalization. Deng agreed to establish diplomatic relations one year before the termination of the treaty and without Washington's commitment to terminate arms sales to Taiwan. Deng's concession was not without controversy within the party. Former foreign minister Huang Hua revealed that, in the winter of 1982, the CCP central leaders received a report complaining that China's policy toward the United States was wrong. Deng wrote in the report that "I am presiding over the work on the United States. If there are problems, I take full responsibility."[20] Deng's authority and determination pushed the policy through.

Shifting the policy priority away from preparing for war to focusing on economic growth, Deng made another significant but controversial decision in 1985 to dramatically cut one million troops and the military budget as a percent of GDP, reduce the number of military regions from eleven to seven, open many bases, ports, and airfields to civilian use, and order defense factories to switch part of their production to consumer goods. The action caused intense personal feelings among the top ranks of military officers. But Deng's personal involvement ensured execution of the tough policy reorientation.[21]

Jiang Zemin and Hu Jintao: Transactional Leaders

Jiang Zemin and Hu Jintao were handpicked by Deng Xiaoping as successors. Continuing Deng's policy line, Jiang made Deng's low-profile guidance public at his meeting with a US Congress delegation in Beijing in November 1992.[22] Although Chinese power rose significantly after the 2008 global financial crisis, defying the prediction of structural realism, Hu did not waver on Deng's low-profile policy and was committed to peaceful development.

They played the role of the paramount leaders primarily as the officeholders of the CCP general secretaries. Preserving the newly established term limit, they served only two terms and followed the rules of collective leadership to build consensus. Jiang formalized the rules of collective leadership as individual preparation (个别酝酿), division of responsibility (分工负责), and decisions at meetings (会议决定).[23] Significant issues were discussed among all members of the leadership, information was prepared and distributed, opinions were exchanged in advance, and important decisions were reached at formal meetings.

As first among equals of the Politburo Standing Committee (PSC) members, Jiang and Hu had the foreign and security policy portfolio as their responsibilities. Other PSC members respected their policy preferences in exchange for the general secretary's support of their preferences on issues under their purview. Without a foreign and national security policy-making portfolio, they did not have a special interest in these issues. Deference to the general secretary was politically expedient. Additionally, the collective leadership was confined to the strategic issues brought to the PSC. Routine and daily foreign and security matters were primarily the responsibility of the general secretary.[24]

As many new and complex foreign policy issues emerged that required professional and specialized knowledge, they relied on advisors, bureaucrats, and experts to provide information and intelligence and draw on broad knowledge and experience. Foreign policy decisions were no longer made with a vertically fundamental unity but a reflection of different horizontal interests coordinated at the center.[25] Their transactional style diminished the degree to which decisions were personalized and arbitrary and helped the continuity of Deng's developmental diplomacy, making China's international behavior pragmatic and predictable.

Xi Jinping: A Supreme Leader

Touting his "China Dream" of Great Rejuvenation, Xi Jinping has elicited a nostalgic conception of a historically resplendent China that, after long and miserable travail, is now on the verge of recapturing its lost grandeur and centrality in the world as an admired and benevolent empire. Pledging to return China to the pinnacle of the past, Xi declared the arrival of a new era in which profound changes unseen in a century created the opportunity for China's inevitable rise. Putting forward a series of proposals and initiatives such as the Community of Shared Future for Mankind and the New Type of

International Relations, Xi has brought China's external relations to a new height of activism and presented himself as the leader absorbing unprecedented global respect and expanded China's global reach as a linchpin for the Great Rejuvenation.

Calling for the fighting spirit to proactively shape the external environment rather than passively reacting to it, Xi has steered Chinese foreign policy gingerly beyond low-profile position and asserted China's interests to prevail even at the expense of appearing the villain. Chinese diplomats have been turned into warriors to win diplomatic battles. China's peaceful development is now contingent upon other countries' respect for China's core national interests.[26] Behaving as a muscle-flexing big power, China no longer bends to America's pressure and accommodates its interests without conditions and works assiduously to dominate its periphery. Although the ingredients and the strategic rationale for China's assertive behavior were already built up by his predecessors, Xi's vision helped seize the opportunity to capitalize on China's clout and bolster China's big power position. Such things as the Belt and Road Initiative (BRI), the Asian Infrastructure Investment Bank (AIIB), and the artificial island buildup in the South China Sea would not have happened if a different leader were in his place.

Assuming the CCP general secretary at the 18th Party Congress in 2012, Xi convinced his colleagues to reduce the size of the PSC from nine to seven members to enhance his decision-making ability. A series of scandal cases involving Politburo members revealed shortly before the Party Congress gave Xi an opportunity to launch an anticorruption campaign and purge political rivals to instill fear in the bureaucratic hierarchy. The campaign also helped increase his popular appeal by combatting the reviled scourge of official graft and political privilege. Eliminating the factional pluralism that his predecessors had tolerated, he locked-down prominent rivals, including Bo Xilai, a Politburo member armed with a strong personal network among princelings; Ling Jihua, a member of PSC very close to Hu Jintao; and Zhou Yongkang, a Politburo member in charge of the Central Political and Legal Affair Committee.

Xi could not have dramatically consolidated power without the consent of the ruling elite who had complained that the Hu leadership was too weak and the factional makeup of collective leadership too divisive to curb massive corruption and ineffectiveness of governance, establish civilian authority over the military, and push through contested reforms. Coping with the unprecedented challenges and severe threats of the scale that led to the collapse of the Soviet Union, the party-state might collapse if they did not support an all-powerful leader to break through the logjams and rein in special interests.[27]

As a shrewd visionary and purposeful leader with strong motives and political wisdom, Xi has augmented his personal authority in the name of unified party leadership by the adoption of a series of new rules guiding the interactions among the top leaders, such as "The CCP Politburo's Regulations on Strengthening and Maintaining the Party Center's Centralized and Unified Leadership" and the "Code on Seeking Instructions and Reporting on Important Matters." The stated goal of these rules is to tighten the organizational discipline of the party-state. In practice, they have recentralized the policy-making authority to the party center, with Xi as the core, and established personal loyalty to Xi as the most important political principle.[28]

Starting a performance-review system that grades leaders on loyalty to the party as the top metric in 2018, Xi has required all other Politburo members, including PSC members, to make annual work reports (述职) in writing to him on behalf of the party center. The Politburo work report system was initially established by Hu Jintao in 2003 for the Politburo as an institution reporting its work to the Central Committee as part of Hu's efforts to promote democracy within the party. Xi changed the system and required party members who held the top party and government positions to submit their work reports to him on behalf of the Party Central Committee. In addition, all party members must maintain "four consciousnesses" (四个意识) to line up (看齐) with him and practice the "two safeguards" (两个维护) of Xi as the core of the leadership and as the unrivaled leader of the party's Central Committee. The phrases "four consciousnesses" and "two safeguards" have become a standard political language in government and CCP documents and led to numerous officials publicly declaring fealty to Xi.

No longer first among equals, Xi has dismantled the norm of reaching a consensus in decision-making. With Xi as the strongman at the top, collective leadership has become a remote memory. Effectively creating a cult of personality, Xi pushed through a resolution on the CCP history at the Sixth Plenum of the Nineteenth Party Congress in 2021 to introduce "Xi Jinping Thought" as "Marxism for the 21st century" and extoll his accomplishments as an epoch-making leader who did what his predecessors wanted but could not: achieved party unity and discipline and started a new era in which China becomes a prosperous society and a global power. China's state-run media were awash with articles blatantly glorifying Xi's leadership before and after the plenum. This is the third such resolution in CCP history. The first one, in 1945, sealed Mao Zedong's status as the definitive party leader. The second one, in 1981, admitted fault by the party, including the horrors of the Cultural Revolution, to pave the way for Deng Xiaoping's market-oriented reform. Given Mao's lamentable record in the cult of personality, many Chinese people still have an appetite for the strong, omnipotent leader because Xi's appeals match the mood of the times in China, one of renewed nationalism, confidence, and self-assertion.

Important power balances in the CCP elite politics existed before: between Mao Zedong and Liu Shaoqi, between Deng Xiaoping and Chen Yun, between immortal retirees and frontline leaders. Running the country without interfering with elders or any credible rivals, Xi has become as untouchable as Joseph Stalin or Mao Zedong after the brutal purges each carried out during the Great Terror and the Cultural Revolution, respectively. Expressing his leadership temperament and impatient with the incremental bureaucratic process, Xi has proposed the top-level design (顶层设计) to develop strategic visions, conduct strategic planning, and make tough decisions. Taking personal charge of all-important leadership positions and policy matters he cares about, big and small, he has become a supreme leader of micromanagement.

Xi personally approved and followed through a deal with Washington to ensure the safe return of Huawei CFO Meng Wanzhou in 2021 after nearly three years of detention in Canada and personally made the last-minute decision to cancel fintech giant Ant Group's public offering in late 2020. After giving detailed instructions on improving public toilets, he was praised for leading a "Toilet Revolution"; he required artists and writers to practice morality and decency, have good taste, and be responsible, honest, and clean.[29] He personally planned, proposed, deployed, and promoted many policy decisions because he believed that many officials were not competent to deal with complicated issues, and little would get done if he didn't issue so many instructions.[30]

Xi has taken a strong personal interest and devoted an equal amount of time and energy to foreign affairs.[31] Energetically informing Chinese people of their country's success, Xi traveled all over the world, received visiting foreign

potentates, and ushered in new initiatives, concepts, and discourse with dazzling speed before the pandemic started in 2020. During his first five years in
office, he flew over 350,000 miles, with an accumulated traveling time of 198
days, visited more than fifty-seven countries and international organizations
on five continents, and delivered more than one hundred speeches. Before
each visit, Xi's office prepared an article to be published in the mainstream
media of the target country to "make China's voice heard."[32]

Becoming the first Chinese leader to outpace his American counterpart
in quantity, duration, and breadth of presidential trips to foreign countries,
Xi averaged 14.3 foreign visits annually and spent around 34 days abroad
before 2020, notably surpassing his US counterparts Barack Obama's annual
visits to 13.9 countries and 25 days of foreign travel and Donald Trump's 12.3
countries and 23 days abroad.[33] Although COVID-19 interrupted full-throttle
presidential trips, Xi kept an active schedule of phone and video meetings with
foreign leaders. Attending over 20 multilateral conferences via video link, Xi
had more than 80 phone calls and virtual meetings with foreign leaders in
2021. In Chinese media, Xi's "cloud diplomacy" (云外交) was accorded with
a similar level of prominence as past foreign visits. Chinese people read and
watched Xi's busy schedule of diplomatic meetings every day and could not
tell the difference between his in-person trips and his virtual ones.[34]

Shaping Ideational and Institutional Conditions

In addition to their visions and power/authority, transformational leaders have
effectively manipulated ideational forces and policy institutions to empower
their policy agendas. Ideationally, they have constructed historical memories
and exploited nationalist aspirations to shape public opinions. Selectively
remembering the glory of the imperial past and the national trauma of modern humiliation, they have drawn historical lessons to help unite the Chinese
people. One most important lesson is that "the backward will be beaten" and
"the weak state cannot have diplomacy" in the Darwinist world.[35]

Taking this lesson, Mao Zedong populated the narrative of self-reliance
to make China completely independent so that no external powers could
humiliate China again. Deng Xiaoping attempted to make China prosper
to eventually beat the Western powers. Celebrating the continuous greatness
of imperial China based on the reinvented Chinese benevolent normative
hierarchy, Xi Jinping has called for the "self-reliance and self-strengthening"

glory of selective memory of
of imperial past to century of humiliation

(自立自强) to make China the strongest nation in the world. He has used the memory of past splendor to create an imperial nostalgia as a master narrative to legitimize China's global centrality as a natural continuity of history.

Mao and Deng used the memory of national trauma to promote a strong sense of victimization and righteousness in foreign affairs. Although China has become a big power and cannot be humiliated by any foreign country, the conviction that China is denied the "rightful place" has focused much of Xi's foreign policy agenda on overcoming the legacy of a century of humiliation, including consolidating Beijing's rule in former foreign colonies of Macao and Hong Kong and winning back the lost territories of Taiwan and the islands in the East and South China Seas.

Nationalism is another ideational force manipulated by Chinese leaders. Mao's revolutionary diplomacy was wrapped with communist rhetoric but followed nationalist instincts. Deng and his protégés openly exploited nationalism to build broad-based national support for developmental goals. Chinese nationalism has been driven not only by the state from the top-down but also by popular forces from the bottom-up. While the state-led nationalism was primarily affirmative and emphasized an exclusive and positive "us" during Jiang Zemin and Hu Jintao's years, popular nationalism was emotional and assertive. Making sure that the emotional popular nationalism did not disrupt developmental objectives, Jiang and Hu controlled the expression of popular nationalism and followed a prudential policy based on Deng's sober assessment of China's domestic and global challenges.

Inflaming nationalist sentiments to rally Chinese people, Xi Jinping has called for a patriotic struggle against Western powers and values, producing a state-led popular nationalism that has targeted the negative "others." With a deeply-rooted suspicion of the Western powers, this nationalist perspective has reacted stridently to all perceived slights to China's national pride and interests, making Chinese foreign policy combative.

While the political parties and leaders in electoral democracies must rely on the expertise of bureaucracies to translate their foreign policy visions into tangible action, and thereby are subject to bureaucratic constraints,[36] the CCP holds the direct and ultimate authority over the government and foreign policy bureaucracy. The primary role of bureaucracy is information gathering and analysis, policy implementation, and recommendations for the CCP leaders.

Chinese foreign policy bureaucracy has been growing vastly. The central issue for the leaders has been how to coordinate it for their policy agendas. Each transformational leader has structured the bureaucratic institutions in his own way.

In the name of strengthening the party leadership, Mao Zedong created the CCP Central Foreign Affairs Leadership Small Group (LSG) to centralize the foreign policy bureaucracies. As an increasing number of agencies in the state, party, and military developed stakes in foreign affairs and new players have emerged in the 1980s, Deng Xiaoping decentralized decision-making authorities and oversaw the pluralization and professionalization of Chinese foreign policy bureaucracy. Xi has recentralized the authority over bureaucratic institutions and personalized China's big power diplomacy. Staking his claim to power on the party in a way that none of his predecessors could, Xi Jinping has strengthened the coordinating institutions and set up new LSGs with himself as the head to bypass entrenched interests and cut through bureaucratic roadblocks.

As a result, Chinese bureaucrats have performed only for the audience of the supreme leader, who does not want to admit any mistakes or hear anything that contradicts his views. His colleagues and subordinates who dare to criticize or disagree with his policy have been labeled "arbitrarily against the center" (妄议中央) and punished accordingly. In this process, he has enlarged Chinese diplomacy far beyond the traditional diplomats by elevating the Communist Party diplomacy and asserting his authority over military diplomacy. If anything happens to Xi, China would have a weakened institutional ability to manage the distribution of interests and factional rivalry, and consequently foreign-policy-making. The uncertainty may cause it to release political pressure through international aggression because leaders tend to rally domestic support for an aggressive foreign policy when a succession crisis occurred in a nationalistic domestic environment.

Exploiting External Environment

Creating ideational and institutional supports, transformational leaders have strategically exploited the global distribution of power and the rule and norms of world order. Mao Zedong took advantage of the heightened bipolar rivalry between the United States and the Soviet Union and made flexible alignment to reduce security threats. Deng Xiaoping played the game of the strategic triangle, in which China acted as the much-coveted balancing third force. Resisting the posited US unipolar moment after the Cold War, Deng's protégés appealed to opponents of US hegemony and pushed for a multipolar world. After the global financial crisis of 2008, which seriously damaged the economies of the United States and other Western powers, Chinese leaders were flattered by the G2 concept but avoided endorsing it because they did not believe the United States was ready to share global leadership with China.

Narrowing the power gap with the United States and widening the gap with the rest, China has become a global power with interests spanning its regions and beyond and built the capacity to act on them to challenge US hegemony. As the Sino-US strategic rivalry has affected virtually every aspect of international politics and caused significant global power realignment, Xi Jinping has constructed an "anti-hegemonic" coalition with Russia and Iran that has shared the sentiments against US hegemony and made every effort to lessen China's economic and technological dependence on the United States. Although China cannot achieve hegemony any time soon, Xi has attempted to place China as an indispensable power in the emerging bipolar competition.

Transformational leaders have also pondered if they are discontented to overhaul or contented to preserve the post–World War II world order constructed under US leadership. Although China's relative power was constrained, Mao Zedong's revolutionary diplomacy attempted to overthrow the US-led order because it excluded the newly founded PRC. Deng Xiaoping's developmental diplomacy benefited immensely from the liberal rules and norms underpinning the order. China became a stakeholder. A powerful China under Xi, however, has become a revisionist state demanding the reform of the order that has conformed American values and helped project American power. Rejecting Western values as universal, challenging US dominance in international institutions, and taking an à la carte approach to reforming the order, China has launched new initiatives such as the Asian Infrastructure Investment Bank (AIIB) and supported international economic institutions that served its interests, turned others to its purposes, and weakened the human rights regimes that might pose a challenge to its values.

existential threat to post WWII order?

The alarmists have, therefore, warned that China's rise and objection to liberal values have amounted to an existential threat to the post–World War II order. But the world has not rushed into a China-led order because China can hardly mobilize enough resources to provide sweeping global public goods or offer alternative values universally accepted to rewrite the rules of the order. *hmmm not rushed n Chinese alternative?* Remaining a beneficiary, China is a revisionist stakeholder and has primarily aimed at advancing its status in the hierarchy of the international system rather than a wholesale rejection of the existing order. While US global leadership has been challenged, China has not demonstrated the global leadership or worked with the United States to meet the global challenges. With the power vacuum, the world faces an uncertain future.

Structure of the Book

This introduction to the scope and central argument of the book is followed by three parts and a conclusion. The first part is composed of three chapters to explore the roles of Mao Zedong, Deng Xiaoping, and Xi Jinping in setting foreign policy courses during the three periods of PRC history. The second part includes three chapters to examine how these leaders have manipulated the ideational forces and restructured foreign policy institutions for their policy agenda. The third part has two chapters to analyze how these leaders strategically exploited the external environment. The conclusion wraps up the book and explores the what's next question in the context of growing Sino-US rivalry to help extend and augment the relevance of the book moving forward.

PART ONE

Setting Foreign Policy Priorities

1

Mao Zedong's Revolutionary Diplomacy
Keeping the Wolves from the Door

WHEN THE PRC WAS FOUNDED IN 1949, the Soviet-American wartime alliance had collapsed into a bipolar Cold War. China's relations with the two superpowers constituted the central security challenge. As the architect of foreign and security strategy, Mao Zedong identified the United States as the principal threat that not only sought to deny the legitimacy of the CCP regime but also encircled the PRC with its allies and a series of military bases and provided the rival Kuomintang (KMT) government in Taiwan with economic and military assistance. Mao, therefore, set the course for Chinese foreign policy as a continuation of revolution against foreign imperialism. Winning the war against Japanese imperialists and the civil war over the KMT regime, Mao believed that the CCP-led revolution was a raging torrent supported by Chinese people and revolutionary forces overseas. His confidence was expressed in the statement that US imperialist power might appear strong and fierce but was merely made of papers destined for the dustbin of history. Acting upon the beliefs that "the East wind was prevailing over the West wind," Mao's revolutionary rhetoric was militant, intransigent, and aggressive.

But Mao was a shrewd strategist keenly aware of the threats from the hostile US power attempting to strike the PRC down. Downplaying the United States as a paper tiger, Mao merely claimed that the imperialist powers were transient. They were both real and paper tigers at the same time. Strategically this tiger must be "despised" but tactically be taken seriously because it had eaten tens of millions of people and could continue to eat people in the future.[1] Preparing to fight tenaciously against the enemy, Mao interpreted the foreign threats in a sinister light and sometimes even exaggerated foreign threats to mobilize domestic support to roll back the US imperialism.

Taking American diplomatic isolation, economic embargo, and military encirclement seriously and believing war with imperialists was inevitable and imminent, Mao decided to lean toward the Soviet Union as the counterweight to the US threat. The Sino-Soviet alliance changed the global geopolitical landscape and extended the Cold War to Asia. Worrying the US-led United Nations (UN) forces might invade China after the Korean War broke out, Mao convinced his colleagues to enter Korea and fight the United States.

The result of the Korean War secured China's northeast border but deferred China's military takeover of Taiwan because the war reversed the United States' prior determination to stay out of the Chinese civil war and established the American protection for Taiwan that has endured in one form or another through the current day. Mao thereby designed a "Noose Policy" to maintain the ties between Taiwan and the mainland. The fallout from the Korean War also significantly reduced Beijing's freedom of action and room for maneuvers. Confronting the US economic and political blockade, Beijing's dependence on the Soviet Union was heightened. Increasingly uncomfortable as a junior brother, Mao redefined the relationship to diminish Beijing's dependence, eventually leading to the Sino-Soviet split. Facing the Soviet military buildup along the borders when the United States was preoccupied in Vietnam, Mao made a strategic decision to align with the US and build an International Anti-Soviet United Front. The Sino-US rapprochement brought a power re-alignment in East Asia in favor of Beijing. Without abandoning revolutionary rhetoric, Mao's balance-of-power maneuvers served his foreign policy priorities of the regime and border security.

Reluctant Alliance and Missed Opportunity

The founding of the PRC marked the beginning of a unified China on the mainland under a single authority to mobilize resources for the reconstruction for the first time since the collapse of the Qing dynasty. Running the world's most populous country, the CCP leadership confronted an array of pressing problems. Industrial production after more than a decade of war had fallen to roughly half of its prewar peak and agricultural output was down by a quarter. Hyperinflation also gathered momentum.[2] Confronting the US-backed KMT forces in Taiwan that vowed to retake the mainland, the new regime had to build a nationwide state hierarchy, restore social order, suppress the armed resistance from the KMT forces left on the mainland, secure border regions, and take control of Tibet and Taiwan.

Under these imperatives, Mao sought Soviet economic and military assistance. Although the excessive dependence on the Soviet Union was hardly desirable, the potential gain for Chinese security far outweighed the risks. An exclusive alliance with the Soviet Union was not Mao's first choice because the Soviet Union and CCP had never worked hand in glove before the founding of the PRC. Repeatedly giving Chinese comrades self-serving advice, Stalin took a two-pronged policy to assist both the KMT and the CCP in the 1920s. Moving the Soviet forces into northeast China to accept the Japanese surrender, Stalin signed the Treaty of Friendship and Alliance with the KMT government in 1945. Cooperating with the CCP to take large stockpiles of weapons and ammunition surrendered by the Japanese in Manchuria, Stalin remained apprehensive about an all-out CCP drive to seize power because he did not want a strong and unified China, which might contain Soviet expansion.[3]

Cabling Mao twice in late August 1945 and shrewdly employing a policy of "divide and rule," Stalin proposed the region north of the Yangtze be ruled by the CCP and the area south by the KMT. According to Wang Jiaxiang, the first Chinese ambassador to the Soviet Union, Stalin's policy was not because he underestimated the CCP, but because he feared communist China's independent stance and future competition with the Soviet Union.[4] A weak and divided China would be a better buffer against the United States while not posing a threat to the USSR. Soviet Deputy Prime Minister Anastas Mikoyan traveled clandestinely to north China in May 1948 and advised the CCP not to cross the Yangtze River.[5] The CCP ignored Soviet advice. The People's Liberation Army (PLA) staged a dramatic crossing of the Yangtze River on April 20, 1949, and captured Nanjing, the capital city of the KMT regime, within days. The KMT government abandoned the mainland and fled to Taiwan. When the communists entered Beijing on February 3, 1949, no Soviet weapons were seen when the communist troops paraded through.[6]

Unlike their ambiguous attitudes toward the Soviet Union, the CCP leaders had favorable opinions of the United States due to the American assistance to China during the Anti-Japanese War from 1937 to 1945 and through their personal experiences. Mao told his comrades that George Washington was one of the greatest heroes in the world. He would like to make China rich, strong, and independent, just as Washington did for America.[7] Planning on America to be the first country with which the PRC was to establish diplomatic relations, Mao intended to visit Washington and discuss the postwar future with President Franklin Roosevelt.[8] Zhou Enlai revealed Mao's intention in a 1946 speech that "It has been rumored recently that Chairman Mao is going to pay a visit to Moscow. Learning this, Chairman Mao laughed and half-jokingly said that if he would ever take a furlough abroad, which would certainly do much good to his present health condition, he would rather go to the United States because he thinks that there he can learn lots of things useful to China."[9]

After the fall of Nanjing to the PLA in early 1949, American ambassador John Leighton Stuart stayed in the embassy and met twice in May and June with Huang Hua, Stuart's former Yenching University student and now personal aid to Premier Zhou Enlai. Huang agreed to arrange for him to meet Premier Zhou in Beijing to discuss diplomatic recognition. Stuart cabled Secretary of State Dean Rusk on July 2 and requested permission. The highly ideological Rusk replied tersely, instructing him to close the embassy and come home.[10] Stuart left China quietly on August 2. The US State Department on August 5 published the China white paper *United States Relations with China: with Special Reference to the Period 1944–1949*, to address critics of the administration for "the loss of China." The window was completely closed as the white paper declared a policy of nonrecognition of the PRC.

In response, Mao wrote five commentaries for Xinhua News Agency. Their titles express Mao's comprehension: "Cast Away Illusions, Prepare for Struggle," "Farewell, Stuart," "Why It Is Necessary to Discuss the White Paper," "'Friendship' or Aggression?," and "The Bankruptcy of the Idealist Conception of History." For Mao, the white paper exposed the imperialist nature of US policy, and the departure of Ambassador Stuart marked the total failure of the US policy in China. Mao, therefore, called for the fight against US imperialism until victory.[11]

A Chinese scholar, therefore, claimed, "Due to the wrong choice made by the American government, the communist party and the Chinese people led by Mao Zedong were pushed into an anti-American position."[12] Although many Chinese scholars blamed the United States for missing the opportunity, one American scholar argued that there was no chance for friendship between the US and China during the period.[13] Indeed, the opportunity might not be there to be missed at all because Mao's terms for opening relations with the United States were too onerous. Mao's decisions to "restart the stove" and "clean the house before inviting guests" meant that the PRC did not recognize the diplomatic relations that the KMT regime had established, and the PRC would start diplomatic relations with foreign countries on the condition that they had to cut relations with the KMT regime first.[14]

The CCP leadership did not pursue American recognition because the United States was not likely to terminate relations with the KMT regime. Mao's Report to the CCP Central Committee on March 5, 1949, stated clearly that because the United States would not change its hostility to the CCP, "we should not be in hurry to resolve the US recognition issue."[15] The CCP leaders were convinced that "Washington's continuous support of the KMT regime" confirmed "the United States was the enemy of the Chinese revolution." Mao believed that in a moral sense the United States and other Western powers owed the Chinese a heavy debt. As the first step toward establishing an equal relationship, the US had to end and apologize for its unequal treatment of China and years of imperialism. These conditions were unacceptable to American leaders.[16]

Under this circumstance, Mao entered the Soviet orbit after Stalin apologized to the Chinese delegation, led by Liu Shaoqi in May 1949, for the Soviet Union not offering as much help to the Chinese communists as it should have—and even hampering the Chinese revolution to some extent because it did not understand China's situation well. He told Chinese comrades, "The victors should not be blamed."[17] Mao then made the historic announcement on the eve of the CCP's twenty-eighth anniversary on June 30, 1949, that China would "lean to one side" in the global struggle between the socialist and capitalist camps. To make his position clear, he stated that China must ally itself "with the Soviet Union, with every New Democratic country, and with the proletariat and broad masses in all other countries."[18]

The Soviet Union terminated the diplomatic relationship with the KMT government and recognized the CCP regime the day after the founding of the PRC on October 1, 1949. Following the Soviet Union, other socialist countries, including Bulgaria, Romania, Albania, Hungary, Poland, East Germany, Czechoslovakia, and North Korea recognized the PRC. In December 1949, Mao left China for his first foreign trip to Moscow. After about two months of negotiation and despite many twists, the Sino-Soviet Mutual Assistance and Friendship Treaty was signed in February 1950. Zhu Zhongli, the wife of Ambassador Wang Jiaxiang, wrote that the treaty formalized the Sino-Soviet alliance, which would not only give China the political capital to confront the imperialist countries and guard against possible imperialist invasion, but also promised Soviet economic, technical, and military assistance.[19]

The Moscow-Beijing alliance changed the Cold War landscape by giving the communists control of the Eurasian landmass stretching from the Baltic Sea to the South China Sea. For Beijing, as Zhou Enlai said on March 20, 1950, the alliance made it less likely that the United States would start a new war of aggression in East Asia.[20] One month later, speaking to the Central People's Government Council, Mao claimed that because reactionaries still existed in the world, China needed friends. With the alliance, "if the imperialists prepare to attack us, we already have help."[21] The CCP leadership looked ahead for a period of peace in the international front for domestic reconstruction and power consolidation.

Keeping the Wolves from the Door

When the PRC was about to shift to peacetime economic recovery and demobilize a large number of soldiers, the Korean War broke out. To the surprise and dismay of the United States, China entered the war. The Truman administration's explanation of China's decision emphasized Beijing's alliance with Moscow and Mao following Stalin's order.[22] But Mao's decision was more nuanced.

The war began after North Korean leader Kim Il-sung visited Moscow in March-April 1949 to gain Stalin's support for the takeover of South Korea. According to Khrushchev's memoir, Stalin doubted the sagacity, but Kim convinced him that the war could be won quickly before the United States could intervene. Mao approved Kim's plans since the war was an internal matter that the Korean people would decide for themselves.[23] For many years, Khrushchev's memoirs were the most detailed and authoritative source for the roles of Stalin, Kim, and Mao in connection with the Korean War. But new studies have falsified the assertion that Mao approved Kim's war initiative in advance. Mao opposed Kim's proposal because it would provoke US involvement. China would be dragged into the conflict.[24]

Despite its intimate cultural and strategic links to China, Korea did not figure prominently in Mao's priority list of domestic and external policy imperatives. Recovering from the destruction of the wars against Japan and the KMT, the CCP regime was badly in need of a break for reconstruction. A war with the United States would delay the reconstruction. Mao understood that Kim attempted to follow China's example to unify Korea by force. But China's national unification, i.e., taking over Taiwan and Tibet, should be given priority.[25] When Kim Il-sung visited Beijing on May 13, 1950, to inform Mao about his agreement with Stalin for the plan to unify the Korean Peninsula, Mao was caught by surprise and requested an urgent meeting with the Soviet ambassador to verify with Stalin. The next day, Stalin's telegram confirmed the matter. Mao accepted the decision but cautioned Kim about possible US intervention.[26]

Kim's conviction that the United States was unlikely to commit itself to the defense of South Korea was supported by the US withdrawal of forty-five thousand troops from the South on June 29, 1949. Leaving only an advisory group of about five hundred officers, the US action gave the impression that the United States accorded "little strategic significance to Korea."[27] In January 1950, a bill for US military and economic aid to South Korea was defeated in the House of Representatives, adding to the impression that US commitment to Korea did not have congressional support.[28] In a National Press Club speech in the same month, Secretary of State Dean Acheson defined the American "defensive perimeter" in the Pacific as a line running through Japan, the Ryukyus, and the Philippines. South Korea and Taiwan were excluded. Pyongyang regarded the speech as the "green light" to pursue forcible reunification because the United States had ruled out military intervention to defend South Korea.[29]

North Korea launched a massive attack on June 25, 1950, expecting a quick victory because the military power balance became favorable to the North.

While the United States was withdrawing its forces from the peninsula, Stalin agreed to furnish equipment and provide training of North Korean troops and massive military assistance.[30] Superior in number and equipped with Russian-made tanks and artillery, North Korean troops advanced rapidly and occupied most of the Korean Peninsula within six weeks.

To the surprise of Kim and Stalin, the Truman administration initiated the collective security motion through the UN two days after North Korean troops crossed the 38th parallel. The UN Security Council (UNSC) adopted two resolutions to mobilize UN forces contributed by sixteen nations to restore peace and security in Korea. On June 27, General Douglas MacArthur was authorized to use American naval and air forces to prevent the Inchon-Kimpo-Seoul area from falling into unfriendly hands. On September 15, MacArthur's successful amphibious landing of Marines at Inchon altered the course of the war. Seoul was recaptured. Crossing the 38th parallel, American forces captured Pyongyang on October 20. A week later, American troops reached the Yalu River, which divides the border between Korea and China. Chinese cities along the border were exposed to US bombardment.

The Chinese leadership was forced to make a difficult decision. According to one Chinese scholar, "The war, which was completely against Mao's will, not only disrupted his overall plan of domestic economic recovery and liberation of Taiwan but also evoked US military intervention that greatly concerned him."[31] But Mao had prepared for the worst-case scenario. As soon as North Korea launched the war, Mao assembled the Northeast Border Defense Force of 250,000 troops and stationed them along the Yalu River. After US-led UN forces were authorized to use ground forces to intervene, Mao began to consider sending Chinese troops to Korea. General Deng Hua was summoned to Beijing from Guangzhou on July 19 and met Mao for the later appointment as the deputy commander in chief of the Chinese People's Volunteer Army (CPVA) in Korea. Mao told him that "your task is not only to defend the northeast border but also be prepared to fight the Americans in an unprecedented battle and possibly a nuclear war."[32]

Mao made his mind known to his colleagues at a Politburo meeting on August 4, 1950, saying, "We must help North Koreans because if the US won, it would threaten China. Timing and format can be considered but we must be prepared."[33] Mao restated this position at the Ninth Meeting of the Central

People's Government Council on September 5: "The US has entered the war in Korea. It would fight wars in other places. We must be prepared to fight a big war, long-term war, even nuclear war."[34] In the same month, Mao ordered to increase the Northeast Border Defense Force to seven hundred thousand troops plus two hundred thousand replacements.

The US-led UN troops moving north toward the Chinese border were enough impetus for Mao to make a final decision. Upon receiving personal letters from Stalin and Kim requesting China to send troops to assist North Koreans on October 1, 1950, the CCP Politburo convened urgent meetings on October 4 and 5. Mao made a case to enter the war, but some of his comrades were hesitant to agree with him. Peng Dehuai, soon to be the commander-in-chief and political commissar of the CPVA, supported Mao. His argument was very powerful: "American occupation of Korea, separating from China only by a river, would threaten Northeast China." If this happened, the United States "could find a pretext at any time to invade China."[35]

MacArthur's advance toward the Chinese border also raised the CCP's worry about the rise of internal counterrevolutionaries. While land reform in rural areas started peacefully in 1950, many landlords, hoping the KMT regime would be restored after the outbreak of the war, stiffened their resistance. China's Public Security Ministry archives revealed that counterrevolutionaries "made use of all possible means to intensify all kinds of destructive activities." No longer restricting themselves to regions adjacent to the Korean peninsula and Taiwan, they became omnipresent. At the Politburo meeting, Peng Dehuai persuaded his comrades not only by the possible US invasion but also that China's intervention would be a "heavy blow to the reactionary momentum and pro-American factions at home."[36]

The Politburo meeting made the decision that "if we don't enter the war and the enemy reaches to the bank of the Yalu River, domestic and international reactionaries would be swollen with arrogance, which would be a disadvantage to China. The entire northeast defense army would be trapped, and the south Manchurian electric supply would be cut. Therefore, we should and must enter the war. Entering the war would be immensely beneficial and not entering the war would be immensely harmful." On October 8, Mao, as the chairman of the Central Military Commission (CMC), ordered the CPVA to cross the Yalu and "keep the wolves from the door."[37]

The Chinese entered the war when North Korean armies had virtually collapsed, and UN troops were close to the Chinese border. Chinese leaders clearly remembered that Japanese imperialists had first annexed Korea, then penetrated and occupied China's northeast, thus beginning a war of aggression. For Beijing, the American invasion of Korea was part of the US strategy to invade China. MacArthur reinforced CCP's fear by saying publicly that he wanted to extend the Korean War into China and return the KMT to power on the mainland.[38]

Considering MacArthur's advance to the border a serious threat to China's security, Beijing made the point clear that "to safeguard the independence and security, China could not but spearhead its struggle against the United States. 'To resist the United States and aid Korea, to defend the country and protect peoples' homes' was the greatest strategic decision made in the struggle against the United States."[39]For the purpose of domestic mobilization, the government did not tell Chinese people that North Korea started the war and lied that MacArthur's amphibious landing of US Marines at Inchon started the war to seize North Korea and ultimately cross the Yalu River into China.[40]

Beijing's decision thus had very little to do with the Sino-Soviet alliance. In fact, Stalin was not very helpful. Agreeing to provide Chinese troops with support and military supplies before China entered the war, Stalin changed his mind and told Zhou Enlai on October 10 that the Soviet Union could not send troops because it would lead to a confrontation with the United States.[41] After receiving a telegram from Zhou from Moscow, Mao put the movement of Chinese troops temporarily on hold. The Politburo held an urgent meeting on October 13. Weighing the pros and cons, participants decided that the Chinese had to fight the Americans even without the Soviet air coverage. Relying on Mao's principles of self-reliance, an army with higher morale could beat an enemy with superior equipment.[42] Crossing the Yalu River on October 19 and fighting the first battle against UN troops on October 25, the CPVA recaptured Pyongyang and pushed the battle line back to the 38th parallel by December.

US officials publicly blamed themselves for not realizing the depths of Chinese "deviousness" and privately blamed MacArthur's intelligence failure. The General took "credit" for exposing Chinese perfidiousness but blamed Washington for not allowing him to use the full US military arsenal against the

Chinese because the Truman administration was much more concerned than General MacArthur over a clash with the Chinese communists.[43] Neither the Truman administration nor the UN could support MacArthur's plan because they thought it would bring a general war. General Omar Bradley, chairman of the Joint Chiefs of Staff, made the famous statement that the United States would be involved "in the wrong war, at the wrong place, at the wrong time, and with the wrong enemy."[44]

With the danger of general war heightened while the military stalemated, the United States was inclined to settle the war by political means. So was Beijing, because China's economy was exhausted by the lengthy civil war and its involvement in Korea. The CPVA was extremely tired, badly in need of rest and reorganization. Their supply line was too long to be secured. Most troops had no winter clothing and were running short of ammunition. Medicine and food were in short supply.[45]

The negotiations started in July 1951. An armistice agreement was reached on July 27, 1953. Fighting US-led UN forces to a truce, China defended its border and preserved an anti-American regime in North Korea. A Chinese scholar observed that "forcing the US to accept a truce in Korea and achieving remarkable economic and political progress on the domestic front, Mao and his colleagues attained greater confidence."[46] One American scholar confirmed: "The battle in North Korea was the first great victory won by Chinese forces over a major power which had a lasting effect on the outcome of an international war since the Opium War opened the modern era in China."[47]

The Noose Policy

But the truce failed to expel the US forces from the Korean Peninsula and deflected the focus of America's hostility from the Soviet Union to China. Demonstrating its ability to resist the US forces and constituting a constant menace to the Americans and their allies, China became the major target of the US containment line, erected through bilateral and multilateral alliances along the fringes of East and Southeast Asia, where the ground forces of the communist bloc on the mainland confronted the air and naval power of the United States over the island perimeter. Taiwan became a focal point.

Before the war, the United States did not see much strategic value in Taiwan and was ready to draw it out of the US defense perimeter. In the

January 1950 Statement on Formosa (Taiwan), President Harry Truman announced that the US government would not provide military aid to Chinese forces on Formosa because it would be deemed intervention in the
Chinese civil war.[48] The outbreak of the Korean War led the United States
to see geostrategic value in Taiwan. The Truman administration reversed its
policy and dispatched the Seventh Fleet to patrol the Taiwan Strait to avoid
the misperception about the lack of US commitment. General MacArthur
famously referred to Taiwan's value as an unsinkable aircraft carrier and submarine tender that could help project American power along China's coast
in a containment strategy.[49]

The Korean War cost Mao the opportunity to take back Taiwan without
facing US opposition. The island's strategic position and its ties to the United
States became an important cause: Mao must bring it under CCP rule to not
only achieve national unification but also eliminate a major security threat.
Beijing reacted forcefully to America's dispatch of the Seventh Fleet to the
strait. Zhou Enlai declared on June 28, 1950: "The fact that Taiwan is part of
China will remain unchanged forever. This is not only a historical fact but
affirmed by the Cairo Declaration, the Potsdam Declaration, and the existing
conditions after Japan's surrender. The Chinese people will surely be victorious
in driving off American aggressors and recovering Taiwan."[50]

The US Seventh Fleet patrol forced Beijing to delay its offensive campaign
to recover Taiwan and the offshore islands Penghu, Jinmen (Quemoy), and
Mazu (Matsu) slated for 1951.[51] But even if Mao gave up on the liberation of
Taiwan for the moment, his civil war rival Chiang Kai-shek had not given up
on the mainland and remained determined to retake it. For years, Chinese
leaders were alarmed about a possible KMT invasion of the mainland from
Taiwan with American support. After the Korean armistice agreement was
signed, Beijing renewed its military campaigns. *The People's Daily* published an
editorial, "We Must Liberate Taiwan," on July 23, 1954, and stressed that after
the cease-fire in Korea, the Chinese people would not tolerate the separation
of Taiwan from the mainland any longer.

The PLA started a twelve-day bombardment of Jinmen on September 3,
1954, to focus the world's attention on the Taiwan issue and remind the world
that Taiwan was part of China. In the meantime, the PLA launched an attack on the Dachen Islands, the northernmost of the KMT-occupied islands.

Although Beijing halted military activities after taking over the Dachens, the atmosphere of hostility increased. Believing that Chinese actions constituted one of the most serious problems of the first eighteen months of his administration, President Dwight D. Eisenhower submitted the Formosa Resolution to Congress in January 1955, which would give the president the right to order military aid for the defense of Jinmen and Mazu.[52]

Anticipating American armed intervention, the Chinese leaders conducted diplomatic maneuvers to support military actions. At the Bandung Conference of Afro-Asian nations in Indonesia on April 18–24, 1955, China proposed the "five principles of peaceful coexistence," including noninterference in the internal affairs of other countries. Zhou Enlai made a public statement at the conference that "the Chinese people do not want to have a war with the United States. The Chinese government is willing to sit down to discuss the question of relaxing tension in the Far East, and especially the question of relaxing tension in the Taiwan area."[53] The United States accepted Zhou's posture and started ambassadorial-level talks with China in Geneva on August 1, 1955. The talks continued for more than two years, with seventy-three meetings. There were many issues on the agenda, but the Taiwan issue was at the center of the discussion. No agreement was reached. The talks terminated on December 12, 1957.[54]

Increasingly suspicious of the Americans intentions, Chinese leaders believed that America's hidden goal was to delay the resolution of the Taiwan issue and eventually force China to accept the existence of Taiwan as an independent state, like the divided states of Germany, Korea, and Vietnam after World War II. Showing determination to take back Taiwan, China began bombarding Jinmen and Mazu for a second time on August 23, 1958. In response, President Eisenhower made a public statement on August 27 that, exercising the power under the Formosa Resolution to assist Taiwan in the defense of Jinmen and Mazu, he instructed US naval forces to implement the convoy-escort plan on August 29. He amassed in the Taiwan Straits the largest single concentration of US nuclear support forces in history by mid-September.[55] Military leaders pushed for authority to conduct nuclear strikes deep into China if the PLA intensified their attacks on the offshore islands. Ultimately, Eisenhower decided to rely on conventional weapons first. To avoid another protracted conventional conflict like the Korean War, there was a "unanimous belief that this would have to be quickly followed by nuclear strikes unless the Chinese communists called off this operation."[56]

But Beijing was not deterred. Mao assessed that neither China nor America was willing to fight a war, but the United States was "more afraid of a war" and would have to abandon the islands if war was imminent. Hence, war was unlikely to break out. Indeed, as military tension in the Jinmen-Mazu area escalated, American officials became dubious about the US commitment to the offshore islands. The chairman of the Joint Chiefs of Staff recommended to President Eisenhower that American forces withdraw from Jinmen and Mazu because they were a strategic liability within range of PLA artillery and difficult to defend. But Chiang Kai-shek believed they would be a useful stepping-stone to reconquer the mainland. Abandoning the islands would seriously imperil the KMT regime's legitimacy in Taiwan. The United States suspected that Chiang intended to intensify the crisis to drag America into his war with the mainland.[57]

Seeing the possibility of US withdrawal from the offshore islands, Mao designed a "Noose Policy" (绞索政策) to postpone the "liberation" of Jin-men and Mazu and maintain a tie between Taiwan and the mainland.[58] On October 6, in the name of Minister of Defense Peng Dehuai, the *People's Daily* published "A Message to the Taiwan Compatriots" drafted by Mao, which stated that "we are all Chinese. Among thirty-six tactics, the peace is the top tactic [三十六计，和为上计]. The bombardment is to call your attention that Taiwan, Jinmen, and Mazu are parts of China, a position shared by all Chinese people." The "Message" announced a unilateral seven-day cease-fire. At the end of the seven days, Beijing announced that bombardment would occur only on even days.[59]

This change in military action was based on Mao's strategic calculation that the KMT retaining Jinmen and Mazu was a noose to affirm Taiwan's ties with the mainland. Believing that Chiang's position was different from the United States' on Taiwan's status,[60] he told his comrades, "Chiang is a patriot. He opposes the US trusty of Taiwan or two Chinas." For Mao, the bombardment of Jinmen was, therefore, to help Chiang defend Jinmen and tighten the noose.[61]

One senior PLA intelligence officer reported to Mao that Chiang was indeed not panicked at all after learning about the bombardment. He proclaimed repeatedly saying "wonderful." Mao told the officer that "this is exactly what I expected. My old rival is very smart. The bombardment helped his bargain with his American boss." The officer revealed that Chiang urged the United States to help defend Taiwan and the offshore islands, but the US wanted him to abandon the offshore islands so that Taiwan could become an independent republic. The bombardment helped Chiang drag on Americans in Taiwan to confront directly with the CCP and thereby maintain the tie between Taiwan and the mainland.[62]

The Sino-Soviet Split

The Sino-Soviet split was misleadingly clad in an ideological garb at the time but was fundamentally an assertion of Chinese national interests against Soviet tutelage. The conflict emerged prominently in July 1958 when the Soviet ambassador to Beijing, Pavel Yudin, conveyed a proposal to Mao for a joint navy to use Chinese harbors but be commanded by a Russian admiral. Mao rejected the proposal because he had long guarded against the Soviet attempt to restore the czarist Russian sphere of influence in northeast China and ensure Soviet access to an ice-free port in the Pacific. Yudin reported to Moscow. Khrushchev requested and held a meeting with Mao at Beijing airport. Khrushchev explained that the Soviets weren't talking about a joint navy but rather long-range wireless stations in China to communicate with their fleet in the Pacific. Mao replied that China had no objection to communication stations, but they must be China-built, China-operated, and China-controlled. Otherwise, the Russians were demanding "military bases on Chinese soil."[63]

At this critical juncture, Beijing asked Moscow to take a tough response to the United States after the PLA started shelling Jinmen island, but the Soviet Union played "a vital off-stage role, avoiding direct involvement in the crises."[64] According to Yu Zhan, former Chinese ambassador to Moscow, in the face of a nuclear threat from the United States, Khrushchev refused the Chinese request for nuclear protection. Warning Chinese leaders about the dangers of a war with the United States, he sent his foreign minister, Andrei Gromyko, to Beijing to show the Chinese leaders a film about the devastation of nuclear weapons.[65]

Mao's decision to switch development strategy from following the Soviet model of bureaucratic command to the mass mobilization of the Great Leap

Forward (GLF) also caused tension. Reacting cautiously to Mao's initiatives, Khrushchev made subtle criticism of people's communes in his report to the CPSU Twenty-First Congress in January 1959.[66] The GLF suffered a vital setback and provoked complaints from Mao's colleagues. Refusing to face the dire reality, Mao launched the counterattack and purged Peng Dehuai, the outspoken defense minister who wrote a long personal letter to Mao and spoke at the CCP leadership's Lushan conference on July 17, 1959, to criticize the Great Leap. Coincidently, Khrushchev made remarks in Poland to attack GLF as "petty-bourgeois fanaticism" on the same day of Peng's criticism. Mao distributed Peng's letter to participants together with a Foreign Ministry report on Khrushchev's remarks claiming that the CCP had made mistakes.[67] Mao could not tolerate Soviet leaders siding with critiques in CCP's internal debate, and he made the clashes open. During Khrushchev's visit to China in October 1959, the two sides staged intense arguments. Sending Khrushchev off at the airport, Mao talked about what the GLF had achieved, how the masses had initiated the people's communes, and what advantages the latter had in comparison with communes in the Soviet Union's past.[68]

Making pressure on Beijing, the Soviets abruptly abrogated the agreement by which the Soviets pledged to assist China in developing nuclear weapons in June 1959; in August 1960, the Soviet Union terminated its economic and military assistance and withdrew 1,300 advisors from China. A Chinese scholar indicated that "the coercive policy of the Soviet Union was seen as extremely insulting by China's leaders who felt much nationalist pride for winning China's independence and raising China's international status."[69] Beijing was further upset that, during the Sino-Indian border dispute in 1959–62, the USSR sided with India instead of supporting its ally, China.[70] Khrushchev's policy for "peaceful coexistence" also caused Mao's concerns. As China confronted the United States over Taiwan, Mao could not accept the Soviet detente with the United States. Khrushchev's withdrawal of missiles from Cuba at America's behest, and the Russo-American agreement on the Nuclear Test Ban Treaty (NTBT) in 1963, deepened Beijing's suspicion that the détente was at the expense of China's interests and fostered the encirclement of China.[71]

The outside world began to see the Sino-Soviet tension through the ideological polemic during 1960–63, which was reminiscent of medieval theological disputes. Each side looked upon the other as an arch-heretic. The April 1960 issue of *Red Flag* magazine run by the CCP Central Committee published an editorial—"Long Live Leninism," the first in a series of articles in the dispute—which asserted Beijing as the true heir of Lenin's legacy while the Soviet Union was held as undertaking revisionism.[72] This editorial was followed by three open letters to Soviet leaders in spring 1963, battering the Soviet agreement to sign the NTBT with the West and warning that a one-sided reduction of the international communist movement to peaceful coexistence and a peaceful transition to socialism betrayed the revolutionary principle.

Worrying about the intensification of tensions, Wang Jiaxiang, the former ambassador to Moscow and the minister of the International Liaison Department (ILD) of the CCP Central Committee at the time, sent a letter to the central leaders in 1962, contending that China should adhere to the principle of peaceful coexistence among countries with different social systems. Mao severely criticized Wang for advocating a revisionist line to accommodate the Soviet Union. Wang's proposal was labeled as "three reconciliations and one reduction" (三和一少), meaning reconciliation with imperialists, revisionists, and international reactionaries, and reduction of support for nationalist liberation war and revolution.[73]

Making its opposition to Soviet revisionism known to the world, Beijing rejected the Soviet leadership in the communist camp and strove to lead the cause of developing countries in their "just struggle against imperialism, neo-colonialism, and the big power monopoly over the handling of international affairs."[74] While Beijing and Moscow worked in tandem organizing the first Afro-Asian conference in 1956, Chinese foreign minister Chen Yi bluntly asserted before the second Afro-Asian conference in March 1965 that the Soviet Union was not an Asian country and had no business at the conference. Competing with the Soviet Union over aid to North Vietnam in its war against the United States, Beijing accused the Soviets of aid not commensurate with their strength. The Soviets accused Beijing of needing a long conflict in Vietnam to keep up the tension and portray China as a besieged fortress.[75]

Enlisting the Soviet Union and its followers as revisionists, Mao made imperialism, revisionism, and reactionaries together the primary targets of Chinese revolutionary diplomacy. Welcoming a stream of leaders of Maoist parties from the developing countries to visit China, Mao encouraged insurgents to carry out armed struggles, committed himself to support all revolutions against imperialism, and opposed any attempt by communists to gain power through peaceful means or to compromise with the US imperialists.[76] Defense Minister Lin Biao portrayed North America and Western Europe as "world cities," and Asia, Africa, Latin America as the "world countryside." Calling for a people's war to establish rural base areas and surround the "cities" from the "countryside," and then capture the cities, Lin claimed that such a people's war had universally applicable values for the world revolution.[77]

The 1964 coup that removed Khrushchev briefly silenced the dispute. But the anti-Soviet course intensified after the Cultural Revolution started in 1966. A vigorous, unrelenting campaign against the Soviet Union provoked noisy demonstrations in front of the Soviet embassy in Beijing. The militant tone was exemplified in the headline of the *People's Daily* editorial, "Hit Back Hard at the Rabid Provocation of the Filthy Soviet Revisionist Swine."[78] Beijing labeled the Soviet Union interference in Czechoslovakia in 1968 as new czarism of and the Brezhnev Doctrine that aimed at the justification of Soviet intervention anywhere in East Europe for the purpose of defending socialism.[79]

The Sino-Soviet split exploded prominently over border disputes. The two countries share the longest boundary in the world. The Chinese claimed that 12,700 square miles of territory north of the Amur River were ceded to czarist Russia under an unequal treaty in 1860 following China's defeat in the Second Opium War. The Chinese government also claimed land in the Ili Valley in the Pamir mountain range that borders China and Afghanistan, which was taken by Russian troops in 1867. Although the Soviet Union argued that the boundary of the Pamir was established in a series of diplomatic notes in 1894, the Chinese introduced documents to prove that the disputed Pamir boundary remained unsettled.[80]

The split of national minorities in their border regions further complicated the antagonism. Both Russians and Han Chinese had chauvinistic and imperial tendencies, opposing self-determination and secession of their border minorities and desiring their cultural assimilation to the dominant nationality. Of the border nationalities, the largest Turkic nationality in China was the Uighurs in Xinjiang; only a few Uighurs lived in the Soviet Union. The three Soviet republics of Kazakhstan, Kyrgyzstan, and Tajikistan had substantial numbers of Kazakhs and Kyrgyz, while on the Chinese side these people were minorities and resented the suppression by China.

In 1954, when Mao attempted to reopen with Khrushchev the issue of separating Outer Mongolia from China, Khrushchev reminded Mao that the majority of Kazakh people lived in the USSR, while only some Kazakhs and Kyrgyz resided in China. The Soviet Union was in favor of self-determination and wanted disputed issues to be settled on this basis.[81] This was an ominous threat to China, which had faced challenges in Xinjiang due to the aspirations of some of the national minorities. On April 22, 1962, about sixty thousand Kazakhs, Kirghiz, and Uighurs in Xinjiang crossed the border into the Soviet Union. Labeling this incident as "Ili Counter-revolutionary Riot," Beijing blamed the Soviet KGB for its role of agitation.[82]

Border confrontation surfaced in March–September 1963 when a spate of Chinese editorials and open letters raised the question of the unsettled frontier north of the Ili Valley in Xinjiang.[83] The Soviet Union responded by presenting an account of Chinese violations of the border from 1960 to 1963, including smuggling and other illegal entries. Amid charges and countercharges, Chinese and Soviet troops clashed over the Ussuri River's contested Zhenbao Island (as it's called by the Chinese; called Mamansky by the Soviets) in March 1969. These clashes were deliberated ambushes of each other's border patrols, resulting in casualties on both sides and intensifying fortification of military installations and armaments along their borders.[84]

Resisting America and Assisting Vietnam

The Sino-Soviet split did not produce an immediate Sino-US rapprochement because American leaders saw Communism as a monolithic global conspiracy. For Washington, no matter how serious China and Russia disagreed, their rift would not divide them in opposition to the United States. The Sino-Soviet dispute was not necessarily a welcome phenomenon because the loss of Soviet control over China could incur more intransigence on the part of the Chinese.[85] Ironically, the United States escalated the war in Vietnam to check communist expansion when China and the Soviet Union, the two communist giants, were on the verge of war.

Motivated by the crude assumption of the "domino theory" that "the loss of any single country would probably lead to relatively swift submission to or an alignment with communism by the remaining countries of this group,"[86] the United States began a military intervention in Vietnam to stop the next domino from tumbling after France withdrew from Indochina in 1954. Each succeeding president did not want to lose a country to communism in his watch against the backlash from the bitter "who lost China" debate. Soon after taking office, Lyndon Johnson said, "I am not going to be the President who saw Southeast Asia going the way China went."[87] Alleging that the US destroyer *Maddox*, on routine patrol in international waters near the Gulf of Tonkin, was attacked by North Vietnamese torpedo boats, Johnson on August 4, 1964, asked Congress for special power to allow the president, without congressional approval, to use forces to assist any member or protocol state of the Southeast Asian Collective Defense Treaty requesting assistance in defense of its freedom. Within hours, Congress passed the Gulf of Tonkin resolutions. America's commitment to Vietnam escalated, paralleling the American perception of China as the most dangerous threat.

Worrying that America might drive the war into China, Mao made the momentous decision to shift China's overall strategic priority from economic construction to defense construction. Preparing for the fight of war along the First Front of the coast and the Second Front of the northeast areas of China, Mao mobilized fifteen million people for the construction of the Grand Third Front (大三线) in thirteen inland provinces in 1964.[88] A top secret, massive military-industrial complex was built in the mountains to keep hidden from enemy bombers. The Third Front received more government investment than any other developmental initiative of the Mao era and militarized Chinese economy, linking millions of everyday lives to the war preparations.[89]

Pinning US troops down in Vietnam, Mao announced that China was ready to provide all necessary material assistance and send Chinese people when needed to fight together with the Vietnamese people.[90] North Vietnam leader Ho Chi Minh made a secret visit to China in April and May 1965. Mao told him that "seven hundred million Chinese people are the powerful backing up to Vietnam. The broad Chinese territory is the reliable rear areas to Vietnam."[91] Beijing secretly sent about 320,000 logistic, engineering, and construction personnel and antiaircraft artillery troops to Vietnam from 1965 to 1973. The first eighty thousand Chinese road-construction troops were dressed in Vietnamese army uniforms and crossed the border on July 9, 1965. The last Chinese military units withdrew from Vietnam in August 1973.[92]

The Vietnam War brought Beijing and Washington to the brink of their largest military confrontation since the Korean War. Operating in uncertainty, both sides prepared for the worst. Washington made contingency plans for a large-scale Chinese intervention in Vietnam. Beijing mobilized its people to defend against a possible US invasion and contemplated the contingency of "fighting on two fronts" with Soviet revisionism and American imperialism.[93]

To isolate the two superpowers, Mao developed the theory of "two intermediate zones." One intermediate zone was the underdeveloped countries in Asia, Africa, and Latin America. The second zone included developed countries, such as Japan, Europe, Japan, Australia, New Zealand, and Canada. Countries in both zones were opposing the control of the United States and the Soviet Union.[94] Working mostly with the countries in the first zone during the 1950s, China paid serious attention to the second zone in the 1960s. Mao told the colorful, wiry British field marshal Bernard Montgomery, "We don't feel any threat from Britain and France and hope you become stronger." He also told visiting French parliament members, "Let's be good friends. You are not in the communist party and I am not in your party. But we have two things in common: the first is that we don't allow any superpower to control us, and the second is that we want to strengthen our economic and cultural exchanges."[95]

Ready to mobilize countries in the two intermediate zones against both superpowers, China, however, headed steadily for a mortal internal turmoil and turned inward, isolating itself from the rest of the world after the Cultural Revolution started in 1966. Calling back Chinese diplomats and students abroad, Beijing declared an increasing number of foreign governments the targets of revolutionary diplomacy. Even relations with North Korea became strained, as China accused Kim Il-sung of revisionism. The only governments with which China remained friendly were those of Albania and North Vietnam.

The International Anti-Soviet United Front

The international isolation compelled Mao to rethink China's security priority. The Soviet threat came to the top of Mao's minds as the Soviet Union dramatically increased the deployment of troops along the border and thrust into Vietnam and Afghanistan to encircle China. Taking seriously the alleged Soviet threat of making a surgical attack to destroy China's infant nuclear capability, Mao laid out the strategy of "digging the cave deeply, accumulating grain extensively, and preparing for war and famine" (深挖洞,广积粮,备战备荒) and ordered the transfer of CCP central leaders and organizations from Beijing to the provinces in October 1969.[96]

Searching for strategic options, Mao entrusted four veteran marshals—Chen Yi, Ye Jianying, Nie Rongzhen, and Xu Xiangqian—who had been sidelined during the Cultural Revolution, to research future policy toward the two superpowers in June 1969. The marshals submitted two reports to the central leadership, on July 11 and September 17, pointing out that Soviet-US contradictions were sharper and bigger than Sino-Soviet contradictions. They proposed aligning with the United States to resist the Soviet Union. Beyond the reports, Chen Yi, the former minister of foreign affairs, verbally proposed to Zhou Enlai that China should proactively initiate ministerial or higher levels of meetings with the United States.[97]

Mao accepted the proposal because America was preoccupied with Vietnam and became less of a threat to China. Mao told Edgar Snow, his old friend and leftist American journalist, that "it is good to have the Americans in South Vietnam," and "China would fight only against a direct attack by the U.S. on her territory."[98] Chinese negotiator informed the US envoy at the ambassadorial talk in Warsaw on February 20, 1970, that Beijing would welcome the United States sending a ministerial-level representative or presidential envoy to Beijing. But the US invasion of Cambodia on March 30 suspended the contacts. Mao attended the mass anti-America rally in Beijing on May 20 to denounce America.[99]

While China was compelled by the Soviet threat to seek realignment with the former adversary, the Vietnam War created an environment in the United States to rethink relations with China. The Fulbright Hearings in 1966 "depoliticized" the China issue, "legitimized" the airing of views that would have been considered "heresy" in the 1950s, and "emboldened" the advocates of China policy reform to push that agenda.[100] At this juncture, Hanoi mounted a massive counterattack, the Tet Offensive, on January 31, 1968, making it clear to the Johnson administration that a quick victory was beyond their reach.

President Johnson rejected General Westmoreland's request for sending more troops to Vietnam, signaling a beginning of de-escalation.

The US withdrawal from Cambodia in June 1970 cleared the way for Beijing to resume rapprochement with the United States. Signaling to the US for reconciliation, Beijing, on July 10, 1970, released Bishop James Walsh, an American citizen who had been imprisoned in China since 1958 on espionage charges. In September 1970, Zhou Enlai sent a message to Nixon via the Pakistani president saying that Nixon's special envoy would be welcome in Beijing. Mao also sent his signal by inviting Edgar Snow and his wife to stand beside him atop Tiananmen Gate during the National Day parade on October 1, 1970. Snow was the first American to be given such an honor. This was followed by the invitation in April 1971 of the US ping-pong team competing in Japan to visit China.[101]

Taking these signals to gain an advantage in relations with the Soviet Union and put pressure on Hanoi to negotiate seriously on the conditions to end the war, President Nixon made an "announcement that shocked the world" on July 15, 1971: his national security advisor Henry Kissinger had undertaken a secret mission to Beijing to arrange for the president's trip to China.[102] Nixon arrived in Beijing on February 21, 1972 and started the week-long visit to "bridge a gulf of almost 12,000 miles and 22 years of non-communication and hostility" that had riven the Asian political landscape since the Korean War.[103] Shaking hands with Nixon at Beijing airport, Zhou told his visitor, "Your hands have crossed the widest ocean in the world."[104]

Common ground for Sino-US alignment was to counter the Soviet threat. This understanding was embodied in the Sino-US Joint Communiqué signed in Shanghai, which provided that "neither should seek hegemony in the Asia-Pacific region and each is opposed to efforts by any other country or group of countries to establish such hegemony." In effect, this was a promise by China not to support Soviet policies against the United States, and a promise by the United States to use its influence to prevent a Soviet attack on China.

The United States agreed to align with China so that it could concentrate its military resources to deter the Soviet Union and reduce the cost of the "two-and-a-half-war strategy."[105] If China were smashed in a Sino-Soviet war, Moscow would be able to shift its entire military weight against the Western alliance.[106] For China, improving relations with the United States was intended to reduce the cost and danger of a possible "two-front war" and concentrate its resources against the more dangerous adversary. Beijing concluded that the American withdrawal of ground troops from Vietnam would ease American military pressure on China's southern flank. China also wanted to find a solution for the reunification with Taiwan through Sino-US rapprochement.[107] The roadmap for the Taiwan issue was stated in the Shanghai Communiqué: "The United States acknowledges that all Chinese on either side of the Taiwan Strait maintain there is one China and that Taiwan is a part of China. The United States Government does not challenge that position."

Resuming relationship with the US, Beijing did not tone down its anti-imperialist and revolutionary rhetoric immediately and continued calling for opposition to the hegemony of the two superpowers. During the negotiation of the Sino-US Joint Communiqué, the American side wanted to include "peace and security" in the document. To avoid the impression that China was compromising with the United States on revolutionary principles, the Chinese side emphasized "revolution, the liberation of the oppressed peoples and nations in the world, and no rights for big powers to bully and humiliate small countries."[108]

Although Mao later acknowledged to his American visitors that stressing these goals was no more than "firing empty cannons" (放空炮), he insisted, "All of these points must be highlighted, and anything short of that would be improper." In Mao's words, "Fight is fight and diplomacy is diplomacy." The rapprochement with the United States would not affect China's position of assisting world revolutionary movements. At Mao's insistence, the joint Sino-US communiqué contained contrasting statements. While China affirmed its support for wars, national liberation, and socialist revolution, the United States affirmed its commitment to peace.[109]

Mao's principled flexibility on ideological issues and the motivation to align with the United States were revealed in his meeting with Henry Kissinger in 1973. Kissinger told Mao that the US and China "face the same danger. We may have to use different methods sometimes but for the same objectives." Mao responded, "So long as the objectives are the same, we would not harm you nor would you harm us." Mao was pleased that the Sino-US rapprochement produced "a horizontal line linking the US, Japan, China, Pakistan, Iran, Turkey, and Europe" against the Soviet Union.[110]

Geopolitical Revolution

Nixon's historic visit generated a realignment in East Asia. Three members of the Association of Southeast Asia Nations (ASEAN)—Thailand, Malaysia, and the Philippines—swiftly established diplomatic relations with Beijing. But the most dramatic consequence was the sudden normalization of Sino-Japanese relations.

The unexpected Sino-US rapprochement was referred to as a "Nixon Shock" in Japan because the Japanese were not forewarned and had to accommodate the new development virtually overnight, although Japan thought of the United States as a mentor and a guarantor of its security.[111] Kissinger later admitted that it was a serious mistake and a lack of consideration to Japan, but the Americans were hardly able to mitigate the blow, which was all the more severe as Prime Minister Sato withstood persistent public pressure for normalizing relations with China and refused to disrupt America's policy of containment.[112] Having been kept completely in the dark by their mentor and ally, Japanese people were genuinely alarmed by the fact that America and China would collude to shut Japan out of further development. Given the Japanese pragmatism to go the Japanese way in accommodating the profound geopolitical transformation, Tokyo soon began preparing for its rapprochement with Beijing and was ready to move fast and outdistance the United States. As the old wartime slogans on "not missing the bus to China" were once again revived with the intent of encouraging all and sundry to make haste to Beijing, "the scramble within and between Japan's political parties to win the race to Beijing was on, and the pace quickly proved deadly."[113]

Beijing was as eager as Tokyo for normalization, partially because the Nixon visit was not as rich in substance as the press coverage suggested. The United States proved a tough negotiator on many issues, particularly the Taiwan issue. Beijing hoped that the ideologically less-committed Japanese would prove more amenable to their wishes. Although there were complicated issues and obstacles in Sino-Japanese relations, especially Japan's historical aggression and the atrocities committed against the Chinese, the Chinese leaders chose not to press Japan's war guilt question nor demand reparation payments. These issues could be raised in the future. For the moment, the crucial thing was to build on the momentum of the Sino-US rapprochement and consolidate it by adding Japan to the picture.[114]

Under the mood on both sides, Prime Minister Tanaka Kakuei wasted no time plunging himself into the normalization fever after taking office on July 5, 1972. The job was not difficult because Sino-Japanese ties were never cut off entirely. Due to historical and cultural affinities, the active unofficial trade and people-to-people exchanges were maintained. The Sino-Japanese relationship was characterized by the separation of politics from economics. Moreover, it was helpful that China did not insist on any modification of US security arrangements with Japan as a precondition for the Nixon trip.

On September 29, 1972, five months after the Nixon trip to China, Prime Minister Tanaka and Premier Zhou signed a joint communiqué in Beijing, declaring the normalization of diplomatic relations. It stated that Japan was aware of its responsibility for causing enormous damages to the Chinese people in the past war and deeply reproached itself. On the Taiwan issue, Japan agreed with the position of the Chinese government that "Taiwan is an inalienable part of the territory of the People's Republic of China."[115] The Chinese government gave up its claim to war reparations on the ground that by being generous on this scope, Japan could be induced to offer various types of economic assistance and cooperate with China in promoting regional stability. Zhou told Tanaka that the Chinese must see the Japanese militarists as outliers and not as representatives of the Japanese people. Both the Chinese and Japanese nations were traumatized during the war. Avoiding the political disputes over historical memory made way for the immediate Sino-Japanese strategic collaboration.[116]

The normalization of Sino-Japanese relations offered China the greatest diplomatic opportunities since 1949. Turning to the United States and Japan, Beijing built a broader international anti-Soviet united front. China had begun to diversify its commercial and diplomatic relationship with non-communist countries even before Nixon's visit. China's trade with non-communist industrial countries reached 45 percent of its total trade by 1968. Japan, West Germany, Britain, Australia, Italy, and Canada were among Beijing's top ten trading partners.[117] Following the establishment of Sino-French diplomatic relations in 1964, seventeen countries established diplomatic relations with China by 1972. Japan was prominent among them.

Beijing was admitted into the UN General Assembly in 1971 on a vote of 76 in favor, 35 opposed, and 17 abstentions. Although Chinese propaganda said that China was brought to the UN by the votes of developing countries, particularly African countries, the countries in relatively developed Europe and Asia provided the highest percentage of in-favor votes for China's entry. Twenty-three European countries, including France and the United Kingdom, voted in favor and only one opposed. The in-favor rate was 95.8 percent. 19 Asian countries in favor and 4 opposed. The in-favor rate was 82.6 percent. Twenty-six African countries were in favor and fifteen opposed. The in-favor rate was only 63.4 percent. Upon entering the UN, Beijing began to move away from the domination by revolutionary rhetoric, play down its ambition to lead world revolution movements, modify its commitments to insurgency movements in third world countries, and depart from economic autarky.

2

Deng Xiaoping's Developmental Diplomacy
Biding for China's Time

WHEN DENG XIAOPING RETURNED TO POWER after the terrors of the Cultural Revolution that plunged China into national calamity and mayhem, China was beleaguered, politically perturbed. The economy was in shambles. Although China's relative power and relations with the two superpowers did not undergo fundamental change, Deng Xiaoping envisioned that war with imperialist powers could be deferred or avoided. He shifted policy priority from preparing for war and revolution to creating a peaceful external environment for rapid economic development. Reflecting deeply about what went wrong and what needed to be done, Deng set out to open China to the outside world while learning from positive experiences and gaining access to the markets and capital in developed (capitalist) countries. Deng did not see the opening as the adoption of capitalism but instead as a way to develop China, best build socialism, and boost regime legitimacy.

The starting point of the new course was normalization of diplomatic relations with the United States, the most advanced economy in the world. The normalization opened the door for China to access US science, technology, capital, and markets. Holding high expectations for normalization, Deng, however, quickly discovered that the inherent ideological and political differences between China and the United States prevented them from developing a close partnership. To mitigate the vulnerabilities of dependence on the US,

Deng adopted an independent foreign policy to improve the relationship with the Soviet Union and build leverage in the relationship with the United States. The end of the Cold War and the demise of the USSR removed the original pillar undergirding the Sino-US rapprochement. Wrestling with the prospect that the United States would curtail support for China's modernization, Deng made a low-profile policy to live with the hegemon and focus on domestic development. Building leverage to balance the United States, China devoted great attention to good neighboring relations and active participation in multilateral institutions.

Deng's developmental diplomacy helped create a favorable external environment for China's rise in the twenty-first century. His handpicked successors, Jiang Zemin and Hu Jintao, faithfully followed his course. Struggling hard to balance the moderation and big power aspiration after China was widely recognized as a rising power, Hu Jintao pledged for China's peaceful development in the harmonious world to assure the international community that China's rise would offer opportunities and benefits rather than conflicts and threats. Although China remained a reluctant rising power and selectively took on global and regional obligations, Chinese foreign policy became omnidirectional, multilevel, and multidimensional. At the Central Foreign Affairs Work Conference in August 2006, Hu made the four phases statement about the importance of an array of foreign relations for China's developmental objectives: big powers were the key, periphery countries the priority, developing countries the foundation, and multilateralism the stage.[1]

Un-knocking the Key for Development

As the architect of China's reform and opening up, Deng was anxious to normalize the relationship with the United States, the key for his economic growth strategy. The negotiation had stagnated after President Nixon's visit because of the political development inside and outside of China. Internally, the power struggle between the radical Gang of Four, led by Mao's wife Jiang Qing, and the moderates, led by Premier Zhou Enlai, dragged out the conclusion of the Cultural Revolution. Purged by Mao for leading toward the capitalist road during the Cultural Revolution, Deng was brought back as vice-premier and PLA chief of staff in 1975 to help Zhou's "Four Modernizations" of agriculture, industry, defense, and science and technology. But Deng was accused of being the black hand behind the massive protests of the Gang of Four and suffered a second purge in early 1976. Deng returned to power only after the death of Mao and the coup d'état that removed the Gang of Four in September 1976. Winning the power struggle against Mao's designated successor Hua Guofeng in 1978, Deng became the paramount leader.

Building a strong leadership consensus that development had to be the top priority and reform and open-up were the pathway for development, Deng led Chinese delegations to visit six Asian countries, including Japan and Singapore, in 1978 and dispatched multiple delegations of senior leaders at the central and provincial levels to Japan and Europe to investigate their economic modernization. The purpose was to emancipate the minds of his colleagues, which would allow them to be aware of how backward and poor China was and aware of the need to focus on economic development. Vice-Premier Gu Mu led the first Chinese government economic delegation to visit Western Europe in May and June 1978 and was shocked by the technological advancement of capitalism and the development of industry and commerce. After returning to China, he gave a brief to the Politburo and State Council. The meeting started at 3:30 p.m. and did not end until 11 p.m. To catch up and modernize fast, Gu reported, China must introduce, digest, and absorb advanced technology from the West.[2] Deng learned that the new dynamos of Asia—Japan, South Korea, Taiwan, Hong Kong, and Singapore—relied heavily on the United States to grow faster than any country ever had. Many patents for goods produced in Europe were held by US individuals and companies.[3] Deng, therefore, took personal charge of the normalization negotiations with the United States.

Outside China, President Nixon was not able to follow through with normalization because the Watergate scandal forced him to resign. In addition, the Soviet Union's countermove to the Sino-US rapprochement by approaching the United States for détente reduced Washington's incentive to move forward in normalization. The Soviet insecurity strengthened the overall position of the United States.[4] Jimmy Carter's administration announced a withdrawal of American ground troops from South Korea in 1977 (later reversed). As a result, the strength of American military forces in the West Pacific would decline.[5]

Having secured détente with the United States and its European borders via the Helsinki Agreement, the Soviet Union turned eastward. In April

1978, Leonid Brezhnev announced that the greater part of the expanded defense budget was going to the Soviet Far East. For the first time, Soviet defense expenditures for Asia moved ahead of those for Europe.[6] The increased Soviet threat alarmed Beijing. Foreign Minister Huang Hua warned that "with American power shrinking and isolationism surging, the revisionist Soviet-imperialists are filling the vacuum to make expansionist and infiltrative moves." He proposed to win the United States over so that China could concentrate all forces to deal with the archenemy, the Soviet Union.[7]

The Americans were at first reluctant to convert to China's united front. President Carter and his secretary of state, Cyrus Vance, sought to pursue an "even-handed" policy and improve relations with Moscow and Beijing simultaneously. But such a policy backfired because both China and the Soviet Union resented the American approach. While Beijing-Washington relations declined, no significant progress was achieved in Soviet-American relations. The failure resulted in a shift from Vance's "evenhandedness" to Zbigniew Brzezinski's "balance of power" policy.[8] Brzezinski, the newly appointed national security advisor to Carter, visited Beijing in May 1978 and told Deng that the United States was ready to achieve normalization as quickly as possible.[9] After six months of negotiation, the United States accepted Deng's "three conditions" regarding Taiwan but expected a peaceful resolution and could not promise to suspend arms sales in Taiwan.

Deng refused to commit China to resolving the Taiwan issue peacefully but agreed that the two sides could express their ideas independently.[10] On the arms sale, Deng maintained that the US commitment to "one China policy" required the United States to stop selling weapons to Taiwan as soon as the relationship normalized. The Carter administration promised a one-year moratorium on arms sales after normalizing relations but could not go beyond the agreement to handle arms sales cautiously and prudently and transfer only defensive weapons. At this last-minute communication, Deng pushed Leonard Woodcock, the director of the American Liaison office in Beijing, to stop the arms sale before announcing normalization. Woodcock comforted him that, with time, the Taiwan issue could be resolved. The important first task was normalization. Deng agreed. Ezra Vogel, the author of Deng's biography, interpreted that Deng implicitly agreed to leave the reunification unsolved for the moment because Sino-US ties were essential to prevent a further shift of the global balance of power in Moscow's favor. More importantly, Deng was eager for China to have access to knowledge, capital, and technology from the United States.[11]

The normalization permitted the rapid development of strategic and economic ties. Deng became the first high-level PRC leader to make a state visit to America in January 1979. American officials were surprised by the number of bilateral agreements Deng was prepared to conclude during the visit and his eagerness for expanded relations with the United States.[12] After the visit, US secretary of defense Harold Brown and Chinese defense minister Geng Biao visited each other's country in 1980. Beijing agreed to allow the United States to establish electronic listening stations in Xinjiang to monitor Soviet rocket firings in Central Asia, which would replace the US listening posts in Iran shut down by the revolution. In exchange, the United States authorized the sale of military and civilian dual-use technology and nonlethal military equipment to China.

Most significantly for Deng's policy priorities, the normalization opened the doors for trade, investment, and technological exchanges. Relaxing restrictions on the export of advanced technology to China, Washington extended Most Favored Nation (MFN) status, which exempted high tariffs from Chinese exports and helped China's labor-intensive products enter the United States. Bilateral trade doubled from US$1.1 billion to $2.3 billion in 1979 and more than doubled again to US$4.9 billion in 1980. Additionally, the United States did not insist on numerical reciprocity in academic exchanges nor channel scholarly exchanges through a single national organization, as was the case with the Soviet Union. Opening its universities and research institutions to deal directly with their counterparts, the United States welcomed millions of Chinese to study the most advanced science and technology. They returned and became the backbone of China's economic modernization.

The normalization resulted in changes in all aspects of China. Mao suits gave way to jeans and shirts. Starbucks, Coca-Cola, McDonald's burgers, and KFC chicken became part of China's lifestyle, as were Hollywood movies and music. US degrees were a symbol of status. More importantly, it allowed China to follow the East Asian path of export-led growth and takeoff rapidly. China adopted the first "Law on Joint Venture using Chinese and Foreign Investment" in July 1979, which helped attract and absorb foreign technology and capital from the United States and other advanced countries and expand its exports to these countries. Getting rich by learning from and collaborating with the United States, China's subsequent rapid economic growth benefited immensely from the relations with the United States and other Western countries.

The Punitive War and Diplomatic Setback

Using normalization as a source of insurance, Deng launched a pedagogical war against Vietnam with the expectation of US endorsement. But the United States made only a lukewarm response. The relationship soured after the US Congress passed the Taiwan Relations Act (TRA) to help defend and maintain a semi-official relationship with Taiwan. Deng began to see the United States as an insincere and patronizing partner that promised more than it delivered, abandoned previous commitments, and treated China on unequal terms.[13]

Beijing's idea for war with Vietnam was evolved before Deng's US visit. China assisted Vietnamese communists to set up a buffer zone against possible US encirclement from the south during the US-Vietnam War. But Sino-Vietnamese relations experienced dramatic changes from comrades to rivals after the US withdrawal. Knowing that Vietnam had heavily depended on the Soviet Union, Beijing was concerned about the strong Soviet influence in the region "if Vietnam became a protectorate of sorts under the aegis of Moscow as guardian of the socialist camp."[14] China was also apprehensive that Vietnam proclaimed itself "the world's third-largest military power" by its military strength grown in the anti-American war and "pursued a regional hegemonic policy in an attempt to annex Cambodia, control Indochina, and carry out its ambitious plan of setting up the Federation of Greater Indochina."[15] In July 1978, the Politburo discussed possible military actions against Vietnam to disrupt Soviet strategic deployments. Two months later, the PLA General Staff recommended punitive actions.[16]

The breakdown came in November 1978 when Vietnam joined the Council for Mutual Economic Assistance (CMEA) and signed the Treaty of Friendship and Cooperation with the Soviet Union. With closer ties to the Soviet Union, Vietnam called for the formation of a special relationship between the three Indochinese countries to establish its dominance throughout Indochina. The Democratic Kampuchea (Khmer Rouge) regime rejected the proposal. On

Christmas Day 1978, precipitating a blitzkrieg, Vietnam invaded Cambodia, overran most of the country within a month, and placed Heng Samrin as the head of the new government. The Khmer Rouge units were forced to seek refuge in the isolated forests of the northwest and the rugged mountains near the gulf of Thailand. China was caught by surprise. The Chinese embassy in Phnom Penh moved and stayed with the Khmer Rouge in the jungle for fifteen days.[17]

Beijing reacted angrily to the invasion because if Vietnam dominated Indochina, the Soviet Union would have completed the encirclement of China's southern border. Mobilizing five hundred thousand troops and eight hundred aircraft to strike in what they hoped was a quick and devastating blow, China invaded Vietnam on February 14, 1979.[18] Beijing justified the invasion to counterattack Vietnamese troops that repeatedly crossed into Chinese territory and provoked those living along the border areas. With a degree of condescension, the Chinese viewed their influence in Vietnam as generous and civilizing. This minor tributary state had been in China's orbit since the second century BC. China would not tolerate its insolence. Deng vowed to "teach a necessary lesson" to the disrespectful Vietnamese who enjoyed substantial Chinese support during the Anti-American war but sided with the Soviet Union to challenge China now.[19]

Chinese forces moved six miles into Vietnam in four days, fifteen miles in six days, and twenty-five miles in nine days. The invasion was costly. Two weeks into the war, China suggested a truce and general cessation of hostilities. Vietnam agreed on peace talks but made them contingent on a withdrawal of Chinese forces. On March 4, China captured the town of Long Son and claimed victory. The following day, China announced withdrawal.

Deng's visit to the United States coincided with the Vietnam invasion in Cambodia. One of China's primary concerns for launching a punitive war was possible Soviet intervention. Deng wanted to get the US endorsement to deter the Soviet Union. Deng openly stated and made clear in private talks with the Carter administration that, regarding the Vietnamese invasion and provocation along the Chinese borders, China could not accept Vietnam's "wild ambitions" and was prepared to teach it a necessary lesson. Brzezinski revealed that President Carter reserved judgment but "the Chinese seemed to have construed this as tacit approval."[20]

Securing a joint communiqué that reiterated Sino-US opposition to hegemony, China felt that it had the "implicit support of the United States and the Soviet Union would be reluctant to be engaged in direct conflict with both China and the United States for the sake of Vietnam."[21] Deng made the final decision to invade Vietnam at the CMC meeting on February 9, the day after his return from the United States.[22] The proximity in the timing of the military thrust to Deng's US visit suggested Deng deliberately contrived to take advantage of the normalization to bluff the Soviets with a nonexistent US endorsement.

However, Deng miscalculated. Although China and America agreed to contain the Soviet Union–backed Vietnamese expansionism, they could not agree on how to achieve this objective. One aspect of disagreement was on the Khmer Rouge, who seized power from the pro-American Lon Nol regime in 1975. To the United States, any link to the regime was politically unpalatable in the wake of the urban resettlement policies of 1975–78, which resulted in the deaths of an estimated 1.5 million Cambodians.[23] Taking an ambivalent position during Deng's visit, Washington never endorsed China's military action. Playing down the international outcry against the invasion by putting it in perspective, Washington took an even-handed approach and called for "two withdrawals": Vietnam from Cambodia and China from Vietnam.[24]

The outcome was a disappointment to both the Americans and the Chinese. To the Americans, the Chinese had resorted to "pedagogical war" in defense of a morally indefensible regime, demonstrating that Beijing could act boldly and unilaterally without much concern for American sensibilities. Americans were disconcerted by a Chinese predilection for the role of agent provocateur. In addition, the United States found that China's armed forces were backward, could be modernized only at prodigious expense, and posed no threat to Soviet naval and air bases on the Pacific coast or Soviet territory in Siberia.[25] China was disappointed in the United States' passivity only months after the euphoria of normalization. American backing off from a venture in which China bore the main risk was a coward action, clouding prospects of further joint action into question. Beijing was particularly dismayed about the US statement that "America will not be directly involved in the armed conflicts among communist countries in Asia. The US immediate interests and the securities of American allies in Asia are not threatened by the conflicts."[26]

As mutual dissolution developed quickly, the US Congress passed the TRA in April 1979 and approved the sale of $292 million in military equipment to Taiwan in 1980. Beijing believed the TRA seriously violated the normalization agreement because it not only stated that the US decision to open diplomatic ties with the PRC "rests on the expectation that the future of Taiwan will be determined by peaceful means," but also stipulated that the United States would provide Taiwan with arms necessary to defend the island. Beijing viewed these clauses as the covert reinstitution of US military protection over Taiwan. The carefully negotiated and finely balanced compromise embodied in the normalization agreement was overturned by unilateral US actions.[27] The Sino-US relationship suffered a severe loss of momentum when the Reagan administration promised to upgrade relations with Taiwan and increase the arms sales in 1981.

The Independent Foreign Policy

As the relationship with the United States stagnated, China took note of the signals of the Soviet Union to restore relations with China. The Soviet digest of anti-Chinese articles *Opasnyi Kurs* (Dangerous course), published in 1969, produced its final issue in 1981. The polemics against China in the Soviet press virtually ceased after 1982.[28] Premier Leonid Brezhnev's speech on March 19, 1982, acknowledged "the existence of a socialist system in China." He pointed out that, unlike the United States, the Soviet Union had consistently supported "the PRC's sovereignty over Taiwan." He also offered to discuss the resolution of the border dispute and resume economic, scientific, cultural, and political relations with Beijing.[29]

Brezhnev's speech caught Deng's attention immediately. He instructed the Ministry of Foreign Affairs (MFA) to make an initial response. Qian Qichen as the MFA spokesperson made a guarded statement on March 26 that Beijing considered "deeds, rather than words" to be the true measure of Soviet intentions.[30] Deng called upon other top leaders to meet in his home and decided to send the director-general of the Department of the Soviet Union and East Europe in the MFA to Moscow on August 10 to pass on Deng's message that China was willing to explore the possible normalization of the relationship.[31] The next month, General Secretary Hu Yaobang at the CCP's Twelfth Congress declared that China adopted an "independent foreign policy" and would never "attach itself to any big power or group of powers." He explicitly stated, "The Chinese people had a long history of friendship with the Soviet people. It doesn't matter what status of the relationship is now, we will make efforts to develop the friendship."[32]

The speech was reassuring enough for Moscow to resume the bilateral talks that had been suspended after the Soviet invasion of Afghanistan. The first round of talks started in Beijing on October 5, 1982. Deng instructed the Chinese delegation to move slowly and not be too rushed in making changes. China repeated the three demands that Hu Yaobang raised earlier: withdrawal of Soviet troops from Mongolia; withdrawal of Soviet troops from Afghanistan; and cessation of Soviet support for Vietnam's occupation of Cambodia.[33]

The rapid succession of Soviet leaders— Brezhnev died in November 1982, his successor Yuri Andropov died in February 1984, and Konstantin Chernenko died in March 1985—created an opportunity for the "funeral diplomacy" to build the momentum of Sino-Soviet rapprochement.

At Brezhnev's funeral, Chinese foreign minister Huang Hua held talks with his counterpart, Andrei Gromyko, but Vietnam's foreign minister met only Leonid Ilichev, a vice foreign minister. At Andropov's funeral, China was represented by Wan Li, a Politburo member and vice-premier, signaling China's positive assessment of the deceased Soviet leader as well as hopes for better relations. For Chernenko's funeral, Beijing sent Vice-Premier Li Peng, who was educated in the Soviet Union and spoke Russian. New general secretary Mikhail Gorbachev received him twice and reaffirmed the Soviet Union's desire to significantly improve the relationship.[34] At the meeting, the two sides began referring to each other as comrades, "a word suggesting that no serious ideological difficulty exists between them."[35] Li Peng congratulated the Soviet Union's achievement of a "socialist course." The Soviet leaders interpreted the term as China's willingness to reunite with the Soviet Union under the banner of a socialist big family. But the Chinese side made it clear that China was willing to improve the relationship but not return to the "big family." China would maintain an independent foreign policy and develop a normal state-to-state relationship.[36]

The primary cause of the Sino-Soviet détente was the changing strategic perceptions of both sides. To avoid the nightmare of two-front wars with the United States and China, Moscow wanted to strengthen its strategic position against the United States. Positioning itself independent of the United States, thereby threatening to defect from the anti-Soviet camp, Beijing wanted more maneuvering room to make Washington more sensitive to its concerns, especially regarding Taiwan.[37] As the Soviet Union had largely spent the international momentum generated in the 1970s and was increasingly preoccupied with its domestic problems, the greater internal stability and economic growth in the post-Mao era made China much less vulnerable to Soviet threat.[38] Pursuing the equal distance between the United States and the Soviet Union, Deng was aimed to build leverage to tilt the balance of power.[39]

In the meantime, Deng's market-oriented economic reform and Gorbachev's perestroika faced similar challenges. Deng saw compelling economic grounds for the reduction of tensions with the Soviet Union so that China could devote all available resources for economic development. Gorbachev wanted to have a more peaceful relationship with China to reduce the Soviets' heavy burden of military expenses.[40] Additionally, China's experiences with economic reform intrigued Moscow. Gorbachev told the readers of a Chinese magazine, "We take special interest in China's ongoing economic and political reforms. Our two countries are now faced with similar problems. This will open a broad horizon for useful mutual exchange of experiences."[41]

Personnel changes in the two countries also facilitated the détente. The appointment of Soviet-educated Li Peng to the premiership was significant. One-third of his cabinet members were Soviet-trained, including Foreign Minister Qian Qichen. Just as Huang Hua and Qiao Guanhua, both Americanists, headed the foreign ministry at the time of Sino-US rapprochement, the "Soviet-trained foreign minister Qian's promotion signaled Beijing's intention in further improving Sino-Soviet relations."[42] On the Soviet side, Brezhnev's team of Sinologists recruited in the 1960s helped formulate a pressure-oriented policy toward China. In 1985, Gorbachev replaced old-guard foreign minister Andrei Gromyko with Eduard Shevardnadze, who had virtually no foreign policy experience and no ties to old policies.

The increasing commercial relations showed one aspect of accelerated Sino-Soviet rapprochement. Bilateral trade almost tripled from $960 million in 1983 to $2.36 billion in 1986 and then to more than $3.2 billion in 1988.[43] In his Vladivostok speech of July 28, 1986, Gorbachev promised concessions on two of China's three obstacles by announcing the imminent withdrawal of six

Soviet regiments from Afghanistan and the removal of a significant portion of the Soviet troops from Mongolia. He also indicated a willingness to negotiate a mutual reduction of the remaining forces along the Sino-Soviet border.[44] Beijing published Gorbachev's speech on the front page of *People's Daily*. Deng on a September 1986 broadcast of the US news program *60 Minutes* offered to meet Gorbachev if he was willing to persuade the Vietnamese to withdraw from Cambodia, the last major impediment to improved relations.

In spring 1988, Hanoi announced the withdrawal of all its forces from Cambodia in September 1989. This move cleared the way for Gorbachev to make a historic visit to Beijing on May 15–18, 1989. For the protocol of the meeting, Deng instructed the MFA that he and Gorbachev would only shake hands but not hug each other, which positioned the relationship on the normal state-to-state base rather than as members of a socialist family.[45] When the first Sino-Soviet summit meeting in thirty years took place in Beijing, it was hailed as marking the restoration of both normal state-to-state relations and party-to-party ties.[46] To the dismay of both leaders, however, the massive antigovernment demonstrations in Tiananmen Square deflected attention from the historic meeting.

Learning to Live with the Hegemon

China's strategic leverage between the two superpowers was lost after the end of the Cold War. The massive pro-democracy demonstrations on Tiananmen Square and the bloody crackdown in 1989 that preluded the end of the Cold War were followed by the dramatic fall of the Berlin Wall and the disintegration of the Soviet Union. China was left as a lonely communist state, subject to the outpouring of Western outrage on the human rights violation and the repressive government.

The condemnation was a shock to Beijing because the Western countries had judged China by different moral criteria than other countries on human rights. The United States began restoring diplomatic contacts with China during the Cultural Revolution, the worst period of repression. Deng's crackdown on Beijing's Democracy Wall Movement in 1979 was followed by the invitation from President Carter for his upbeat visit. Deeply impressed that Deng was "small, tough, intelligent, frank, courageous, personable, self-assured, friendly," Carter failed to challenge Deng when he said that Chinese people had been permitted substantial freedom of speech and expression.[47] Carter's attempt to raise China's human rights issue was silenced by Deng's jocular offer to provide as many as two hundred million Chinese, if necessary, to the United States for protection of human rights.[48]

The Tiananmen crackdown locked Chinese leaders in an unwelcome struggle against Western sanctions. France froze relations and became a haven for Chinese dissidents from Tiananmen. Australia cut back on aid and loans. Sweden put aid on hold and banned military shipments. Switzerland likewise banned military sales. Norway froze credits and new exports. West Germany delayed the signing of the already completed financial assistance agreement. In the United States, while the George H. W. Bush administration tried to save the relationship, it had to suspend all exports of weapons and high-level changes. Promising not to coddle tyrants to Beijing and chastising his predecessor for conducting business as usual with those who murdered freedom in Tiananmen Square, President Bill Clinton issued an executive order in 1993 to link human rights conditions for the extension of China's MFN status beyond July 1994.

Conditioned by circumscribed capabilities and geostrategic isolation, Deng proposed the "twenty-four characters guidelines" for China to go through the difficult time: observe carefully (冷静观察); secure China's positions (稳住阵脚); calmly cope with the challenges (沉着应付); hide China's capacities and bide its time (韬光养晦); be good at maintaining a low profile (善于守拙); and never claim leadership (绝不当头).[49] "Learning to live with the hegemon" by adapting to the reality of the US dominance in the world,[50] China would conduct shrewd diplomacy, which "requires rationality and calmness," and avoid becoming the second "Mr. No," and repeating the failure of the Soviet Union in a competition for hegemony that exhausted its economic and military capacity.[51]

Deng met twice with President Bush's National Security Advisor, Brent Scowcroft, who had been secretly dispatched to Beijing and privately urged the Bush Administration to help rescue the rapidly sinking relationship. Deng also allowed prominent dissident Fang Lizhi, who had taken refuge in the US embassy in Beijing, to leave China in June 1990. Most prominent political prisoners were released. As a friendly posture, China did not veto the UN vote for the US military intervention in Kuwait on August 2, 1990.

In response, the Bush administration lifted the sanctions that prohibited high-level official contacts with China and invited Foreign Minister Qian Qichen to visit Washington on November 30, 1990. The US secretary of state James Baker visited Beijing in November 1991. Responding to the accusation that Beijing had transferred nuclear technology to such countries as Algeria, Iran, Pakistan, and North Korea, Jiang Zemin assured him that China would abide by international agreements banning nuclear proliferation. The next month, China signed the Nuclear Non-proliferation Treaty (NPT).[52]

The warming of relations was tested by a crisis after the US Navy stopped a Chinese container ship, *Yinhe*, on suspicion it carried chemical weapons components to Iran in July 1993. China denied the allegation, but the United States unilaterally cut off the civilian GPS signals on the ship, causing it to lose direction and anchor on the high seas for twenty-four days until it agreed to inspection. No chemicals were found. But the United States declined Chinese demands for a formal apology and compensation in damages.[53]

Despite the humiliation, President Jiang downplayed the effect and attended the inaugural Asian Pacific Economic Cooperation (APEC) summit in Seattle to meet with President Clinton in November 1993. Before the trip, Jiang proposed a "sixteen-characters formula" to work with the United States: "enhancing confidence, reducing troubles, expanding cooperation, and avoiding confrontation" (增加信任, 减小麻烦, 加强合作, 不搞对抗).[54] Demonstrating a goodwill posture, Jiang presented to Clinton a carefully selected gift, a beautiful saxophone, which the Chinese leader learned that Clinton was good at and loved to play.

Clinton delinked China's MFN and human rights records in 1994. Jiang and Clinton exchanged state visits in 1997 and 1998 respectively and issued a joint statement to build a constructive strategic partnership toward the twenty-first century. During Clinton's visit to Shanghai, he declared the "three nos'": not recognizing two Chinas (or one China, one Taiwan); not supporting independence for Taiwan; and not backing Taiwan to join international organizations that require sovereignty for membership.[55]

The relationship was tested again after the US-led NATO bombed the Chinese embassy in Belgrade on May 7, 1999, which blasted outrage among the Chinese people who could not accept the US explanation that it was accidental. The Jiang leadership did everything it could to pacify the outrage because the relationship with the United States was considered too valuable to sacrifice to the emotion of the moment.[56] Manipulating the events to China's advantage, Beijing pushed for significant US concessions on its entry into the World Trade Organization (WTO). The two countries reached an agreement in November 1999 and the US Congress endorsed the agreement in 2000. China concluded the WTO negotiation in 2001.

President George W. Bush came to office and claimed China strategic competitor rather than a strategic partner. A mid-air collision of a Chinese jet fighter with a US EP-3 reconnaissance plane over the South China Sea on April 1, 2001, touched off a tense crisis. While the crisis created negative feelings and stoked nationalist sentiment in China, President Jiang accepted US Secretary of State Colin Powell's expression of very sorry for the loss of the Chinese pilot and aircraft as the formal apology it demanded and released the American crew. After President Bush approved the largest package of $5 billion arms sales to Taiwan and abandoned Clinton's strategic ambiguity to state unequivocally that he would do whatever it took to defend Taiwan, Jiang followed Deng's tactic of "criticism, struggle, and then turn around" (一批 二斗 三转弯) in response to Bush sr.'s sale of F-16 fighters to Taiwan a decade ago and maintained the relationship.[57]

The September 11 terrorist attacks provided an opportunity for Beijing to improve relations. Hours after the attacks, Jiang sent a telegram to Bush to express condolences as well as the Chinese government's opposition to terrorism. George W. Bush telephoned Jiang the next day and stated that he looked forward to combating terrorism together with Jiang and other world leaders. A week after the attacks, Chinese foreign minister Tang Jiaxuan arrived in Washington to prepare for Bush's October state visit to Beijing. Because he was overseeing the military operation in Afghanistan, Bush canceled his state visit but came to Shanghai for the APEC summit and met with Jiang. Proposing a "constructive, cooperative, and candid" relationship with China, Bush made up the state visit to Beijing in March 2002.[58] While it was unprecedented that a US president visited China twice within five months, a third summit took place at the Bush family ranch in Crawford, Texas, on October 25, the highest frequency of meeting between the presidents of the two countries in history.

The war on terror profoundly changed the focus of US security concerns. While the Pentagon's *Quadrennial Defense Report* in September 2001 identified

China as the long-term threat to the United States, the administration's National Security Strategy in September 2002 identified global terrorism as a primary threat and asserted the need for working closely with China to combat terrorism. When Vice President Hu Jintao visited Washington in October 2002, he was invited and became the highest-ranking Chinese official to visit the Pentagon. The dramatic change was due to the "most important adjustment in Chinese foreign policy toward the United States and US interests in world affairs since the end of the cold war, strongly emphasizing the positive while eschewing pressure, confrontation, and conflict."[59]

Beijing was noticeably relieved after the United States launched the Iraq War, which tied up much of US national resources. Beijing believed that "the United States now needs China's help on issues such as counterterrorism, nonproliferation, the reconstruction of Iraq, and the maintenance of stability in the Middle East."[60] The US preoccupation was conducive for China's continuing focus on domestic development and stability. At the Sixteenth CCP Congress in October 2002, Hu Jintao presented the goal of quadrupling the 2000 GDP by 2020 and transforming China into a *Xiaogang* society, in which the Chinese people would enjoy an abundant and comfortable life. China was to "devote wholeheartedly to development and construction" and build up comprehensive national strength, composed of international competitiveness, efficient and flexible diplomacy, and a compatible military capability.[61] China was not to challenge US dominance in the world because the United States remained the sole superpower in terms of its economy, scientific and technological strength, military might, and foreign influence.[62]

Beijing was pleased when the Bush administration was upset with Taiwan after Chen Shui-bian was elected president in 2002 and made a series of provocations. As President Bush made crystal clear his opposition to a declaration of Taiwanese independence, the Chinese saw "Washington as playing a role in restraining Taipei's separatist movement."[63] This positive relationship continued in the first year of the Barack Obama administration. The Chinese leadership was pleased to hear from Secretary of State Hillary Clinton before her first Asian trip that "some believe that China on the rise is, by definition, an adversary. On the contrary, we believe that the United States and China can benefit from and contribute to each other's successes."[64]

Good Neighboring Policy

Keeping a low profile policy in relations with the United States, China used an array of balancing techniques to expand its international engagement. The priority was on the periphery. Beijing embraced the prospect of a "Pacific Century" with the hope that fast economic growth in the region could offer new energy to China's prosperity. The emergence of "new Arianism," which claimed that the success of Asian modernization was based on its unique values, also resonated in the hearts of Chinese leaders. Beijing would take advantage of the regional activism to face the West.[65] While Deng started formulating good neighboring policy in the 1980s, Jiang Zemin intensified the effort after the Cold War to stabilize periphery (稳定周边), expand diplomacy (开拓外交), and alter the situation (扭转局面).[66] Specifically, Beijing would explore the common ground with periphery countries in economic and security arenas to convey the image of a responsible power willing to contribute to stability and cooperation in the region.

Luring trade and investment from Japan and other East Asian newly industrial countries, Beijing looked for shared security interests with its neighbors. One Chinese strategist divided China's periphery countries into three categories: those who shared China's interest in reducing the pressure of the United States intervening in their internal affairs; those who hoped to maintain the US strategical advantage but did not have major conflicts of interest with China; and those who wanted to prevent China from becoming a security threat. China shared strategic interests with most of the periphery countries and could work with them to build a favorable security environment.[67]

Bordering fourteen countries, China has more than thirty "neighbors" if nearby states that don't border China are counted. Perceiving some of its neighbors as a threat due to border disputes or their alliances with hostile powers, Beijing was on constant alert against possible invasions by hostile powers via its neighboring countries and also fought wars in neighboring countries. When the United States was perceived as the most hostile power, China was alert against US allies in the region, including Japan, South Korea, and Thailand. When the Soviet Union became a serious threat, Beijing regarded Mongolia and Vietnam as contributing to the encirclement of China.

Making important adjustments to implement the good neighboring policy, Beijing abandoned ideology as the guidance to develop friendly relations with neighbors regardless of their ideological tendencies and changed the practice of defining China's relations with its neighbors according to their relations with either the Soviet Union or the United States. China would develop normal relations with neighboring countries regardless of their relations with other powers.[68] Chinese leaders also showed a benign face to settle border disputes through consultations and negotiations. During the century of humiliation, Western powers took over China's tributaries and pushed the frontiers forward into areas that China would have preferred to control itself. After the founding of the PRC, Beijing found itself in a series of territorial disputes and fought border wars with India, the Soviet Union, and Vietnam. Taking a set of relatively conservative, stability-seeking initiatives and practices to negotiate border disputes, China deemphasized the use of confrontational claims and made use of diplomatic measures and legal agreements in the 1990s.[69]

China signed a border agreement in November 1988 with Mongolia, which had long been perceived as a Soviet satellite in China's northern frontier, and realized the ice-breaking visit of Indian prime minister Rajiv Gandhi to Beijing in December 1988, the first such visit after the Sino-India border war in 1962.[70] The Tiananmen crackdown in 1989 led to the deterioration of China's relations with Western countries but had little negative impact on relations with Asian neighbors, as the human rights records in most of these countries were not better than China's. To a certain extent, they were sympathetic to China's struggle against pressures from Western countries. While China's relations with Western countries soured, its relations with periphery countries improved.

Beijing's relationship with Russia improved spectacularly. Following President Boris Yeltsin's first official visit to China in December 1992, Beijing and Moscow institutionalized a twice-a-year summit meeting system at the president and premier levels. Jiang and Yeltsin met five times by the end of 1997. Despite Yeltsin's critical health situation, the sixth summit was held in a Moscow hospital in 1998 and Yeltsin visited Beijing for the seventh summit in 1999, culminating in a landmark joint communiqué criticizing American hegemony and denouncing the use of "human rights interventions" by foreign countries. China declared Chechnya a matter of Russian internal affairs. Russia supported China's sovereignty over Taiwan.[71] The Sino-Russian relationship was defined as a "constructive partnership" in 1994, "strategic" was added in

1996, and was finalized as a "strategic cooperative partnership towards the 21st Century" in 1997.

After the retirement of Yeltsin, Chinese leaders continued the partnership with President Vladimir Putin. At the July 2001 summit, they signed the Good Neighborly Treaty of Friendship and Cooperation. Article 9 of the treaty notes that "when a situation arises in which one of the contracting parties deems that peace is being threatened and undermined or its security interests are involved or when it is confronted with the threat of aggression, the contracting parties shall immediately hold contacts and consultations to eliminate such threats." This could be construed as an implicit commitment to mutual defense. The partnership resulted in the demarcation of the eastern section of the Sino-Russian border in November 1997 and culminated in the 2008 treaty in which Beijing acquiesced to Moscow's historical claim to thousands of square kilometers of Chinese-claimed territory to settle a dispute over the world's longest land border.

Beijing's normalization of relations with Southeast Asian countries was also impressive. Settling the land border with Vietnam in 1991 and establishing diplomatic relations with Indonesia and Singapore in 1990 and Brunei in 1991, Beijing consolidated its position after the Asian financial crisis in 1997. As a wave of defaults and devaluations hit the region, many East Asian countries looked for assistance from the United States and Japan to bail them out. But both countries responded slowly. In contrast, China made a highly symbolic move to firmly refuse the devaluation of its currency. A Chinese devaluation would set off competitive devaluation and have devastating consequences for the whole region. Beijing also contributed an estimated $4 billion to its ailing neighbors through bilateral channels and participation in bailout packages put together by the International Monetary Fund (IMF). A World Bank report in 1999, therefore, appraised China as "one source of stability for the region."[72]

As a result, many Southeast Asian countries not only sided with China against US pressures on the human rights issue but also accepted Beijing's position that reunification with Taiwan was China's domestic affair. President Jiang was invited to meet with his ASEAN counterparts to start the annual ASEAN+1 summit and then joined the leaders of Japan, South Korea, and ASEAN countries at the first ASEAN+3 summit, in which he announced the Sino-ASEAN Good Neighboring and Mutual-trust Partnership Toward the Twenty-first Century. While China's long-term power potential was still viewed with trepidation, China was welcomed by many neighbors as a partner.

Additionally, Beijing secured balanced relationships with both Koreas by focusing on trade and investment to normalize the diplomatic relationship with South Korea in 1992 while making every effort to keep strategic relations with the North.[73] The relationship across the Taiwan Strait was also significantly relaxed. Shifting from "liberating Taiwan" by force to a peaceful offensive, Beijing proposed three links of commercial, postal, and travel, and four exchanges of academic, cultural, economic, and sports to gradually eliminate antagonism.[74]

The success of China's good neighboring policy coincided with American relative inattention to the region. China participated in the inaugural East Asia Summit (EAS) in 2005, while the United States was not invited and appeared virtually moribund. One commentator wrote, "The U.S. is perceived as the pushy, intrusive troublemaker in the region, making demands on a range of issues from human rights to intellectual property to the environment. Meanwhile, Beijing is refraining from pushing ideology on its neighbors. Rather it is pledging pragmatic partnerships for mutual benefit while rebuilding its traditional prestige as the Middle Kingdom and capitalizing on the natural desire among Asians for self-reliance and freedom from outside interference."[75]

Compared with George W. Bush, Hu Jintao was more adept at maintaining relationships while tamping down concerns of China's rise. At the APEC summit in 2007, when Bush addressed an audience of the business elite on the war on terror, Hu talked about the business opportunities from China's growth. The messages "underscore how Washington and Beijing are now being perceived in the Asia-Pacific region, where the U.S. role seems to be slipping, while China is seen as the power of the future."[76]

Many analysts confirmed this observation when they wrote that "The US is suddenly no longer the only power to which lesser nations pay tribute. Strengthened by the relentless growth of its economy, China wields more influence among its Asian neighbors with every passing year."[77] "China is more popular and the target of less suspicion than in the past among many Asian governments, elites and popular opinion, and its economic importance as an engine of Asian growth has increased."[78] Providing the economic engine for regional growth and wagering its neighbors' reliance on its economy for trade and investment, Beijing built goodwill, close ties, and space for strategic posturing to ease suspicion over China's geopolitical intentions.

Regional Multilateral Initiatives

Beijing also evoked enthusiasm for multilateral regional institutions to expand international engagement. Becoming a member of the ASEAN Regional Forum (ARF) in 1994 and ASEAN's comprehensive dialogue partner in1996, China institutionalized its participation in what they called the three-meeting mechanism: ASEAN Foreign Ministerial Meeting, Enlarged ASEAN Foreign Ministerial Meeting, and ARF. China participated in the first ASEAN+3 summit in December 1997, took a lead to establish the EAS in 2005, and donated $20 million to the Asian Development Bank (ADB) for a regional poverty reduction center in 2005, the first fund set up by China at an international institution.

Most significantly, China initiated two regional security institutions: the Shanghai Cooperation Organization (SCO), which has developed successfully into a regional security institution; and the Six-Party Talks on the denuclearization of the Korean Peninsula, which failed but left a legacy for China's strategic leverage over the United States.

Beijing signed the Treaty of Enhancing Military Mutual Trust in the Border Areas with Russia, Kazakhstan, Tajikistan, and Kyrgyzstan in Shanghai in 1996. The treaty intended to prevent Islamic militancy from fueling separatism in Xinjiang, and to secure relations with the newly independent Central Asian states after the disintegration of the Soviet Union. Inaugurating the annual meeting in 1997, the "Shanghai Five" began to meet under the name of the SCO after Uzbekistan was accepted in 2001. Mongolia received observer status in 2004; Iran, Pakistan, and India became observers the following year. India and Pakistan received full memberships in 2017.

Covering three-fifths of the Eurasian continent and nearly half of the human population, the SCO has become the largest regional organization in the world in terms of geographical size and population and evolved into a semi-alliance in which the member states have agreed to take actions on political, military, and intelligence cooperation for the purpose of cracking down on the so-called "three evils" of terrorism, separatism, extremism. It established the Heads of State Council as the supreme decision-making body and the Regional Antiterrorism Organization, which is capable of speedy intervention in a crisis. After the first counterterrorism joint military exercises in Kyrgyzstan in 2002, the SCO has conducted regular military exercises among member states.

Beijing has played a leadership role to strengthen mutual trust and good-neighborliness among member states to stabilize the frontier and defend its security in Eurasia, open-up new development space, and provide strategic support for China's role on the international stage.[79] To balance US power, Beijing promoted its new security concept (新安全观): that no single state, even the most powerful country, could cope with all the challenges alone.[80] Sharing the grievances over US dominance in the region, China and Russia had strong motivation to take advantage of the SCO to balance US power and stop US "color revolutions" in their neighborhoods.[81]

The Six-Party Talks of China, the United States, North and South Koreas, Japan, and Russia were meant to end North Korea's nuclear program after US intelligence uncovered North Korea's uranium-enrichment program in summer 2002. The talks called for regional countries with a stake to work together and compel North Korea to abandon its nuclear program. Suspecting the United States' main objective was regime change, Beijing was initially reluctant to join the multilateral effort. But China changed its position over concerns the United States might launch a preemptive strike on North Korea's nuclear complex after North Korea reactivated its nuclear power plant in Yongbyon, withdrew from the NPT, and expelled the International Atomic Energy Agency (IAEA) inspectors.[82] In addition, China hoped the negotiations could develop into a kind of multilateral security mechanism in Northeast Asia so that China could play a leading role.[83]

Beijing dispatched former vice-premier Qian Qichen as a special envoy to Pyongyang in early 2003 to persuade the Democratic People's Republic of Korea (DPRK) to join multilateral talks. The DPRK participated in the first trilateral meeting with the United States and China in April 2003. The talks were expanded into six parties in August 2003. A joint statement in September 2005 committed Pyongyang to abandon its quest for nuclear power, eventually dismantle all nuclear weapons and existing nuclear programs, rejoin the NPT, and allow IAEA monitors to return. In exchange, the United States affirmed that it had no intention to attack or invade North Korea and would provide North Korea with food and energy assistance.[84]

The joint statement, however, quickly fell apart because Washington and Pyongyang seized upon its ambiguity to start a round of disagreement about what constituted a "dismantling" and a "freeze" of nuclear enrichment. The talks came to a halt in November 2005 when the US Treasury Department requested the Macao government to freeze $25 million of North Korean funds in Banco Delta Asia for alleged money laundering. As the talks fell apart, North Korea stepped up provocations and announced a successful nuclear test on October 9, 2006. In response, the UNSC unanimously adopted Resolution 1718, condemning North Korea's action and imposing sanctions on certain luxury goods and trade of military units, Weapons of Mass Destruction (WMD)-related parts, and technology transfers.

China voted in favor of the UN resolution because the North Korea nuclear test amounted to a major failure for one of China's most extensive diplomatic efforts. The Chinese Foreign Ministry statement expressed its anger in unusually strong terms: "The Chinese side strongly demands the DPRK side abide by its commitment to going nuclear-free, halt all the activities that will possibly lead to the further deterioration of the situation and once again return to the track of the Six-Party Talks."[85] But China quickly returned to its previous position of calling for dialogue, eschewing confrontation, and warning against comprehensive sanctions because China was concerned about growing US influence close to home.

China's interest in the North Korean nuclear issue was different from the United States'. For Washington, nuclear disarmament was the fundamental issue and likely could only be achieved by a regime change. Beijing would like to see a denuclearized North Korea but insisted in "three nos": no chaos (不乱), no wars (不战), and no nuclear (不核), which meant the survival of the North Korean regime, the stability in the peninsula, and stopping the nuclear domino effects in Northeast Asia. Beijing was concerned that the United States used non-nuclearization as an excuse to make regime change.[86] Beijing needed North Korea as a buffer against US troops in South Korea. Moreover, if the regime fell, the risk of North Korean refugees flooding across the border into China was a frightening prospect. Frustrated with US inflexibility and suspicion of its real intentions, while China criticized the nuclear test with the strongest expression in the history of its relations with North Korea, China urged the United States to show flexibility to resolve the standoff.

After a few months of hiatus, North Korea agreed to return to the talks in December 2006. The sixth round of Six-Party Talks in Beijing hammered out a denuclearization accord on February 13, 2007. The implementation of the accord seemed to go well for about a year. Hopes ran high that the Six-Party Talks would produce a regime of arms control and regional security.[87] This hope, however, was shattered during the last months of the Bush administration as Pyongyang failed to agree to the details of a verification protocol. Weeks before the inauguration of President Obama, North Korea revived its rhetoric for a nuclear weapons power status and demanded that normalization of relations with the United States must be achieved before it would fully dismantle its nuclear weapons program.

Although the Obama administration signaled its readiness to engage Pyongyang, North Korea responded with multiple missile tests. After the failed launch of its Kwangmyŏngsŏng-2 missiles on April 5, 2009, the UNSC unanimously passed a resolution to condemn the rocket launch. One day after the UNSC's statement, North Korea kicked international monitors out of their nuclear facilities and announced that it "will never again take part in the six-party talks and will not be bound by any agreement reached during the talks."[88] After Pyongyang conducted a nuclear test in May 2009, the United States pushed for tougher sanctions through a new UNSC resolution, which blew up the prospects for resuming the Six-Party Talks.

The talks failed not only because North Korea had no intention of abandoning its nuclear programs, but also because all the parties placed their own agendas above the multilateral approach. Chinese scholars described the talks as a "Face-Mask Dance Party" in which North Korea played the game for the regime's survival while each of the other parties used the nuclear issue for their geopolitical objectives.[89] One South Korean observer commented that "the out-of-focus six-party talks failed to follow up agreements as each member state spends time coordinating its different policy position toward the North's provocative behavior." The talks, therefore, became "a structure that cannot turn a wolf into a sheep."[90]

China's role in the Six-Party Talks was very complex. As Pyongyang's long-standing ally and main supplier of energy and food assistance, Beijing had the leverage to bring North Korea to the negotiating table. But China's principal objective was peaceful denuclearization without damaging the strategic relationship with North Korea. It would be a nightmare if the DPRK nuclear program caused an American military strike or full-scale war. But a unified Korea led by the South was also undesirable: China was afraid of US troops in a unified Korea overlooking Chinese territory.

China's leadership role in the Six-Party Talks boosted its leverage over Washington. Working with China to maintain peace and stability in the Korean Peninsula, the United States found it difficult to use force, which would destabilize the region at China's doorstep. In addition, the United States on occasions had to consider the potential impact on Beijing's cooperation on the Six-Party Talks when deliberating on other issues. As one study found, although "China did not blatantly put pressure on Washington or threaten to curtail cooperation on North Korea unless the U.S. took a specified action, U.S. diplomats simply became more mindful of avoiding actions that would irritate Beijing, especially at sensitive junctures in the Six-Party negotiations."[91]

Beijing was upset when North Korea announced its withdrawal from the Six-Party Talks on May 25, 2009, because China would lose leverage over the United States. Joining the United States and other parties in adopting UNSC Resolution 1874 that imposed new sanctions on North Korea in 2009, China posed a travel ban and asset freeze on some North Korean officials as proposed by the United States and other Western nations. China, however, became very alert when it discovered that these actions caused tensions in its relationship with North Korea and the Obama administration proposed direct US–North Korean talks in early September 2009. To avoid being sidelined, Beijing sent State Counselor Dai Binguo as President Hu's special envoy to Pyongyang to repair its relations. The Six-Party Talks failed or not, Beijing wanted to be included and play a role.

A Reluctant Rising Power

Wrapping its great power aspirations in modesty and focusing on domestic development, China boasted the world's fastest-growing economy, which caused anxiety among neighbors. Making a preemptive effort to build an image of a peace-loving and responsible power, President Hu's aid, Zheng Bijian, put forward the concept of China's peaceful rise at the March 2003 Boao Asian Forum—an annual high-level gathering of political and business leaders from Asia-Pacific countries on China's Hainan Island. Premier Wen

Jiabao endorsed this concept in his New York City speech in December 2003. But some Chinese scholars and officials expressed the concern that "rise" sounded too provocative and might imply attaining a superpower status that could intimidate some of China's neighbors.[92]

Hu, therefore, used the bland phrase "peaceful development" in his speech at the 2004 Boao Forum. To reconcile rise and development, Zheng Bijian in his 2005 Boao speech elaborated: "China has chosen a strategy to develop by taking advantage of the peaceful international environment, and at the same time to maintain world peace through its development. This is a strategy of peaceful rise, namely, a strategy of peaceful development."[93] Rhetoric aside, the declared commitment to a peaceful development reflected Chinese leaders' recognition that China's rise still required a peaceful and stable external environment. Although the concept was transitional and instrumental, China would not give up the rhetoric before it secured a big power position.

The rhetoric of peaceful development was accompanied by Hu Jintao's another brainchild concept, the "harmonious world," derived from traditional Chinese thinking that harmony was at the core of dealing with everything from state affairs to neighborly relations. Chinese scholars described that the key attribute of a harmonious world was building and accepting a world of divergence in national development strategies and political systems.[94] The world of harmony signified the importance of the coexistence of diversified civilizations and consultation among all countries involved, not unilateralism driven by hegemonic ambitions.[95] During an overseas visit in early 2009, Vice President Xi Jinping made an unguarded remark to a Chinese audience in his visit to Mexico that foreign powers had nothing better to do than messing around and pointing their fingers at China's affairs. When the remarks caused a sensation in the international media, Chinese domestic media were banned from reporting his comments.[96]

Emphasizing the peaceful development in the harmonious world, the Hu leadership played down the pretense of being a big power meddling regionally and globally. While China was regarded as a rising power by people outside China, the topic remained delicate in China at the time. The official discourse avoided referring to China as a power. Assuring China's rise would bring opportunities and benefits instead of a threat to peace and stability; Beijing worked hard to cope with the criticism over its relations with some of the troubled third world friends that most Western countries shunned. Finding a balance between relations with its third world allies and being responsive to Western concerns, China voted to impose and tighten sanctions on Iran, supported the deployment of an UN–African Union force in Darfur, and even sent its military engineers to join the force in 2007. China also condemned the brutal crackdown in Burma in 2008 and quietly overhauled its policies toward pariah states; China was "willing to condition its diplomatic protection of pariah countries, forcing them to become more acceptable to the international community."[97] Avoiding the banner as the leader of the third world countries against Western interference, China was very selective in taking on global and regional leadership responsibilities. Some in China even suspected that the Western call for China to take greater responsibility was intended to dictate China's international performance.[98]

China's reluctance to be a visionary and magnanimous global power looking beyond its own often desperate and narrowly focused interests to meet the expectation of its rising great power responsibility was criticized as reflecting a "me first" notion. China was characterized as "a reluctant follower not a leader," "not psychologically prepared to play a full 'great power' leadership role in confronting problems such as climate change, genocide, civil war, nuclear proliferation, much less abusive governments." China was accused of a "global free rider" reluctant to take on more burdens.[99]

China justified the behavior as following the principles of making commitments according to its ability, and combining China's interests with the common interests of the international society.[100] President Hu emphasized the "shared responsibility": China's contributions to the global commonwealth could not adversely affect China's core interests; and China's international commitments were conditional to the inputs of other nations, especially the developed countries and regions.[101] Struggling between its emerging power aspiration and parochially defined national interests, the Chinese leadership was torn between seizing their moment in the geopolitical spotlight and shying from it. Cherishing rising power status, China focused mostly on its immediate interests and avoided heightened international expectations.

This contradiction caused the internal debate about whether China should continue to follow the low-profile policy. Aspiring to explore the "new thinking" and take on more proactive diplomacy, one view urged the government to abandon what they perceived as passive low-profile policy and take "big power" responsibility to ensure a "just" world order. The second view called for a modified low-profile policy to emphasize "striking for achievements" (有所作为). The third view insisted on continuing the low-key policy. The first view received the most attention in the media at the time. The second view became the actual policy practice. But government officials held the third view. As Premier Wen Jiabao stated, "Precisely by not raising our banner or taking the lead internationally, we've been able to expand our room for maneuver in international affairs." Therefore, "there is no reason whatsoever to alter this policy."[102] As a result, a perception gap existed between Chinese officials and many Western observers. While many Westerners were anxious about China's rise, the Hu administration continued to follow the course set by Deng Xiaoping to develop and modernize China, which still faced enormous internal challenges and needed a benign international environment.

3

Xi Jinping's Big Power Diplomacy
Showing China's Sword

TAKING ADVANTAGE OF THE POWER and wealth accumulated during the previous decades of reform and open-up, Xi Jinping has abandoned Deng Xiaoping's developmental moderation and advocated big power diplomacy to achieve the China Dream of Great Rejuvenation. The term "big power diplomacy" started to appear in Chinese foreign policy discourse in the 1990s. But Xi's predecessors were reluctant to endorse the concept. Cherishing China as inherently a big power by the virtue of its history and rising power status and expected to be treated as such, they emphasized that China was a developing country, which had "neither the material strength nor genuine interest to play a role commensurate to its great-power self-image."[1] China's extraordinary performance during the 2008–10 financial crisis increased the confidence of Chinese elites about the shift in the global power balance. But Hu Jintao continued to walk on a tightrope between moderation and assertion.

Envisioning the profound global change in which China is on the rise and the West in decline, Xi Jinping began to advocate the big power's thinking, sense of responsibility, and manner, and to accentuate China's big power status.[2] Taking the driving seat of global affairs, Xi Jinping has moved the center of gravity in Chinese foreign policy toward more proactively shaping the external environment rather than passively reacting to it, and forcefully safeguarding national interests rather than compromising them.

Xi Jinping has called on Chinese diplomats to demonstrate the fighting spirit and show their swords to fuel the power ambitions and unnerve the rivals to prevail. In response, Chinese diplomats have become wolf warriors to win diplomatic battles and counter any criticism of the CCP regime and its development model. Setting the tough tone and embarking on the full enunciation of a proactive approach to foreign relations, Xi Jinping has laid the baseline that other countries cannot cross; no longer accommodated US interests without conditions; vowed to build into a maritime big power to take back Taiwan and other "lost" territories; and aimed to carve out a sphere of influence in the enlarged periphery as a pathway for global preeminence.

The changing course of Chinese foreign policy has alarmed the United States and generated a pervasive level of insecurity among some of China's neighbors. Without simply submitting to China's power ambition, these countries have pushed back. Beijing has interpreted these reactions as a threat to its vital interests and mobilized its power resources to respond forcefully. China's big power diplomacy has, therefore, contributed to the rise of twenty-first-century Hobbesian power politics in which might makes right, raising the question of China as not just seeking its place in the sun but becoming a bellicose big power.

Rising Confidence and Frustration

The turning point from developmental diplomacy to big power diplomacy was set in 2008 when Beijing successfully hosted the largest Summer Olympic Games in history. While the foreign audience was astonished by the live TV pictures of modern China, for many Chinese, the Olympics was a symbol of the national resurgence from a dark cocoon of decline and isolation into the light of international recognition.

The Beijing Olympics was followed by the global financial meltdown, which started in the United States and sputtered the global economy. Maintaining GDP growth at 8.7 percent in 2009 and 10.41 percent in 2010, China blamed the crisis on the "inappropriate macroeconomic policies" of Western countries and "their unsustainable model of development."[3] For about three decades, the Chinese were on the receiving end of patronizing lectures from Western leaders about the superiority of their capitalism. The tables were turned. While Western countries struggled in the difficult economic recovery, the Chinese contended that they faced none of the problems many Western countries grappled with. While the political gridlock in the United States delayed the adoption of a stimulus to prevent the deep economic contraction, a Politburo meeting in October 2008 made a swift decision to adjust China's macroeconomic policies from "preventing overheating and curbing inflation to maintaining growth through expanding domestic demand."[4] Deploying its enormous state capacity to ward off the recession, the State Council announced a 4 trillion yuan (US$586 billion) stimulus package on November 9, 2008, and pumped money throughout the economy, sparing China from the liquidity crunch and credit collapse savaging other nations.

The crisis revealed the fallacy of liberal supremacy, generating confidence in the China model, which adapted the market economy to its design by the powerful one-party state.[5] In some cases, this new confidence took on an arrogant triumphalism. At the April 2009 Boao Forum, a Western journalist reported that "there seemed scarcely a moment when a top Chinese official wasn't ridiculing the world's financial institutions, demanding major concessions from the United States, proposing new Asia-centric international architecture or threatening to turn off the taps of Chinese capital which the rest of the world so desperately needs."[6] As China's economy played a substantial role in determining the path of the global economy, a new wave of celebration occurred to boost the success of the China model for fast growth and great stability.[7] As an intellectual symbol of national pride, the China model surged as a popular term in the "discourse of greatness" that included such terms as "China in ascendance," "the China path," "the China pace," "the China miracle," and "the rise of China."

Liu Yunshan, a CCP Politburo member and the minister of the CCP Central Propaganda Department, claimed, "Chinese-style socialism has exhibited nonpareil superiority and the China model has demonstrated strong vigor and energy."[8] A Chinese economist wrote, "The financial crisis shows that a twenty-first-century market economy requires the government participation to function." The Chinese government played an active role in avoiding the difficulties that the Western economies experienced.[9] A Beijing University professor declared that China was the largest winner of the global crisis. The Western criticism of China lost its appeal and the world opinion was transformed to recognize the unique characteristics of the Chinese system in contrast with bankrupted Western institutions.[10]

With Western leaders desperate for cash-rich China to come to their aid, Chinese leaders became confident in their ability to deal with the West on China's terms. Enhancing their belief, President Obama reached out to China's leadership quickly, early, and personally, put human rights concerns on the back burner, and delayed meeting with the Dalai Lama after coming to office in 2019. A new term, "core national interests," suddenly became popular in China. Chosen with intent to signal the resolve in China's sovereignty and territorial claims that it deems important enough to go to war over if necessary, core interest refers to the issues that are essentially nonnegotiable. While China's official statements on the core interests of sovereignty and territorial integrity used to refer almost exclusively to Taiwan, Hong Kong, Tibet, and Xinjiang issues, Chinese leaders expanded the core interest issues to include territorial claims in the South and East China Seas and developmental interests.[11]

Confident in their accomplishments, Chinese were frustrated by the suspicions of, and resistance to, China's rise from the so-called foreign anti-China forces. One example was the perceived conspiracy to slow down China's rise by blocking its global search for natural resources and acquisitions of foreign assets. China National Offshore Oil Corporation (CNOOC) offered an $18.5 billion takeover bid for Unocal Corporation in 2005 but was demonized as the advancing guard of a plan by Beijing to buy up America's industrial crown jewels and control its energy supplies. Chevron Corporation acquired Unocal for $1.5 billion less than CNOOC's offer.[12] This ignominious setback was repeated in 2009 when Rio Tinto walked away from a tentative agreement with Aluminum Corporation of China Limited, which would pay $19.5 billion to increase its stake in the Anglo-Australian mining giant. Rio Tinto rejected the deal because "there are lots of Aussies in high political places who don't want . . . land and resources sold to China."[13]

These incidents were perceived as coordinated actions to stop China's rise. While the United States claimed that the main point of friction was due to China's authoritarianism and therefore pressed China on issues of human rights and democracy, the Chinese wondered whether the conflict would remain and perhaps grow starker even if China became democratic because the

United States would not want to see even a democratic China becoming richer and stronger than America. Testing US intentions, the Chinese assumed that a weakened United States in debt to China would make concessions because the recovery of the US economy depended to a great extent on China's purchase of US bonds and jointly stimulating the world economy. They, however, were frustrated by the United States "ungrateful" position, which did not reflect the nature of the new symbiosis.[14] The troubled relationship confirmed the United States' hidden agenda of preventing China from rising to a peer power. The perception of a troubled United States still attempting to keep China down made many Chinese elites ready to fight back.

The China Dream and the Profound Change Unseen in a Century

This peculiar combination of confidence and frustration provided a breeding ground for Xi Jinping to present the China Dream in a visit to "The Road of Rejuvenation" exhibition at the National Museum days after he became the CCP general secretary. The China Dream blended resentment over past abuses by foreign powers, as well as their continued malign intentions, with references to China's glorious history, growing strength, and future greatness. Great Rejuvenation (伟大复兴) is a grand process after the enormous suffering and sacrifices to take back China's rightful place in the word under the CCP leadership.[15] This vision for Chinese people striding the stage of world history is to stake Xi and the CCP's persistence in power and create an alternative to the American Dream.

The dream of wealth and power has been the central theme of the political discourse of every Chinese communist leader. Mao declared China's independence and pulled it out of the nadir of national humiliation. But his Great Leap Forward and Cultural Revolution resulted in the Great Famine and brought China to the brink of social and economic collapse. Deng started modernization to invigorate China, creating a favorable environment for Xi to invoke the China Dream. Xi spelled out a timeline of two centennial targets to achieve the China Dream. By the CCP centenary in 2021, China should have built a moderately prosperous society and doubled its 2010 GDP and income per capita, which Xi declared completed in his speech to celebrate the one-hundredth birthday of the CCP on July 1, 2021. By the PRC centenary in 2049, China should have ascended to global power in all aspects, including cultural, economic, and military prowess. Between the two centennials, in 2035, China should have built into a modern economic, technological, and military power.[16] The China Dream has reached global resonance and imagination under the rubric of these goals.

The China Dream is featured as a collective dream of the Chinese nation to reach common prosperity and claim China's place at the top tier of the international power hierarchy. The personal dreams of Chinese people, fueled by their search for wealth, must be subsumed into those of the state. The China Dream is fulfilled through personal commitment, but personal success is not earned by dint of hard work and ingenuity and would not be complete without China becoming a powerful nation to rid the past and forge a happy, sanguine story of revival. The China Dream is thus distinguished from the American dream in that people can pursue individual dreams and contribute to the national dream at the same time.[17]

A strong military is the pillar of the China Dream. Only one month after taking the helm of the CCP general secretary in November 2012, Xi Jinping boarded a guided-missile destroyer patrolling the South China Sea and told the sailors that the China Dream for the armed forces is "a dream of a strong military." The prosperous nation and strong military were "two foundational stones" for the China dream.[18] Casting himself as a strong military leader, Xi made a clear break from his predecessors. Jiang Zemin kept the military focused on building the capacity to defend borders. Hu Jintao kept a low military profile, focusing on China's peaceful development. But Xi made high-profile visits to the army, air force, space programs, and missile command facilities in his first one hundred days in office. One of Xi's first moves was to issue orders for the military to focus on "real combats" and "fighting and winning wars."[19]

The strong military dream played well with military hawks. Col. Liu Mingfu's sensational book *The China Dream* was removed from the shelves after its initial publication in 2010 over concerns from the Hu leadership that it could damage relations with the United States and alarm China's neighbors. The day after Xi made his China Dream speech, Liu's book was on display in the "recommended books" section of state-run bookstores. An English edition was released in 2015, with the cover having a line from Henry A. Kissinger's *On China*: "In Liu's view, no matter how much China commits itself to a 'peaceful rise,' conflict is inherent in U.S.-China relations." Praising President Xi by saying that "China finally has a leader who is bold enough to resist the US,"[20] Liu claimed that a rich nation without a strong military was an insecure and hobbled power. Only by becoming a military power could China maintain its security. China's military must be more powerful than any rival's so that no nation could contain China's rise.[21]

PLA commanders have been pleased because the dream of a strong military means the defense-spending increases. Despite the economic slowdown, the Chinese military budget has continued to increase, outpacing economic growth, since Xi came to power.[22] While Hu struggled under pressure from military hawks to take assertive actions, Xi has established clear authority over generals and endorsed the muscular national security posture.

Xi's confidence has built upon his belief that "China is in the best development period since modern times and the world is in a state of the profound change on a scale unseen in a century." Believing that "the time and momentum are on the China side,"[23] he pointed to three unprecedented changes: the rising speed of the emerging and developing countries; the rate at which new technologies replace older ones and the resulting fierce competition; and the changing nature in global governance.[24] Although Xi has never elaborated these changes, Chinese scholars have rushed to decode Xi's statement.

The first change is the geopolitical rise of the East and decline of the West, and the geo-economic rise of the South and decline of the North. In other words, emerging powers, particularly China, have become the engine of global growth while the Western countries, particularly the United States, have failed to maintain their dominance in the world because they have become aged with an increasing number of internal problems. As the gravity of the global economy has shifted from the developed world to developing countries, and the center of global power has moved from the West to the non-West, the Western countries' ability to intervene in world affairs has declined.[25]

The second change is the new round of technology revolution, in which China has taken the commanding heights. Leading the first technology revolution of the steam engine, England emerged as a global empire. Leading the second tech revolution of electricity, the United States leaped to the global hegemon and continued to lead the third tech revolution of information technology to maintain its hegemony. China has invested heavily and built comprehensive and complete industrial capacities while the US manufacturing industries have been hollowed out. Catching up quickly, China is positioned better than the United States to turn innovation into industrial capacity. Taking "advantage of the late-development" to leapfrog forward, China's political leadership is stronger and more effective to make and implement strategic decisions than the Western democracies. Attaching great importance to science and technology, the powerful government has made tough decisions and mobilized resources to build the world's largest expressway and high-speed rail that are unthinkable in the Western democracies.[26] While US leaders have wished to bring the sun-set industries of the textile, steel, and coal back to the United States, Xi has embraced the economy of the future to seize the opportunities of digital industrialization and launched the New Infrastructure Construction initiative to replace traditional infrastructure such as construction of railways, highways, and airports.[27]

Chinese scholars have described the third change as the emerging world disorder due to the rise of populism, nationalism, racism, hegemonism, unilateralism, protectionism, and religious fundamentalism. Uncertainty and unpredictability become the norm, and the possibility of tragic crisis and human spiritual conflict has risen. At the crossroads of history, China has played a positive role to maintain the world order by strengthening regional cooperation and promoting multilateralism, injecting tremendous stability into the world, and becoming the engine of world growth and the new impetus for global governance.[28] As China offers order in contrast to US chaos, and effective governance instead of Western ineffectiveness, the world has expected China to assume great responsibility and promote fairness.[29]

The New Direction of Chinese Foreign Policy

These intertwined and turbulent changes have laid the groundwork for Xi to set a new direction for Chinese foreign policy at the Central Conference on Peripheral Diplomacy in October 2013. Unlike his predecessors, he did not mention "low-profile diplomacy" but emphasized that "the primary theme of China's foreign policy should be the striving for achievements (奋发有为), moving forward along with time changes (与时俱进), and acting more proactively (更加主动)."[30] Foreign Minister Wang Yi, in his inaugural press conference in March 2014, characterized the new direction as "proactively striving for achievements to let the world hear of the Chinese solutions and Chinese voices."[31] Xi's speech at the Fourth Central Foreign Affairs Work Conference in 2014 elaborated the new facet of Chinese foreign policy as "a distinctive diplomatic approach befitting its role as a big power to show Chinese features, Chinese style and Chinese confidence," and to effectively use China's strength to achieve the double centenary objectives of the China Dream.[32]

As an indication of the changing mood, Xi's once censored, unguarded accusation of the Western powers during his visit to Mexico City in February 2009 reappeared prominently in the official media in 2013.[33] The "harmonious world" propagated by Hu to calm Western anxiety was no longer part of the foreign policy lexicon. "No" and "not" as keywords that Hu used to express China's moderation disappeared or were modified. For example, "not take the lead" is replaced by "international leadership with Chinese characteristics"; "not export Chinese political ideologies" is replaced by "sharing the Chinese experiences of governance." The buzzword now is "new," such as the new era, the new type of big power, the new international relations, and the new model of big power relations.[34]

Xi's commitment to a peaceful rise is now conditioned by the external accommodation to China's core national interests and premised on reciprocity. Forcefully protecting China's core interests is given greater importance than peaceful rise. Instead of following Deng's low-profile dictum, China reminded the West of the tough statement that Deng once made: "No one should expect China to swallow the bitter fruit that hurts its interest." China used to state what it hoped other countries would do but has moved toward "baseline thinking" by setting red lines that other countries could not cross.[35] While Beijing's tough stances generated concern outside China, for Beijing, establishing baselines reduced strategic uncertainties and prevented other countries from misjudging China's intentions and its resolve to protect its national interests.[36]

Insisting on baseline thinking, Xi Jinping has required Chinese diplomats to demonstrate their fighting spirit, enhance their fighting skills, and dare to attack and win,[37] which highlights one new feature of Chinese foreign policy that conceives diplomacy as a war against enemies that must be defeated. Chinese diplomats used to be known for their courtesy but have now become wolf warriors, a term derived from China's top-grossing movie in 2018, in which a Chinese soldier defeated Western mercenaries in defending China's overseas interests. A line from the movie found popularity among Chinese audiences for promising that anyone who attacked China would be killed, no matter how far away the target was.

Proud of being a wolf warrior standing in the way of the "mad dogs," Chinese ambassador to France Lu Shaye claimed that the rise of the wolf-warrior diplomacy reflected China's rising national strength and the changing external environment. Becoming a giant, China could no longer hide its ability. Facing suppression by the United States and other Western countries, China must shift from lamb diplomacy (羔羊外交) to wolf warrior diplomacy and fight with strength and courage.[38] Chinese ambassador to Sweden Gui Congyou gained notoriety with his unusually strident posture in a blistering criticism of the host country over anything deemed sensitive by Beijing. The Swedish foreign ministry summoned Cui more than forty times in the first two years of his stint to protest his controversial remarks. There were repeated calls in Sweden for him to be declared persona non grata. But for Chinese diplomats, wolf warrior diplomacy is a natural response to the Western plot to contain China. Growing increasingly impatient with what they see as nitpicking criticism of China, they refuse to accept that China could be in the wrong.[39]

Wolf warrior diplomacy made headlines around the world amid COVID-19. As the world watched the outbreak in China, Beijing raised the stakes of its foreign relations by forcing foreign countries to make a choice to either be with China or against China. Deflecting blame for China's initial missteps and countering the accusations that the coronavirus originated in China, Zhao Lijian, a Foreign Ministry spokesperson famous for his sharp and abusive language, publicly floated a conspiracy theory that the American military brought the virus to China during the Military World Games in Wuhan in October 2019. This unsubstantiated claim went viral in the tightly controlled media across China. The conspiracy theories temporarily disappeared from official media after the Chinese ambassador to Washington, Cui Tiankai, who could see from the front lines the damage to China's relationship with the United States, said to American media that "the job of finding the source of the virus is one for scientists, not diplomats and journalists."[40] Cui's reasonable statement, however, did not clear the continued speculations in Chinese media.

With China locked in a blame game with the United States, wolf warrior diplomacy performed well in convincing the Chinese that the United States was biased with ideological and racist tinges against China. Beijing would need to escalate its countermeasures toward Washington. In response to US secretary of state Pompeo's use of the term "Wuhan virus," Chinese official media labeled him the "public enemy number one of mankind." When China stabilized the outbreak and the pandemic went on a rampage in Europe and the United States, Chinese diplomats stationed all over the world inundated international newspapers with op-eds to hail the sacrifices that China made to buy time for other countries and compare the chaos in America with the success in China.

Waging an all-out "discourse" war to beat back critics, Chinese diplomats lashed out at any foreign leaders who criticized China's pandemic responses. Demonstrating his fighting spirit, Foreign Minister Wang Yi labeled the criticism of China as a "political virus" born of prejudice and ignorance, and slammed US politicians for "jumping at any opportunity" to scapegoat China for the consequences of their disastrous mismanagement of the crisis.[41] A *Global Times* editorial declared, "The days when China can be put in a submissive position are long gone. As Western diplomats fall into disgrace, they are getting a taste of China's Wolf Warrior diplomacy."[42]

The Shining China Model of Authoritarianism

While wolf warrior diplomacy did not play well with overseas audiences, it hit the right notes back home: China had become a big power and must be recognized as such. Xi Jinping has highlighted the superiority of the China model to demonstrate China's success. While his predecessor cautiously avoided endorsing the China model, reflecting the hesitancy to engage in ideological debate, Xi declared that China's path offered "a new option for other countries and nations who want to speed up their development while preserving their independence."[43] He also proposed "four confidences"—the theory of socialism with Chinese characteristics, China's socialist path, political system, and culture—to refute the universal applicability of liberal democracy.

In his first overseas visit to Russia as president, Xi Jinping stated, "Only the wearer knows if the shoe fits his foot. Only the people of the country know best whether or not the development path is appropriate for the country."[44]

Advocating Chinese exceptionalism, he then spoke in Europe that "China's unique cultural tradition, unique historical fate, and unique national conditions have determined that China must follow the road of development that fits Chinese characteristics."[45] At Peking University, he said, "We cannot forget our ancestors and copy the foreign model. Nor can we accept any instructions imposed by foreigners."[46] Because every country is exceptional in its way, each should have the right to choose its model, including taking inspiration from the China model. The consolidation of the China model proved the existence of a "post-democratic future" and challenged the Western conventional wisdom that the march of democracy went in lockstep with market capitalism and economic modernization.[47]

China's early success in containing the outbreak of COVID-19 provided an opportunity to prove the China model. The outbreak was initially predicted as China's "Chernobyl moment," a mishandled disaster in which the Chinese leadership might lose political legitimacy, with geopolitical consequences.[48] Although the government discouraged the early and transparent recognition of the threat, the state went into crisis mode quickly once it realized the scale of the threat. Xi's centralization of power generated strong capacity for the state to take zealous and heavy-handed actions to quarantine the epicenter of Wuhan, a city of more than eleven million people, and extended the quarantine to the entire country.

The world marveled at China's ability to construct temporary hospitals at lightning speed. Large swathes of public transportation, factories, shops, and schools were shut down. People were blocked at home. Declaring a "People's War," Xi launched an arsenal of propaganda campaigns and used harsh control measures, including community policing, that forced people to be hygienic and follow orders. In a high-tech country where privacy was limited, authorities developed health-monitoring apps to gather data on individuals' body temperatures, movements, and social contacts. Citizens were assigned health-rating codes on cell phones based on their medical history, contacts with infected people, or visits to high-risk places.

The scale and speed of these measures were unseen in history, a testament to the untrammeled state power to mobilize resources and restrict citizens' rights in times of crisis. These stringent actions were highly effective in limiting the spread of the coronavirus and preventing healthcare systems from being crushed. Chinese society returned to a certain degree of normality once infection numbers came under control. China announced zero new domestic cases on March 18, 2020 and reported zero coronavirus deaths on April 7. The seventy-six-day Wuhan lockdown was lifted on April 8. After success in this herculean fight, the Chinese propaganda machinery went into overdrive to declare war against COVID-19, and to portray even a single infection as a failure on the part of the local government. The state's ability to roll out compulsory mass testing each time new cases were detected, to impose city-wide lockdowns, and to suppress every local outbreak proved the success of the China model.

The early success also helped Beijing orchestrate a diplomatic offensive to boost China as a generous and responsible power. Owning most of the global medical supply chain, the government launched "mask diplomacy" by sending medical equipment and doctors to many pandemic-ravaged countries. Chinese media dutifully reported every delivery and highlighted the airport ceremonies in which receiving nation's dignitaries went out to meet the Chinese experts and uttered words of gratitude and relief.[49]

Mask diplomacy was followed by vaccine diplomacy. Despite the lack of complete data and other deficiencies, China rolled out its vaccines quickly to developing countries for their urgent need amid a global shortfall in supplies. Framing it as the solution to rather than the origin of the pandemic, China advanced vaccine diplomacy primarily because the leaders in Western democracies faced horrifying virus infection rates at home and had to meet their voters' need to inoculate domestic populations first. China faced neither of the problems. China's infection rates were low enough that they could afford to send vaccines abroad. Chinese leadership did not have to worry about public opinion backlash. Just by showing up and helping plug the colossal gaps in the global supply, China gained ground.[50] Like mask diplomacy, Chinese media covered every delivery of the shipments that were greeted by senior local leaders, often the presidents, fawning over the vaccine cargo to express gratitude to the government and people of China.

In the gambit to turn the pandemic into a celebration of the strong capacity of the state, the diplomatic offensive buttressed the claim in the superiority of the China model based on social control, harsh confinement, and surveillance in a favorable light in contrast to the Western democracies for their incapacity in the crisis. COVID-19 tallies became a league table for the state to overcome the crisis. China began at a low spot but soon overtook the United States and European countries to win the championship. From this vantage point, Xi called "to take initiatives and effectively influence international public opinion by telling the stories of China's fight against the epidemic and showing the spirit of the Chinese people united and worked together."[51] The Chinese government published a white paper to rebut the accusation of China's initial cover-up and to document its successful practices fighting the pandemic.[52]

The American failure in response to the pandemic under President Trump reinforced Chinese views on the dysfunction of democracy and contributed to their confidence in the single-party system as better designed to undertake tough but necessary sacrifices in times of crisis. Creating collective obedience, orderliness, and respect for life, the Chinese leadership was said to have played the chess game with remarkable coordination because of institutional advantages of "concentrating capacities on accomplishing big things" and "strictly following orders for highly effective collaboration."[53]

Many Chinese scholars joined the propaganda campaign and stood out for the unabashed, often flashily erudite advocacy of one-party rule. Fortifying China for an era of deepening ideological rivalry, they described the United States as an overreaching shamble in the wake of the pandemic and Western liberal ideas as a dangerous mirage that could hobble the party, and they extolled Xi as a strong leader guiding China through the crisis. Taking a victory lap to celebrate the ascendance of authoritarianism and decay of democracies, one Chinese scholar concluded that this "control group experiment" confirmed that the Western model of limited government could not cope with the crisis. A strong and decisive state was necessary. "Because abnormality and normality are a pair of blurred concepts, a system that cannot deal with an abnormal crisis is not a good system."[54] Another Chinese scholar agreed that it did not matter if a state was democratic or authoritarian. What mattered was the governance. Winning the turnaround battle against COVID-19, China demonstrated its outstanding governance ability.[55]

Believing that the pandemic marginalized the United States in the world, Chinese people no longer regarded the US economy, political system, ideas, and popular culture as the benchmark of the world. The United States is no longer a model for the future of the world. As the charm of the United States was tarnished and the US model declined, many people altered their perception of the United States and increased their confidence in the CCP regime, making Beijing less concerned about the damage by its wolf warrior diplomacy.[56]

A New Model of Big Power Relations

China has categorized foreign countries, according to their geopolitical power and location, into big powers, peripheral countries, and developing countries. The relations with big powers have been the top priority and an important leitmotif running through China's relations with other countries. One conceptual building block undergirding big power diplomacy is the new model of big power relations. Although the new model covers China's ties with all big powers, none of them rises to the level of Sino-US relations. Xi proposed three essential aspects of the new model: no confrontation; mutual respect; and win-win cooperation. Mutual respect of core interests is the baseline. The new model, therefore, is not just another façade on the rhetoric of peaceful coexistence. China and the United States can coexist peacefully only if they do not break through the baseline of the other side and make their strategic aspirations compatible.[57]

During the Deng Xiaoping era, China reluctantly acceded to conditions demanded by the United States, however grudgingly, because the primary objective of Chinese diplomacy was to exploit external conditions to facilitate rapid and sustained economic development. China has grown faster than America for decades and narrowed the gap quickly. Hu Angang of Tsinghua University famously argued that China's national strength had surpassed that of the United States on all fronts by 2014.[58] The perceived rising strength of China and the decline of the United States made it possible and urgent to address a more dangerous US that would not accept its fall from grace and would do whatever it takes to forestall its decline and thwart China's rise. A declining hegemon may be more dangerous than it was as an unchallenged superpower. Beijing, therefore, no longer bends to America's pressure or unilaterally accommodates its interests without conditions. The United States must concede to China's core interests in exchange for China's collaboration in managing a range of challenges that the US has faced in the world.

The Obama administration initially responded positively to the new model proposal because it seemed to resonate with the long-standing US policy to integrate China into the international community. President Obama said in 2014, "We are committed to the shared goal of developing over time a 'new model' of relations with China defined by increased practical cooperation and constructive management of difference."[59] Obama's conciliatory stance, however, was interpreted as a sign of weakness by Chinese leaders.[60] Shifting the attitudes from looking up (仰视) to looking levelly (平视) toward the United States and from the sense of inferiority to equality, if not superiority, Beijing has pursued its interests without worrying much about American concerns.

While China promised market liberalization after accession into the WTO decades ago, Beijing has strengthened the position of state-owned enterprises (SOE) and protected domestic "champions" to compete with American companies, compelled American firms to transfer technology as a condition of operation in China, and blocked American internet businesses. When President Trump complained to Premier Li Keqiang in his 2017 Beijing visit, Li "dismissed U.S. concerns over unfair trade and economic practices, indicating that the U.S. role in the future global economy would merely be to provide China with raw materials, agricultural products, and energy to fuel its production of the world's cutting-edge industrial and consumer products."[61]

The United States had expected engagement with China would lead to liberal reform, but Xi has rallied Chinese people not to the promise of greater freedom, openness, and constitutionalism, but to the vision of China's great wealth, authoritarian power, and global clout. Making use of high-tech for authoritarian control to access ubiquitous data gathered about Chinese citizens, China has accelerated the construction of an unprecedented surveillance state by deploying millions of facial-recognition cameras to document good and bad deeds for personal social credit score. Advocates for civil and political rights were arrested with greater intensity; civil society groups harassed; and controls on free expression tightened.

The Obama administration in the second term became reluctant to endorse the new model without having agreed with its concrete contents and finding solutions on the controversial issues first. Giving cold shoulder to the rising aspirations of China, the Obama administration launched a strategic rebalance to the Asia-Pacific theater. The Trump administration started a trade war and escalated the relationship to a full-scale clash. But Xi Jinping did not back off. While Beijing emphasized "confrontation will lead nowhere" in response to the US threat to unleash a trade war against China's copyright piracy in 1996, Beijing now stated that "China does not want to fight the trade war but is not afraid and would fight back if necessary to the end and see who would endure longer."[62] A video comparing the shift from "confrontation will lead nowhere" to "we'll see who will last longer" was widely circulated across Chinese social media platforms.

Turning American pressure to political advantages, Xi used the trade war to blame America for the slowdown in China's economy and other problems. External pressure has historically helped mobilize Chinese nationalism against any concessions that could be regarded as surrender to foreign powers. Proud of their accomplishments through hard work, tremendous sacrifices, dogged determination, and well-crafted policies, many Chinese are fed up with US criticisms that China's rise is because it did not play by rules, violated international commitments, and tilted the playing field to advantage Chinese firms. Portraying the acrimonious trade war as part of an American conspiracy to contain China, Chinese media was filled with emotional stories that China was forced to take tit-for-tat actions and dared to show its sword. Mao Zedong was once again celebrated for having boldly gone to war against the Americans in Korea. People critical of China's assertive stance were criticized as having a soft bone disease (软骨病), of worshiping America and kneeling to America: "A self-reliant China is the best medicine for this kind of rickets."[63]

Pursuing the China Dream of restoring China to wealth and power based on historical grievances and considerable resources, many people accepted the government propaganda because the broader anti-China trend in the United States was an intensely unwelcome surprise. They were convinced that the United States was driven by fear and envy to contain China in every possible way. The government and public opinion became surprisingly consistent in their resistance toward Western criticism. As the overall distrust and resentment toward the United States reached an unprecedented level since the establishment of diplomatic relations, the tolerance to US challenges was greatly reduced. Throwing away its illusions and preparing for the worst, China fought back proactively and resolutely.[64]

The public has supported and pushed the government to force America to toe the official line. For example, after Daryl Morey, the general manager of the NBA's Houston Rockets, tweeted "Fight for freedom. Stand with Hong Kong" in December 2019, social media protests pushed the authorities to demand Morey's immediate firing, cancel all the licensing deals for the Houston Rockets, and ban NBA games from being televised in China. The state-owned CCTV canceled the showing of an Arsenal soccer game because the club's star, Mesut Özil, criticized the Chinese crackdown in Xinjiang.

While China was the passive target of US sanctions in the past, China has used sanctions increasingly often in retaliation. In response to the US decision to sanction Chinese media in February 2020, Beijing expelled more than a dozen American journalists, giving them ten days to turn in their press cards and prohibiting them from working in Hong Kong and Macau, marking the most sweeping press expulsions from China since Mao's death in 1976. After the United States sanctioned top officials of the Chinese government for their actions in Xinjiang and Hong Kong, China announced sanctions against US senators Marco Rubio, Ted Cruz, and other officials. China also imposed sanctions on Lockheed Martin, Boeing Defense, Raytheon, and other US companies involved in the arms sales to Taiwan in October 2020. Within minutes of President Biden's inauguration on January 20, 2021, China announced the sanction of twenty-eight former Trump administration officials, prohibiting them and their immediate family members from entering China and restricting them from doing business with China. Mirroring America's sanctions tool kit for export controls, national security investment screening, and visa sanctions, China passed an "Anti-Foreign Sanctions Law" in June 2021 to criminalize the sanctioning of China by any organizations and individuals, adding legal ground to its response to sanctions.

China also punished the US allies that challenged China on sensitive issues. In April 2020, Australian foreign minister Marise Payne called for a global independent inquiry into China's handling of the outbreak and the origins of the coronavirus. Being afraid of the snowball effect, China launched an increasingly shrill campaign to denounce Australia with a palpable sense of anger and resentment. Urging Canberra to "grow up and reflect on its wrong deeds,"[65] China applied duties of between 116.2 percent and 218.4 percent on Australian wines in March 2021 until 2026, imposed high tariffs on the imports of Australia's beef, barley, coal, copper ore and concentrate, sugar, timber, and lobster, and warned its tourists and students to reconsider Australia as a destination.

At the first high-level meeting with the Biden administration in Alaska in March 2021, Beijing's top diplomat, Yang Jiechi, confronted his US counterparts by saying that "the United States does not have the qualification to say that it wants to speak to China from a position of strength," and "the United States must stop advancing its democracy in the rest of the world" when it was dealing with discontent among its population. Foreign Minister Wang Yi added: "It is time for the US to correct the long-standing bad practice (老毛病)" of willfully interfering in China's internal affairs.[66] These comments circulated widely on China's social media, resonating with the belief that China's "rise to great-power status entitles it to a new role in world affairs—one that cannot be reconciled with unquestioned U.S. dominance."[67]

Beijing demonstrated its position of strength again when US deputy secretary of state Wendy Sherman visited China in July 2021. Dedicating much of the meetings to the venting of its anger at Washington and demanding the United States take actions to repair the damaged relationship, Vice-Minister Xie Feng said of the Biden administration: "The collaborative aspect is just an expediency, and the competitive aspect is a narrative trap." He presented the United States with two lists, one of "errors" to be addressed, and the other of issues Beijing considered important. Foreign Minister Wang Yi set out three red lines for the United States in the meeting: do not challenge China's political system, do not disrupt China's development, and do not interfere in China's sovereignty issues such as matters in Hong Kong, Tibet, Xinjiang, and Taiwan.[68]

Beijing also embarrassed Special Presidential Envoy for Climate Change John Kerry when he visited China the next month. Kerry was offered only video meetings with senior officials who reiterated that the United States should actively respond to the "two lists" and "three bottom lines" put forward by China.[69] These chilly treatments reflected China's increasingly assertive approach to Washington, a stark departure from Beijing's long-standing restrained style. While Chinese diplomats had been scorned by the Chinese public for being weak, the wolf warrior diplomats have showed their sword and demonstrated their fighting spirit.

The Enlarged Periphery Strategy

The big power diplomacy has paid special attention to the so-called enlarged periphery (大周边), which expands China's neighborhood beyond the geographic belt of adjacent areas of Northeast Asia, Southeast Asia, South Asia, and Central Asia to include the South Pacific and West Asia.[70] Because regional primacy is a precondition for China's global power aspiration, Xi Jinping has worked assiduously on the enlarged periphery, like the United States beginning in the Western Hemisphere to build global primacy. The enlarged periphery is regarded as the indispensable path, compulsory course, the foothold and basis, the starting point, and "big rear area" for China's power ascendance.[71]

Imbibing this path, Xi Jinping has advanced the concept of the Asian Community for a Shared Future. Speaking to the Boao Forum, he proposed the concept of the "Asia-Pacific Dream," a mirror to the China Dream, for the Asian Community, reflecting Beijing's intention to shape the enlarged periphery in China's image. Many of China's neighbors are alarmed when Chinese leaders talk about the shared future in the context of the China Dream, recalling the old days when imperial China dominated much of East Asia. China's enlarged periphery strategy has provoked the possibility of China's version of the Monroe Doctrine. Like the Japanese insistence in the Greater East Asia Co-Prosperity Sphere, because its constituent units were either integral parts of the most advanced state or willing supplicants to benefit by following Japan's lead, China has insisted that many states would benefit from following China's lead because they share China's grievances over Western-imposed liberal values and intervention in their domestic affairs.

China cannot dominate the region if it remains surrounded by US allies and partners. China has used a mixture of inducement, coercion, and manipulation to push the United States out. Xi demonstrated this intention at the 2014 Shanghai summit of the Conference of Interaction and Confidence-Building in Asia (CICA) by announcing the New Asian Security Concept: "Asian issues should be taken care of by Asians; Asian problems should be handled by Asians, and Asian security should be maintained by Asians." This "Asia for Asians" idea implied that Asia can take care of its security without the meddling of the United States. This little-known regional summit had languished for years. Xi invigorated the organization because its members did not include the US allies.[72]

China has launched new initiatives to help pursue the enlarged periphery strategy. The Belt and Road Initiative (BRI) is the most important one, which weaves a China-led network of bilateral relationships with more than one hundred countries and international organizations. Spending billions of dollars on the construction of infrastructure projects in partner countries, BRI is to cover two-thirds of the world's population by building six economic corridors across Eurasia, the Indian Ocean, and the Pacific. Although China has framed BRI as global public goods and China's goodwill to offer other countries aboard the Chinese development express train, it is an expression of Beijing's newly found pride in the nation's power to advance China's geo-economic and geopolitical interests.

Xi Jinping hosted the First Belt and Road Forum for International Co-operation (BRFIC) in Beijing in May 2017. It was attended by twenty-nine heads of state and representatives from about one hundred governments and international organizations. The second BRFIC in 2019 was joined by thirty-seven heads of state and five thousand other representatives. Chinese media coverage of the BRFICs showed that all world leaders praised China's investments in their countries, demonstrating China was a global leader and all roads led to Beijing. In a set piece of imperial power and benevolence for which the Chinese capital seems designed, Xi stood in front of a giant landscape painting titled *This Land Is So Rich in Beauty* and shook hands with the heads of state lining up in the Great Hall of the People. These images encapsulated China's growing political and economic influence and Xi's leadership on the world stage. China was positioned as a benign empire, receiving tribute from neighbors and harking back to the glory days when the imperial reach was at its peak.

Focusing on infrastructure construction to meet the desperate needs in many developing countries, the BRI has helped China open emerging markets by connecting with an expansive geographic scope and building a web of connectivity spanning multiple continents, and by strategically constructing supply chains with China as the hub. Connectivity is the focus because China's economic growth is powered by massive export-oriented industries and the import of large amounts of intermediate components and raw materials through land transportation and maritime shipping. BRI has invested in strategically vital transit corridors and seaports all over the world to help control the world's busiest trade loops.

These outposts have broader strategic significance. For example, the China-Pakistan Economic Corridor and the Chinese-invested Pakistani port of Gwadar, a political bulwark of BRI, is aimed to circumvent the problem of overly relying on its transit from the Persian Gulf and Africa through the Malacca Strait under the patrol and surveillance of the US Navy. China has also built its first overseas military base in Djibouti to advance a mix of commercial and security investments outside the Western Pacific. Additionally, China has constructed transborder highway and expressway networks to almost every neighboring region and direct rail services across Eurasia. With generous government subsidies, freight express train lines between central Chinese cities to the heart of Europe are considerably cheaper than air and faster than the sea. The rail expressway got off to a sluggish start but accelerated dramatically after the pandemic started in 2020, which caused congestion in air freight, sea shipping, and access to ports.

The funding for the BRI projects has helped advance China's strategic interests. Chinese investment has created a pattern of clientelism with these projects both as incentives to garner support and as means to punish recalcitrant countries. With the condition that these countries defer to China on sensitive issues such as Taiwan, Xinjiang, and Hong Kong, China has been successful to such an extent that Taiwan is left with diplomatic ties to only a dozen small countries. Most of the nations that supported China's Hong Kong suppression were BRI partners.[73]

The Digital Silk Road, which includes technology investments and bilateral joint research, has advanced China's goal of becoming a "tech-superpower" by deploying Chinese technologies, setting standards, and securing commercial advantages for Chinese firms. China's provision of communications and surveillance systems not only assisted the foreign leaders to track and suppress opponents but also caused recipient countries to rely on Chinese providers and gave China a multiregional base to project its systems and networks to the wider global market.[74]

The enlarged periphery strategy has targeted particularly the "developing big powers." The term initially appeared in the 1990s when Chinese scholars tried to understand how some big developing countries were successful in taking a unique path of industrialization different from the West. Chinese scholars began to use the term in the twenty-first century to explore how emerging economies played an increasingly important role in international organizations, geopolitics, and the reform of global governance. After the global financial crisis in 2008, the Chinese government has joined Chinese scholars to explore how China could work with these developing big powers for its geopolitical objectives.[75]

China's list of the developing big powers includes a handful of large, rapidly emerging, and politically influential nations called the Emerging 7 (E7): China, India, Russia, Indonesia, Turkey, Mexico, and Brazil, which have challenged the dominance of Group of Seven (G7) of the United States, Canada, France, the United Kingdom, Germany, Italy, and Japan. While the aggregate economic size of the E7 was only half of G7's in 1995, it reached the same level in 2015 and could double the size of G7 by 2040.[76] China has developed strategic relations with the emerging big powers through collective action, such as the BRICS countries of Brazil, Russia, India, China, and South Africa, and collectively engaged subsets of them through multilateral forums such as the G20. China has also concluded bilateral "strategic partnership" agreements with all emerging big powers and engaged with each of them bilaterally. Among them, China's partnership with Russia and Iran has gained global significance, to be analyzed in chapter 7 of this book.

A Strong Maritime Big Power and Taiwan Contingency

Building China into a maritime power with a world-class navy, a large and effective coast guard, and an ability to harvest and extract important maritime resources and defend its overseas interests is a bellwether of Xi's big power diplomacy. Following Alfred Thayer Mahan's ideas about sea power to defend the "maritime rights" derived from "maritime interests," China has expanded its security perimeter to ensure access to the Pacific Ocean and the Indian Ocean and defined its national security to have enough space for defense, including the control of the maritime peripheries.

After the founding of the PRC, Mao Zedong focused on defense of the coastline via the "People's War" of building a maritime great wall.[77] Deng Xiaoping proposed the "near-sea defense" beyond the coastlines in the 1980s.

Jiang Zemin began to emphasize the need to defend China's maritime rights and resources in the 1990s.[78] Hu Jintao expanded the PLA's missions to protect China's overseas interests and for the first time in 2012 called for building China into "a strong maritime power" with the capacity to "exploit marine resources, develop marine economy, protect the marine ecological environment, and resolutely safeguard China's maritime rights and interests."[79]

Xi Jinping has moved forward to state in 2013 that "the oceans and seas have an increasingly important strategic calculus concerning global competition in the spheres of politics, economic development, military, and technology."[80] China's Defense White Paper in 2015, the first one released by the Xi administration, contained unprecedented maritime emphasis. Stating that "the traditional mentality that land outweighs sea must be abandoned," it required the People's Liberation Army Navy (PLAN) to move from "near seas defense" to "the combination of 'near-seas defense' and 'far-seas protection.'"[81] As China's overseas investments span the globe, China's Defense White Paper in 2019 expanded the missions of armed forces to "effectively protect the security and legitimate rights and interests of overseas Chinese people, organizations, and institutions."[82]

Xi has presided over the major overhaul of the PLAN, which overtook the United States in the number and total tonnage of vessels launched yearly and became the world's largest navy in 2019.[83] Xi reviewed a major naval parade in the South China Sea through mist and rain to mark the seventieth anniversary of the PLAN in 2019. Xinhua revealed that "President Xi has attached great importance to the construction of the People's Navy, repeatedly inspected the naval forces and issued a call for striving to build the PLAN into a world-class navy."[84]

A continuing theme in Chinese maritime strategy is to break through the First Island Chain stretching from Japan to Taiwan to the Philippines and the Second Chain through the Marianas, including Guam, with free access to the Pacific. The phrase "Island Chain Strategy" was first used by John Foster Dulles in 1951 to contain China. While the phrase did not become part of US doctrine, it has become part of China's strong maritime power strategy.[85] The PLAN began sailing through the First Island Chain in 2009 and has conducted routine exercises and operations beyond the First Island Chain through the years. With its first aircraft carrier, the *Liaoning*, entering the fleet in 2012 and the second carrier, the *Shandong*, in 2019, the Chinese fleet has developed the capability to operate far seas-defense. China has launched warships, government vessels, and aircraft over the oceans and major sea lanes, built military outposts across the disputed maritime waters, and frequently resorted to sanctions, ship-ramming, and aerial intercepts in territorial disputes with its neighbors. Investing heavily in advanced air defenses, submarines, and other anti-access/area-denial capabilities, China intends to keep US ships and planes away from its shores and eventually dominate the Western Pacific.

Taiwan contingency is the lead planning scenario for China's maritime power development. An integral part of the First Island Chain, Taiwan is not just a "lost territory" to be recovered; it is of critical geostrategic value and a key forward defense position for the PLA to defend China's maritime interests and its highly industrialized and urbanized eastern seaboard, help PLAN dominate the shipping lanes, and give Beijing powerful leverage over Japan and South Korea. Although Deng Xiaoping told Americans during the normalization negotiation that Beijing was not in hurry to resolve the Taiwan issue, Chinese leaders have become increasingly impatient with the prospect of peaceful unification. Jiang Zemin started to articulate that China would not wait forever, but the country did not have military power to back up the implicit threat.[86]

The military balance across the Taiwan Strait has moved in China's favor since then. Becoming confident in China's capacities to resolve the Taiwan issue in his term, Xi Jinping made a blunt statement in October 2013: "The issue of political disagreements between the two sides must reach a final resolution, step by step, and cannot be passed on from generation to genera-tion."[87] His Political Report to the 19th CCP National Congress in 2017 listed the national unification with Taiwan as a condition for achieving the China Dream of Great Rejuvenation. Setting a linkage between the China Dream and national unification, Xi Jinping implied a timetable of the unification by 2049, the one-hundredth anniversary of the PRC.[88] For China to remain a "divided nation" simply does not sit well with Xi's China dream. National unification has become a capstone to his legitimacy and legacy.

Xi has become disappointed that Beijing's economic and political engage-ments have not wooed Taiwanese people to identify more closely with China. He has also been concerned that the United States has ratcheted up support for

Taiwan. Turning up the pressure, China's military activity in the Taiwan Strait has become more frequent and intrusive since President Tsai was reelected in January 2020. The PLA has staged live-fire combat drills in the vicinity, sailed aircraft carrier and warship through the strait, and ramped up the number of fighters crossing the median line, which carries no legal force but both sides had respected in the past to avoid conflict. Chinese foreign ministry spokesman denied the existence of the media line.[89] Routinely sending fighter jets and bombers to Taiwan's air defense identification zone (ADIZ), the PLA has increased its combat preparedness by making its exercises more complex and by considering possible US and Japanese interventions. These military actions make the island's status and relationship to the United States among the thorniest points of friction in the increasingly tense Sino-US relationship.

The official website of the Taiwan Affairs office published an article amid COVID-19 and claimed that strong public outrage raised the voice of unification by force. The article proposed six triggering conditions for military unification. In addition to the three conditions for using the "non-peaceful measures" stipulated in the 2005 Anti-Secession Law—declaring independence; a major event that may cause Taiwan to secede from China, and the possibility of peaceful reunification completely lost—the article added three more: organizing an independent referendum; a military attack on the mainland; and large-scale unrest in Taiwan.[90] In his government report to the NPC in 2020, Premier Li Keqiang left out the word "peaceful" in front of "reunification," departing from the standard expression that Chinese leaders had used for four decades in the government reports. Although he used "peaceful reunification" in his press conference, the absence of the word "peaceful" in the report caused considerable fluttering in Taiwan. In his 2021 NPC report, "peaceful" disappeared again before "unification." One official publication explained: "Due to Taiwan secessionists and US interference, the mainland would have no choice, and must push the process with non-peaceful efforts, including a military one."[91]

One retired PLAN rear admiral explained that the changing mode from peaceful to military unification came along with the changing military power balance across the strait. He had avoided talking about the possibility of war when China's military equipment was not only behind the United States' but also behind Taiwan's. Beijing had to avoid talking about the war. Now the PLA obtained full control power over the air and sea and could take back Taiwan within one week, Beijing must "accelerate preparation for military unification".[92] A former Deputy Commander of Nanjing Military Region made the claim earlier that modern warfare was about enduring ability. Taiwan, as an island close to the mainland without a strategic heartland, could not endure the war. The PLA could easily destroy all strategic targets in Taiwan as soon as the war started.[93]

It is hard to know if Xi Jinping is ready to take Taiwan by force. Although Xi has appeared unnerved by Putin's battlefield setbacks in Ukraine, Russia's stumbles should have taught Xi how important it is to be ready militarily, politically, economically, and diplomatically before conquering Taiwan by force. China is not ready until its national power significantly exceeds that of the United States, it is well positioned to resist the international push back, and it is certain in winning the war and retaining the island. Before then, Xi Jinping may still prefer to accomplish national reunification peacefully. In addition to the three conditions for non-peaceful measures in the Anti-Secession Law, and besides an explicit declaration of independence, it is unclear what constitutes a major event that may cause Taiwan to secede from China, or if the possibility of peaceful reunification is completely lost. Beijing has set vague provisions that can leave room to maneuverer before it must take non-peaceful measures. Beijing's intensified military pressure may remain part of the strategy to undermine confidence in Taiwan's ability to hold out against China. Xi wants fear over the threat of invasion to be reinforced in order to stop or at least slow Taiwan's drift toward independence. But the risk of war has increased in the context of China's strong maritime power aspiration.

Might Makes Right

China's fast-growing maritime power has important implications for the territorial disputes in the East and South China Seas. Believing some of its neighbors capitalized on China's self-constraints to assume control of disputed islands when China was relatively weak, Beijing has taken a tough position as a big power. Complying with China's demands or suffering the consequences is the unequivocal message. Representing an imperious attitude toward the small states, Foreign Minister Yang Jiechi said at an ASEAN meeting, "China is a big country and you are small countries and that is just a fact."[94]

China is in dispute with Japan over what the Chinese called Diaoyu and the Japanese call Senkaku islands in the East China Sea. China's claim is based on the discovery of the unclaimed territory, which Chinese fishermen used back in the fourteenth century. It was ceded to Japan in 1895 by the Treaty of Shimonoseki as part of Taiwan. The United States controlled the islands after the Pacific War in 1945 and transferred administrative power to Japan as part of Okinawa in 1972, but the United States did not take a position on their sovereignty. The Japanese government asked the United States to amend its stance in April 1978, but the American government declined because "it could become embroiled in a Sino-Japanese territorial dispute."[95] US Department of Defense press secretary John Kirby got into trouble in February 2021 when he stated that the United States supported Japan's "sovereignty" over the Senkaku, only to correct it four days later by saying there was "no change in policy."[96] But Japan has claimed sovereignty based on effective administration.

Beijing agreed to defer the resolution of the dispute during the diplomatic recognition negotiation in 1972. An advisor to Premier Zhou Enlai recalled that Japanese Prime Minister Tanaka raised the islands issue. Zhou responded that "it would not be good to talk about it at this time."[97] At the ceremony to sign the Treaty of Sino-Japanese Peace and Friendship in 1978, Deng Xiaoping enjoined Prime Minister Fukuda Takeo to "follow our established policy and postpone the solution for another twenty or thirty years" because "the issue is too complicated to discuss at this time."[98] Shelving the dispute, Chinese leaders handled incidents related to the islands in a relatively cool-headed way to ensure that they did not escalate into major crises.

China's position shifted in a standoff after a clash between a Chinese fishing trawler and a Japanese Coast Guard vessel near the Diaoyu/Senkaku islands on September 7, 2010. Japanese officials detained the Chinese captain to pursue the matter through a Japanese court, violating the Sino-Japanese Fisheries Agreement, which specified that the areas around the Diaoyu/Senkaku islands were treated as the high seas in which vessels were subject to flag-state jurisdiction. The Chinese government acted quickly to demand Japan "immediately and unconditionally" release the captain. China's top-ranking foreign policy officials, including State Councilor Dai Bingguo, summoned the Japanese ambassador six times to express outrage and to protest. While such aggressive summonses were themselves unprecedented, Beijing sharply raised the stakes by displaying its coercive power of diplomatic paroxysm and economic blackmail.[99]

Seeking a face-saving solution two weeks after the clash, a Japanese official brought a message to Dai Bingguo in Beijing that Japan could release the captain swiftly if he would pay a simple fine for ramming into the Coast Guard vessel. China turned down the proposal because it would allow Japan to retain jurisdiction over the proceedings. After China arrested four Japanese nationals in Hebei Province, accusing of them illegally entering a defense zone and videotaping military targets, Japan released the Chinese captain. Taking an unprecedented hard-line position, China got its way.[100]

The two countries were knocked into another crisis after the Tokyo governor, Shintaro Ishihara, made a bid to purchase the islands from a private Japanese owner to build infrastructure there in April 2012. Preempting Ishihara's provocative plan, the Japanese government decided to purchase three of the five islets in September 2012 to keep them as they were for the time being.[101] Whereas the Japanese government viewed its actions as preventing a likely crisis, China interpreted it as an imaginative act to strengthen Japan's claim through government control. Declaring that "long gone are the days when the Chinese nation was subject to bullying and humiliation from others,"[102] the Chinese government displayed coordinated coercion. Upping the ante further, Beijing declared an ADIZ in November 2013 that covered the Diaoyu/Senkaku islands as well as the greater part of the East China Sea.

Prime Minister Abe requested a meeting with President Xi to talk about the dispute. But Beijing set two preconditions: Japan had to acknowledge the existence of a dispute over the sovereignty of the Diaoyu islands, and Abe stated his commitment not to visit the Yasukuni Shrine that honored the souls of Japanese soldiers who died in the service to Japan, including the war criminals in the Pacific War. Although Abe managed a brief encounter and shook the hand of Xi on the sidelines of the APEC summit in Indonesia in November 2013, Xi did not formally meet Abe until Japanese national security advisor Yachi Shotaro reached a four-point agreement with the Chinese government that was spun by Chinese media as signaling Japan's admission that it did not have sole administrative control of the islands.[103] The media showed Abe walking toward Xi, who stood soberly and appeared to be condescending as he looked off in a different direction at the meeting in November 2014.

FIGURE 1   Shinzo Abe walked toward Xi Jinping who stood soberly and appeared to be condescending. The *Japan Times*, credited to AP. https://www.japantimes.co.jp/news/2014/11/11/national/politics-diplomacy/awkward-looks-reveal-hard-work-come-abe-finally-meets-xi/.

FIGURE 2   Xi Jinping shaking hands with Shinzo Abe and looking off in a different direction. NBC News. https://www.nbcnews.com/news/world/chinas-xi-jinping-japans-shinzo-abe-meet-apec-summit-n244951.

But the meeting has not been accompanied by any serious attempt at resolving their fundamental differences. Forcing Japan to accept its claim over the disputed islands through attrition and fatigue, China has enlarged its maritime activities around the Sankaku/Diaoyu islands. The bigger and better equipped Chinese ships have sailed more numerously and stayed longer in the contiguous zone than ever. China passed the Coastguard Law on January 23, 2021, empowering the Chinese coastguard to use weapons when sovereign rights or jurisdiction are infringed or threatened.

In the South China Sea, China's U-shape nine-dash line claim that includes about 80 percent of the water has been disputed by Vietnam, the Philippines, Malaysia, Indonesia, and Brunei. For a long time, Beijing took a delaying strategy and a position of ambiguity to avoid officially stating the extent, meaning, nature, and legal basis of its claims to prevent the other claimants from making counter claims and starting the process of clarification and negotiation.[104] Xi Jinping switched the ambiguity to a clarity strategy. Expanding maritime law enforcement and sending combat-ready patrol ships regularly to escort fishing fleets, China scaled up land reclamation on and around the disputed islands and turned small islets into seven man-made islands with giant dredging ships, adding a total of 290,000 square meters of landmass between 2014 and 2017. Among them, Fiery Cross Reef, Subi Reef, and Mischief Reef have featured runways, hangars for fighter planes, ammunition bunkers, barracks, and deep-water piers, and became the largest islands in the Spratly Islands chain.[105]

Beijing also built a rugged power projection platform on Yongxing Island and significantly upgraded the installation with an airstrip and expanded the infrastructure, including a 2,700-meter runway that can accommodate most Chinese fighter jets. While some Southeast Asian claimant states also engaged in land reclamation activities, these were on a minuscule scale compared with China's construction of much larger landmasses. China has maintained that the construction was to ensure safety at sea, including navigation assistance, search and rescue, and fisheries protection. But these facilities have enhanced China's ability to conduct long-distance patrol operations, hinder US military operations, and overwhelm the military forces of other claimants in the event of war.

Frustrated with the lack of viable alternatives to stop China's actions, the Philippines filed a Notification and Statement of Claim at the International

Tribunal for the Law of the Sea (ITLOS) in January 2013 to seek determination if certain features in the disputed waters were entitled to the legal definition of islands and the two-hundred-nautical-mile Exclusive Economic Zone (EEZ). China rejected the legal action because Beijing optionally excluded itself from compulsory arbitration when it ratified the UN Convention on the Law of Seas (UNCLOS) in 2006. When the ruling was imminent in 2016, Beijing launched a campaign to convince governments around the world that the tribunal was illegitimate. Speaking in a Washington think tank, former state councilor Dai Bingguo described the forthcoming verdict as "merely a piece of wasted paper."[106]

The tribunal ruled in favor of the Philippines in July 2016 that China has no legal basis to claim historic rights in the areas within its nine-dash line. All the features in the areas are either low-tide elevations or rocks that cannot sustain human habitation or economic life. Accordingly, none of the features can generate two-hundred-mile EEZs and there are no areas of overlapping EEZ claims between China and the Philippines. The tribunal also ruled that Mischief Reef is a low-tide elevation in the EEZ of the Philippines. Consequently, the installations and structures built by China there are legally under the jurisdiction of the Philippines.

The Chinese government rejected the ruling by declaring "four nons": non-participation, non-recognition, non-acceptance, and non-enforcement.[107] Chinese foreign minister Wang Yi used "Three Illegals": illegal initiation of the arbitration, illegal formation of the arbitration court, and illegal ruling of the arbitration, to claim that the tribunal lacked jurisdiction, was biased, and had no legal basis.[108]

Beijing is a signatory of the UNCLOS but refused to take part in and accept the arbitration because a big power would not surrender its territorial claims under international pressures. The Chinese government had promised that a rising China would be capable of recovery of all lost territories and would not be bullied by others. Backing down would not only leave China locked out of the resources in the South China Sea but also diminish its legitimacy in the eyes of the Chinese people. Ignoring the ruling indicated China's exercise of big power privilege. As Graham Allison indicated, "None of the five permanent members of the UN Security Council have ever accepted any international court's ruling when (in their view) it infringed their sovereignty or national security interests. Thus, when China rejects the Court's decision in this case, it will be doing just what the other great powers have repeatedly done for decades."[109]

Demonstrating Chinese power and resolve, Beijing maneuvered and stopped other countries from calling China to comply with the verdict.[110] Washington had urged China to honor international law. Coming hot on the heels of the ruling, Secretary of State John Kerry met Chinese foreign minister Wang Yi on the sidelines of the Sixth EAS Foreign Ministers' Meeting on July 26, 2016, and said that "the international community needs to be patient and flexible and not put China in a corner, while China must reformulate its policy in line with international law."[111] Wang agreed that it was time to return things to the "right track" and "turn the page" on the ruling.[112]

As the United States kept mum, the twenty-eight members of the European Union failed to endorse the ruling as legally binding in the statement that took three days of protracted negotiations. As Greece, Hungary, and Croatia opposed any strong language, the European Union (EU) statement did not support but merely "acknowledged" the ruling and took a neutral position to call on all parties to clarify their claims and pursue them by international law.

Beijing also successfully prevented the ASEAN Foreign Ministers' Meeting on July 24, 2016, from mentioning the ruling in the joint communiqué. China triumphed after Philippines' President Rodrigo Duterte visited Beijing to mend fences and boost trade in October 2016. Duterte promised that the two sides were "to seek a settlement on the South China Sea issue through bilateral dialogue," the stance Beijing had insisted on. After the visit, President Duterte not only stopped pressing China to abide by the arbitration but also played down concerns about China's dredging work and building activity on reefs.[113] Manila in return received vast inflows of Chinese investment.

The muted and embarrassed response of the Western countries and the calming down of the Philippines as the most vociferous claimant showed Beijing could get around the observance of the verdict of international arbitration. In the eyes of many Chinese, Beijing's success in brazening out legal censure, intimidating Southeast Asian states into silence, and achieving de facto acquiescence of the West confirmed the success of Xi's big power diplomacy.

The validity of the arbitration has, however, remained a source of friction between Beijing and its neighbors. New Zealand defense minister Gerry

Brownlee said at a security forum in Beijing in October 2016, "As a small maritime trading nation, international law and particularly the UNCLOS is important for New Zealand. We support the arbitral process and believe that countries have the right to seek that international resolution." Fu Ying, former Chinese deputy foreign minister, rebuked New Zealand by reaffirming China's official position that countries "not involved in the disputes" should not interfere.[114] On December 12, 2019, Malaysia made a submission on an extended continental shelf to the UN Secretary-General, claiming sovereign rights and jurisdiction of the natural resources of the seabed and subsoil in their two-hundred-nautical-mile EEZ in the South China Sea. The Philippines, Vietnam, and Indonesia submitted their notes verbally to support Malaysia, referring to the 2016 decision on the dispute between China and the Philippines as an authoritative interpretation of the law. These actions signal that the dispute over the legality of China's claims is not going away.

PART TWO

Shaping Ideational and Institutional Conditions

4

Power of the Past over the Present
The Imperial Glory versus the Century of Humiliation

POLITICAL LEADERS IN DEMOCRACIES are constrained by public opinion in making foreign policy decisions. Failure to respect public opinion can be politically expensive. But in China's authoritarian state, leaders are not only relatively free from the constraint but also able to create and shape public opinion to mobilize support to their policy agenda. One way to do so is the reconstruction of the collective memories of China's mythologized history. As one of the world's longest civilizations, history is inscribed in China's mental terrain. The collective memory of the past binds the Chinese people to form their national identity and shape their views on and relations with the outside world. Looking at the past to guide the future, Chinese leaders have drawn lessons from historical instances and used the vocabulary and questions developed historically to interpret international affairs, find policy objectives, and justify decisions. John K. Fairbank, therefore, insisted that historical perspective is not a luxury, but a necessity to understand the actions of Chinese leaders.[1]

But historical memories as recollections and representations of past events can be strategically reconstructed by political elites. Because most witnesses of the historical events have passed away, current and future generations of the public are connected to them through stories told by the media, family members, and classrooms. Michel Foucault famously said that "if one controls people's memory, one controls their dynamism."[2] George Orwell confirmed that "who controls the past controls the future, who controls the present controls the past."[3]

Historical discourse has been extremely politicized in China. As Chinese official historians have often said, history study is a mirror for today (以史鉴今) and an instrument to govern and educate people (资政育人).[4] In other words, historical memories are not necessarily about the truthfulness or objective reflections of the past but whatever the CCP chooses to remember. China's sharply contrasting historical experiences have left rich legacies for their maneuver: the imperial glory of the past millennia has left an ethnocentric world outlook, while modern humiliation resulting from the invasion of the foreign imperialist powers has created a unique sense of victimization and insecurity.

After the founding of the PRC, Mao Zedong focused on the national trauma to build the nationalist credential of the CCP and set course for his self-reliance and revolutionary diplomacy. His attitude toward imperial China was ambivalent because the Chinese empire expanded vast territories and left controversial legacies, such as territorial disputes and cultural chauvinism, complicating its relations with neighbors. Following the communist ideology that emphasized class struggle between the exploited and the ruling classes, Mao blamed the ruling classes for imperial warfare and expansion.[5]

The national trauma remained a backbone of Deng Xiaoping's developmental diplomacy to help build national consensus for economic modernization through reform and opening up to the outside world. The narrative became that China had been strong when it was open and drawn deeply in the achievements of other peoples and civilizations. When China closed itself, it became complacent and fell behind. Breaking from Maoist autarky that locked China in poverty and attributing the national humiliation to China's lack of development, Deng popularized the historical lesson that "the backward will be beaten" and focused on economic development to overcome the vulnerability.6

As China has reemerged as a big power, Xi Jinping has become more willing to celebrate China's thousand years of imperial glory to boost national pride and fuel nostalgia for national rejuvenation. While many foreign observers have used the term "rise" to describe China's emergence in the twenty-first century, Xi Jinping has emphasized rejuvenation to the past greatness rather than a rise from nothing. This glory was interrupted by the invasion of Western powers during the century of humiliation. The time has come for China to restore its ancient greatness. What Xi has celebrated, however, is a reinvention of imperial China as the benevolent center of East Asia to advance the agenda of China's rise as a return to the natural state in which a powerful China would be benign at the center of the world. The imperial wars and conquests have been selectively forgotten. The chosen glory, chosen trauma, and chosen amnesia have mutually reinforced each other and served as the backdrop of Xi's imperial restitution and an all-purpose gripe in his justifications of China's aspirations as a big power.

China, with thousands of years of history, cannot be reduced to simplistic villains, saints, or victims. China has been the powerful and expansionist conqueror, the inward-looking hermit, the victim of Western and Japanese imperialism, the beacon of order and good governance, and the antipode to Western civilization. As one observer suggested, "China is no more constrained by its history than any other country. But insofar as its leaders prefer to cast their efforts as a culmination of what has gone before, there are ready examples to justify nearly any path they choose."[7]

Imperial Glory and the Chinese World Order

The memory of China's mythological history has been evolving in modern times. The conventional paradigm of imperial China's foreign relations has been "the Chinese world order" coined by Harvard Sinologist John Fairbank in the 1960s. It was a Sinocentric order, with "China being internal, large, and high and the barbarians being external, small, and low."[8] All countries were arranged hierarchically around the Chinese emperor as the Son of Heaven that entitled to enjoy the reign of the world. Fundamentally different from the contemporary world order based on the Westphalian principles of state sovereignty and diplomatic equality, the Chinese world order was regarded as an ethical hierarchy, maintained by the power of the Chinese civilization and self-sufficient agricultural economy, with its smaller neighbors to be civilized by learning to accept Confucianism as the most advanced ethical system.[9]

For example, Chinese culture dominated the literature, written languages, and spoken tongues of Vietnam and Korea. Confucianism, along with its ex-amination system, influenced their political and intellectual life. Even though some countries, such as Japan, never fell under China's political domination, they could not escape from the strong influence of Chinese culture. China's relations with its neighbors were thus culturally superior-inferior. The Sinitic zone was at the center, including the core of China proper and the most nearby and culturally similar tributaries, Korea, Vietnam, and the Ryukyu Islands. Tibet and Central Asia, whose cultural developments were independent of Chinese civilization, were located next. At a further distance were barbarians. The Chinese culture and civilization demarcated the boundary between China's sedentary agricultural society and the barbarians' nomadic steppe societies. Clear legal boundaries of jurisdiction did not exist.[10]

China's cultural superiority was due to the Chinese imperial system and Confucianism that preserved domestic social order and political stability and therefore extended to the surrounding areas.[11] China was occasionally invaded by nomadic tribesmen, which brought about the rule of the Mongols and the Manchus during the Yuan and the Qing dynasties respectively. But Chinese culture was so powerful that the Mongols and the Manchus had to rely on Chinese bureaucracy and Confucianism to maintain their rule. The vitality of Chinese civilization proved capable of absorbing the changes thrown at it in the form of invasions and new dynasties. Dynasties came and went but the pattern of governance succeeded in reasserting itself. Chinese civilization as lasting power bridged periods of disunity and infused new governments. The term "culturalism" has thus been used to describe the dominant worldview of imperial China. Culturalism did not regard the boundary between the Chinese and barbarians as static or fixed. All those who accepted Chinese culture could be incorporated into the cultural bounds and become Chinese.[12]

Putting special emphasis on the virtue of the rulers, "The Chinese, with their Confucianism, created an elaborate intellectual structure of an ethical order which all enlightened peoples were expected to acknowledge and respect."[13] Harmony was the product of the emperor's virtue. If the emperor violated the virtue, the rivers would flood, the mountains shake, the people revolt, and the order would crumble. The Chinese order was thus sustained by heavy stress on ethical orthodoxy and proper norms in virtuous conduct. Right conduct was to move others by example. According to this mystique, the Chinese emperor's superior position gave one prestige among others and power over them.

China's central position was manifested in the tributary system, a term used by John F. Fairbank in the 1940s, as the institution for foreign relations.[14] The tributary system was highly developed during the Ming and Qing periods when Korea, the Ryukyus, Annam (Vietnam), Burma, Laos, and Nepal sent tributary missions regularly to China.[15] Imperial China dealt with external affairs through the Board of Rites Reception Department (礼部) in the Ming dynasty and the Barbarous Affairs Department (理藩院) in the Qing dynasty. The envoys of tributary states were expected to appear in the Chinese capital, make obeisance to the emperor, and present tribute in the imperial court.

The Collected Statutes of the Great Qing described the operation of the tributary system in a very ceremonial way. The Qing court, in most cases, paid for the expenses of the tributary missions from their arrival at the Qing border to their departure. The tributaries were escorted to court by Qing officials. After performing the appropriate ceremonies, they presented tribute memorials and a symbolic tribute of their precious native products. As a consolation, they were usually given more valuable presents, most often highly portable silk cloths and imperial gifts. Finally, Chinese missions were sent to visit them in return.[16]

Although the tributary system sometimes embarrassed the tributary states and bore a heavy cost to imperial China, it was valuable for both. For tributary states, it enabled the legalization of controlled trade along their frontiers with China and validated their political power from the Chinese emperor. For the Chinese court, the ritual acknowledged the superiority of Chinese culture, recognized the greatness of Chinese civilization and the existence of Chinese authority, and, consequently, the inviolability of China's frontiers. Economically, China was able to trade for items necessary without admitting its dependence on these items of trade, preserving "the myth of China's self-sufficiency."[17]

The hegemonic nature of Chinese culture gave rise to a false sense among the Chinese that the hierarchy was universal. There were no other hierarchies or other sources of power in the world. All countries within the tributary system were culturally subservient. The countries that were geographically too distant simply lived in a kind of limbo or cultural vacuum. Within the order, a great deal of "self-determination" existed, but opposition to the Chinese empire was considered rebellion against the established order.

A Nostalgic Futurology

China's reemergence as a great power in the twenty-first century has renewed the interests of Chinese leaders and scholars in the ancient order. Although traditional ideas like harmony were criticized as a contradiction to the Marxist class struggle in Mao's years, Hu Jintao proposed the concept of the harmonious world derived from the traditional Chinese order. Xi's China Dream has appealed to nostalgic futurology to recast the millennial history as characterized by peace and prosperity to justify China's power ambition as a continuity of the glorious past. In Xi's narrative, "China has never engaged in colonialism or aggression. China's unswerving pursuit of peaceful development represents the peace-loving cultural tradition for thousands of years."[18]

The Chinese world order has been presented as a *tianxia* (all under heaven) system. *Tian* is heaven, *xia* is earth, and *tianxia* is the universe under heaven. The Son of Heaven ruled all below and brought order to the world. The official media has portrayed Xi Jinping as bearing the "*tianxia* feelings and minds" (天下情怀和胸怀) to seek the rejuvenation of the Chinese nation and the peaceful development of the mankind.[19] Rebuilding the normative hierarchy operated in harmony with its neighbors and a superior civilization that used nonmilitary means to spread its influence, China's reemergence has created an opportunity to reshape the unjust Western-centric world.[20]

Zhao Tingyang, a Chinese philosopher, made his name known by the reconstruction of tianxia as the universal system inherited from the Zhou dynasty about three thousand years ago.[21] Tianxia presupposed the universe of "inclusion of all" and implied the acceptance of the diversities in the world, emphasizing the harmony of reciprocal dependence maintained by cultural attraction and ruled by virtue to achieve perpetual peace.[22] Notably different from the aggressive empires in other parts of the world, imperial China was more concerned with establishing itself as an everlasting power than with the plight of endless expansion because of the unaggressive and adaptable characteristics of the Chinese culture.[23]

Tianxia is thus presented as "the Chinese normative principle of international relations in contrast with the principles of sovereignty and the structure of international anarchy which form the core of the contemporary international system."[24] Tianxia's moral appeal is distinguished from the *realpolitik*, which is regarded as conducive to discord and war. The tianxia system is thus superior to the UN system, which is more of a political market for nations and only capable of working with national interests.[25] Committing to a universal mandate, tianxia aspired to the principle of binding all under heaven and across all geographies. Its validity rests not on the power to impose on others, but on its potential as a critique of parochial interests and structures of domination.[26] "Tianxia is where nature and humanity intersect, a space where political authority and social order interact . . . Within the Tianxia system, the structure is hierarchical because only such an arrangement could sustain its stability and harmonious order."[27] In the Tianxia community, the center protected the periphery, and the periphery subordinated to the center, forming a pattern of interdependence, coexistence, and common prosperity between China and its neighbors. China never interfered in the internal affairs of tributary states. The traditional East Asian international system remained stable for more than two thousand years.[28]

According to Yan Xuetong, a leading scholar in Beijing, the rulers in the Tianxia system relied on humane authority (王道) that focused on peaceful means to win the hearts and minds of people. Humane authority was distinguished from hegemony and tyranny that used military force and inevitably created enemies. Humane authority created and maintained perpetual peace. Ancient Chinese rulers appealed to justice (道), benevolence (仁), and morality (德) to win the world.[29] Providing a roadmap for current affairs, Yan argues that great powers that seek international respect must wield humane authority rather than exert hegemony.[30] Another Chinese scholar confirmed that humane authority played an invaluable role in the stability and prosperity of the Chinese cultural areas because it started with an internally holy process (内圣) to reach harmony rather than an external imposition. Humane authority achieved external authority (外王) by reaching harmony among different peoples, nations, and civilizations. Harmony was not uniformity, but rather seeking common ground while preserving differences (和而不同).[31]

According to this reconstruction, imperial China developed a very prudent and defensive strategic culture to arrive at their objectives without using force and worked within the premise of humane authority and sustained the political centripetal forces of the surrounding regions through morality, not coercion. As the celebrated Confucian philosopher Mencius stated, "A just cause enjoys abundant support, while an unjust cause finds little support."

Chinese rulers cautiously waged just wars based on moral rather than material interests. The goal of just wars was not only to punish war criminals but also to establish universal moral authorities.[32]

The CCP's contemporary reconstruction of the just war tradition went back to Mao Zedong, who held that if a state acquired *dao* (justice) it would eventually win no matter how inferior it was in physical strength to its opponent. If a state did not acquire dao, it was doomed to failure no matter how powerful it might be.[33] Two Chinese military scholars generalized three paradigm differences between the Chinese and the Western statecrafts: "justice" vs. "interests," "human factors" vs. "weapon factors," and "stratagem" vs. "strength." The Chinese tradition stressed moral and human factors and believed that the killing power of weapons was not decisive. If China demonstrated domestic harmony and a resolve to fight, no enemy would risk a general war against China. Moreover, the Chinese preferred winning by wisdom over brutal force. Concealment, deception, and secrecy had much more to do with China's traditional culture than with its political system.[34]

In comparison with Western countries that used coercive power to build colonies, one Chinese scholar finds that the Chinese world order caused the tributary states to admire Chinese culture without using force. Sharing the Chinese cultural ideals and values that emphasized "peace, harmony, and a middle way," China developed relations with East Asian countries based on benevolent governance.[35] From this perspective, imperial China's relations with surrounding regions were far more advanced than the colonialism of Western countries. Imperial China resisted the temptation of expansion and won the admiration of its neighbors because it was pedantic and cared about morality and principles.[36]

Some Western scholars have joined the chorus. Martin Jacques has become prominent in China because his book presents China as a civilizational state, an inheritor of the oldest continuous history in the world. Its underlying cultural unity and self-confidence were without equal. Its rulers created the first modern bureaucracy, imbued with a Confucian outlook, controlling domestic subjects more by moral education than force and organizing adjacent regions into a consensual tributary system. Redrawing contemporary ideas of racial hierarchy, China's rise signals the end of global dominance by the West and the emergence of a world disconcerting and unfamiliar to those in the West.[37]

David Kang echoes that although China was the hegemon in the region, the tributary order afforded its participants' immense latitude and played a positive role in maintaining stability and fostering diplomatic and commercial exchange. Criticizing those who downplayed the role of political cultures, he suggests that a rising China is a stabilizing force due to its unique cultural tradition and values. East Asian states grow closer to China because Chinese preferences and beliefs are responsible for maintaining stability in the region.[38]

In a collection to celebrate the lifelong scholarship of Wang Gungwu, a contributor to Fairbank's Chinese world order volume in 1960, Brantly Womack finds that the historic centrality of China produced an East Asian pattern of asymmetric relations based on "attention" rather than power, with leadership asserted by the soft means of prestige and authority. He hails Wang Gungwu for revealing three unique traits of Chinese imperial diplomacy: virtuous superiority, impartiality, and inclusiveness, providing "rituals and routines that met the needs of both the center and the various policies on the periphery." James C. Hsiung agrees that, unlike the power-balancing model of the Eurocentric system, the Chinese order "consisted of formal hierarchy but informal equality," leading to fewer wars in Asia than Europe.[39]

The Symptom of Amnesia

Imperial nostalgia has suffered the symptom of amnesia, which ignored the fact that the current Chinese territory was produced by imperial conquest and expansion, not much different from other empires. Before the Qin dynasty, China was divided into many small warring kingdoms. The Qin emperor expanded the geographical scope immensely by force. The Han dynasty and the Tang dynasty sent armies marching from north to south. The Yuan dynasty, under Kublai Khan, the successor to the legendary Genghis Khan, expanded the empire by the military expedition, stretching across Central Asia, Burma, and Vietnam. In 1263, Kublai Khan made Korea his vassal and aspired to the conquest of Japan. His fleets twice reached the shores of Japan in 1274 and 1281 but were shipwrecked by typhoons, which were to become legendary in Japan as the *kamikaze*, or "divine wind."[40]

The Han people moved southward from their origins in north-central China toward the Yangtze River and down to the area around Hong Kong and Yunnan. The last great gambit south was in the Ming dynasty to the

Western Pacific and Indian Oceans under admiral Zheng He. What stopped China from controlling these areas was domestic turmoil, which forced the Ming court to concentrate on pressure from northern nomadic tribes instead of venturing into far-flung seas.[41] The Qing dynasty expanded to unprecedented size, nearly doubling land from the Ming dynasty. During the 1750s Western Expedition into the Zungharia in Central Asia and the Mongolian heartland, the Qianlong Emperor ordered his army to kill all Zunghar elite. "He incorporated most of eastern Zungharia and the minor Khanates to its south into China, creating one region that Qianlong, triumphantly, referred to as China's new frontier (Xinjiang)." These expansions witnessed several of the most hair-raising bloodbaths in human history.[42] But the lands acquired by the Qing emperors are now considered indisputable parts of the PRC.

Imperial China had to use force because its territorial domain was not always accepted by its neighbors. When imperial China was powerful, it followed the policy of fusion and expansion (融合扩展) and expanded its frontiers and territories (开疆扩土), claiming suzerainty over its smaller neighbors. An empire without durable rivals in its region sustained the illusion and sometimes the reality of superiority. Protected by high plateaus and mountains and the broad expanses of the Pacific Ocean, and surrounded by culturally and often militarily inferior peoples and thinly populated, inhospitable steppes, imperial China deployed various instruments of persuasion and coercion to maintain and expand its rule, including the art of statecrafts. When troubles did occur in the frontiers, Chinese emperors usually could use either militarism or pacifism to suppress them. Such practices worked successfully when the empire was unified and strong. When the empire was weak and divided, the neighbors in turn conquered it.

Sun Tzu's *Art of War* was thus written for the complex political and military struggle to prevail by either nonmilitary or military means. While President Xi drew repeatedly on a phrase from the "Methods of the Sima"—that "a warlike state, however big it may be, will eventually perish"—to emphasize China's peaceful intention, he also emphasized the phrase that "those who forget warfare will certainly be endangered." The two phrases together tell that imperial China was both war-averse and war-ready because warfare was constant.[43] One scholar, therefore, distinguishes two strands of imperial traditions in China's relations with neighbors: the tradition of Mongols of the Yuan dynasty and the Manchus of the Qing dynasty that expanded through military campaigns and a bullying form of diplomacy; and the tradition of the Han emperors who claimed the benevolent authority within tianxia, which had no territorial limits and was extended beyond the lands directly administered by the emperors to all other territories near and far.[44]

Peter Perdue, therefore, claims that the techniques of the Qing to legitimize its rule and claim superiority over rivals were not radically different from the Russian, Mughal, and Ottoman imperial formations. The concept of "colonialism" could be usefully employed to describe certain aspects of the Qing practice.[45] Some Chinese historians admitted that the formation and maintenance of imperial China were more by force than by cultural appeal. Fan Wenlan wrote in 1962 that conflict rather than harmony produced the Chinese nation. Wars were conducted among different states rather than ethnic groups of China. Their relations were determined by their relative power. Bigger and more powerful states always tried to conquer smaller and weaker ones.[46] Fan was brutally attacked. His article was not published until 1980, ten years after his death during the Cultural Revolution. Shortly after Fan's article was published, another Chinese historian argued that there were many hostile nations and states fighting wars in Chinese history. The current boundary of Chinese territory was created by the victory of the Chinese empire against other states.[47]

It is, therefore, a myth that China possessed a unique strategic culture disinclined to force and coercion, seeking nonviolent solutions to interstate disputes and favoring peace over expansionism and war. Viewing war as a central feature of interstate relations and justifying behavior in culturally acceptable terms, Chinese politicians claimed that force should be applied defensively, minimally, only under unavoidable conditions, and in the name of the righteous restoration of a moral-political order. But the operational decision rule assumed that conflict was a constant feature of human affairs. The application of violence was highly effective for dealing with the enemy. This preference was tempered by an explicit sensitivity to one's relative capacity, demanding coercive actions against the enemy as relative capacities became more favorable, consistent with Western realpolitik.[48]

Chinese strategic culture has two strands: one is pacifist and defensive-minded; the other, a realpolitik favoring military solutions and offensive actions. The combination of the two produced a "Chinese cult of defense," which presented the Chinese as a peace-loving people who only used force in self-defense. In the Chinese cult of defense, realist behavior dominated but was justified as defensive. China has assertively protected and aggressively promoted its national interests, up to and including acts of war, but that rationalized all military moves as purely self-defensive.[49] Realpolitik calculation and a notable willingness to use violence when the balance of force permits represents the "bones" underlying the ideational "flesh" of China's strategic culture.[50]

The Fairbank paradigm was thus criticized as an "idealized version of a hierarchical Sinocentric world order" and a nostalgic "half-idealized, half-mythologized past."[51] It reflected the political concern of some scholars writing with Fairbank in the 1960s in opposition to prevailing views that China was merely another totalitarian communist state. They argued for China's distinctive history as a long and civilized society, with the implication that the current communist direction might be temporary, and that long-term historical trends would prevail.[52] The Chinese world order based on a Confucian-Legalism imperial state and the authoritarian Qin-Han polity justified and defended its rule with the Mandate of Heaven.[53] "Supporters of the revival of tianxia as a model for today's world are essentially misrepresenting the past to reconfigure the future, distorting it to advance a political agenda that is at best disingenuous and at worst dangerous."[54]

The tributary system as a key component of the Chinese world order was conducted sometimes only in a ritualistic sense. Tribute is a translation of the Chinese term貢, meaning the presentation of gifts. It was more of a trade. One study reveals that the letters to the Qing court brought by the tributary missions from the Siamese (Thai) court in the 1780s were written in language that portrayed them as an independent kingdom equal to the Qing court. When the missions arrived in the Chinese port, Guangzhou, the Chinese officials edited the letters in their translation to comply with the hierarchical ritual before presenting them to the emperors. The Qing letters to the Siamese court, written in hierarchical terms, were similarly edited in translation and arrived in the Siamese court as documents between equals. The major role of the tributary missions was commercial. Since trade with China was vital to the Siamese, they were willing to send tributary missions, but the Siamese court never accepted the canonization from the Qing court.[55]

A Korean scholar confirms that Chinese hegemony was accepted, defied, and challenged by its East Asian neighbors at different times, depending on these leaders' strategies for legitimacy among their populations.[56] A Chinese scholar, therefore, distinguishes the tributary system, which was on a case-by-case basis and equal footing for trade, from the patriarchal-vassal system, which was institutionalized hierarchical relationships. The local rulers who accepted the canonization of the Chinese court were vassals and paid tributes regularly. During the Ming and Qing periods, only three vassal states, Korea, Annam (Vietnam), and Ryukyu, institutionalized patriarchal-vassal relations.[57]

Although scholarly works have demonstrated that the harmonious Sino-centric world order is a myth, the Chinese government has insisted that imperial China was uniquely peaceful with war employed only as a last resort for defensive purposes. China has maintained control over a territory forged through a great deal of conquest and the borders carved out by the Qing dynasty. Chinese scholars have rejected the comparability of the Chinese empire with the empires in other parts of the world and accused the Western scholars who have described the Qing dynasty as having an expansion tendency as trying to discover the aggressive characters of ancient China to demonstrate the inevitable aggression of today's China.[58] Labeling them historical nihilists and imperialists in a new guise, the CCP calls for Chinese historians to produce a gusher of new scholarship to meet the needs of the party and the people.[59]

The Clash of Civilizations?

The empire collapsed in the nineteenth century. The Qing court already suffered serious social, economic, and political decay. The heavy burden of military and luxurious life expenses and corruption led to massive uprisings such as the White Lotus Rebellion (1796–1805). With its weaknesses exposed, the empire began to lose power over its tributaries. The tributary system began to disintegrate when the Tay Son Rebellion in Vietnam in 1771–1802 threatened to sweep away the entire Confucian establishment of Vietnam; fought off the Qing army; and united the country for the first time in two hundred years. The crushing defeats that the Qing army suffered in a series of military confrontations with Western powers delivered the final blows to the dynasty already in decline.

The encounters were often described as the clash of civilizations. As one scholar wrote, "The Sino-Western conflict in the 19th century was not so much an international conflict as it was a system-to-system conflict, a mismatch between Western nationalism and Chinese culturalism."[60] Another scholar confirmed that the collapse of imperial China resulted from the clash of the principles of international orders. As the tributary states became the colonies of the Western powers, imperial China was downgraded from a tianxia system to a sovereign state and reluctantly accepted sovereign equality. "Imperialist powers defeated China and repudiated the Chinese benevolent governance."[61]

The opposed concepts of cultural hierarchy and diplomatic equality were indeed a cause of conflict. Imperial China was condescending toward the "uncivilized" barbarians within and outside its spheres alike. When European expansion challenged China's cultural superiority, the perception of cultural hierarchy precluded the Chinese from accepting other cultures as equals, making it intellectually difficult to adjust to the new reality. The Westerners were "overwhelmingly impressed by the stubborn persistence" of the Sinocentric perception during the late nineteenth century, when China faced the new and unprecedented challenge of Western powers with their absolutistic claims.[62] The collapse of the Chinese empire was a process of "struggle to resist aggressive European expansion, to adjust itself to the changing international realities, to meet its problems without totally abandoning its imperial tradition, and finally to accept, slowly and gradually, though sometimes reluctantly, some of the European standards, institutions, rules, and values."[63]

But the conflict was also a result of imperial China's resistance to European powers' attempts to incorporate it into the global commercial system. From the geographical location of Europe, China was imagined as the rich and grand "Far East." During Europe's medieval period, China boasted several cities of greater size and wealth than most European cities. Chinese goods, especially tea, silk, and porcelain, were in great demand in the Roman Empire and were carried over the legendary silk routes winding through Central Asia. Starting with Matteo Ricci's travels in the sixteenth century, Europe looked to China for commerce. But imperial China was closed and had very limited interest in the outside world. Trading with far-off Rome along the silk route and the

Eurasian coast through middlemen, Chinese exports were coveted in the Mediterranean world, but China only collected such curiosities as jugglers, acrobats, and giraffes. China's self-sufficiency was never seriously challenged from the outside. James Legge, a Scottish Sinologist, bitterly criticized Chinese people in 1872 for their failure to "realize the fact that China is only one of many independent nations in the world."[64]

Despite the Chinese ignorance, the Europeans kept looking for trade opportunities. Following the "geographical revolution," Christopher Columbus convinced the Spanish crown to provide him with a small fleet to look for a sea route to China. His journey in 1492 gave him credit for discovering America. However, when he first landed on the American continent, he mistook it for India, located midway between Europe and China. The Portuguese were the first to establish a presence in East Asia by its rule of Macao on China's coast, followed by the Dutch in Taiwan and Japan and the Spaniards in the Philippines. Europeans began arriving in large numbers by the sixteenth century when they circumnavigated the globe and set up provisioning stations and trading posts in different parts of the world.

Professing little need for Western goods, the Qing rulers were confident in their self-sufficiency and assumed an aloof and patronizing attitude toward the Europeans. Perceiving the Europeans as no different from their Asian neighbors, the Qing court held that the Western barbarians "should observe the rules of the tributary system and fit themselves into the civilized Sinocentric world order in their pursuit of foreign trade."[65] Early European traders and missionaries were rebuffed and confined to small enclaves known as factories in the port cities of Macao, Hong Kong, and Guangzhou (Canton), where they dealt exclusively with a small guild of licensed Chinese merchants. They were forbidden to trade outside these factories and not allowed to enter the city of Guangzhou. Any request to Qing officials went through those merchants. They could not even reside permanently in these buildings and had to leave China at the end of the trading season.[66] This pattern of relationship, known as the Canton system, "was built on a central theme of contempt for foreigners and disdain for merchants."[67]

Despite these restrictions, the British East India Company developed a profitable trade by monopolizing all British trade and dealing with a comparable monopoly on the Qing side, a licensed guild of about a dozen firms. Each side effectively had a body that could represent and discipline its members. At the heart of British imports was Chinese tea. The British shipped cargo of woolens and lead from England, raw cotton from Bombay, and tin rattans from the Strait of Malacca in exchange for soaring tea imports.[68]

While "the old Canton system proved mutually profitable within the limits imposed by two, Chinese and foreign, systems of trade regulation,"[69] European expansion and free trade disrupted the Canton system. The East India Company's monopoly was lost in the 1833 parliamentary reforms. The deregulation brought about a flood of new merchants. They found the trade constraints intolerable. It was against the principle of free trade if foreign traders had no direct access to markets and had to accept the prices offered by Chinese merchants.[70] In addition, as the quantity of teas taken by the British went up, lead, rattans, and cotton fell short of covering the cost. The gap in the balance of payment had to be filled with silver, which grew scarcer than ever in the early nineteenth century of the mercantilist time. The British thus discovered a new commodity, opium, that was in large supply for massive numbers of consumers to balance the payment.

As the flourishing opium trade produced devastating consequences for Chinese society and national wealth, a policy debate took place in the Qing court. One side wanted to legalize and tax the opium trade to relieve the treasury's problem. The other side advocated the suppression of both opium dealers and addicts.[71] The hard-liners prevailed. When the spread of opium addiction and large-scale opium imports became a menace to drain on the country's silver supply, Lin Zexu was appointed commissioner with broad discretionary powers in 1839 to stop the drug trade. He forced the British merchants to surrender vast opium stocks and destroyed them without compensation.

In response, the British government demanded indemnity for the loss and began a series of naval assaults after the Qing court refused this demand. The Opium War broke out in 1840 because of Chinese resistance to the opium trade and the British insistence on its commercial expansion. The Qing court had little appreciation of its weakness when it sent a fleet of ships to fight the British fleet in the water of Hong Kong. The British easily destroyed the Qing fleet and went on to blockade and bombard Guangzhou and other coastal cities. When Nanjing lay at the mercy of the British fleet in 1842, the Qing court was forced to sign the Treaty of Nanjing, making concessions to end the war.[72]

The National Trauma

The Opium War was the violent encounter between the declining Qing dynasty and industrialized Britain. The miserable defeat was a milestone of the imperial collapse and came as a heavy blow to the sense of Chinese superiority. The official history textbooks of the PRC have set the Opium War as the starting point of the century of humiliation, the period when China experienced internal fragmentation, was attacked, bullied, torn apart and "carved up like a melon" (瓜分), made major concessions to foreign powers, and endured brutal occupation. It fell from a powerful, proud, and unified empire into a weak, humiliated, and divided semicolonial country.[73]

The humiliation was recorded in the Treaty of Nanjing, by which China ceded Hong Kong to the British as its colony and opened five ports for trade. The Qing court could not regulate this trade, nor could it impose tariffs in the treaty ports where the Westerners enjoyed "extraterritoriality," i.e., foreign rather than Chinese laws would apply to foreigners living in China. To add insult to injury, China was required to pay Britain a huge amount of silver as compensation for the destroyed opium.

Prompted by complaints about the execution of a French missionary by Chinese local authorities in Guangxi Province, which at that time was not open to foreigners, the French joined the British for more privileges and started the Second Opium War. A joint British-French expeditionary force sailed northward to Tianjin and proceeded to fight their way to the imperial capital Beijing. Xianfeng Emperor dispatched ministers for peace talks in the outskirt of Beijing. The British envoy, Harry Parkes, insulted the imperial emissary by demanding one thousand Anglo-Franco military forces march into Beijing and be received by the emperor with the Western military ceremonies. Xianfeng imprisoned Parkes and his entourage. Half of them were allegedly murdered in a gruesome fashion: by slow slicing with the application of tourniquets to severed limbs to prolong the torture.[74]

The Anglo-Franco army was infuriated to discover the bodies unrecognizable after entering Beijing and proceeded to sack and burn the imperial Yuanming Palace to the ground as a personal punishment to the emperor. The Qing court was forced to sign the Tianjin Treaty in October 1860. In addition to increased monetary compensation, the Qing court accepted the diplomatic representation of Western powers in Beijing. Britain wrested away from China the Kowloon Peninsula, incorporating it into the newly prosperous colony of Hong Kong.[75]

China suffered another military defeat by Japan in the 1894–95 war for supremacy in Korea, a longtime tributary state of China. In the Treaty of Shimonoseki that ended the war, China recognized the independence of Korea and ceded Taiwan, the adjoining Pescadores, and the Liaodong Peninsula to Japan. The defeat was particularly heart-wrenching. At the time, "China was already accustomed to rapacious Western powers squabbling over its riches but had remained self-confident in the knowledge of these powers' irrelevance. However, the assault from Japan, a speck of dust in its backyard, shattered this self-assurance and was experienced as a shocking and intolerable humiliation."[76]

China's humiliating defeat by Japan, a tiny country that the Chinese dismissively called 倭人 (dwarfs), was fundamental to the rise of the first generation of Chinese nationalists. Liang Qichao stated that the defeat effectively awoke the Chinese people "from the dream of 4,000 years."[77] One observer argued that "This was the point at which the fear of the loss or the death of China . . . took hold. Theories of Social Darwinism filled many Chinese with foreboding."[78] A British scholar discovered that "China was besieged, and an easy target for any industrial power bent on war."[79] The growing sense of national humiliation was particularly intense as China had considered itself superior to Japan, which had derived its own culture from China. It was as if the world was suddenly turned upside down. Strange and inferior barbarians suddenly defeated the Chinese empire out of nowhere and broke their ramparts with superior firepower.

Imperialist powers started to split up China into spheres of interest. The British carved out a sphere of influence in the Yangtze Valley, France in Guangzhou, Germany in Shandong, Japan in southern Manchuria, and Russia in northern Manchuria and Outer Mongolia. In September 1899, Secretary of State John Hay of the United States dispatched the Open-Door notes to Germany, Russia, England, Japan, Italy, and France, requesting formal assurances that they would grant traders of all countries' equal treatment concerning harbor dues and railroad charges.[80] In July 1900, he sent a circular to these powers, stating the US intention to "preserve China's territorial and administrative entity" and "protect all rights guaranteed to friendly powers by treaty and international law, and safeguard for the world, the principle of equal and impartial trade with all parts of the Chinese Empire."[81] As a result, a legal provision, known as the Most Favored Nation (MFN) clause, was inserted into every treaty signed by China with foreign powers. Beijing's concessions granted to any foreign country would automatically be extended to all of them. The MFN clause prevented the Qing from playing one power against another by offering one power concessions for help in fending off the other.

In the seventy years after the Opium War in 1840, the Qing court was forced to sign one treaty after another and accept the Westphalian concept of diplomatic equality. Although the Qing court resisted as much as it could, the fact that China signed these treaties affirmed the principle of diplomatic equality, shattering the fictive remnants of cultural superiority. China's official recognition of legal equality was found in an imperial edict issued by Xianfeng Emperor in 1860 that "England is an independent sovereign state, let it have equal status (with China)."[82] This recognition was borne by the initiation of the General Ministry (总理衙门), a prototype of a foreign office. As "barbarian affairs" became foreign affairs, China was brought into line with the principle of the nation-state system.

Although China adopted European diplomatic institutions and practices, China came to the world not as the center of prominence but as a target of humiliation. When China began to accept the idea of diplomatic equality and struggled to defend its sovereignty, the world had come under the domination of imperialist powers that did not treat China equally. The formal diplomatic equality masked a host of provisions in what the Chinese labeled the "unequal treaties," which disadvantaged China and lacked reciprocity.[83] Whereas imperial China had previously existed in relative isolation from the rest of the world, it was now brought into a global system, which was almost entirely out of its control but would determine its fate.

The death knell of the Chinese empire was loudly sounded by China's loss of its tributary states. China was at its knees, no longer constituting a world unto itself. The blow to its prestige was to reverberate, expand, and be exacerbated by a variety of internal rebellions. The Fists of Righteousness and Harmony (义和团 or Boxers) rebellion started as a xenophobic and anti-Christian movement in Shandong in 1897 and extended to other areas. The Boxers practiced martial arts and performed rituals that purportedly made them immune to bullets. Empress Dowager Cixi was initially hostile to the Boxers but changed her mind to use them and declared war on foreign powers in 1900. "Support for the Qing and extermination of the foreigners" (扶清灭洋) thereby became the slogan of the Boxers. Annihilating everything related to "Western" influence and culture, the Boxers killed both foreign missionaries and Chinese Christians, foreign engineers, and their families and destroyed Western goods and properties.[84]

Protests by Christian churches led to the Eight-Nation Alliance of the United States, United Kingdom, Russia, Germany, the Austro-Hungarian Empire, France, Japan, and Italy sending troops to Beijing to crush the Boxers. Although both sides committed atrocities, the massive executions of Chinese civilians believed to be Boxers is a painful memory in China. The Qing court was forced to sign the Boxer Protocol on September 7, 1901, which included the "Boxer Indemnity" of reparations of 450 million taels of silver (about 18,000 tons) to the eight powers over thirty-nine years.[85] The protocol and indemnity delivered a devastating blow to the Chinese economy. The Qing court never recovered.

The domestic rebellion and foreign humiliation cumulated in the Nationalist Revolution that brought down the Qing dynasty and established the Republic of China in 1911. But the country continued to sink even deeper into turmoil and could not regain international standing. China entered World War I as part of the Allied coalition, only to suffer more humiliation at Versailles when the former German concession in Shandong was given to Japan. The wave of anti-imperialist protests that followed, including the May Fourth Movement of 1919, accumulated in the founding of the CCP in July 1921. Holding on to the banner of anti-imperialism, the CCP finally founded the PRC in 1949.

The Lesson of History

The historical experiences of the modern humiliation and the ancient glory have been kept alive in the official historical discourse from which the CCP leaders have drawn historical lessons. One of the most important lessons pervading China's political discourse is "the backward will be beaten" (落后就要挨打). A related phrase is "the weak state cannot have diplomacy" (弱国无外交). This mnemonic construction has presented a diehard realist view of world politics for its lonely self-help character. If one state lags others, it will be suppressed, bullied, or invaded. The strong powers always bully the weak (持强凌弱) but fear the stronger (欺软怕硬). If China does not want to be beaten, it must become powerful enough to defend its sovereignty and interests.[86] In the social Darwinian jungle, China must observe the iron law of the strongest survived and the weakest eliminated and make the nation the strongest.[87]

Chinese political elites have disagreed about the sources of China's weakness and the most effective approach to revitalize China. The mixture of the historically derived cultural superiority and the sense of humiliation has resulted in the tension between nativism and anti-traditionalism. Nativism regards the impact of imperialism on Chinese self-esteem and the subversion of indigenous Chinese virtues as the root of weakness. China can become strong only when it no longer relies on the outside world, particularly Western countries. Reaffirming the durability of traditional cultural superiority, it advocates a staunch adherence to Confucian orthodoxy for a successful rejuvenation. Extreme nativism takes the position of general xenophobia and antiforeignism. In contrast, anti-traditionalism argues that Chinese culture has little relevance to the modern world. Holding tradition as the source of weakness, anti-traditionalism calls for boundless adoption of advanced foreign models and accommodation to the world dominated by progressive or modern powers.

The tension between nativism and anti-traditionalism dominated China's political discourse for the twentieth century. Its repercussion has continued in the twenty-first century. While this persistent tension is hardly unique to China, the tension in China has been unusually acute because it derives from the memory of an unusually long and powerful tradition of imperial greatness in contrast to its deep wounds inflicted by the Western powers. This tension has produced a two-fold dilemma for Chinese leaders: on one side, to avoid the problems of self-reliance that leave China poor and weak; and on the other, the swamp of international involvement that may compromise China's independence and ideals and values.

In the early days of the PRC, communist leaders brought with them traumatic memories of China's inability to determine its fate. Facing containment from the Western countries, Mao Zedong called for self-reliance to defend

China's independence while adopting the Soviet model. China accommodated the Soviet-led communist world, and accepted the Soviet assistance to build China's industrial base. Self-reliance became a necessity after China split with the Soviet Union. Confronting both superpowers, Mao turned China almost completely inward. The isolation and autarky stagnated China's economy and kept the PRC in poverty.

Deng Xiaoping abandoned self-reliance and opened China to the outside world because he recognized that "isolation would prevent any country's development. We suffered from this and so did our forefathers."[88] Although foreign economic exploitation and cultural infiltration caused China's weakness, the lack of economic development was the reason why China became an easy target. Asking the Chinese people to bear in mind that stagnation, weakness, disunity, and disorder at home would invite foreign aggression, the phrase "the backward will be beaten" became a political icon of Deng's modernization drive. The Western countries were regarded simultaneously as advanced economies that China should learn from and as perpetrators that humiliated China in history and deserve to be resented. Deng's developmental pragmatism made "positive compromises," which distinguished from "passive compromise" or one-sided accommodation, to avoid international conflicts that could hurt China's development.[89]

Adapting to the world dominated by Western countries for regeneration, Deng watched with caution for the unintended and unwanted social and political consequences. At the very outset of opening-up, Deng made clear that China must insist on the four cardinal principles: CCP leadership, the socialist road, Marxism, and proletarian dictatorship.[90] Deng also guarded against nativism, which never lost ground and resurfaced with resentment at the Western sanctions after the end of the Cold War.[91] Facing the challenge from both international isolation and domestic nativism, Deng urged Chinese people to focus on economic modernization and avoid confrontation with the United States and other Western countries. In the asymmetric game, while the United States as the more powerful player took a boxing position to hit China directly, China played the martial arts of *taiji* (tai chi) with its strength hidden in the soft performance and bite for its time until the boxer exhausted itself.[92]

As China's power grows, Chinese leaders have become increasingly willing to reveal their historical views of the Sino-centric world. This message was sent loudly at the opening and closing shows of the 2008 Beijing Olympics, which showcased China's reemergence by placing modern technological innovation in the context of five thousand years of history. Xi Jinping is not a straightforward nativist, but his big power diplomacy reclaims the moral duty and the historical role China once played by tapping into the strong sense of pride in ancient achievements and values. Visiting Confucius's birthplace in Qufu, Shandong Province, in November 2013, Xi emphasized that "the prosperity of a country and a nation is always supported by cultural prosperity. The Great Rejuvenation of the Chinese nation requires the development and prosperity of Chinese culture."[93] Xi appealed to Confucianism to reject the Western liberal values as universal and help focus on the longevity of Chinese civilization. The nostalgia for national rejuvenation has played well to the minds of Chinese elites who have never stopped thinking of returning China to the center of the world.

Posing the China Dream and launching the BRI and other initiatives to re-create the Sino-centric world, Xi has revamped the past for the present quest for power and prosperity. The historical memory is reconstructed to create a narrative that helps support China's status as a global power. During President Trump's only state visit to China in 2017, the American guests received a history lesson as they toured the Forbidden City, which served as the backdrop for Xi to remind them that Chinese dynasties had long stood at the center of the earth and "the CCP was making the efforts to extend China's influence along its frontiers and beyond to regain the honor lost during the century of humiliation."[94]

China has dreamed of establishing a sphere of geopolitical and cultural centrality even though the rest of the world would not accept the Sino-centric vision. China's formidable economic performance has made China stronger and alarmed many countries about China's long-term intention. But China has refused to recognize this reality and blamed the United States and other Western countries for attempting to prevent China from rising to its rightful place. Nativism has emerged powerfully after the United States launched a trade war and imposed sanctions on Chinese tech companies. Xi has recalled the Mao-era slogan of self-reliance. When Mao proposed self-reliance, China was poor and faced an external threat. Xi's China is no longer poor and aims at leading the new technology revolution. China is huge, Chinese people are intelligent, and its national market is big. China is to rely on its market and indigenous innovation to drive growth and reduce reliance on foreign technology and the international market. Although Xi's self-reliance is not retreating China into Mao-era isolation, Xi's call represents the feeling of threat by the so-called "hostile foreign forces" and his determination to fight back. Xi aims to prepare the Chinese people for a long struggle and self-sacrifice should China's rise encounter barriers set by internal and/or hostile foreign forces.

The Sense of Victimization and Righteousness

Drawing from the historical experience of subjugation and internecine strife after the fall of the Chinese empire, Chinese political leaders throughout modern history have been preoccupied with an overarching goal of redeeming the humiliation, which nurtured a strong sense of "victimization" and righteousness in foreign affairs. Chiang Kai-shek kept a diary for over twenty years starting in 1928, and every single entry in the diary contained the two words "avenge humiliation" (雪恥) in the top right corner. One of his entries in 1934 was called "Recover Korea. Recover the land that was part of the Han and Tang dynasty." Four years later, his Ministry of Internal Affairs published a "Map of National Shame," in which Mongolia as well as parts of Siberia and all of Indochina continuing down to the Strait of Malacca were marked as "lost territories."[95]

PRC leaders have equally committed to avenging humiliation. The wars, "unequal treaties," humiliations, and territorial losses were the painful road that China walked into the modern world. But Chinese leaders have embraced the Western concepts of equality and sovereignty to vigorously defend Chinese interests, producing an obsession that obtained an inherent and almost self-reverential value in Chinese political discourse. Portraying modern Chinese history as the struggle to defend Chinese sovereignty, Mao Zedong took the Opium War in 1842 as the watershed that prepared the founding of the CCP to wage struggles for an independent China. Lin Zexu was praised as a national hero to represent China's legitimate assertion of sovereignty in front of British imperialism.[96] Deng told British prime minister Margaret Thatcher that China would take back Hong Kong in 1997 no matter what, otherwise he would be no better than the traitors of the Qing dynasty.[97] Xi Jinping is determined to win back Taiwan and the islands in the East and South China Seas. Although the nation-state as a territorial specificity is a recent phenomenon and imperial China was not a nation-state, Chinese leaders have claimed the never-existed Chinese nation-state, creating a mythology in which the making of national territory is embodied in the making of the Chinese nation-state.

The CCP leadership has learned from the historical dynasty cycle in which an old dynasty lost the Mandate of Heaven because it descended into mediocrity and nepotism. The water system went unrepaired, famine broke out, wars and banditry appeared. A conqueror, either Chinese or foreign (Mongol or Manchu), then took over a demoralized empire and regained the Mandate of Heaven by putting an end to the chaos and initiating economic progress. The door opened for the next dynasty. The CCP regime is fully aware of the revolving door. Xi Jinping has examined the collapse of the Soviet Union and the dismembering of the Soviet communist party thoroughly to forestall something similar. The lesson is to strengthen the prerogative of the party and stop any kind of uncertainty about its right to govern China. Any kind of interference from abroad is judged by its impact on social stability and regime legitimacy. Social unrest must be suppressed. Chinese leaders have thus insisted on the absolute right to govern their country. Hypersensitive to issues of sovereignty and territorial integrity, they have harbored irredentist sentiments and objection of the interference by any foreign forces in China's internal affairs.

China has become a big power and cannot be easily humiliated, but China's accomplishments have strengthened and activated, not assuaged, the memory of past humiliation. The conviction that China is denied its rightful place in the world has focused much of China's foreign policy agenda on overcoming the legacy of China's unjust treatment by foreign powers. Seeing a relationship with the world in terms of bullying and humiliation, Xi Jinping repeated the invented historical memory at the celebration of the CCP one-hundredth anniversary in 2021: "We Chinese are a people who uphold justice and are not intimidated by threats of force. As a nation, . . . we will never allow any foreign force to bully, oppress, or subjugate us. Anyone who would attempt to do so will find themselves on a collision course with a great wall of steel forged by over 1.4 billion Chinese people."[98]

The victimization narrative has not only supported the widely and deeply shared commitment to redress past grievances but also placed China on the moral high ground vis-à-vis Western countries. Justifying whatever policy is entirely in its legitimate restoration of justice, Chinese leaders have seen any problems China faces as caused by Western powers and have little patience with the complaints and calls for China to compromise. The morally driven foreign policy imperatives have made it impossible for China to admit any mistakes and make compromises on issues China deems as vital. Showing the curious mixture of great power and weak power attitudes, Beijing has insisted that China be accorded due respect by other powers while demanding special privileges due to its past victimization.

Through the lens of the century of humiliation, an isolated and accidental event or misstep by other nations could quickly touch on sensitive Chinese feelings. For example, the demands of some US Congress members for compensation from China for coronavirus-related damages in 2020, a *gengzi* (庚子) year in the Chinese lunar calendar cycle of sixty years, were quickly linked to the historic memory of Boxer Indemnity in 1900, another *gengzi* year 120 years ago. The Boxer War is still a living memory partially because the Chinese propaganda has portrayed the Boxer Rebellion as a patriotic movement against foreign imperialism and deliberately ignored the Boxers' goal of extermination of the foreigners and their violence. The propaganda has also downplayed the US goodwill gesture tantamount in 1908 to waiving its rights to the Boxer Indemnity and reinvested the remaining share of the indemnity for scholarships to Chinese students studying in the United States and setting up Tsinghua College, which has become China's top university.[99]

Chinese propaganda amid COVID-19 distorted history that the Boxer War was caused by the Eight-Nation Alliance invasion of China. They burned and looted in Beijing, slaughtered ordinary people, ransacked the royal palace, destroyed cultural relics, and demanded huge compensation. An editorial in *Global Times* stated that "120 years later, in this Year of the Gengzi, the descendants of the Eight-Nation Alliance shamelessly demand compensation, evoking our historical memory of humiliation."[100] A *People's Daily* article accused Western countries for continuing to bash, coerce, and use derogatory remarks to humiliate Chinese nationals, like what happened 120 years ago.[101] Claiming that "China today is not the Qing dynasty and Xi is not Cixi," Chinese propaganda warned that a bare-knuckled approach would be a mistake. "When push comes to shove, China will punch back with more force than that from a band of Boxers armed with swords, spears, shields, prayers, and magic rituals."[102]

Reducing the complicated historical event to a black-and-white opposition between inherently "good" Chinese and "evil" foreigners, the CCP successfully proposed a paradigm to interpret the criticism of China through the lens of Western countries' historical wrongdoing and turned the conflict into a patriotic battle. Chinese writer Fang Fang published *Wuhan Diary*, a daily chronicle of life and death in her home city during the early days of the pandemic, and incurred harsh condemnation for "giving a knife to Western anti-China forces" and called a "traitor" for defaming the heroic image of Wuhan, thus helping Western countries claim the second *gengzi* indemnity.[103] The constant reference to such a dark period strikes a peculiar behavior for a nation on the cusp of regional and global dominance. But the chosen trauma is part of a narrative of redemption that legitimizes the CCP's one-party rule and credits the party with restoring its great power status and taking whatever policy that suits China's need. Deng Xiaoping took a low-profile policy when China was not strong enough. Xi Jinping has flexed muscle when China becomes a big power.

This victim narrative has sustained a deep-rooted geopolitical belief in securing its peripheral areas because the loss of control on the periphery had rendered the core vulnerable to penetration and attack by foreign imperialist powers. Xi's foreign policy is praised as demonstrating a new tianxia strategy, in which China has rebuilt its centrality in its periphery through the diplomacy of fan-like diffusion (辐辏外交).[104] Although Xi has claimed that China has never practiced imperialism, he has looked back to the country's earlier apogees of power and acted in ways that can evoke aggressive realpolitik behavior. The national shame of the past justifies belligerent actions. Chinese leaders cannot forget that the Middle Kingdom enjoyed power diffusion in its periphery. The Western imperialist expansion overwhelmed the position of China even in its own region. The imperiousness that dictated ancient China's policies has manifested itself in Xi's BRI to build a modern-day version of the tributary system. China's massive infrastructure investments across the Indo-Pacific, Eurasia, and beyond are aimed to place China at the center of trade routes and communications networks.

While much of Chinese leaders' public rhetoric was couched in terms of condescension toward the intruding foreign imperialists, their private calculations by contrast often employed the vocabulary of strategic rivalry and the balance of power.[105] Functioning in an amoral interstate system characterized by constant maneuver and ruthless competition, Chinese leaders have dug into Chinese history to find models of statecraft, from the lofty imperial style to shrewd Machiavellian cunning, to achieve foreign policy objectives. The appeal of the ancient Warring States model has been particularly strong since China's rise as a big power. Chinese leadership has rediscovered the old model of unbounded power politics, a twenty-first-century Hobbesian struggle of all against all.

Selectively remembering the best and the worst of their past, the Chinese leaders' frame of reference to China's reemergence as a big power is strikingly historical and often told from the comparative analysis of historical long-term cycles (历史长周期比较分析).[106] China's historical fall and contemporary rise have presented not just a cautionary tale about past experiences but a source of beliefs about how the world works. Civilizations and powers rise and fall, with new forms of government and political organization created in response to changing conditions, time and again. Searching for the historical opportunity of reemergence, they have expected the decline of the United States in the light of China's own historical experience, which was marked by sudden and radical interruptions. The parable of every dynasty in China followed a script that foresaw, after growth and stabilization phases, a collapse.

The prediction of inevitable eclipse of the US power gained momentum after the 2008 financial crisis. The very ascent of President Trump to discredit American democracy was a symptom of a profound systemic crisis. The poor performance of the United States during the early days of the COVID-19 pandemic further revived the perception of US decline. The indelible images of the US withdrawal from the Afghanistan debacle in 2021 strengthened the belief that the United States was a declining power. The chosen glory, trauma, and amnesia have, thus, reinforced the power of the past over the present and the future and shaped public opinions for the support of Chinese foreign policy priorities.

Defining China's National Interests
State versus Popular Nationalism

THE PRC HAS BEEN LED BY A COMMUNIST PARTY. Communism as the official ideology is supposed to provide perceptual prisms for CCP leaders to view the world, analyze foreign relations, and find solutions to conflicts. But its universal orientation has created tensions with China's national interests. While Mao Zedong tried to practice communist internationalism, he followed nationalism to protect Chinese interests. Deng Xiaoping downplayed communist ideology and focused on nationalist themes of wealth and power to rebuild the CCP's legitimacy. After the end of the Cold War, Chinese leadership launched a patriotic education campaign to compensate for the tarnished communism.

Nationalism has been driven from two directions: by the state from the top-down and by popular forces from the bottom-up. For many years after the end of the Cold War, the state-led nationalism was affirmative in emphasizing exclusive but positive "us" for the survival of the lonely communist state subjected to international isolation in the post–Cold War world. Exploiting nationalism to build broad-based national support and hold the world's most populous country together during the turbulent transition, Chinese leaders made effective efforts to control the expression of popular nationalism, which was more assertive and hostile to the Western powers. Tempered by prudence, Chinese foreign policy was not dictated by the emotional rhetoric of popular nationalism, and it maintained cooperative relations with Western powers and Asian neighbors that China's economic success depended heavily upon.

The pragmatic control of popular nationalism began to loosen up after the financial crisis in 2008 as Chinese leaders became sympathetic to the beliefs of popular nationalists that the financial trouble in the Western countries provided a historic opportunity for China's big power aspirations. Xi Jinping came to office in 2012 and has intensified the patriotic education campaign and tightened information control to rally support for resuming China's historic role of preeminent power in Asia and beyond. Chinese nationalism has therefore become assertive to target negative "others." Xi's patriotic education has been empowered by the narratives of the national trauma during the century of humiliation and national pride in the collective achievements for rejuvenation by the collective sacrifices and hard work of the Chinese people under the CCP leadership. Xi's assertive turn has resonated among popular nationalists and inculcated a state-led popular nationalism characterized by intolerance to any criticism of the CCP regime and its policies, muscular hostility toward Western powers and values, and assertiveness in pursuing expanded national interests. Inflaming nationalist sentiments, Xi Jinping's patriotic campaign and information control have produced combative patriots standing firm behind Xi's foreign policy agenda.

Historically, nationalism has inspired nations to gain independence, be free from alien rule and contribute to modernization. But extreme ultra-nationalism has driven nations to catastrophic destruction and made them responsible for brutal wars and violence. Nationalism has reinforced Chinese national pride and turned past humiliation into a driving force for modernization, but it has also produced xenophobia characterized by fear, hatred, and hostility toward foreigners. The emergence of state-led popular nationalism has fed a roiling sense of anxiety in many countries about the possibility of belligerent nationalism fanning China into wider geopolitical conflicts. While some scholars cautiously explored the limits of Chinese nationalism,[1] many scholars have found a reckless assertive nationalism empowered by traditional Sino-centrism, victim narratives, and China's contemporary power aspirations, and became a virulent force driving Chinese foreign policy toward an inflexible direction.[2]

Communist Internationalism and
Chinese National Interests

The CCP party-state is a goal-rational political system where legitimacy is claimed, and to some degree granted, in terms of its ability to achieve declared goals of communism. Although the precise content of the framework varies considerably over time, the tenets of communist prescriptions on foreign affairs include that the world is divided into two camps of socialism and capitalism; countries in the socialist camp practice communist internationalism to achieve the goal of communism; relations among socialist states are based on the common course rather than transitory interests; and Communism will eventually prevail over capitalism.[3]

China joined the Soviet-led socialist camp in the 1950s, but Mao Zedong was reluctant to follow communist internationalism because the Soviet Union saw internationalism as the unconditional compliance of other socialist states to Soviet policy. China would have to take joint actions with other socialist countries under Soviet leadership. China leaned toward one side of the Soviet Union not because of communist internationalism but because of the complementarity of Chinese anti-imperialist nationalism and Soviet socialist internationalism at the time. The Sino-Soviet Mutual Assistance and Friendship Treaty served China's security interest through the Soviet commitment to military assistance.

Mao followed both communist internationalism and Chinese nationalism when they could be reconciled. When they collided, Chinese nationalism most often won over communist internationalism. China's policy decision to leave Hong Kong for British rule is one example. Allowing China's arch-imperialist foe in modern history, Britain, to continue the rule of Hong Kong after 1949, communist leaders took a significant exception to its ideological lines to ameliorate the pain inflicted by the US containment. Hong Kong functioned to circumvent the US blockade and became the largest contributor of foreign exchange; the only entrepôt for sanctioned Western technology, equipment, and medicines; and a business operation base for Chinese enterprises.[4] Mao's decision to enter the Korean War in 1950 is another example. The Chinese feelings of "proletarian solidarity" and the strong ties forged with the Korean communist comrades were not enough to dispose the Chinese troops toward intervention. The Chinese leaders were convinced of the necessity of intervention only after Mao made support of the war a patriotic crusade to defend the motherland.[5]

Mao exercised maximum pragmatism and forged a nation-state that included a broad range of "the working class, the peasantry, the urban petty bourgeoisie, and the national bourgeoisie" to define the communist state in a united-front style to line up the broadest possible national support for the regime in the early years of the PRC.[6] The CCP regime achieved an impressive rate of economic growth and noticeable progress in raising the living standard of the Chinese people and restored national unity and state power to a degree unknown since the collapse of the Qing dynasty. The rise of China's international status satisfied nationalist aspirations.

The pragmatic nationalism, however, became shrouded by an overlay of Mao's Utopian communism after the Sino-Soviet split in the late 1950s. Rejecting the Soviet version of communist internationalism, Mao developed his radical version of socialism in the decade of polemics with the Soviet Union for the leadership of the world revolution, exported the Chinese model of socialism to third world countries, and competed for the influence in North Korea, Vietnam, and revolutionary movements elsewhere. The radical socialism led to China's isolation and insecurity, and it scared and drove many of its Asian neighbors away from Beijing. The worst debacle was the bloody Indonesian coup of 1965 after Beijing tried to foster the local communist party. Thousands of ethnic Chinese and suspected communists were slaughtered. Soon after, the ASEAN was formed with Indonesia at its core to resist Chinese influence.[7]

Mao's ideological fanaticism and extremism led not only to international isolation but also domestic purge, persecution, antirationality, and social chaos. After Mao's death, Deng Xiaoping began to reassess Maoism and eradicate ideological obstacles for market-oriented economic reform. Unexpectedly, the campaign resulted in the widespread demise of communist ideology. Deng replaced it with expedient slogans, such as "to get rich is glorious." People were urged to develop themselves as entrepreneurs. In this case, when reform brought about such hardships as high inflation, corruption, and unemployment, and the regime could not find ways to compensate people for their losses, the state was left without an effective vision to inspire people to bear the hardship for the sake of a better future. This situation not only weakened mass support for the regime but also turned some Chinese intellectuals to Western liberal ideas, producing the massive antigovernment Tiananmen demonstrations in spring 1989.[8]

State-led Nationalism

How to rebuild the regime's legitimacy became the most serious challenge to the post-Tiananmen leadership. Nationalism was rediscovered. Deng's successor, Jiang Zemin, began to wrap the communist regime in the banner of nationalism, the most reliable claim to the Chinese people's loyalty and the only value shared by the regime and its critics. A historical sense of injustice at the hands of foreign powers is deeply rooted in the national psyche, and the dream of a strong China is shared among all walks of Chinese people. Moving quickly to position the regime as the defender of China's national pride and interests, the regime's nationalist credential was bolstered in the fight against sanctions and for China's entry into the WTO, stopping Taiwan's independence, and winning the opportunity to host the 2008 Olympic Games in Beijing.

The nationalism championed by the CCP portrays the state as the embodiment of the nation's will and identifies the Chinese nation closely with the communist state. The nationalist sentiment is expressed as *aiguo*, meaning loving the state, or *aiguozhuyi* (patriotism), which is love and support of China indistinguishable from the communist state. Seeking the loyalty and support of the people that are granted to the nation, the state speaks in the name of the nation and demands citizens to subordinate their interests to those of the state as the embodiment of the nation's will. This conceptual manipulation is coupled with political control of nationalist sentiments and expressions, thus making nationalism subordinate to party-state interests.

Making maximum use of nationalism, Jiang launched a patriotism education campaign in the 1990s to ensure loyalty in a population that was otherwise subject to many domestic discontents and external influences. The core of the campaign was the affirmative *guoqing jiaoyu* (education in national conditions), which held that China's national conditions were unique and not ready for adopting Western-style democracy. Following Deng's instruction to Jiang soon after he was picked as his successor, that "stability is above everything. The people's democratic dictatorship, therefore, cannot be given up,"[9] the campaign stressed that the one-party rule helped maintain political stability, a precondition for rapid economic development.

The campaign was affirmative also in the recasting of China's modern history as striving and prospering with increasingly high levels of international prestige under the leadership of the CCP. This nation still faced many constraints due to modern historical turmoil and foreign imperialist exploitation. The leadership of the CCP was indispensable because the success of economic development depended on political stability, which could be maintained only by the authoritarian rule of the CCP.[10] In this way, the campaign not only affirmed the CCP leadership but also effectively rejected the demands for democratic reform on grounds that democracy would bring turmoil and political instability and thereby delay economic development.

The nationalist appeal was particularly effective when Chinese people felt threatened by external forces. It was revealing to see that although corruption and some other social and economic problems undermined the legitimacy of the communist regime, many Chinese people sided with the government against sanctions by Western countries that were said to be hostile to China. No matter how corrupt the government was, foreigners had no right to make unwarranted remarks. Many people were upset by US pressure on issues of human rights, intellectual property rights, trade deficits, weapons proliferation, and Taiwan because they believed that the United States used these issues to demonize China and prevent it from rising as a peer power. Redefining the regime's legitimacy on the basis of providing political stability and economic prosperity, the communist state, which would otherwise be hardly acceptable to the Chinese people after the collapse of communism in other parts of the world, was justified by the unique national condition. Because of a volatile mix of rising pride and lingering insecurity during the profound transformation, nationalism represented an aggregation of various political forces to hold China together.[11]

Patriotic education refocused Chinese foreign policy on national interests, a concept that the Chinese government rarely used for a long time.[12] Entrenching in PRC's political discourse during Deng's years, the concept of national interest replaced internationalism in China's foreign policy discourse in the 1990s. Yan Xuetong, a Berkeley-trained Chinese scholar, published the first Chinese language book in 1996 that systematically explored China's

national interests. Yan argued that national interest rather than class interest or internationalism was the sole guide of international relations. China
should always take national interest as its priority. This scholarly book gained
unusual popularity because it was a very fresh idea to the Chinese audience
that China must prioritize its national interest rather than follow communist
internationalism.[13]

Pursuing national interests as the cornerstone, Chinese foreign policy discourse undertook a steady transformation. In response to the rising nationalist
sentiment longing for power and prosperity, Jiang Zemin and Hu Jintao fostered nationalism as a source of regime legitimacy, a means of communication
within the regime and between the regime and the people. Communist ideology was transformed from functioning as a guide for policy action into a set
of abstract principles and rhetorical norms. The revolutionary, transformative
rhetoric of communist ideology was shelved in favor of a language of pursuing China's national interests. A new term, "core national interests"—those
that are essentially nonnegotiable and not to be compromised—suddenly
became popular in China after 2008. State Councilor Dai Bingguo specifically
stated that China's number one core interest was to maintain its fundamental
political system and state security; next was state sovereignty and territorial
integrity; and third was the continued stable development of the economy and
society.[14] The survival of the CCP regime became the core national interest
because Chinese leaders had a deeply rooted sense of political insecurity over
the fear that its one-party system would never be accepted by the West and the
problems of political legitimacy in an increasingly pluralistic society. Foreign
anti-China forces joining hands with domestic adversaries would threaten the
survival of the CCP regime.[15]

Popular Nationalism

Nationalism is not an endogenous construct by the state. Popular sentiments
were part of the nationalist orchestra. Popular nationalism defines the nation
as composed of citizens who must support the state in safeguarding national
rights but also the rights of political participation in foreign-policy-making.
Including liberal ideas against the authoritarian state, popular nationalists are
more vocal than the state in resisting the bullies of foreign powers. Holding
the state accountable to fulfill its promise of safeguarding China's national

interests, popular nationalists have often charged the state as too soft to the provocations of the United States and Japan and called for the government to stand firm in completing the historical mission of national reunification.

The rise of popular nationalism was expressed powerfully in the instant bestsellers of "say no" books in the mid-1990s, such as *China Can Say No*, *China Still Can Say No*, and *How China Can Say No*. Because most popular nationalists were young, they were known as "angry youths" (愤青). Connected mostly by the internet, the angry youth movement gained momentum. With a quick and automatic conviction that the US bombing of the Chinese embassy in Belgrade that killed three Chinese journalists was deliberate, they led the demonstrations that damaged the US embassy buildings in Beijing in 1999. They also led the anti-American protest after the midair collision between a Chinese fighter jet and the US surveillance airplane along China's coast in 2001. Mobilizing the twenty million people internet signatures to oppose Japan's bid to join the UNSC, they organized massive anti-Japanese demonstrations in Beijing and other major cities in 2005 to protest Japan's approval of history textbooks that they said whitewashed Japanese wartime atrocities and Prime Minister Junichiro Koizumi's visits to the war tainted Yasukuni Shrine.

Popular nationalist sentiments were invoked particularly strongly when the Chinese government was preparing for the showcase of the Beijing Olympics Games. Caught by the surprise of the Tibetan riot in March 2008 ahead of the Olympics, Beijing dispatched a large number of troops to suppress the protests, which led to wide Western media condemnation. The demonstrations of international human rights groups and Tibetan exile communities plagued the Olympic torch relay in London, Paris, and San Francisco. Global protests became a public relations disaster for Beijing. This event was followed by the embarrassing announcement of Hollywood director Steven Spielberg that he was quitting as an artistic consultant to the Olympic Games to protest Beijing's failure to use its influence to help resolve ethnic and political conflict in Sudan that left 200,000 dead and drove another 2.5 million from their homes. Nine Nobel Peace Prize laureates signed a letter to the Chinese president, urging China to uphold Olympic ideals by pressing Sudan to stop atrocities. The international scrutiny of China's Sudan policy was related to the criticism of China's relations with many of its third world friends for undermining the international efforts to promote transparency and human rights.

China invested heavily to stage the Olympics and built the world's largest airport terminal to welcome foreign visitors. Thousands of newly planted trees and dozens of colorful "One World, One Dream" billboards lined the main roads of a spruced-up capital. Chinese people looked forward to the Olympics as a demonstration of their newfound modernity and as a chance to reinforce their engagement with the wider world. When Western media portrayed China in their Olympic reports as a showcase for violent repression, censorship, and political persecution, the Chinese people became frustrated at what they believed was the apparent failure of foreigners to understand them, and feared being robbed of the hoped-for harmonious tone of the Games.

Nationalist heat was generated in cyberspace and spilled over into city streets. Huge crowds gathered outside some of the more than one hundred stores of the French supermarket chain Carrefour to protest the rough treatment of a handicapped young Chinese athlete who grimly clung to the Olympic torch on her wheelchair as a pro-Tibetan protester tried to snatch it from her in Paris. The French company was singled out because Chinese media televised the scene and an internet rumor accused it of supporting the Dalai Lama to undermine Chinese rule in Tibet.

Popular nationalists were frustrated that the throbbing media soundtrack about a rising China brought about not only the celebration of China's achievements but also the intensified international scrutiny of many of China's awkward domestic and external challenges.[16] With the anxiety of unsatisfied nationalist aspirations, they were angry over the criticism by the Western powers as an uncomfortable reminder of the historical humiliation when China was weak. At the root of their complaints was a sense of wounded national pride China had suffered before but was not prepared to suffer again.

The boiling popular nationalist rhetoric called for participation in foreign-policy-making, an arena long monopolized by the state. Longing for a powerful China, popular nationalists routinely charged the state as not competent in dealing with foreign powers. Wang Xiaodong, a leading popular nationalist, was angry at the failure of the state-controlled media to report the $2.87 million settlement Beijing paid for the damage inflicted on US diplomatic properties by anti-American demonstrators in 1999.[17]

A Double-Edged Sword

Although the outpouring of popular nationalism was a propaganda bonanza for the state, Chinese leaders had to be cautious because its emotional nature was often linked with "Confucian fundamentalist nationalism" featured by antiforeignism, hypersensitive to perceived foreign insults and militant in its reaction to them. This emotional nationalism held other nations either inferior or threatening and attempted to deal with them harshly.[18] Nativist-tainted popular nationalism was thus irrational and emotional xenophobia and posed a daunting challenge to the developmental diplomacy that prescribed extensive interactions with foreign countries to secure a wide range of inputs essential to economic development.

Guided by Deng's saying that "it doesn't matter if it is a black or white cat as long as it can catch rats," Jiang and Hu made an all-out effort to gain access to the world's most advanced science and technology while rejecting anything they deemed threatening to communist party rule. In response to perceived foreign pressure that was said to erode, corrode, or endanger the national interest of China, they were flexible in tactics, subtle in strategy, and avoided appearing confrontational, but they were uncompromising with foreign demands that involved vital interest or triggered historical sensitivities. Emphasizing the principles of peaceful coexistence, peaceful rise, and peaceful development, they wanted to make sure that popular nationalism would not jeopardize the overarching objectives of political stability and economic development.

It was, therefore, not difficult for them to realize that nationalism was a double-edged sword: both a means to legitimate the CCP rule and a means for the Chinese people to judge the performance of the state. If Chinese leaders could not deliver on their nationalist promises, they would become vulnerable to nationalistic criticism, which the state had not yet learned to control in the cyber age, with the result that the regime had to play catch-up with nationalist emotions. It was not unlikely that the Chinese people would repudiate the government for nationalist reasons after a conspicuous policy failure. The cost of overplaying nationalism could be disproportionately high.[19] Without constraints, nationalism could become a dangerous Pandora's box and release tremendous forces with unexpected consequences.

Balancing the positive and the negative aspects, the state adopted a two-pronged strategy. Tolerating and even encouraging the expression of popular sentiments to defend China's vital national interest, their nationalist rhetoric was often followed by prudential policy actions. Describing nationalism as a force that must be "guided" in its expression and genuinely fettering popular nationalism, the government took repeated actions to restrain the antiforeign expressions of popular nationalism and even ban the antiforeign demonstrations.

Chinese leaders learned lessons the hard way from handling the US bombing of the Chinese embassy in 1999. With an emotional burst of popular nationalism, university students gathered at the front of the US embassy and consulates, throwing eggs and stones. The Chinese government tolerated and encouraged demonstrations until they spiraled out of control. In a televised speech, Vice President Hu Jintao praised students' patriotism but warned against extreme and destabilizing behavior. The *People's Daily* reported that various Western countries issued advisories against traveling to China, hurting tourism and foreign investment. Meeting with foreign visitors, Jiang Zemin stated that life in China should now return to normal for economic necessity. A tight police cordon was put up around the embassy. Students were bused back to their campuses.[20]

The crisis was a wake-up call for the danger of falling victim to uncontrolled popular nationalism. When a US Navy EP-3 plane landed in China's Hainan Island after the midair collision between the plane and a Chinese jet fighter in the South China Sea took place in 2001, Jiang was determined to avoid a repeat of the anti-American demonstrations one year earlier. Uncompromising on its demands that the spy plane crew would only be released after a formal apology by the US government, Beijing accepted Secretary of State Powell's "very sorry" as a close equivalent to full apology and released the crew after 10 days of detention. It was a testimony to Chinese pragmatism that the official media translated "very sorry" as *baoqian* (抱歉), which is one Chinese word different from but has almost identical meaning as *daoqian* (道歉), the Chinese expression of "apology." Chinese leaders interpreted the expression of "regrets" and "sorry" only for the loss of the pilot and aircraft as applicable to the whole incident of the collision. Without altering their tough rhetoric for a domestic audience, they did everything they could to avoid confrontation with the United States.[21]

Hu Jintao used similar tactics in response to the anti-Japanese demonstrations in April 2005. Initially tolerating the demonstrations, the government was alarmed when it discovered an internet call for larger-scale demonstrations on the anniversary of the May Fourth Movement, which was an anti-imperialist movement triggered by anger over the Versailles Treaty that gave Japan control over parts of China's Shandong Province in 1919 and a symbol of resistance to foreign aggression.[22] Walking on a tightrope, Beijing ordered a stop by blocking anti-Japanese text messages and online postings calling for more protests, and sending a blizzard of text messages to mobile phone users in major cities, warning against joining illegal demonstrations. Several organizers of the online petition and popular protests were detained. Police in major cities throughout the nation went on full alert. Tiananmen Square was closed to the public for a government-organized coming-of-age ceremony for eighteen-year-olds on May 4 to thwart any protests. Shanghai authorities closed the area around the Japanese consulate to traffic.[23]

Talking tough but acting in a calculated manner, Chinese leaders prevented the rise of popular nationalism from damaging China's relations with the United States and Japan. They could do so because of their power in determining information available to the public. The CCP Propaganda Department held almost absolute authority over what the public could read and see through its control of the media. On current foreign affairs concerning China, the Ministry of Foreign Affairs and the Xinhua News Agency jointly decided the content and tone of news reports to make sure they were in line with China's official positions. On important foreign policy issues, domestic media outlets were required to use the official stories and lines from the state-run Xinhua News Agency.[24] The party-state, therefore, monopolized the discourses of nationalism and its expression to decide its direction, content, and intensity. It appealed to nationalism whenever it so wished and dismissed it whenever it needed. Holding the "safety valve," the state assured the effects of popular nationalism on foreign policy were under control.[25]

The Strident Turn

Chinese nationalism made a strident turn after the global financial crisis in 2008.[26] With the West in financial turmoil and China maintaining economic growth, popular nationalists urged Chinese leaders to take the opportunity and resume China's place as a big power, leading to the rise of Geopolitik nationalism. Its key elements included the strategic control of territory and space and the call for strong leaders to build a strong military and use force against separatists and enemies.[27] This sentiment was expressed powerfully in a 2009 popular nationalist book, *China Is Not Happy*. Claiming that the crisis could result in an envious West doing whatever it could to keep China down, the authors tapped into a widespread public feeling of disgruntlement with the West and urged China to assert itself and grasp its great power place.[28] The book sold half a million copies in a few months after its release and immediately shot to the top of the bestsellers list.

Facing rumblings of discontent from those who saw the global downturn as a chance for China to assert itself stridently, the Hu leadership became reluctant to constrain the expression of popular nationalism. Even active-duty military officers could openly urge the government to take tough positions on foreign policy issues. A group of bellicose military officers became media stars and online performers, catering to a vast domestic audience eager for news about China's growing military power and instilling a sense of national pride that China had become strong and a force to be reckoned with by other powers.

Colonel Dai Xu's popular book and provocative speeches claimed that China was encircled by hostile or wary countries beholden to the United States and could not escape the calamity of war. Because the United States put a fire in China's backyard, he called for the Chinese leaders to light a fire in the US backyard.[29] Senior Colonel Liu Mingfu's book *The China Dream* stood out for its boldness in the chorus of nationalist expressions. Reflecting on China's swelling ambitions, the book called for China to abandon modest foreign policy and build the world's strongest military to deter the wary United States from challenging China's rise while the West was still mired in an economic slowdown.[30] Hawkish voices and nationalistic commentators found an easy target during the standoff between Chinese surveillance ships and a Philippine warship near Scarborough Shoal, as it's known to the Philippines (and as Huangyan islands to the Chinese), in 2012. The beat of the war drums was unusually strong as the Chinese believed that the Philippines was weak and could not punch back. Major General Luo Yuan urged China to take "decisive actions," including "war at all costs," to reinforce Beijing's claim on the Scarborough Shoal.[31] The *Global Times* warned the countries disputing China's maritime claims to be prepared for "the sounds of cannons" if they did not change their ways of working with China.[32]

The relatively unconstrained expression of popular nationalism partially reflected the weakness of the second-term Hu administration, white-knuckling the way through the final years before handing over to Xi Jinping. As the succession process geared up, hard-line nationalist policies were popular because they could become springboards to power for ambitious and unscrupulous leaders during a caustic period. Increasingly sensitive to popular views on hot-button issues involving state sovereignty, Hu understood that mishandling these sensitive issues could lead to social instability and undermine state legitimacy, leading to the tough position on the issues that defined China's core national interests.

Additionally, the Hu leadership was not sure if the global financial crisis would batter China's economy and produce social unrest. Rapid growth in the previous decades had raised expectations by the Chinese people for the performance of the government. Facing serious challenges from growing public discontent on economic and social inequality, corruption, pollution, emaciated health care, and shredded social services, they had to deal routinely with tens of thousands of civil protests from those robbed of their land for development, from laid-off workers, and from those suffering from the side-effects of environmental despoilment.[33] As the financial meltdown swept across the globe, they did not know what would happen to the millions of migrant workers who lost their jobs and the many white-collar workers who were laid off or had their wages cut. With the uncertain future, the leadership demonstrated their nationalist competence to divert attention from domestic problems.

Moreover, due to the commercialization of a large portion of Chinese media in the Hu years, papers found nationalist expression one of the powerful approaches to attract readers' attention and raise profile and revenues. As popular nationalism was expressed vocally in commercially driven press and internet, Chinese leaders found themselves with less room to operate on sensitive issues, creating a dangerously stunted version of a "free press," in which a Chinese commentator could more safely criticize government policy from a hawkish, nationalist direction than from a moderate, internationalist one.[34]

Patriotic Struggle in the New Era

Although China's rise in an interdependent world requires it to be more open, inclusive, and tolerant, and thus gradually edging away from emotional popular nationalism, Xi Jinping has exploited nationalism not only for the regime legitimacy but also for big power diplomacy. The CCP regime has maintained legitimacy primarily based on two pillars since the end of the Cold War: economic performance and nationalism. While the rapid growth of the Chinese economy sustained the regime's performance legitimacy for decades, nationalist legitimacy has become more important than ever as economic growth has slowed down.

Highlighting China's rising national strength as a backbone and promising that the Chinese people would return to the historical apogee of power, Xi Jinping has intensified patriotic education campaigns. Never hesitating to tell the Chinese people how they should think, Xi's campaign has inoculated the youth and engineered their souls through penetration into the curriculum of the education systems. A directive from the Ministry of Education in 2016 ordered across-the-board patriotic education to suffuse each stage and aspect of schooling through textbooks, student assessments, museum visits, and the internet. Patriotism was required to merge into university, secondary, and primary school exams and courses. Proselytizing beyond China's borders, the document demanded Chinese students abroad be immersed in classes and textbooks that promoted loyalty to the communist party.[35]

Speaking to mark the one-hundredth anniversary of the May Fourth Movement in 2019, Xi called for the youth to carry on patriotism and revolutionary fervor: "Think about where your happiness comes from and understand how to repay it with a grateful heart," and to "thank the party, thank the country and thank society and the people."[36] The Outline on Patriotic Education in the New Era adopted by Politburo in September 2019 even insisted on starting patriotic education from babies, "focusing on consolidating the roots and concentrating on the soul."[37]

Making a clear transition from affirmative to assertive nationalism, the campaign has adamantly targeted Western liberal values. A joint directive from the CCP Central Organization and Propaganda Departments called for "carrying forward the spirit of patriotic struggle," a new term used by Xi to require the Chinese people to fight against any "unpatriotic" ideas and behaviors.[38] While Jiang emphasized "public opinion guidance" (舆论导向) and Hu talked about "public opinion channeling" (舆论引导), Xi has called for "public opinion struggle" (舆论斗争), making the stakes much higher.[39] The terms "guidance" and "channeling" in Chinese were primarily invocational to urge Chinese people to follow the party line, but the word "struggle" was more assertive in calling Chinese people to proactively fight external forces.

The "patriotic struggle" has targeted primarily liberal intellectuals in the education sector. Curricula and speech at universities have always been tightly controlled, but students and faculty have pushed the limits from time to time. While these pushes at times opened up space for freer expression during the Jiang and Hu years, Xi has gone into overdrive to impose a uniformity of thought among university teachers and students. The CCP Central Committee issued the infamous "Document no. 9" in April 2013, ordering officials to combat the spread of subversive currents that could undermine the party's rule and instructing "Seven Don't Speaks," including Western constitutional democracy, universal values of human rights, Western-inspired notions of media independence and civil society, ardently pro-market neoliberalism, and nihilist criticisms of the party's traumatic past. Xi's speech at the national propaganda work conference on August 9, 2013, warned that because the disintegration of a regime often started from the ideological sphere, the party had to uphold leadership, management, and discursive power in ideological work to avoid "irreparable historical mistakes (颠覆性历史错误)."[40]

The patriotic struggle gained momentum with the publication of an article in November 2014 in *Liaoning Daily*. Accusing university teachers across China of being too "negative" about the country and universities of being troubled by ideological laxity, the article found that many teachers were overly critical of Chinese society and the party but overcomplimentary of Western liberal ideas. The phenomenon of "being scornful of China" existed to a definite degree, and in some cases was quite excessive.[41] The article was a dangerous encroachment on academic freedoms that were already under serious threat. But the attack was reinforced by Xi's response at the National Higher-Education Party-building Conference in December 2014, in which he called for "positive energy" and a "bright attitude" toward the party and state.[42] Xi's speech was relayed through the CCP Central Committee and the State Council "Document No. 30," which demanded strengthened party control and cleansing Western-inspired liberal ideas from universities.[43] Following the guidance, universities cracked down on teaching Western concepts of individual rights, freedom of expression, representative government, and the rule of law. Faculty and students must now take lessons in Xi thought, which is the subject of the popular apps and requires users to sign in with their cell phone number and real name to earn study points by reading articles, writing comments, and taking multiple-choice tests.

While Jiang and Hu tolerated limited expression of liberal ideas, university teachers who dared to deviate from textbooks in Xi's new era were reported by student informants who kept tabs on their professors' ideological views. Professors were punished for making comments critical of the government. Numerous writers, rights lawyers, and activists who served as the conscience of the nation were silenced. Some of them were forcibly exiled or disappeared. In July 2015, the authorities rounded up and interrogated about three hundred rights lawyers, legal assistants, and activists across the country.[44] After openly criticizing Xi for his initial mismanagement of COVID-19, Professor Xu Zhangrun in Tsinghua University was detained for six days on bogus and laughable "soliciting prostitutes" charges. He was then fired from his university.

The Inflated Sense of Empowerment

Pushing a resentful strain of nationalism that targeted the vicious "others" as the backdrop of Xi's big power diplomacy, the campaign has celebrated the victorious "us." Making this point, Xi announced in 2013 the creation of a new national holiday: the Victory Day of the Chinese People's War of Resistance against Japanese Aggression on September 3 to celebrate the Japanese surrender in 1945. The first Victory Day in 2015, coinciding with the seventieth anniversary of Japan's surrender, was featured by a military parade in Tiananmen Square. Reviewing the parade from a "Red Flag" limousine, Xi celebrated a "great triumph" that had "crushed the plot of the Japanese militarists to colonize and enslave China and put an end to China's national humiliation." While the parade ended with a flock of seventy thousand peace doves ascending into the skies, what caught everybody's attention were the DF-21D ballistic missiles built to destroy American aircraft carriers. The muscle-flexing was designed primarily to arouse a domestic audience, inspiring them with ceremonial cannon fire and giving them confidence with rockets pulled along on wheels.[45]

Kicking off the patriotic buildup to the military parade, the government inaugurated the "Great Victory and Historical Contribution" exhibition at the Museum of the Chinese People's War of Resistance Against Japanese

Aggression on July 7, 2014, the seventy-eighth anniversary of the Marco Polo (Luguo) Bridge Incident, in which a skirmish between Japanese and Chinese troops near the granite bridge on the outskirts of Beijing developed into full-scale war. Xi and the other six members of the Politburo Standing Committee attended the ceremony and pledged to "firmly remember history, graciously value peace, never forget the national shame of humiliation, and realize the China dream."[46] In the run-up to the military parade, the CCP propagandists prepared a stream of nationalist movies, concerts, performances, and exhibitions to highlight "the spirit of patriotism, uprightness, and heroism in their creations, artists can help the public to strengthen their values on history, nationalism, and culture, [and] therefore increase their self-confidence and dignity as Chinese."[47]

Chinese leaders have never passed over the history of the Japanese invasion. The two countries completed diplomatic recognition in 1972 and signed the peace treaty in 1978. But the memories of Japanese cruelty still hover over China's collective consciousness. Chinese people have remained resentful for what they perceived as whitewashing of Japan's aggressive history, lack of sincere efforts toward restitution, and failure to atone for its war crimes. The government has made them fresh by constantly replenishing propaganda in schools and media. Highly publicized quarrels with Japan over wartime atrocities as well as contemporary territorial disputes in the East China Sea have only added to Chinese distrust and even hatred of Japan.

For most of PRC history, China's public discussion of the Anti-Japanese War focused on the experience of victimization. As China grows powerfully, the meaning of the war has been expanded. Celebrating the victory, wartime China has emerged more as a victor. Public sites of memory, including museums, movies, and television shows, have emphasized national cohesion and patriotic loyalty that contributed to the victory and greatness of the Chinese people. Even the depiction of the KMT's role in resisting Japanese aggression is changed from mocking degradation to increased honesty about its forces bearing the brunt of the fighting and casualties. The shifting story has nurtured a new narrative that China was the creator and protector of the international order that emerged from the war. China's reconstruction of its collective memory of the war has created a new victorious foundation for Chinese people to shape nationalism.[48]

Enjoying an inflated sense of empowerment supported by China's new quotient of wealth and military capacities, the patriotic education has promoted the idea that the leadership of Xi and the party has earned China's success in taking over Western rivals. A sweeping propaganda blitz to promote China's accomplishments such as eradiating poverty, maintaining peace, and avoiding the unrest that plagued much of the developing world is an important part of the campaign. *Amazing China*, a documentary produced by China's state broadcaster, elevated both China's achievements to leading the world and Xi's role in driving progress. It became the highest-earning documentary ever shown in the country. The documentary ended with a fervidly patriotic song performed by pop singer Sun Nan with lyrics that include: "We are confident! We are going forward! Watching the Chinese sons and daughters walking towards a new universe!" Since then, "Amazing China" has become a popular term in Chinese daily conversation along with other sensational ones that boasted China's achievements, such as "China number one" (世界第一), "China produced globally first" (全球首款), "the US scared" (美国害怕了), "Japan scared stupid" (日本吓傻了), "Europe regretted" (欧洲后悔了).

The success of the documentary came along with similarly jingoistic blockbusters. *Wolf Warrior II*, a story of a Chinese special forces agent saving a war-torn African country from the hands of Western mercenaries, became the country's top-grossing film of all time in 2018. In response to the Western criticism of it as a "nationalist action movie," a Xinhua editorial stated that there was nothing wrong "with having faith in one's country to carry out the quintessential job of protecting its people."[49] *Operation Red Sea*, a film about the Chinese navy rescuing hostages from terrorists in a fictitious Arab nation, was as popular one year earlier. While Chinese nationalistic films of the past tended to tout communist ideals with some revolutionary elements, these films used national pride to rally the Chinese population behind the state.

In a grand parade to celebrate the seventieth anniversary of the PRC in 2019, Xi stood on the Tiananmen Gate and declared in front of jubilant crowds cheering and waving Chinese flags that "no force can shake the status of our great country and no force can stop the Chinese people and nation from marching forward."[50] He then presided over a vibrant and colorful parade displaying the PRC's socioeconomic achievements, advances in science and technology, and state-of-the-art new weapons. One highlight was the first public appearance of the Dongfeng-41 intercontinental ballistic missiles, which can carry ten nuclear warheads with a range of up to 9,300 miles to strike anywhere in the United States. The display sent a dramatic, carefully rehearsed message: China had emerged as a global military power and a formidable rival to the United States. The dazzling parade drummed up nationalism and showcased Xi's power as military commander in chief. Reenergizing the Chinese people with deeper loyalty to the party and the PLA's ambitions to become a world-class military, the anniversary unleashed a wave of excitement and fervent patriotism and mobilized the country emotionally.

The patriotic education has mastered the power of symbols and symbolism in the mass and social media to instill Chinese with patriotic zeal. Blurring the line between love for the country and love for the party, the flags of the communist party and the PLA for the first time appeared in the military parade along with, and were marched ahead of, the national flag in 2019. Chinese people, particularly young people, displayed a strong nationalist spirit in response to the power of national symbols. Many people rushed to add a national flag logo to their profile photos on WeChat. On Douyin, the Chinese version of TikTok, China's biggest entertainment stars and ordinary people alike posted videos of themselves cupping their hands into a heart shape over their chests for loving the party-state.

State-Led Popular Nationalism and Information Control

The themes of Xi's patriotic education have echoed the assertive sentiments of popular nationalists and catalyzed the convergence of state nationalism and popular nationalism into a state-led popular nationalism. Like earlier popular nationalism, state-led popular nationalism is raw and conspicuous in calls for a more muscular foreign policy and public outrage in the wake of perceived foreign threats. While popular nationalism showed a liberal tendency in critical of the authoritarian government, the state-led popular nationalists have been genuinely proud of the performance of the party-state and defended its domestic and external policies.

State-led popular nationalism has been especially successful at getting its message across to the youth. Young people across the world should be the most anti-establishment, open, and alive in their thinking. But it is not so in Xi's China. Chinese youth are more fiercely patriotic and loyal to the party-state than the earlier generations because they have grown up witnessing, and proud of, China's rise in living standards and rapid modernization; they have no memory of anything other than steady growth and increasing opportunity under the party-state.

While the regime had enjoyed performance legitimacy for the decades of high economic growth, the economy has slowed and the largesse to dispense benefits diminished. Xi Jinping has, therefore, invested more in social policies and emphasized absolute poverty eradication. One Harvard University survey published in July 2020 found that Chinese citizens' satisfaction with the government had increased across the board since 2003 and rated the government as more capable and effective than ever before because of the real, measurable changes in individuals' material well-being.[51] One survey in September 2020 revealed that over 90 percent of more than 580 college teenagers used terms such as "lucky and satisfied" to describe how they felt about growing up in China. Many people who had admired the United States were now convinced that they lived in a country that others looked up to in admiration because of the advantages of the Chinese system in advancing the people's welfare.[52]

This performance-based legitimacy is reinforced by patriotic education. The new generation of nationalists started secondary school and college with a heavy dose of the education that taught a version of history that highlighted all the accomplishments of the CCP in the contest of the century of humiliation while omitting the party-produced disasters, including the Great Leap Forward and the Great Famine, the Cultural Revolution, and the Tiananmen protests. They have been exposed to the propaganda that Western countries are hostile and foreign criticism of the Chinese government is reflexively backed by the anti-China forces. Against the backdrop of China's economic rise and growing influence around the world, the party has promoted the idea that a diminishing West is determined to thwart China's rise.

The regime's overwhelming control of information has enhanced the effects of patriotic education. The CCP and the government have owned the state media and censored all information flows. After the internet emerged as an alternative source of information, the state acted quickly and has made China's internet environment one of the most restrictive in the world. Beijing began to build the Great Firewall of censorship and surveillance aimed at restricting content, identifying and locating individuals, and providing immediate access to personal records in 2000. The firewall initially blocked only a handful of sensitive Chinese-language websites. It was relatively easy to circumvent the blockage to discuss social and political issues and pass on information about the unofficial versions of Chinese politics and history. Netizens still became irritated. In May 2011, a student at Wuhan University threw eggs and shoes at Fang Binxing, the architect of the Great Firewall, when Fang was giving a speech there. Numerous netizens cheered the student's action and called Fang "the enemy of netizens."[53]

But the firewall has been built up tighter in Xi's era. Griping on the media, expanding surveillance efforts to control the thinking of the people, and ratcheting up the pressure for journalists to speak with one voice to support party policies, Xi started unrelenting crackdowns on the internet and blocked channels through which people could gain perspectives different from official narratives. Other than the CCP Propaganda Departments at all levels, various government agencies, including the Ministry of Public Security, the State Council Information Office, and the State Internet Information Office, are all responsible for regulating the internet. They have issued directives to websites to monitor the content of posts, forums, blogs, and microblogs and not to publish "problematic" information. The Ministry of Public Security has set up "cyber security police stations" so that it can "catch criminal behavior online at the earliest possible point."[54]

Additionally, the government has established a huge internet army to advance its narratives and block "unhealthy content." The most renowned internet army is the 50 Cent Party, the internet-literate youths who are paid 50 Chinese cents for each post of negative news and opinion they delete in the web, then counter with positive information. Blocking access to all sensitive websites and filtering keywords typed into search engines, the government has used Artificial Intelligence (AI)-powered censors to scan images and find sensitive words and phrases. The unauthorized use of Virtual Private Networks (VPNs) as proxy servers is illegal and shuttered.

As a result, internet tools that people across the world use to stay connected, including Gmail, Google, YouTube, Facebook, and Twitter, all fell under the censors' blade and are replaced by the heavily monitored Chinese counterparts, such as Baidu, WeChat, Weibo, QQ, and Youku, among others. The Chinese internet police have censored and filtered all news and commentaries, producing the bizarre uniformity of the discourse. As no messages or posts deviating from the official position could be displayed, truth and fiction are often reversed inside the firewall or the LAN (local area network).[55] Full of often sensational nationalist information about the CCP leadership in the defense of China's national interests, the internet has become a powerful instrument of Xi's patriotic education, making the youth more nationalistic to the exclusion of liberal values.

Instead of bringing democracy to China, the internet is no longer a channel for new thinking and greater openness or a place for the users to learn and debate China's historical mistakes and political systems. Chinese netizens cannot go online to expose government corruption and criticize leaders. Ruthlessly censoring alternative versions of history, suppressing any dissenting voice, and closing alternative sources of information, government propaganda becomes more believable and changed the public conversation. Having grown up without access to international platforms such as Twitter and Google, they believe the firewall has protected them from false information and the country from social instability, and that it created the necessary conditions for the rise of China's tech giants. Instead of creating a more open society, the internet has fostered nationalists who have accepted and even preferred a strong and authoritarian state above the frightening possibilities of disorder. Young Chinese, once conduits for new ideas that challenged the authorities, are increasingly part of Beijing's defense operation.[56]

Combative Patriots

As the state has administered a hefty dose of patriotism and depicted a competitive world filled with danger and national security threats from the United States and other Western powers that conspire to besiege China, state-led popular nationalism has instilled a mentality that any criticism of China by foreign countries is instigated by anti-China "black hands." Without the recognition that China's actions may prompt counteractions by others, the peril of real or contrived threats has sparked popular nationalist demands for the government to fight back on any unwarranted foreign criticism and actions. Treating the United States, Japan, India, Southeast Asian countries, and others with full disdain, they have taken a militant position toward the Taiwan pro-independence forces and protesters in Hong Kong. Proud of the accomplishments of the party-state, many people genuinely believe that the disloyalty of Hong Kong people is both incomprehensible and a threat to China's security; and that US blame for the COVID-19 crisis betrayed an ulterior motive, to block China's accession to its rightful place in the world. They believe that they have a sense of duty to guard their country against unwelcome criticism.

The "little pinks" (小粉红) gained momentum and replaced the term of "angry youth" after early January 2016, when Chinese netizens flooded social media platforms after Chou Tzu-yu, a sixteen-year-old Taiwan-born pop singer, waved Taiwan's national flag on a television show. Chinese netizens swarmed Chou's Instagram account, accusing her of supporting Taiwan's independence and forcing Chou to apologize. After Tsai Ing-wen won Taiwan's presidential election on January 2021, Chinese netizens bombarded Tsai's Facebook page as well as the Facebook pages of Taiwan- and Hong Kong–based media organizations viewed as pro-independence. The large-scale and unprecedented nature of nationalistic expression in the cross-strait memes war shocked outside observers. These young digital warriors were labeled "Little Pink" with an ideological connotation—the communist party is red, and the young "crusaders" are in lighter red, or pink, which makes them the agents of the party. Unlike the "angry youth" throwing rocks at the US embassy and overturning Japanese cars, or the paid shills of the 50 Cent Army whose lack of basic internet savvy can be truly baffling, the little pinks were well versed in the ways of digital dialectic and used the internet as a battleground while brushing off attacks with sangfroid and snark.[57]

Demonstrating the pride in China's accomplishments in contrast to the failure of the United States, one Beijing artist in his early twenties depicted China as a high-tech superpower and the United States as a humbled country that embraced communism in one digital illustration of the future world. Manhattan, draped with the hammer-and-sickle flags of the "People's Union of America," has become a quaint tourist precinct. A caption says, "To take in the changes of history and feel the afterglow of the imperialist era head to North America." The cartoon caught fire on Chinese social media because this triumphant vision resonated among Chinese who believed that China's system proved itself superior, and the Western powers were in irreversible decline.[58]

One survey in 2017 revealed a majority of Chinese urban residents were supportive of the government using force to take back the disputed Diaoyu islands from Japan even though such an action risked a potential war with the United States.[59] A survey in 2018 confirmed the hawkish attitudes that endorsed greater reliance on military strength, supporting greater spending on national defense, and approving of sending troops to reclaim disputed islands in the East and the South China Seas. Respondents who grew up under patriotic education were more hawkish than their elders. The post-1980s generation was more hawkish than those born in the 1970s, which were, in turn, more hawkish than those born before the 1970s.[60]

Showing that the firewall has created an information bubble, a survey research in 2020 found that a majority of respondents thought most Hong Kong residents had positive views on the Beijing government despite Hong Kong's massive protest. Being immersed in China's information bubble about the country's power and popularity made the public overly sanguine and even complacent about the country's global standing.[61] Most Chinese people knew little about what happened in Hong Kong, and to the extent they did know, most accepted the official story that Hong Kong people were unpatriotic, ungrateful for Chinese support, and dupes of foreign meddling and incitement. State-led popular nationalists have, therefore, supported Xi's policy shift to pull Hong Kong fully into China's internal security system, including bypassing the Hong Kong legislative process to introduce the National Security Law, requiring the Legislative Council members to demonstrate allegiance to Beijing. Hong Kong's pro-Western orientation, its people's desire for greater autonomy, and its extensive connections with the West set the perfect scene for Xi to flex the nationalist muscle to control Hong Kong over utilitarian calculations of the territory's financial contribution. Although the policy changes sparked massive protests in Hong Kong, popular nationalists blamed the protesters, believing they were instigated by anti-China foreign forces.

Angry demonstrators in Hong Kong showing their dislike of the Chinese government left Chinese nationalists defensive and outrageous. Supporting the government's full-blown smear campaign to frame the protests as a secessionist conspiracy, China's celebrity-obsessed young nationalists patrolled cyberspace, ready to pounce on perceived slights and defend their motherland. Nicknamed "fangirls" because they exhibit the same fervor most often reserved for pop-culture icons, they called out Houston Rockets general manager Daryl Morey for supporting Hong Kong protesters, prompting state broadcasters to drop NBA games. The onslaught of vitriol they directed at Hong Kong pop star Joey Yung forced her to apologize for a single Facebook selfie of herself on a plane wearing a surgical mask, which Chinese netizens interpreted as supporting the anti-Beijing protesters who commented that "Wearing a mask to fly with you too." But she was still banned from a high-profile gala. While many Westerners saw Chinese people as forced into supporting Beijing or muzzled from expressing their true feelings, these combative patriots suggested earnest and resilient backing for their government against what they perceive as mistreatment and misrepresentation by outsiders.[62]

Chinese nationals abroad are particularly ardent in the defense of the government. A group of Chinese students in their Ferraris, McLarens, Porsches, and Aston Martins adorned with Chinese national flags ran their dragsters alongside a pro–Hong Kong rally in Toronto, calling the Hong Kong protesters "poor garbage." A shouting match erupted at a rally at the University of South Australia in Adelaide. In response to chants of "Hong Kong, Stay Strong," Chinese students countered in unison, "Cao ni ma bi"—an obscene Chinese insult that's made its way into the Urban Dictionary. The Chinese students involved in these incidents pushed their nationalist narrative and were widely celebrated on China's highly censored Weibo platform.[63] With the emboldened nationalist fever, Beijing has successfully imposed direct rule over Hong Kong against the "scheme" to turn the city into a fulcrum for the United States to contain China.

State-led popular nationalism surged amid COVID-19 as the CCP pushed the narrative that China stamped out the coronavirus with a resolve beyond the reach of flailing Western democracies. China's economy revived quickly, defying fears of a deep slump from the pandemic. The theme of China as triumphantly vindicated against critics had real public appeal, particularly among the youth. While international public opinion polls showed China's image as unfavorable amid COVID-19, many Chinese people responded to criticism with scornful disdain. State media were filled with how amazing China successfully contained the spread of the pandemics and was praised for assistance to other countries. The effervescent narrative provided a convenient and powerful tool for popular nationalists to join the state and frame criticisms of governmental responses to the crisis as antithetical to the interests of the Chinese nation.

Supporting the government to hit back against Western critics, combative patriots launched a large-scale personal attack on Fang Fang, a Chinese writer, after she published an online diary about the difficulties of life in Wuhan during the early days of quarantine. Attracting a large number of followers, she was accused of betraying her country and empowering Western critics of China. Fang came under heavy fire of the so-called cyber-indignation (网络民愤) after she decided to publish the English and German language versions of the diary. The critics accused Fang of failing to highlight the government's success in containing the outbreak. "Fang's diaries had done more harm than good to China" and "would give Western countries 'justification' for accusing China of mishandling the epidemic."[64] On the microblog Weibo, a user commented that "the West smears us and wants to get together to demand sky-high compensation. Fang passes the sword hilt to them to attack the nation."[65]

Fang was not a political dissident. A former chairwoman of the Hubei Provincial Government-sponsored Writers Association, she criticized only the initial cover-up of the virus by local officials and didn't raise any questions about the response of the central government or the authoritarian system. Her diary was published at a time when many people across China were enraged by the death of Li Wenliang, a doctor who was punished for circulating an early report of the virus and then died of COVID-19. Many in China were already reflecting on the political system's strengths and weaknesses in handling the virus. The nationalistic attack on Fang helped the state divert the public's attention away from an in-depth reflection on the outbreak.

While Western accusations have created an angry China that seethes and bristles at such criticism, state-led popular nationalists have not only fought back at any criticism but also used disinformation to portray Western countries in extremely dark images. Australia has drawn China's ire for urging an investigation into the origin of the pandemic, a touchy subject in Beijing. A Chinese foreign ministry spokesman tweeted a Chinese artist's fabricated image of an Australian soldier poised to slit the throat of an Afghan child. Australia's prime minister, Scott Morrison, demanded an apology from China over the image, which was a reference to an inquiry by the Australian military that found that its troops had unlawfully killed more than three dozen Afghan civilians. The Chinese foreign ministry scoffed at Morrison's demand. Fu Yu, who created the image under the name Wuheqilin, created another one mocking the Australian leader.[66]

Making a reputation with his scathing images of the United States as a blood-soaked, irrational, medieval realm, the artist published an illustration after the G7 foreign ministers meeting in May 2021 that criticized China's policies in Xinjiang, Hong Kong, Tibet, and Taiwan. Comparing the meddling of the G7 in China's internal affairs to the notorious invasion of China by the Eight-Nation Alliance troops in 1900, the illustration, looking like a yellowing old photograph, was painted based on a real group photo of the G7 foreign ministers and the high representative of the European Union for foreign affairs taken in London, but it depicted them wearing old-style military uniforms and black face masks. The artist posted on social media: "The last time when these guys colluded to [suppress] China was in 1900; 120 years have passed, they are still dreaming." A *Global Times* story praised the artist as a patriot and reported that the illustration went viral on Chinese social media.[67]

After Bloomberg published a survey ranking the United States number one in COVID-19 resilience in June 2021, a Chinese think tank report released in

FIGURE 3   The satire illustration that Wuheqilin posted on social media on May 7, 2021.

FIGURE 4　A group photo of G7 delegates, May 5, 2021.

Further notes

Both photos 3 and 4 are from *Global Times*, a Chinese government newspaper.

The photos are from the public domain.

The full citation of the article is

Huang Lanlan, "'Invaders United Kingdom 1900': Chinese Cartoonist Wuheqilin Mocks G7 Meeting with New Illustration," *Global Times*, May 7. 2021, https://www.globaltimes.cn/page/202105/1222868.shtml.

Chinese, English, Spanish, and French blasted the United States as the world's number one failure in pandemic prevention, as well as the number one failure in seven other areas, including economy, politics, and society. The report was hastily put together and contained obvious errors and emotive language.[68]

In this political environment, public opinion was effectively mobilized in the "narrative war" with evil Western countries. Chinese people cannot even publicly praise anything positive about the United States and other Western countries. Zhang Wenhong, one of China's leading epidemiologists, commented in July 2021 that COVID-19 would not go away soon and China should "learn to live with this virus." Although Zhang did not directly criticize Beijing's COVID-zero strategy, he quickly faced an unusually intense social media backlash for being a traitor in wanting to imitate the West. Zhang was accused of being a fan of foreigners for his earlier comments of "drinking less porridge and eating more milk and eggs" because the typical breakfast in China is porridge; the advocacy of drinking milk is not patriotic. He was, therefore, investigated by his alma mater over accusations of plagiarism in his dissertation his critics leveled at him.[69]

Viewing any criticism of China's handling of COVID-19 as an attack on its honor, the state has engaged in propaganda that scorns Western governments for their mishandling of COVID-19 and Westerners for quiescence in the face of widespread perceptions of foreigners as carriers of the virus and as lacking in discipline. Many Chinese, fed by state media, believe that the virus did not originate in China and that Western governments and media have been spreading falsehoods about China. This position has poisoned relations between China and the West.[70]

These developments demonstrated the success of the state in winning over popular nationalists, especially among the internet-savvy youth who had long been most open to different worldviews, illustrating a striking change in Xi's era. Encouraging rather than suppressing the expression of combative nationalism, Xi Jinping has stirred up domestic public opinion and manufactured an ideational environment to strengthen his foreign policy position and leverage against the foreign criticisms of China's human rights violations and territorial claims. As the state has become more willing to play to the popular nationalist gallery and take tougher approaches, such as forcefully pursuing core interests with China's growing economic, diplomatic, and military muscle, China has reacted stridently to all perceived slights to its national pride and interests, giving rise to wolf warrior diplomacy and fueling ever-sharper demands for deference to China's wishes. Defending wolf warrior diplomacy, Le Yucheng, the Chinese vice foreign minister, warned that "China was not spoiling for fights, but other governments should not underestimate its resolve to push back against criticism. Facing this suppression and containment without scruples, we'll never swallow our pride or stoop to compromise."[71]

Speaking at the one-hundredth anniversary of the CCP, Xi warned that foreign forces who try to "bully, coerce and enslave" China will "break their heads on the steel Great Wall built with the blood and flesh of 1.4 billion Chinese people." One observer noticed that Xi's barbed comments elicited the loudest cheers of his entire speech from the packed crowds on Tiananmen Square. He commented that "If such accolades were sincere and representative of what most Chinese citizens feel, Xi's words may augur a very dangerous era indeed."[72] Xi's turning loose of the wolf warriors indicates he is willing to take a hit in international reputation to feed the increasing appetite of China's nationalists at home.

Empowered by China's rapid reemergence, state-led popular nationalism has launched the Chinese colossus into a global competition to achieve an international status commensurate with China's big power status and the Chinese people's conception of their country's rightful place in the world. Involving a strong sense of morality and righteousness against any policy that might be seen as bowing to foreign pressure, or too solicitous of the United States and other foreign powers that are said to have plotted against China's big power ambitions, the state-led popular nationalism has made compromise extremely difficult if not impossible on issues China deems as a core interest.

The Party-State Hierarchy
Paramount Leaders versus Institutions

POLITICAL PARTIES AND LEADERS in electoral democracies come and go and their ability to set foreign policy courses is often constrained by the interests of bureaucracies that are in place before the parties/leaders arrive and remain so when they leave. But in the one-party state system, the CCP holds the ultimate authority over the government and the military. The CCP leaders have held the ultimate authority to structure bureaucratic apparatus for their policy agenda. The CCP Central Committee is the supreme decision-making institution. The State Council is the executive organ for the implementation of party policy. The PLA is the armed wing of the party rather than a state army. The CCP leadership over diplomacy (党管外交) through personnel appointments and resource distribution has been the political and organizational principle since the founding of the PRC. Premier Zhou Enlai famously told the first generation of Chinese diplomats when the Ministry of Foreign Affairs (MFA) was established on November 18, 1949, that "there is no small matter in diplomacy" (外交无小事),[1] meaning that because diplomacy represented the party-state in fighting for national interests, Chinese diplomats were "the PLA with civilian clothes," subjected to discipline and self-discipline and required to function in absolute compliance to the party policy.[2]

Showing the importance of foreign affairs to the CCP leadership, the paramount leaders have often kept a foreign and national security policy portfolio as part of their official responsibilities. Sitting at the apex of the party-state hierarchy, they have the authority to selectively use and construct foreign policy institutions. Holding the position of the CCP general secretary/ chairman, they can call on the meetings of the Politburo and Politburo Standing Committee (PSC), which are the top decision-making institutions on behalf of the CCP Central Committee. The Politburo has also held regular study sessions, which have been publicized widely since 2002, as a platform for the leadership to promote new policies or directions. The topics of these meticulously orchestrated sessions have regularly focused on foreign affairs.

The paramount leaders are often personally or have their protégés in charge of the central party coordination and elaboration institutions, including the CCP Foreign Affairs/National Security Leadership Small Group (LSG)/Commission, and call on the central work conference on foreign affairs. These opaque party organs have worked behind the scenes to build policy consensus on novel and pressing issues in a timely and interdepartmental manner. The foreign policy bureaucracies in the state, party, and military have been structured in the service of the paramount leaders. New players have emerged since the 1980s, but they have been licensed in a corporatist fashion to the policy process.[3]

Each paramount leader has interacted with the bureaucratic institutions in a unique way. Making policy decisions top-down on strategic and security issues, Mao kept foreign policy bureaucracy relatively small and extremely disciplined. Keeping eyes on the broader picture and strategic issues and involved deeply in decisions on these issues, Mao delegated routine decisions and supervision of bureaucracy to his trusted lieutenant, Zhou Enlai. Repeatedly stressing the importance of the diplomatic corps' limited authority, Zhou always asked for instructions from Mao before making decisions.[4] Following Mao's guidance, Zhou helped devise policies regarding basic principles to establish diplomatic ties with other countries according to their attitude toward Taiwan and traveled widely to promote Mao's revolutionary diplomacy. Going to Moscow in February 1950 to assist Mao in negotiating with Stalin, he signed the Sino-Soviet Mutual Assistance and Friendship Treaty. Zhou also arranged the historic meeting between Mao and President Nixon in February 1972.

Deng Xiaoping's open-up to the outside world brought more players into the foreign policy arena. Building broad consensus or, at least, the perception of it among a myriad of players required an enormous amount of elaboration and bargaining to reach a compromise acceptable to all parties concerned. Deng began to decentralize authorities to the bureaucracy to solicit, digest, bargain, and balance a great number of interests and views, leading to the expansion and fragmentation of the policy institutions and extensive bargaining between bureaucratic units over authority, resources, and influence in the emerging fragmented authoritarianist system.[5] Jiang Zemin and Hu Jintao continued the process to seek consensus in the name of collective leadership,

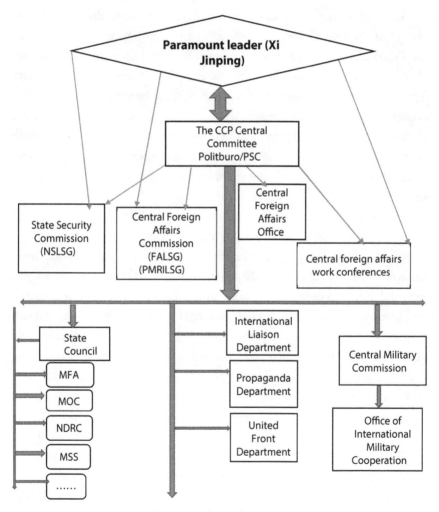

CHART 6-1   Foreign/National Security Policy-Making in Xi Jinping's China

relied on foreign policy professionals, and melded stakeholders into the policy process. As a result, Chinese foreign policy priority kept relatively consistent and predictable.

Becoming the most powerful leader since Mao, Xi Jinping has recentralized policy-making authorities. Regularly summoning the Politburo members, the leading national security and foreign policy bureaucrats, and all of China's serving ambassadors to listen to his instruction, Xi has built new and upgraded existing foreign policy coordination institutions chaired by himself to whip the bureaucracy into shape and provide strong institutional support for his big power diplomacy. Enlarging diplomacy (大外交) beyond the sphere of professional diplomats, Xi Jinping has empowered the state foreign policy bureaucracies, expanded the reach of party diplomacy, and tightened the reins over military diplomacy.

Foreign Policy Coordination in the Party-State Hierarchy

Mao Zedong from the pinnacle of power held the authority over the policy-making apparatus. But bureaucratic institutions often bent their directives on decisions in a manner favorable to their interests. When Mao and his top associates set broad policy guidelines and altered the balance of power among competing bureaucratic interests, the information available to them and the alternatives they confronted had often been shaped by the prior activities of bureaucracies.[6] To enlarge his range of options and enforce his commands in the name of strengthening the party leadership, Mao Zedong decided to establish five Central LSGs along functional lines of finance, political and legal, foreign, science, and cultural and education affairs to assert control over bureaucracy in March 1958. The Central Foreign Affairs Leadership Small Group (FALSG) was among them. Mao wrote in instruction on behalf of the Central Committee that "these groups belong to the Party Central Committee and report directly to the Politburo and Secretariat of the Central Committee . . . The major directions and policies and specific arrangements are unified. There is no separation of party and government."[7]

The FALSG was disbanded in 1970 when the Cultural Revolution withdrew China from the world. It was restored in 1981 when Deng Xiaoping's open-up brought more stakeholders and proliferation and complications of the foreign policy issues. The FALSG was positioned as the central party coordination and elaboration organ (协调议事机构) to provide a forum for the members of the central leadership in charge of foreign affairs to meet regularly with the top bureaucrats within the functional sectors to hash out priorities, reach consensus, and make recommendations to the Politburo.

The FALSG was not a formal institution because it did not appear in the publicly available CCP organization chart. Its activities were not generally reported in media and the lists of its members were not publicized on a current basis. Official media occasionally referred to it in reporting on policy outcomes and a leader's membership in it. Equipped with no regular staff and offices, it existed mostly as ad hoc meetings. Its policy preferences and recommendations had an important impact on decision-making because they were taken to represent a consensus among stakeholders. Once a consensus was reached on the pending issues, "it is submitted to the unwieldy Politburo for *pro forma* approval. This *modus operandi* is further reinforced by the fact that the head of the FALSG is the paramount leader himself and the 'recommendations' were supported by their colleagues in the Politburo without foreign policy responsibilities."[8]

FALSG's membership was semi-institutional, i.e., most members were job slot representatives. Its political clout depended on the position of the leader in the power hierarchy. What it could or could not decide depended on the issue, the confidence and power of its leader, and the circumstances, such as crisis or routine decisions. Without a fixed meeting schedule, it was convened when an important issue arose and the paramount leader wanted to elaborate and coordinate with the stakeholders. Using the FALSG to coordinate policy-making allowed the paramount leaders to control policy formulation and overcome the bureaucratic barriers, thus perpetuating their personal authority.[9]

The FALSG was the only standing foreign policy coordination organ before 2000. After the NATO bombing of the Chinese embassy in Belgrade in 1999, the Central National Security Leadership Small Group (NSLSG) was created in 2000 to coordinate national security crisis responses. The FALSG and NSLSG shared the same general office in the CCP Central Foreign Affairs Office (CFAO) for staff support. When tensions were heating up in the East and South China Seas in 2010–12, Hu Jintao was under pressure to synchronize the disparate maritime law enforcement entities, known as "nine dragons playing with water," to safeguard maritime rights and interests. The Protecting Maritime Rights and Interests LSG (PM-RILSG), was established in 2012. The PMRILSG also relied on the CFAO for staff support.[10]

The CFAO had its origin in the Foreign Affairs Office (FAO) of the State Council created in 1981. Throughout the 1980s, the size of FAO was small and headed by vice-ministerial-level officials. In 1998, Jiang Zemin reorganized the FAO into the CFAO to concentrate foreign affairs power in the party system. The rank of the CFAO director became a full minister. Hu Jintao upgraded the CFAO with the appointment of Dai Bingguo, a state councilor, as the director.[11] As the importance of the CFAO increased, it took more responsibilities. But its staff support to the foreign and security affairs LSGs was not enhanced. The shortage of full-time policy staff constrained the ability of foreign and national security policy LSGs. Ranking highly and represented broadly, they could not function regularly for selecting, summarizing, and judging all types of policy suggestions and worked only on critical and strategic issues. Most of the routine policy issues were left to the autonomy of each line agency. They were more reactive crisis-management mechanisms than daily policy coordination and elaboration institutions based on consistent, effective, and efficient information processing and agency coordination. China's foreign and security policy decision-making authority suffered from the lack of a core team for coordination and consultation.[12]

This situation complicated Chinese foreign policy because the fragmented bureaucracies often manipulated decision-making by recommendations with selective information that supported their positions and presentation of their specific perspectives and missions as China's priority. For example, regarding North Korea, the PLA tended to focus more on traditional security threats, and the CCP's Central Liaison Department (CLD) on party friendship, while MFA hinged more on regional stability and China's international responsibilities. In addition, some of the Chinese domestic actors benefited from cooperation with pariah states, expansive and rigid interpretations of sovereignty claims, and, in some cases, tension with the United States and its allies, while the Ministry of Commerce (MOC) had to respond to the pressure on these issues from the Western countries. The competing viewpoints pulled the decision-making in different directions.

The Top-Level Design

Staking his claim to power on the party in a way that none of his predecessors had, Xi Jinping has stressed the importance of top-level design and reconstituted the LSGs as the true nerve center and the core executive of the party in the strategic policy-making process and set up new LSGs with himself as the head to bypass entrenched interests and cut through bureaucratic roadblocks. Known as the "Chinaman of everything" and relying on LSGs to rule the country (小组治国), Xi has upgraded the status of the coordination institutions, giving Xi substantial control over policy-making on issues he cares about.

Xi's first initiative in building strong institutional capacity to achieve a greater degree of coordination for national security was the creation of the State Security Commission (SSC) in 2013 as a platform to help manage the variety of predictable and unpredictable security risks. The SSC absorbed the NSLSG and functioned much more broadly than LSGs as a decision-making, elaboration, and coordination organization.[13] Domestic and international security issues used to be handled in separate LSGs. The SSC is responsible for issues of both domestic and external security, both traditional and non-traditional security, and both development and security. Claiming that China faced a more complicated internal and external security environment than at any other time in history, Xi at the first SSC meeting in April 2014 proposed a concept of the "holistic national security" (总体安全观) to cope with an array of eleven areas of security threats, including the threats to Chinese culture, cyberspace, ideology, and political security, the coded words for regime security. The holistic national security concept gives the SSC comprehensive authority to consolidate Xi's control over China's vast security apparatus.[14]

Functioning behind the scenes, the SSC has kept low visibility. Xi pronounced at the second SSC meeting in 2018 that "the SSC has solved many problems that had long remained unsolved and achieved tasks that had long remained undone." He mentioned four aspects of accomplishments: the construction of the main architecture of the national security system; the formation of the national security theory system; the improvement of the national security strategy system; and the establishment of a national security coordination mechanism. In particular, the SSC guided the making and implementation of the State Security Law and State Security Strategy Outline.[15]

Unlike the US National Security Council, the SSC has shown a marked orientation toward regime security, including domestic threats with foreign connections. The emphasis is on state security (国家安全), which in the Chinese language shares the same characters as the concept of national security but means protecting the Chinese party-state from domestic and foreign threats, not so much a reference to geography, China, or the Chinese people.[16]

Because of the SSC's internal security focus, the FALSG was upgraded as the Central Foreign Affairs Commission (CFAC) in March 2018. While the precise difference between LSGs and commissions is unclear, commissions are more formalized with more bureaucratic power. Its mandate is also broadened to absorb the responsibilities of the PMRILSG. The upgraded CFAC represents the rising status of foreign affairs in the party-state hierarchy. President Xi is the head, Premier Li Keqiang the deputy head, and Politburo member Yang Jiechi the secretary-general and chief of its General Office. Xi at the inaugural meeting stated that the upgrade was to enhance the centralized and unified leadership of the CCP over foreign affairs, making sure party decisions within its purview are implemented across the bureaucracy.[17]

In addition to SSC and CFAC, Xi has convened high-level foreign affairs work conferences much more often than his predecessors to help bring together the senior bureaucrats and other players germane to the coordination process. These conferences are authoritative gatherings of the entire leadership to build policy consensus on China's national security strategy and foreign policy agenda, synthesize China's official analysis of international trends, and assess how China should anticipate and respond to them in the prosecution of its own national interests. Soon after coming to office, Xi called the Central Work Conference on Peripheral Diplomacy in October 2013, the first high-level conference on China's neighboring relations in PRC history. Outlining the new direction of periphery diplomacy, he said that although China continued to maintain good neighborly relations based on amity, sincerity, mutual benefit, and inclusiveness, China could sacrifice its core interests under no circumstances. Drawing the red line, Xi demanded the periphery policy to safeguard China's core interests, particularly the sovereignty of the disputed territories belonging to China since "ancient times."[18]

Xi held the fourth Central Foreign Affairs Work Conference in November 2014, of which there had previously been only three, in 1971, 1991, and 2006.

While Jiang Zemin and Hu Jintao each held one and on a much smaller scale, Xi held another Central Foreign Affairs Work Conference in June 2018, attended by the entire PSC, plus ex-officio member Vice President Wang Qishan, together with all other Politburo members; the senior officials in the entire Chinese foreign, security, military, economic, trade, finance, cyber, and intelligence communities; and the central think tank community and nearly all Chinese ambassadors. In a visible break from past practice, state media reports on the conference failed to mention previous leaders and their foreign policy concepts but were full of references to foreign policy initiatives and concepts developed under Xi. The emphasis on the party's absolute control over foreign policy was also fresh. Xi emphasized that "diplomatic power must stay with the CCP Central Committee and consciously be consistent with the Central Committee on ideology and on the action."[19]

In addition, Xi Jinping has institutionalized the meetings of Chinese diplomatic envoys to foreign countries. The first meeting of Chinese diplomatic envoys was convened in 1952 and had been held about every five years until the eleventh meeting in 2009. Seven years after, Xi held his first meeting in 2016. But it was not called the twelfth meeting but rather the 2016 annual meeting. Xi met with the participants and spoke in the 2017 and 2019 annual meetings. Communicating his foreign policy vision through top-level meetings is an integrated part of the endeavor to cut across otherwise fragmented bureaucracies.

The Enlarged State Diplomacy

During the early years of the PRC, the MFA was one of the very few agencies that conducted state diplomacy and enjoyed high political status. The first minister of foreign affairs was concurrently held by Premier Zhou Enlai. His successor was Chen Yi, the PLA marshal and vice-premier. Among the first fifteen Chinese ambassadors appointed by Mao in 1951, twelve were PLA generals. Many middle-ranked diplomats were also former military officers. This makeup met the demands of Mao's foreign policy priorities to safeguard China's regime and border security.

Deng Xiaoping expanded China's international interaction and resulted in the proliferation of state agencies that developed international outreach in their respective fields. Chinese diplomacy has been enlarged beyond the sphere of traditional diplomats. In the 1980s, the Foreign Affairs Committee of the National People's Congress (NPC) was established to conduct parliamentary diplomacy; the Ministry of State Security (MSS) was created with the merging of the CCP Central Investigation Department and the counterintelligence elements of the Ministry of Public Security; the Ministry of Education started administering Chinese students/scholars overseas and international education exchanges; and the Ministry of Culture and the Information Office of the State Council expanded the responsibility to promote international cultural exchanges.

Because the management of foreign economic relations required specialized knowledge that most diplomats in the MFA are unfamiliar with, specialized economic agencies gained prominence. The Ministry of Foreign Trade became the Ministry of Foreign Economic Relations and Trade (MFERT) in 1993 and the Ministry of Commerce in 2003. Its function was extended beyond foreign trade and economic assistance to foreign investments, consumer protection, and market competition. The People's Bank of China and the Ministry of Finance began to venture into foreign economic affairs, working with the IMF and the World Bank respectively and managing China's international monetary and financial policy. The State Planning Commission was reorganized to State Development and Planning Commission in 1998 and the National Development and Reform Commission (NDRC) in 2003. Its portfolio was expanded to include coordination and supervision of bilateral and multilateral economic exchanges, including BRI, climate diplomacy, trade, and investment treaty negotiations. The State Oceanic Administration (SOA) rose to prominence after 2013 when China began to assert its claims in the maritime territorial disputes in the South and East China Seas. The agencies associated with law enforcement at sea were integrated within the SOA. It was incorporated into the newly established Ministry of Natural Resources in 2018 and continued to provide the leadership with unique expertise on maritime security.[20]

These agencies have competed for resources and authorities in their support to the policy priorities of the leaders. For example, Made in China 2025 was initially proposed by the Ministry of Information and Industries and the Chinese Academy of Engineering to upgrade manufacturing capability and make China a self-reliant, global champion in ten core strategic innovation sectors. It was adopted in the thirteenth Five-Year Plan and was later formally developed jointly by the NDRC and the Ministry of Science and Technology. Despite initiating the plan, the Ministry of Information and Industries had to share policy responsibilities and budgetary powers with the NDRC and the Ministry of Science and Technology.[21]

As new issues have arisen that fall between the cracks of existing bureaucracy, new state agencies have been established. Xi Jinping's restructuring of the state bureaucracy in 2018 created two important agencies. One was the State Immigration Administration that took over exit and entry, customs, and immigration affairs from the Ministry of Public Security. Another was the International Development Cooperation Administration (IDCA), which centralized the control of China's massive and opaque foreign aid programs as Beijing shifted from foreign aid receipt to one of the world's biggest development assistance providers. The establishment of IDCA represented an attempt to balance commercial benefits of the MOC and strategic interests of the MFA.

As the stage of diplomacy became crowded, the makeups, bureaucratic status, and functions of the MFA have experienced significant change. The sizable transfer of diplomats from the military largely stopped after the 1960s. Diplomats with relatively narrow experiences have gradually dominated the MFA since the 1980s. Although diplomats, like all Chinese officials, must demonstrate their political loyalty to the CCP, they became professionals recruited from elite universities. The senior diplomats worked up from the very bottom during their decades of career in foreign affairs.[22] Specialization and professionalism became the hallmark of the MFA.[23] In comparison with the early generation of diplomats from political and military careers, the elite college-trained diplomats were prudent to follow not only the political lines of the party-state but also their professional training and knowledge.

This development produced a paradoxical transformation of the political status of the MFA: the more specialized and professionalized the Chinese diplomats, the less important their political status. Senior diplomats hardly made it to the top level of the political hierarchy for about two decades before 2017. Post-MFA position of the foreign minister declined from the rank of Politburo member and vice-premier (Chen Yi) to vice-premier only (Qian Qichen) and state councilor (Tang Jiaxuan and Yang Jiechi). In contrast, as the developmental diplomacy empowered MFERT/MOC, two MFERT ministers rose to the ranks of national leadership: Li Lanqing became a member of the standing committee of the Politburo (1997–2002) and vice-premier (1998–2003), and Wu Yi became a vice-premier (2003–2008).

In the enlarged foreign policy arena, the MFA had to compete with other agencies for influence and came under bureaucratic stress by serving too many administrative patrons: serving up to the top leaders; horizontally to the lateral ministries; and down to the exponentially increasing members of the public going overseas. Handling growing expectations with shrinking authority, the MFA, with its long overseas tenure, underpaid staff, adamant emphasis on discipline, and steep climb to top positions, lost its lure. Sidestepped from the top, challenged by lateral ministries, and mocked from below, the morale in the MFA was low.[24]

The political status decline of MFA, however, has been reversed by Xi. Yang Jiechi was promoted to a Politburo member in 2017, the first career diplomat who reached that level and the second ex–foreign minister after Qian Qichen who had ever entered the Politburo after the Cold War. Yang was also appointed as the Chief of the General Office of the CFAC in 2018 with bureaucratic power to help set CFAC meeting agendas and control the flow of documents/information to the paramount leader. He concurrently held the directorship of the CFAO as China's top diplomat. Wang Yi, the sitting foreign minister, was promoted to the position of state councilor in 2018, another first time for decades.

While the elevation of two career diplomats raised eyebrows, the promotion of stellar, seasoned career diplomats aligns with Xi's vision to consolidate foreign-policy-making at the top level of the party. Speaking at the meeting of diplomatic envoys in 2017, Xi required the diplomats be absolutely loyal to the party, the country, and the people, and, in addition, to enhance their professional ability and keep their knowledge up to date. Xi also required the MFA to "forge a politically resolute, professionally exquisite, strictly disciplined foreign affairs corps."[25]

For decades before Xi's reign, China's foreign policy professionals, just like their economic and financial counterparts, saw themselves and were seen by the political establishment primarily as professionals and technocrats. Professional identification has been replaced by political loyalty to the party as the top requirement. Xi has constantly reminded the diplomats that their first loyalty is to the CCP and their first duty is to implement the directives of the Central Committee that Xi himself leads. Dealing with the foreign policy apparatus whose parts were content to move to their tune, Xi has taken dramatic action to tame the machine and create an empowered and disciplined diplomatic corps with one voice.

Xi has also stepped up resources for foreign affairs. While the government's resource allocation for foreign affairs had been conservative in the face of the historically fast GDP growth, foreign affairs resource investment during Xi's first term was maintained at a level substantially above GDP growth. Resources spent on foreign affairs increased almost two-thirds from $5.2 billion at the end of the Hu period in 2012 to $8 billion at the end of Xi's first term in 2017.[26] Additionally, the MFA gained a centralized authority over financial and personnel management at Chinese missions overseas.

These reforms have helped stabilize the personnel in the MFA and, more importantly, enhanced the political loyalty of the diplomats to the party. With the increased political status and the resources, the MFA, which reportedly once received calcium tablets from citizens hoping it would grow some backbone, has recast itself as one of the party's most vocal defenders and become known as the wolf warrior ministry. The rising status of the MFA has come with the rise of a large cohort of wolf warrior ambassadors and senior diplomats who are media-savvy and meticulous, with a clear understanding of what Xi Jinping wants from his diplomats. No longer emphasizing diplomatic protocol, a new generation of Chinese diplomats have competed to demonstrate their fighting spirit with a tough attitude, offensive tone, and confrontational cruelty against foreign rivals.

The Reach of CCP Diplomacy

The CCP has long conducted activities abroad through the CLD, Central Propaganda Department (CPD), and United Front Work Department (UFWD). These party departments have normally been headed by members of the Politburo or its Standing Committee in order to showcase their high status in China's political hierarchy. While these departments functioned most covertly with the limited scope during the eras of Mao and Deng, Xi has expanded their mandate, made them visible, and provided them greater resources to project China's positive image abroad.

The CLD was established in 1951 to manage relations with foreign communist and socialist parties, especially the CPSU, oversee the ties with Maoist parties and organizations, and foment revolution abroad by funneling money and resources to left-wing and rebel groups around the world. Deng Xiaoping gradually suspended its function in the support of overseas Maoist insurgencies and expanded its mission to forge ties with all types of foreign political parties willing to work with China. It was the official agency assigned to handle North Korean issues and network with foreign political parties through hosting conferences, training foreign cadre, and sending official delegations to many parts of the developing world. As most of its activities were not covered in media, the CLD was regarded by the outside world as marginalized.[27]

The media exposure of the CLD has increased significantly since Xi came and emphasized China is a socialist country bound together with other socialist countries by shared values. Stepping up its global outreach, the CLD has been out and proud by keeping regular contacts with more than six hundred political parties and organizations in about 160 countries and dispatching and receiving several hundred delegations annually. Taking a more active role in building and maintaining relations with other socialist countries, CLD minister Song Tao was sent to Cuba, Vietnam, and North Korea to brief their leaders after the CCP Nineteenth Party Congress in 2017.[28]

The CLD distinguishes its diplomacy from that of the MFA as being more long-term-oriented, more flexible, and focused on helping rectify foreigners' "incorrect ideas" on the CCP and China. The CCP diplomacy is to help foreign people accept China's values, support China's development path, understand the Chinese system, and learn from China's experience in governing the country, all of which shows the world how Chinese governance works against Western criticism about China's lack of civil liberties and democratic elections.[29]

Encouraging foreign politicians to recognize the merits of CCP policies and spreading CCP ideas about good governance to receptive elites around the world, the CLD began to send formal "briefing delegations" abroad to explicate CCP policies after the Third Plenum of the Eighteenth Central Committee in November 2013. The delegations were typically headed by a ministerial or vice-ministerial-rank official and composed of policy drafters, academic experts, and officials from CCP central agencies and local committees. It sent such delegations to ten countries after the Fourth Plenum of the Eighteenth Party Central Committee in 2014, to over forty countries each time after the Fifth Plenum in 2015 and the Sixth Plenum in 2016, and to about eighty countries following the Nineteenth Party Congress in 2017. The CLD also held a "briefing" in Nanchang to explain the "spirit" of the Fourth Plenum of the Nineteenth Central Committee in 2019, attended by over two hundred delegates of political parties from almost fifty countries.[30]

With a markedly higher profile to advance a "new type of political party relations," the CLD launched the annual "CCP and the World Dialogue" in 2014 to promote China's experiences in socialist development, known as the China mode, and tell "China's story" to inform, persuade, and inspire foreign political elites.[31] This dialogue received little coverage in the media initially but garnered worldwide attention when it was upgraded into "the CCP in Dialogue with World Political Parties High-level Meeting" in December 2017. Over 600 representatives from nearly 300 political parties and organizations of 120 countries attended the meeting, including Burmese leader and State Councilor Aung San Suu Kyi and President of the Cambodian People's Party and Prime Minister Hun Sen.

It was for the first time that the CCP held a high-level meeting with such a wide range of political parties. Xi Jinping spoke at the meeting and suggested the High-level Dialogue be institutionalized. Although Xi pledge China would not export the Chinese model nor import foreign models, the Dialogue issued "the Beijing Initiative," which praised China's contributions to the world and endorsing Xi's concept of "community of a shared future for mankind and of a better world."[32] As follow-ups, the CLD organized several thematic party dialogues, including the commemoration of the two-hundredth birthday of Karl Marx in May 2018, attended by leaders of seventy-five communist and workers' parties across the globe, the first CCP-hosted communist party conference in China. The CLD also hosted the African Dialogue in July 2018, attended by more than one hundred leaders of over forty political parties from forty-plus African countries.[33]

As a formal follow-up, the CLD held "the CPC and World Political Parties Summit" on July 7, 2021, days after the CCP centennial celebration. More than 500 leaders of political parties/organizations and over 10,000 representatives from 160-plus countries attended the hybrid summit. In a press briefing before the summit, Guo Yezhou, the CLD vice minister, said that the summit aimed to "help the international community adjust more quickly to the rise of China" and for Beijing to gain more "understanding, support and companionship."[34] Xi made the keynote that China's modernization had proven itself as a viable alternative to the Western system of governance. Beijing was willing to share its experiences with other countries.[35] More than twenty heads of state from the developing countries made plenary speeches to congratulate CCP on the one-hundredth anniversary. Some of them thanked China for providing them with assistance and vaccines to fight the pandemic.

The CPD is another important agency for party diplomacy. It oversees ideology-related propaganda to sway domestic and international opinion in favor of the CCP policies. While Mao used the CPD to promote his revolutionary ideology abroad with very limited success, Deng stepped up foreign propaganda activities to focus primarily on encouraging foreign investment and trade. Xi has shifted the priority of the international propaganda to coordinate the enlarged external propaganda (大外宣) in a multimedia environment.[36]

Overseeing virtually every media in the dissemination of information, the CPD has provided staff support to the Central Foreign Propaganda LSG, which sets China's foreign propaganda agenda and oversees external propaganda operations to cultivate foreign politicians and other elites and expand China's international media and cultural presence. It also oversees the State Council Information Office (SCIO, 国务院新闻办公室), which was established in 1991 to improve the Chinese government's international image after the 1989 Tiananmen protests. These party agencies have controlled and used both traditional and social media, censored information flow, and posted news, opinions, pictures, videos, and so forth. The Xinhua News Agency under the CPD was proud of being "the world's largest propaganda agency" with overseas stations to tell Chinese stories and report through their internal channels to the policy-makers.[37]

The UFWD is another party agency with both domestic and foreign operations. The United Front work started from the revolutionary period to rally as many allies as possible to defeat the common enemy. Mao credited the United Front as one of the "Three Magic Weapons" (法宝) alongside the party construction and the armed struggle for the CCP victory.[38] After the founding of the PRC, the UFWD focused primarily on running a network of party and state agencies responsible for influencing celebrity groups outside the CCP in support of the regime. Deng Xiaoping expanded the scope of the UFWD to work on sympathetic foreign celebrities and professional groups with a focus on Chinese diaspora communities to attract foreign investment and trade. Xi Jinping has emphasized United Front work more than his recent predecessors as a "magic weapon" for national rejuvenation.[39] The UFWD has emerged stronger than ever since the 2018 party-state agencies reshuffle, which merged the State Council Overseas Chinese Affairs Office and Religious Office into the UFWD. The UFWD has also taken on responsibility for ethnic minority groups, Taiwan, Hong Kong, and Macao affairs.[40]

Although its overseas operation is often covert or deceptive, the UFWD has become increasingly visible to increase the CCP's influence, suppress dissident movements, and build a permissive international environment for the takeover of Taiwan. The priorities are the new migrants who have gone to study and work abroad since China's opening-up in 1978 and have retained varying degrees of ties with their native land. Appealing to patriotism, the UFWD has tried to win their hearts and minds to support the CCP regime and its policies and increase their antipathy toward the so-called anti-China foreign forces. Making use of community associations and harnessing overseas Chinese to project CCP's influence abroad, it has been successful in fostering positive opinion among overseas Chinese and marginalizing opposition groups within Chinese expatriate communities. Nonethnic Chinese, particularly those with positions of respect in their communities and varying amounts of wealth, are sought out as well.

Because of its success, overseas organizations associated with the UFWD have attracted an unprecedented level of scrutiny by the governments of the United States, Australia, Canada, and some European countries. The UFWD is labeled as the Chinese agency responsible for coordinating foreign influence operations. These governments have taken actions to end China's United Front works in their countries.[41]

The Emerging Military Diplomacy

Military diplomacy emerged in the 1990s when the PLA began participating in UN peacekeeping operations. The term appeared for the first time in the Chinese National Defense White Paper in 1998.[42] Although China's military footprint in the world remains small relative to its economic heft, military diplomacy has expanded steadily to forward China's national defense goals by encompassing a wide range of activities, including a variety of communications and crisis management mechanisms with foreign militaries.

The most institutionalized activities have been a series of security dialogues with China's periphery countries. Beijing has also conducted regular security dialogues with distant states in Africa and the Middle East. The PLA's nascent but growing military role in Africa was highlighted by the commitment in 2015 to provide $100 million military assistance to the African Union, as well as the inauguration of the China-Africa Defense and Security Forum in the summer of 2018, which brought senior military leaders from fifty African states to Beijing.

Joint training and exercises have developed as one of the most important activities of military diplomacy. The most advanced joint exercises have come with Russia. After the first joint exercises in 2005, the troops from both countries have participated in several large-scale exercises every year. The most significant one was China's participation in the largest Russian military exercises since the fall of the Soviet Union, the Vostok 2018, which allowed the PLA troops to gear up alongside a combat-hardened military with considerable battlefield experience. The joint exercise yielded "tangible practical benefits for the PLA beyond political symbolism."[43] A joint China-Russia bomber patrol over disputed territory off the coast of South Korea and Japan in July 2019 pointed to a new level in their military cooperation. Russian and Chinese strategic bombers conducted the second joint patrol and flew over the Sea of Japan and the East China Sea in December 2020.

As an increasing number of Chinese citizens, officials, and enterprises have operated overseas, including in high-risk countries, and China's economy has depended increasingly on resource imports and trade, military diplomacy has served China's expanding overseas interests. Dispatching its first antipiracy detachment to the Gulf of Aden in 2008, the PLA diverted a destroyer from the Gulf to Libya where the Arab Spring led to the civil war and political turmoil, flew aircraft, and evacuated more than thirty-five thousand Chinese nationals over twelve days in February and March 2011, demonstrating Beijing's capabilities to manage and mitigate crises overseas.[44] Military diplomacy has also expanded China's global presence. Establishing a potential network of military bases beyond China's shores, the PLA opened a "logistical support facility" in Djibouti in 2017, adjacent to military outposts operated by the

United States, France, and Japan. It is equipped with maintenance facilities for ships and helicopters, weapons stores, and around two thousand military personnel to protect Chinese interests in Africa and the Middle East, and the Maritime Silk Road.[45]

Military diplomacy is managed top-down by the CMC, which is headed by the paramount leader. Acting as the nexus between the military and civilian decision-making apparatuses, the CMC is responsible to ensure the absolute loyalty of the armed forces to the party. The PLA retains a powerful voice at the highest levels of the foreign and security decision-making process through an institutional arrangement by which top military officers are presented at the Politburo and the central foreign/security policy coordination organs. The military delegates are also an important block at the NPC. But the military has not had a representative in the Politburo Standing Committee since 2002. The PLA is influential in shaping China's defense and security policies, such as relations across the Taiwan Strait and maritime sovereignty disputes. The civilian foreign policy establishment has remained dominant in advancing China's diplomatic and economic agenda since the 1980s.[46]

The civil-military coordination, however, has been complex because the PLA has institutional interests that could conflict with that of the civilian bureaucrats. Military officers also tend to perceive the world differently from civilian bureaucrats because the PLA demographics continue to be predominantly rural and the military claims a higher ideological ground and its indoctrination is more nationalistic. In contrast, the foreign affairs bureaucrats are full of college graduates from elite universities who are cosmopolitan, urban, fluent in foreign languages, and well versed in diplomatic protocols.[47]

The civil-military tension was expressed clearly during the Jiang and Hu eras. While civilian leaders believed the imperative of maintaining economic development posture, military leaders looked for tensions with foreign countries to support more defense spending. In relations with the United States, the civilian leadership was consolatory, emphasizing mutual benefits. The PLA evaluation of the US intentions was foremost influenced by their perceptions of the threat from the United States. China's growing economic ties with the United States prevented the PLA from openly airing its grievances. A consensus of the American threat, however, was openly articulated by the military elite during the second term of the Hu administration. The military officers denounced Washington publicly and linked the US threat closely to China's strategic interests, making it hard for the leadership to present a cohesive policy toward the United States.[48]

Commanding the military affairs without the military background and personalities that would confer absolute authority over the PLA, Jiang and Hu followed a formula of reign without overt rule. The PLA had autonomy in running military administration and operations. Effective channels of consultation existed at the apex of power over strategic policy guidance. But the lack of a coordinated oversight over PLA actions with national security consequences was a problem, highlighted by the surprise antisatellite missile test in January 2007, which the MFA was not able to verify or provide any comment about until more than a week later; and the rollout of the J-20 stealth fighter during the visit by US defense secretary Robert Gates in January 2011. In all these cases, President Hu was not informed in advance.[49]

Without effective oversight, some PLA officers became media sensations for their tough positions in the public debate about national security issues. General Zhu Chenghu in the National Defense University (NDU) told international media in 2005 that if the US missiles targeted China's territory, China would respond with nuclear weapons. Zhu's comments caused a media stir because it was against China's official no-first-use policy.[50] President Hu had to intervene to calm it down. Zhu was transferred from a first-line position at the Institute for Strategic Studies to the second-line Department of Military Training for Foreigners at the NDU so that he would have less opportunity to express his hawkish opinions publicly.[51] Although the hawkish remarks by PLA officers did not represent the official policy or imply divisions within the policy-makers, they were often confused.

The lack of civil-military coordination was in part because the military was not subject to the leadership of the State Council but ranked parallel to it. The PLA reported to the CMC through a closed system and made decisions on defense-related foreign affairs independently. Given the PLA's special political status and military secrecy and sensitivity, generals did not feel obliged to inform or share specific and high-stakes undertakings with their civilian counterparts even though they might have international repercussions. The lack of communication was also due to political taboos. Unauthorized contact between civilians and generals would easily cause serious suspicion.[52]

Xi Jinping has determined to reassert the party and his authority over the military. Launching intense anticorruption campaigns and enforcing ideological orthodoxy, Xi purged many senior military officials, including Generals Guo Boxiong and Xu Caihou, two CMC vice-chairmen under Hu, whom Xi charged with bribery and political misconduct. Xi has required the military officers to be "absolutely loyal, absolutely pure and absolutely reliable" to the party and him personally.[53] As the Chairman of the CMC, he has undergone drastic reorganization of the PLA, handpicked all CMC members on the basis of their proven political and personal loyalty, and established the CMC chairman responsibility system to stress his dominant role over military affairs. "All significant issues regarding national defense and military development shall be decided and finalized by the CMC chairman. The CMC Chairman shall preside over and take charge of overall work of the CMC."[54]

Presiding over the first-ever All-Military Diplomatic Work Conference in January 2015, Xi emphasized "unwaveringly upholding the party's absolute leadership over military diplomacy" to establish the party and his command over the military and military diplomacy. Xi's speech cited several goals for Chinese military diplomacy to establish civilian authority in the civil-military coordination, including supporting overall national foreign policy, protecting national security, and promoting development interests.[55] In a sweeping reorganization of the PLA command structure in 2016, the Ministry of National Defense's Foreign Affairs Office was placed under the direct supervision of the CMC and renamed the CMC Office of International Military Cooperation. The reorganization reflected Xi's heightened emphasis on, and gave him direct authority to control, military diplomacy.[56]

Corporate Pluralization

China's increasing international interactions have brought about new players to the crowded foreign policy arena. The most notable ones are foreign policy think tanks; the sensational media and netizens; local governments; and transnational corporations. The paramount leaders have incorporated them into the policy process.

Government-sponsored research centers and institutes have existed since the founding of the PRC. During Mao's years, they were characterized by a substantial ideological focus and rarely functioned to support foreign-policy-making. Deng's reform and open-up created the opportunities as well as the demands for them to provide empirically based and less ideologically bound policy recommendations and consultations. The Chinese term for *think tank* was a translation from English and introduced to the policy community in the 2000s. As policy-makers have found a great need for in-depth analyses and insights about international affairs, the think tanks have grown rapidly to bring expert knowledge to policy-making in an increasingly complex and information-explosion world.

Xi Jinping has paid special attention to the construction of think tanks. "The Decision of the Central Committee on Comprehensively Deepening Reform for Several Major Issues" adopted in November 2013 set a special section about the urgent need for strengthening the new style of think tanks with Chinese characteristics and constructing and improving the policy-making advisory system (决策咨询制度). This was the first time the term *think tank* appeared in a CCP document. The Central Comprehensively Deepening Reform LSG meeting in October 2014 adopted the Resolution on Strengthening New Type of Think Tanks. Xi at the meeting called for constructing a group of high-level think tanks with international influence.[57]

Differing from the liberal model of the think tanks in Western countries, which advocate independence, autonomy, and transparency, Chinese think tanks are not independent and autonomous. Most of them are run by the party-state in the following three types. The first type is the state academies straddling the fence between advice and academic work. The premier and most comprehensive think tank is the Chinese Academy of Social Sciences (CASS) established in 1977. A cabinet-level government institution under the State Council, its official mission is to "provide important research papers and policy suggestions to the CCP Central Committee and the State Council."[58] The CASS runs many international and area studies institutes, which usually house the national associations of the relevant specialists in academic institutions, allowing researchers and scholars from all over the country to link up with the premier research institutes in their fields and establish networks and possibly joint projects to play the advisory role, build contacts with policy-makers, and provide inputs for relevant topics.[59]

The second type are the research institutes under the auspices of the state and party agencies. The most influential one is the China Institutes of

Contemporary International Relations (CICIR), established officially to the public in 1980. CICIR had its origin in the policy research bureau of the MSS. It is staffed by more than three hundred researchers and covers a wide range of strategic, political, economic, and security issues and country/regional studies. Because of its affiliation with the MSS, its research outcomes can reach the national security apparatus directly. Another influential foreign policy think-tank is the China Institute of International Studies (CIIS) under the MFA. Founded in 1956, CIIS is the longest-standing foreign policy think tank in China and has housed many semiretired and rotational diplomats from the MFA. The CIIS's research and advisory role is primarily for the leaders of MFA. The Xi Jinping Thought on Diplomacy Research Center inaugurated in July 2020 has been hosted in the CIIS. Outside of Beijing, the most important foreign policy think tank is the Shanghai Institutes for International Studies (SIIS) founded in 1960. With more than one hundred research staff, SIIS performed foreign policy advisory roles not only for the Shanghai Municipal Government but also decision-makers in Beijing.

Some important think tanks are affiliated with the ministries on functional foreign policy issues. The Chinese Academy of International Trade and Economic Cooperation under the MOC is a conglomerate with more than six hundred staff members. The China Center for Contemporary World Studies was founded by the CLD in 2010, focusing on the study of foreign political systems, China's global strategy, and development models. It also is the home for China's Silk Road Think Tank Association to coordinate policy research on the BRI.

The third type are international and area studies schools and centers in elite universities to engage in foreign policy research and advice. The influences of these think tanks vary a lot, depending largely on the connections of the institutional heads and individual scholars with the party-state agencies and leaders.[60]

Nongovernment think tanks have emerged in recent years. But they have survived largely by undertaking government-commissioned research projects and serving government needs. The most influential one is the Center for China and Globalization (CCG) founded in 2008 by Wang Huiyao, an overseas returned scholar. The CCG has about one hundred researchers and staff. Focusing on issues of overseas Chinese talent recruitment, the CCG has expanded its research to the study of China's foreign economic and security issues.

Think tanks have presented their views in media and published their research as journal articles or books to rally public support to the party-state policies. But their primary function is to submit the internal reports and references to the top leaders and party-state agencies and present in-person advice through lectures, briefings, and commissions. Think tank specialists have been successful in raising their academic profile and emerged as key players in their fields after their reports received top leaders' comments (批示).[61]

The government affiliation and orientation of Chinese think tanks have limited their ability to provide objective policy recommendations, especially when the research results may go against the official policy lines. As the commissioning government agencies have a clear bias for certain research results, their reports serve as an endorsement for the patron's policy positions.[62] Using this research to promote their interests, their policy recommendation often paints an incomplete picture. Chinese think tanks are, therefore, criticized for the concomitant influence of cronyism on the policy-making process.[63] But Chinese scholars have argued that because of China's unique political environment and cultural tradition, it is difficult to use the Western liberal model to assess China's think tanks that have served the Chinese government well.[64]

Another new player is the sensational media and citizens. China's increasing involvement in the world has helped Chinese people become aware of the relevance of foreign policy to their personal lives. To stay commercially viable and politically correct, the media has often appealed to the nationalistic or even the xenophobic taste of their potential audiences. Chinese media flooded with sensational and nationalist writings and stories can beat competitors and secure more commercial advertisements. *Global Times* has become a constant bestseller throughout the country by its reputation as a voice of nationalist sensation.

Social media as a powerful platform for heated international issues has allowed growing numbers of Chinese people to be part of foreign policy conversations and communicate their opinions back to the upper tiers, which exacerbates public emotion toward certain news items. As a result, the relationship between Chinese media and government was transformed from the throat-and-tongue (喉舌) of the party for mobilizing mass support, to a two-way instrument of not only transmitting information from the top down, but also communicating the public opinion back to the leadership.[65]

This change took place mostly during the second term of the Hu administration. Sensitive to popular views on issues involving China's vital national interests, the Hu leadership allowed the media, especially the internet, to serve as a safety valve to release popular anger toward foreign governments that otherwise might be directed to the Chinese government. Understanding that mishandling some issues could lead to social instability, the Hu administration had to refer to the constraints that the surging nationalist public opinions placed upon them to resist foreign entreaties and make their policy positions more credible. The result was the creation of a heated political environment, in which hawkish and nationalist calling for more muscular foreign policy prevailed over moderate and internationalist ones.

This situation has changed since Xi Jinping came to power. Intensifying media control and censorship, Xi Jinping has manipulated and made use of the seriously distorted public opinion toward the one-sided support to his tough foreign policy agenda and serve as leverage in negotiations on China's sovereignty claims and strategic interests. He has manufactured the public opinions through manipulation of sensational media and citizens as an instrument for big power diplomacy.

Local governments have become players because the decentralization of foreign trade and investment power during Deng's years has brought local governments to direct interactions with foreign countries and produced local liberalism to push for transnational collaboration in the economic, social, cultural, and nontraditional security issues. The paramount leaders tolerated and even encouraged local liberalism because it facilitated developmental diplomacy by promoting international economic interactions and producing political spillover. The provincial/municipal governments, with distinctive geopolitical locations and economic clouts, have been particularly influential. One classic example is that Liaoning and Shandong Provinces. Moth are strategically situated adjacent to South Korea and competed to make the arrangements for the first South Korean trade mission to China in the late 1980s and helped establish Beijing's diplomatic relationship with Seoul in 1992.[66]

As the major gateway to Southeast Asia and South Asia, Yunnan and Guangxi provincial governments have also played an important role in cementing the relations between China and the mainland ASEAN countries and helped bring them into the Chinese political orbit.[67] Shanghai as the economic and financial center has contributed significantly to China's foreign economic policy-making. Recognizing its economic prowess, the paramount leaders have taken advantage of its special position to launch experimental policies. For example, Xi Jinping launched the China (Shanghai) Pilot Free Trade Zone in 2013, making Shanghai the first regional jurisdiction to propose guidelines for implementing the Foreign Investment Law, which is the basis for a new investment framework that promises equal treatment for foreign and domestic enterprises. Through these initiatives, Xi Jinping tested the waters for contested reform policy while Shanghai municipal government pursued local economic interests.[68]

China's transnational corporations, mostly the SOEs and state banks, have become important players in the foreign policy arena since they emerged as globally active at the beginning of the twenty-first century. Using commercial engagement to advance the nation's broad foreign policy and security agendas, Xi Jinping has gone to great lengths to shield the SOEs from foreign competition and help them conquer overseas markets through, for example, the BRI. The global expansion of Chinese companies has, in turn, generated overseas interests that they want the policy-makers to be aware of and protect.

The executives of large SOEs in strategic industries such as petroleum, minerals, nuclear power, electronics, and defense are often consulted when relevant foreign policy issues are deliberated. Some executives of the SOEs have the same bureaucratic status as those of the State Council ministers or provincial governors. Within the party-state hierarchy, bureaucratic ranking is decisive in access to the policy process. The voices of high-ranking SOE executives are heard and the interests of these SOEs are protected. For example, China was reluctant to join the United States and other countries in the sanction of Iran because it would hurt the commercial interests of China's large energy companies and financial institutions. China's largest power utility companies have also resisted setting carbon emission quotas due to their share of the coal electricity generation market. Their opposition has slowed the delivery of Beijing's international commitment to climate change.

Electronic giant Huawei provided one powerful case of a transnational corporation as a player in the making of foreign policy. Huawei was a symbol of China's rise to technological primacy the Chinese telecommunications racing toward dominance of the world's 5G networks. After the Canadian government arrested Meng Wanzhou, Huawei's CFO and the daughter of Ren Zhengfei, the founder of Huawei, per the extradition request of the US government in December 2018 for financial fraud, the entire Chinese foreign policy establishment was mobilized to punish the Canadian government. The Chinese government went to extraordinary lengths to arrest two Canadian citizens, Michael Kovrig and Michael Spavor, as hostages. The case rapidly turned from a legal dispute into a geopolitical battle. Although China publicly maintained that there was no connection between Meng's case and the imprisonment of the "two Michaels," it sent signals that dropping Meng's case would help free the two Canadians and end the diplomatic stalemate.[69]

With Xi's personal involvement toward the end of three years of extradition drama, the US Justice Department announced a deferred prosecution agreement with Meng to drop the case. Meng returned to China as a hero on September 24, 2021. China released the two Michaels hours after the announcement. The blatant display of hostage diplomacy not only demonstrated their conviction that the US justice system was just as subject to political intervention and manipulation as their own, but more importantly, it demonstrated that Xi Jinping would do whatever he could to protect the strategically vital commercial and business interests of China.

PART THREE

Exploiting External Environment

Searching for China's Place in the Sun
International Distribution of Power

CHINESE LEADERS ARE ESSENTIALLY realists. Perceiving the world as a Darwinist jungle in which each state must look out for its survival and security, Chinese leaders have constantly assessed the balance of forces (力量对比), a Chinese term for the distribution of power, and carefully examined the power dynamics or the basic contradictions (基本矛盾) in the world and the changing alignment of political forces. As a Chinese scholar indicated, "Without a study of the balance of forces, policy-makers in Beijing presumably would not be able to adjust foreign policy accordingly."[1]

Chinese leaders have not simply adapted to but strategically exploited external conditions. Mao Zedong took a flexible alignment strategy and played one superpower against another in an unsentimental balance-of-power game during the height of the Cold War. Deng Xiaoping leveraged China's flexible alignment practices and placed China as the much-coveted balancing third force in the strategic triangle and formulated the low-profile policy to survive China's isolation after the Cold War. As China reemerged from isolation, Jiang Zemin and Hu Jintao pushed for multipolarity against the US unipolar moment. Weathering the global financial crisis in 2008 better than the United States and other Western powers, the Hu administration looked forward to the shift of power distribution to a G2 world but continued Deng's low-profile policy because of their perception of China's circumstanced power position.

As the post–Cold War unipolarity and multipolarity give way to an emerging bipolar world driven by the Sino-US rivalry, Xi Jinping has wielded China's newfound heft to pursue China's power ambition. The sharpened Sino-US rivalry has shown some futures of a Cold War.[2] Xi Jinping has rejected the Cold War analogy. But the emerging bipolarity underscored by the geopolitical incompatibility between the rising and incumbent powers has exaggerated hostility against each other. Working with Russia and Iran to build an antihegemony coalition, Xi has tried to consolidate China's position in response to the US attempt to line up like-minded countries in the contest with China.

But the Sino-US bipolarity does not match the classical vision of a colliding set of roughly equivalent great powers. The United States and China are superpowers, but multiple big powers of the European Union, Russia, Japan, India, and some other countries remain independent; each has substantial political and diplomatic influence, or economic weight or military heft, although none has all. With the ability to upset the balance of power, they have prevented the world from splitting into two rigid ideological and geopolitical blocs. Additionally, the power balance remains delicate. Although China is not in the position to achieve global hegemony, it has narrowed the power gap with the United States and others. Building a strong economic, technological, and political foundation, China has sustained itself as a formidable competitor in the rivalry. The two powers incapable of dominating each other have dictated the endurability of bipolar competition.

Exploiting the Cold War Bipolarity

The PRC was founded when the world was dominated by the Cold War rivalry between the United States and the Soviet Union. Taking a balance-of-power strategy, Mao Zedong confronted the United States and allied with the Soviet Union but never in an irrevocable fashion. China's intervention in the Korean War brought it to the front line of a major military conflict with the United States, which imposed blockade and containment, deepening Beijing's dependence on Soviet assistance. China experienced the worst of both worlds: political domination by the far more powerful ally and isolation and encirclement by the world-leading military power.[3]

To improve its position, Beijing initiated ambassadorial dialogs with the United States in Geneva and subsequently in Warsaw in the mid-1950s and

embarked on a more independent foreign policy after the split with the Soviet Union in the 1960s. To broaden China's strategic space, Mao formulated
a three-world strategy to lead the third world countries and cooperate with
the second world of Japan and Western European countries to form an international united front against the two superpowers of the first world.[4] As
the intensified tension with the Soviet Union threatened China's security,
Mao reached out to the United States for a vital breathing space to reduce
vulnerability.

Mao's flexible balance-of-power maneuvers set the stage for Deng Xiaoping to gain leverage from the antagonism between the two superpowers as a
fulcrum for strategic and economic benefits. China acted as if it was a global
power and was treated as such, serving as the lodestar for Deng's developmental
goal. In the strategic triangle, leaders evaluated the respective policies of the
other two and developed their own with attention to the triangular implications. But one of the most notable issues was the asymmetry of national
power. Significantly less powerful than the other two, China was the most
reactive state. Despite the asymmetry, both the United States and the Soviet
Union took China's presumptuous self-esteem seriously and played the China
card against each other whenever they could. Each superpower deemed it
highly advantageous to be aligned with China in a "national love affair" and
deemed China's realignment to be a traumatic event severely jeopardizing its
national security.[5] Becoming a fully accredited player, China benefited far out
of proportion to its real power.

China's attention to the two superpowers was easily comprehensible. But
the American and Soviet attention to China's strategic role was qualitatively
different from their attention to the other party. Both superpowers shared
strategic capacities of mass destruction. China's nuclear power was far more
limited, resembling that of France and Britain. China's strategic position was
not solely a function of its military power but rather the flexible diplomacy
in the bipolar world.

China's modest nuclear deterrence and conventional military capacities
were significant support for its strategic leverage. With the largest population
and one of the largest standing armies in the world, China could tilt the military balance in East Asia and affect the European strategic balance between
NATO and the Warsaw Pact countries. In response, the Soviet Union deployed

fifty-two divisions in its four Far Eastern military districts, about a quarter of all Soviet ground forces, as well as its most advanced military equipment along the Sino-Soviet border.[6] China reinforced its position by pursuing and surviving the self-imposed isolation. Although costs were high, neither the Soviet Union nor the United States could achieve its goals in Asia without taking into consideration the legitimate interests and concerns of China.[7]

China's military weight alone, however, could not explain the preoccupation of both superpowers. China's strategic importance was derived from the demonstrated flexibility in its alignment practices. China was the only major power to have switched sides in the post-1945 East-West confrontation, except for Egypt in its 1972 break with the Soviet Union. China was also the only major country to have engaged, in a series, in military conflict with both superpowers, and the only major country, again excluding Egypt, to have been militarily aligned with both.[8] While France and Great Britain's commitment to NATO eliminated any ambiguity concerning their diplomatic positions, China's flexibility limited confidence in Moscow and Washington that Beijing would maintain its diplomatic posture. The uncertainty surrounding the Chinese alignment policy contributed to its strategic significance.

Exploiting the strategic triangle, Deng Xiaoping responded positively to the US quest as a strategic partner in the late 1970s, aggravating Soviet security frustration. He then responded positively to the Soviet Union's signal of improving relations in the 1980s. With ideological opposition to America and under the pressure of Soviet encirclement, China maintained a distance from the United States to alleviate the Soviet strategic burden. This striking fluidity made Moscow and Washington apprehensive about China's alignments and, in turn, enhanced Beijing's leverage.

The Soviet Union and the United States did not consider Chinese power independent from bipolarity. Their attention to China reflected the appreciation for China's ability to either exacerbate or ameliorate the burden of the superpower conflict. In isolation, China could not pose a significant threat to Soviet interests and was of little immediate value to America. But in the context of heightened threat perception on the part of both superpowers, China assumed exaggerated strategic importance.

Without the persistence of the bipolarity, Washington's patience with China's domestic political system and aspects of its foreign policy would have quickly eroded. Similarly, Moscow would have ceased viewing China's US policy as threatening and would not need to balance China's growing influence. All these factors were crucial in defining China's leverage. Without Chinese military capacity, the power balances would be purely bilateral affairs. Without China's diplomatic flexibility, China's role in world affairs would be sufficiently predictable so that neither Moscow nor Washington would have worked so hard to influence Chinese behavior. And if Chinese flexibility had not emerged during the bipolar hostility, neither Washington nor Moscow would have taken China so seriously.[9]

Resisting Unipolar Moment and Pushing for Multipolarity

The end of the Cold War, therefore, left Chinese leaders without a definition of their place in the world. The United States, once a Cold War quasi-ally, became a powerful and ideologically adversary. Chinese leaders were profoundly frightened by the speculation that the unipolar moment of US dominance was emerging from the ashes of the Cold War. Searching for a niche, Chinese scholars began predicting and pushing for a multipolar world.[10] But the official view was cautious at first. In a December 1990 interview, Foreign Minister Qian Qichen said that the world was in a transitional phase. The old structure dissolved but no new one emerged. Premier Li Peng in March 1991 said that "the old-world structure, which lasted for over four decades, was disintegrated and the new one has yet to take shape."[11] In the 1991 year-end assessment of the international situation, Minister Qian discovered "the initial stage of the evolution towards multipolarity, in which one superpower and several powers depend on and struggle against each other." He became more assured in 1992 that "the breakup of the old-world pattern means the end of the post-war bipolar system. A new world . . . is likely to be multipolar."[12] By the mid-1990s, Chinese leaders were certain that "the world has undergone a transition to multipolarity."[13]

Three scenarios of multipolarity were presented by Chinese strategists. One was a tripolar world of the European Community, North America, and the rising Asia-Pacific. The second was a five-polar structure of the United States, Germany, Russia, China, and Japan. But the most popular scenario was one superpower and many big powers. Bilateral relations varied between these powers. Some were opposed on the ideological level, some were in sharp

political conflict, some had serious economic conflicts, some were political allies but full of economic contradictions, and some had different social systems
but complemented each other economically.[14] The multipolarity narrative
represented Beijing's attempt to resist the posited unipolar world by appealing
to opponents of US hegemony. China was to find a multipolar chessboard
in which US global power declined and regional powers were able to resist
external interference in their respective region. With the rise of non-Western
nations, the domination of the "West over the rest" would decline. No single
power was able to exert an overwhelming influence. China was on a stable
and upward trajectory in contrast to the contradictions and turbulence in
other countries.[15]

In the Chinese lexicon, multipolarity referred to the autonomy or independence of other states to the hegemonic power or freedom from hegemony
rather than the existence of states with the independent capability to challenge
the leading state.[16] A multipolar world was not simply a modus vivendi of the
concert of powers. It meant an imbalance of power to produce new conflicts
between the United States and its allies. After the West lost its common enemy
of the Soviet Union, problems held down by the two blocs' strife surfaced,
making the situation tumultuous and capricious and damaging the Western
alliances. West-West contradictions were involved in economic frictions, political control and anticontrol, and divisions in defense matters. It was no longer
easy for the United States, Europe, and Japan to coordinate their relations.[17]

Playing the role of a balancing force against the backdrop of the unipolar
world, China embraced multilateralism from the perspective of multipolarity
where countries balanced against the prevailing power, whereas the notion
of multilateralism meant a kind of foreign policy that could be carried out
even in a world dominated by a single power.[18] Portraying the emergence
of multipolarity as a natural progression that could not be resisted, Jiang
Zemin designed a network of strategic partnerships that practically covered
China's relations with all major powers and regional organizations. Within
the framework, Jiang appealed to their counterparts to abandon the Cold
War mentality and actively identify common interests. The network was instrumental for China to secure the multipolarity in which the major powers
would interact on equality and check and balance each other. Following the
principle of making partners but not alliances (结伴不结盟), the partnership

network was sufficiently vague enough to allow China to encourage countries to adopt a more independent foreign policy while avoiding the perception of an anti-US alignment.[19]

Emphasizing the desirability and likely emergence of a multipolar world of states mutually respecting the principle of noninterference, Chinese leaders had to admit and adapt to the reality of US predominance and made a steadfast effort to maintain a cooperative relationship with the United States. As one Chinse scholar suggested, "In the long term, the decline of US primacy and the subsequent transition to a multipolar world are inevitable, but in the short term, Washington's power is unlikely to decline, and its position in the world affairs is unlikely to change."[20] The Chinese leaders were relieved when the United States was dragged into the prolonged war on terror after 2001. The US government was not only subject to a strong domestic resistance to foreign military intervention but also failed to enact an effective strategy of controlling the globe unilaterally as a growing number of countries, including American allies, became bold enough to say no to the United States.

The G2 Mirage

In the wake of the global financial crisis of 2008, some American strategists proposed a G2 concept that attracted the attention of Chinese leaders and scholars. Expecting China to quickly match US power, the proposal suggested that the most prominent rising power and the strongest status quo power could cooperate to address global challenges and convince the rest of the world to go along.[21] Some academic fora went further and suggested that the United States and China could solve global problems by dividing the world into two spheres of influence. As uncontested American leadership in Asia became illusory, China could dominate Asia in its place.[22]

Although the Hu Jintao administration cautiously avoided endorsing the G2 concept because they did not believe the United States was ready to share global leadership, they were flattered by the idea and looked forward to the shift of global power distribution to a bipolar affair with America and China the only two powers that mattered. China as a rising power, therefore, was hardly a status quo power. Instead of cooperating with the United States, it became increasingly assertive in challenging US hegemony in the Asia-Pacific.[23]

With conflated confidence in its rapidly accumulated power, China took an unusually hawkish position to confront the Obama administration that proposed to build a positive, comprehensive, and cooperative relationship with China. In March 2009, just one month after Obama took office, China intercepted the USS *Impeccable* in the South China Sea, where the American navy had frequently deployed to monitor China's military activities. While the Chinese always viewed US surveillance operations close to its coasts as a challenge, China had never taken such high-profile actions to stop US ships in its EEZ.[24]

Following this incident, Beijing took an unusual position against the joint US–South Korean military exercise and specifically objected to the aircraft carrier USS *George Washington* deployed to the Yellow Sea in 2010. Although the US Navy had long conducted exercises there, Beijing warned that the deployment would place the Chinese capital within the carrier's striking distance. Between early June when the news was revealed and early July when Washington confirmed the exercises, China issued six protests with successively tougher tones, beginning by calling on involved parties to "maintain calm and constraint," followed by expressing "concern" and "serious concern," then morphing into words such as "oppose" and "strongly oppose."[25]

Although Obama was the first US president to make an official visit to China in the inaugural year and went out of his way to show his goodwill before the visit, his town hall meeting with young Chinese in Shanghai was not broadcast live, whereas the speeches of Presidents Clinton and George W. Bush in Chinese universities were. When the Obama administration announced the postponed arms sale to Taiwan in January 2010, a Chinese MFA spokesperson for the first time stated that it was time for China to sanction the companies in the arms sales to "shape the policy choices of the US."[26] Working assiduously to lay the groundwork for cooperation on global challenges, the Obama administration found itself facing an increasingly assertive China and therefore made an adjustment in the second year to reenergize relationships with allies and partners and wield American leadership in the region.[27]

The timing of the policy adjustment coincided with a deterioration of China's relations with its neighbors as China's maritime neighbors were alarmed as China increased naval patrols, pressured foreign energy companies to halt operations in contested waters, and imposed fishing bans on parts of the sea. Tensions were escalated as Chinese vessels clashed with the ships of other claimants, causing incidents with Vietnamese oil exploration ships, Philippine navy naval patrol vessels, and Japanese coast guard patrol ships. China's relationship with South Korea also soured after it rejected an international investigation report that showed the sinking of the South Korean warship *Cheonan* was caused by a torpedo attack by a North Korean submarine on March 26, 2010. More than thirty South Korean sailors died in the incident. The brutality was followed by the North Korean shelling of the Yeonpyeong Islands in November 2010. China's reluctance to denounce North Korean belligerence frustrated South Korea.[28]

Emerging as the largest trade partner of many Asian countries, China, however, faced serious problems translating the economic clout into strategic leverage. Increasingly wary of China's threats, many Asian countries began hedging against China by seeking US leadership and deepening strategic relations with each other. The United States gained favorable attention even from former enemies like Vietnam and estranged friends like the Philippines and Indonesia, making it relatively easy for Obama's strategic rebalance toward the Asia-Pacific as a pivot.[29]

Beijing interpreted the US strategic rebalance as an attempt to curtail China's influence through strengthened military alliances with US allies and partners to sabotage China's ties with neighbors and undercut China's effort to lead the regional economic integration.[30] As the Sino-US competition intensified, the G2 idea suffered a natural death. Causing great ferment in China and many Asian countries, the concept became a mirage because it raised "expectations for a level of partnership that cannot be met" and exacerbated "the very real differences that still exist between Washington and Beijing."[31]

As the G2 idea lost momentum, the Chinese criticized the notion as "a potential trap for China that could expose it on the world stage."[32] Premier Wen Jiabao rejected the notion as "not appropriate, baseless and wrong" and reiterated that "China remains a developing country despite remarkable achievements."[33] Wen's statement was not simply an expression of modesty to soothe Western worries about the China threat: "It's far more likely that China's leaders are telling the truth" because Wen was aware of China's substantially conditioned national strength.[34]

The Antihegemonic Coalition

When the nascent G2 disappeared, China enhanced strategic partnerships with Russia and Iran to construct what Zbigniew Brzezinski predicted would be the "antihegemonic" coalition united not by ideology but by complementary grievances against the United States, a fearsome enemy.[35] Although these relationships are transactional rather than sentimental, Xi Jinping has taken advantage of these relations to enhance China's position in the rivalry with the United States.

China has nudged closer to Russia for its diplomatic clout and remaining military might. The triangular dynamic has continued to influence the strategic thinking of Chinese leaders. Making the point by choosing Moscow as the destination of his first presidential trip in 2013, Xi Jinping said that the two countries spoke a "common language" and accorded the priority to deepening their comprehensive strategic cooperative partnership.[36] Although Russians initially had reservations, the Western sanction for annexing Crimea and supporting rebel movements in Ukraine in 2014 pushed Moscow toward Beijing. Despite its long-championed principle of sovereignty and territorial integrity, China kept silent on Russia's infringement on these principles. Sensing the geopolitical urgency to break international isolations, President Vladimir Putin approved the sale to China of the S-400 missile defense system and Su-35 fighters it had been reluctant to provide, endorsed the BRI, agreed to link the BRI to the Moscow-led Eurasian Economic Union, and signed the thirty-year contract between Russia's Gazprom and the CNPC for the Power of Siberia gas pipeline to China that had long been held in abeyance.

Sharing the geopolitical distaste for the United States operating in their neighborhood, China backed Russia in carrying out military exercises to intimidate countries in Europe and the Middle East and held the joint naval operations in the Baltic amid the heightened tension between Russia and NATO in 2017 in opposing the pressure by NATO's expansion. In reciprocity, Russia took part in joint naval exercises in the South China Sea in 2016 and started joint air strategic patrol over the Pacific in 2019. Russia invited the Chinese to its largest military exercises since the fall of the Soviet Union, Vostok 2018, the first time Beijing participated in Moscow's simulated war games as opposed to drills under the rubric of counterterrorism cooperation or law enforcement, a groundbreaking sign of heightened trust.

Economically, with Russia offering military equipment, energy, and raw materials and China providing capital and consumer goods, their bilateral trade grew from $10 billion in 2003 to the $100 billion mark in 2018 and reached $107 billion in 2020. China is Russia's top trading partner. Russia supplanted Saudi Arabia as China's biggest crude oil supplier. Making a "de-dollarization" effort, the two countries drastically cut their use of the US dollar and increased the amount of their bilateral trade in yuan and rubles.

The United States rolling back China and Russia's power aspirations contributed to the Sino-Russian collusion. Acting by the geostrategic calculation that "the enemy of my enemy is my friend," their strategic partnership has advanced with mutual empathy at the top political level. Holding summits twice annually and developing a strong personal rapport, Xi claimed that "Russia is the country that I have visited the most times, and President Putin is my best friend and colleague." State media of both countries featured the two leaders making blinis together, topping them with caviar and downing shots of vodka.[37] Xi and Putin signed a Joint Statement in the wake of the Beijing Winter Olympics on February 4, 2022, twenty days before the Russian invasion of Ukraine. Hailing their friendship as without limits for cooperation, the joint statement endorsed each other's foreign policy wish lists, with Russia affirming China's opposition to "any forms of independence of Taiwan" and China denouncing "further enlargement of NATO."

Gushing hyperbole indicative of how China has valued the Russian tie, the Chinese media has been full of puff pieces about Russia's military and new weapons, paralleling the "negative" news about the United States. Foreign minister Wang Yi in a bilateral conversation with his Russian counterpart Sergey Lavrov openly attacked the United States, stating that it "has lost its mind, morals, and credibility."[38] Immediately after the rocky Anchorage meeting with his US counterparts in March 2021, Wang Yi welcomed Lavrov to China. Highlighting the significance of the meeting, Chinese media warned that "it would be disastrous for any country to confront China and Russia through allying with the US."[39] After Russia invaded Ukraine, Beijing not only refused to condemn Russia's invasion but also adopted the Russian narrative to blame NATO expansion for driving Russia into a corner.

Although there is little overt ideological alignment, both leaderships have drawn upon the premises of the Marxist-Leninist theory of imperialism in the construction of worldview and shared a convergent set of political norms and values to resist US promotion of human rights and democracy. Sharing a strong desire to impose tight controls over their societies, Xi Jinping has bolstered the party's role in society, akin to Putin's effort to tame Russian oligarchs and crush political opposition. China was inspired by Russia's legislation cracking down on nongovernmental organizations, while Russian officials expressed admiration for China's comprehensive internet censorship and "social credit" system to rank citizens based on their loyalty and behavior. Believing the West orchestrated subversion of authoritarian regimes and therefore their legitimacy, Moscow has been troubled by the Georgian and Ukrainian revolutions and Beijing by separatist agitation in Xinjiang and democratic protest in Hong Kong. In a phone call, Putin supported China's Hong Kong National Security Law, and Xi supported Russia's revised constitution.[40] Showing their unhappiness about the Democracy Summit hosted by President Biden in December 2021, Russian and Chinese ambassadors to Washington published a joint letter to criticize the summit as an evident product of US Cold War mentality, stoking up ideological confrontation and a rift in the world and creating new "dividing lines."[41]

For many years, Washington held that the burgeoning China-Russia ties were a shallow partnership of convenience and bound to be undermined by diverging national interests and distrust. There is ample evidence to support this view. Both Russia and China see themselves as deserving to be great powers and value highly the independence of their respective decision-making. Never comfortable with the junior brother position and pecking order from the big brother in the 1950s, China is now an economic giant with ambitions for world dominance while Russian global influence is constrained by economic and demographic weaknesses. Deep in the heart, however, Moscow sees itself as a European power. Acting as a junior partner belies Putin's imperial power ambition. Additionally, Moscow has viewed itself as a quintessential Eurasia power and regarded much of Central Asia, the main stage for BRI, as its backyard. Reluctant to cede influence in the region, Russia did not respond to BRI until 2014 when it had to dip into China's deep pockets due to Western sanctions.

On the other side, China is not happy that Russia maintains close military ties with and sold advanced weapons to India and Vietnam; both are locked in territorial disputes with China. China also cannot forget that Russia took the territories in northeast China more than one hundred years ago. On July 2, 2020, the Russian embassy in China posted a video of a party celebrating the 160th anniversary of the founding of Vladivostok, which means "ruler of the east" in Russian and was annexed by the tsarist empire from China in 1860. The post reminded the Chinese of emotions over history and prompted an online backlash with posts such as "Today we can only endure, but the Chinese people will remember!," and "This ancestral land will return home in the future!"[42]

Because Russia is not amenable to accepting a junior role and Beijing cannot forget the unhappy history, a full-blown alliance is not in sight. Great powers do not mate for life. The US policy toward them largely determines their position toward each other. China cannot afford an unexpected rapprochement between Washington and Moscow, and vice versa. As such, the China-Russia relationship is anchored more in shared grievances than in common visions.

Ironically, as Americans have become increasingly aware and concerned about Sino-Russian cooperation undermining US interests, the skeptical view has given way to an emerging American consensus that the Beijing-Moscow axis is built on real commonalities and has a strong foundation and a positive future.[43] The Worldwide Threat Assessment by the US intelligence community in 2017 explicitly pointed out that Moscow and Beijing were "more aligned than at any point since the mid-1950s."[44] China and Russia were also listed together as the top threats in the 2017 US National Security Strategy. The Biden administration's Interim National Security Strategic Guidance published in March 2021 labeled Russia a disrupter and China a challenger. While the Sino-US relationship came to a historical low point, the Biden administration imposed tough sanctions against Russia over its interference in US elections and other malign activities. The United States and Russia grew antagonistic in theaters from the Middle East to Eastern Europe. Simultaneously piling pressure on both China and Russia, the United States compelled them to advance their strategic partnership far beyond convenience.

Iran has joined the antihegemonic coalition because its relationship with China has been crucial to resisting the US sanctions that meant to end its nuclear program, if not the regime itself. The sanction has scared away its badly needed foreign trade and investment, including access to the international banking system, and provided Beijing with a unique, multilayered monopoly over Iran. China bought Iranian oil and the money was deposited in Chinese banks. Chinese businesses offered services and products to Iran banned by the West. Benefiting from working with China, Iran quickly jumped onboard as a Eurasian hub when China launched the BRI. The China-Central West Asia Economic Corridor, the 10,399-kilometer-long "Silk Railway" to link the Iranian capital to Yiwu in China's Zhejiang Province, has carried goods and passengers in only fourteen days, as opposed to the month and a half the same shipment would take by sea.[45]

President Xi visited Iran and signed the Comprehensive Strategic Partnership with his counterpart Hassan Rouhani in 2016. Both countries are authoritarian and reject Western intervention in their domestic affairs. The partnership was enhanced after the Trump administration's unilateral withdrawal from the Iran nuclear deal in 2018. China vocally opposed US sanctions and rebuffed the proposed extension of the UN Security Council arms embargo on Iran. Amid COVID-19, while the United States refused to lift sanctions, the Chinese airlifted supplies and medical personnel to Tehran. A social media spat revealed how invested Iran is in the Tehran-Beijing axis. On April 5, 2020, when the spokesperson for Iran's Health Ministry called Chinese data on coronavirus cases a "bitter joke," many Iranian conservatives attacked him. Just hours after, he retracted the comments and thanked Beijing for standing by Iran during the crisis. The Iranian ambassador to China was quoted in state media: "In this time of sanctions we need to be very careful about what is said about China in Tehran." He even labeled the critique of the Iran-China relationship as those "who do not wish well for the regime and the Iranian people."[46]

Moving from working on ad hoc projects to the commitment for broad and long-term cooperation, China and Iran signed a twenty-five-year comprehensive cooperation agreement in March 2021 to vastly expand Chinese investments. In return, Iran would regularly supply China with oil at a discount. The agreement deepened military cooperation, including joint training and exercises, and intelligence sharing. It also stipulates the joint development of Iran's port of Chabahar. This port, in addition to the Gwadar Port in Pakistan and the Kyaukpyu Port in Myanmar, would be the most prominent in China's chain of ports on the Indian Ocean.

The renewed relationship underscores Beijing's resolve to promote a strategic partnership that goes beyond economic objectives and extends Chinese footprints deeper into the Middle East, a sensitive area with the United States' long-standing dominance. Iran's geographic location at the center of land and maritime trade routes makes it a key component for China to cultivate political and economic leverage in the region. Iran can also serve as a strong connection between China and Central Asia after the US withdrawal from Afghanistan and Russia's inability to meet the developmental needs of these countries. With the expansion of the BRI projects, the geopolitical ties Iran enjoys with Central Asian countries would be a great asset to China in relations with Pakistan and Afghanistan.[47] At a time when Biden was trying to bring Iran back to the nuclear negotiating table, China demonstrated its newfound influence with this action.

The Emerging Bipolarity

An infinitely powerful China rivaling the United States has alarmed Americans to redefine the relationship. While the tipping point came much earlier, the Trump administration publicly unveiled the shift in the US policy toward China by declaring great power competition as the focus of the US national security strategy. Using the language in the Cold War, his secretary of state, Mike Pompeo, incited the Chinese people to topple the CCP regime.[48] Pledging that the United States was not "seeking a new cold war or a world divided into rigid blocs."[49] President Biden has continued many of Trump's get-tough policies. Casting the rivalry as a battle between democracies and autocracies, Biden has increased public criticism of China's human rights violations in Xinjiang, Tibet, and Hong Kong, and countered Chinese operations in the Taiwan Strait and the South China Sea. Demonstrating intentions to further develop the Quadrilateral Security Dialogue (Quad)—revived by the Trump administration among the four democracies of the United States, Australia, India, and Japan as a mini-NATO—Biden's first multilateral meeting was to host the Quad summit as a "critical part of the architecture of the Indo-Pacific."[50] One of the primary objectives of his first overseas trip to Europe was to rally allies to constrain China's influence, including boosting infrastructure projects to counter Xi's BRI.

The Chinese government has criticized the United States for adopting the Cold War mentality based on a zero-sum mindset and ideological prejudice.[51] Xi warned just days after Biden's inauguration that "to build small circles or start a new Cold War, . . . will only push the world into division and even confrontation."[52] China, however, has taken tit-for-tat actions to confront the United States in almost every realm and everywhere with the conviction that "the US will not willingly accept the rise of a power with a very different social system, ideology, cultural traditions and even race and will inevitably try every possible means and spare no effort, even without a bottom line, to suppress, contain, divide and besiege China."[53]

In response to the US attempt to ally with democracies against China, Xi has embarked on an extensive diplomatic campaign to encourage US allies and partners to chart their own course. Taking preemptions with elements that range from trade initiatives around the world to escalating actions against prodemocracy activists in Hong Kong and dissidents at home, China signed with the EU an investment deal before President Biden could even reach out to allies and frame his China strategy. Locking its closest democratic allies into investment and trade agreements to which Washington isn't a party, Beijing signed the Regional Comprehensive Economic Partnership (RCEP) of the fifteen member-countries in December 2020, which includes the US allies and partners of Japan, Australia, South Korea, Singapore, and New Zealand.

As their strategic rivalry has affected virtually every aspect of international politics and caused significant global power realignment, a bipolar confrontation has emerged. Viewing each other as trying to subvert its political system and way of life and eyeing each other as strategic adversaries, each is determined to maximize its position and deter the other from threatening its security and prosperity. Neither can get its way without depriving the other. One observer, therefore, asserts that the clash of systems between China and the United States will define the twenty-first century and divide the world. "China is positioning itself as the world's defender of hierarchy and tradition against a decadent and disorderly West; the United States is belatedly summoning a new alliance to check Chinese power and make the world safe for democracy."[54]

The emerging bipolar world has exaggerated each nation's ideological hostility. Although China's authoritarian state has challenged the Western belief that democracy works best for every country at every level of development, China has not harbored ambitions to lead an authoritarian bloc to conquer the world and undermine democracies or impose its system on other countries to the same degree as the Soviet Union promoted communism and the United States promoted liberal democracy. While the longevity of China's one-party rule has constituted an important source of Sino-US rivalry, Beijing has not built its relations with other countries based on an ideological litmus test. China's authoritarianism and high-tech surveillance state has not offered a morally compelling alternative to liberal democracy for most countries. Without ideological soul mates, committed followers, or dedicated sycophants and messianic ideology to export, China's appeal derives from its economic and political performance, not its ideas.[55]

Beijing is, therefore, more afraid of America's advocacy of expanding democracy and civil liberties into China than the United States is afraid of China's authoritarianism affecting the United States. Instead of engaging in a determined effort to spread autocracy, Beijing has constructed an information firewall and tightened ideological control domestically. Its influence operation in the United States and other Western countries has focused on changing those countries' attitudes and policies toward CCP rule and Beijing's position in Xinjiang, Hong Kong, and Taiwan; China's influence can hardly undermine their democracies. Rejecting human rights, freedom, and democracy as universal values and insisting every country has the right to choose its political system without foreign pressure, China has sought primarily to make the world more accommodating to its authoritarian system.

Western countries have criticized the Chinese brand of state capitalism, but China is the biggest trading partner of most economies in the world and an active participant in global capitalism. Guided by industrial policy, not central planning, Beijing has not coerced other countries to reject US-style capitalism for an alternative economic model in part because the Chinese economy is highly intertwined and entangled with the global economy, including the American and other market economies. Although many liberal economists believe the industrial policy is inefficient and a losing formula in the longer term, government support and industrial policy have played a significant role in development at various stages in many Western countries, the United States included. A showcase of capitalism, China is second only to the United States in its number of billionaires. Beijing has become home to more billionaires than New York City and the new billionaire capital of the world in *Forbes's* World Billionaires List for 2021.[56]

The ideological threat to China posed by the United States is also exaggerated. The US is no longer the beacon of democracy. Once almost-universal admiration of the United States has given way to disappointment over the displays of racial tensions, political polarization, socioeconomic inequality, and xenophobia. The United States has not put its own house in order and yet waged a principled campaign against China. The United States cannot win the competition when its democracy so hangs in the balance and its resources diverted from the internal construction. The internal decay is more damaging to the United States than is the external challenge from China.

While the United States attempts to build exclusive alliances, most US allies and partners don't want to be squeezed in between China and the US, not only because they have deep anxieties about US creditability and capability but also because they have different economic and strategic priorities, threat perceptions, and comfort levels from the United States in contest with China. It is hard to expect the alliances established in the Cold War context to endure once the context has been transformed.

Trump's incitement for the January 6 insurrection against the democratic institutions denigrated liberal values and left many people around the globe questioning the right of the United States to anoint itself as the unblemished democracy. President Biden has faced uphill battles to make US democracy competitive and demonstrate that the United States is reliable after the election in which Trump received more votes than any presidential candidate in history other than his opponent. No longer loyal to the United States on the grounds of shared ideals and trust in US strength, US allies and partners have weighed the costs and benefits and made their decisions accordingly. They have confronted China because of their sense of the threat for their economic and strategic interests and adjusted these calculations as China's power grows and their economic ties with China tighten. Navigating the complex and ever-changing rivalry between the United States and China, many US allies have stood up to China but have not taken a firm side. The Sino-US rivalry, in this case, has not split the world into two rigid ideological and geopolitical alliance systems.

Delicate Balance of Power

The dynamics of the emerging bipolarity have been complicated by the delicate power balance between China and the United States. Although Xi Jinping has indulged China in a state-managed banquet of positivity in its heft, the culture of inflated self-congratulation has become corrosive. The endogenous hubris and narratives of the inevitable rise of China have covered the gap between the rhetoric and reality. Despite rising confidence, China has not matched the US superpower position across the full spectrum of power assets and capabilities.

Economically, China's nominal GDP has come close to and may overtake the United States soon, but its per capita GDP is less than 20 percent of the United States ($10,484 versus $63,416 in 2020) and well below many middle powers. Although overall economic size matters more than per capita income, the low level of income indicates that China's net national wealth, i.e., the resources available to pursue national interests, is not in America's league. Additionally, a superpower must have a currency dominating the international payments and reserves. As one PLA officer realized, "The rise of China relies first upon Renminbi (RMB, Chinese currency) and second upon the PLA, just as the US world dominance has relied on the US dollar and military."[57] Although China has pushed the internationalization of RMB for many years, the share of RMB in global payment has been about 2 percent while US dollar share remains above 40 percent; RMB accounts for a scant 1 percent of global reserves while the US dollar accounts for over 60 percent.

China has spent enormous sums to modernize its military, which has become much stronger but still can hardly project itself globally. China's imperial outposts such as the Piraeus harbor in Greece and activities in other parts of the world are vulnerable without the regional assets anchored by the Chinese military. China's access to the outside is mainly overland through adjacent countries, and its maritime sector is weak. The United States is a two-ocean country: access to the outside world is much easier than it is for China. Xi Jinping has called for China's military to be ready for war and to win, but it has not been tested since its last war with Vietnam in 1979.

Compared with US allies and partnerships of over sixty countries, China has fewer allies and partners of global weight or credibility and has not created anything akin to the Warsaw Pact. Averse to traditional alliances because of damaging historical experiences from the Sino-Soviet alliance that collapsed in acrimony, China has eschewed formal alliances that involve trading some autonomy and flexibility for more security and influence. The balance of power was revealed by the countries that supported and opposed China's imposition of the Hong Kong National Security Law in the UN Human Rights Council (UNHRC) in 2020. The fifty-three countries in hock to China comprised only 4 percent of world GDP. The rich democracies coalesced into a united front against China's Hong Kong policy.

Russia is the most important pseudo-ally, but its economy is only about the size of Australia's or China's Guangdong Province. China–Russia relations are asymmetrical in favor of China, but Russia is far from being subordinate. In addition, their power centers are a continent apart. Russia's center of gravity has been in Europe with a zone of strategic tension of its own to the west. China's geopolitical sore spots are located largely in the Asia-Pacific, thousands of miles away from Russia.

In addition, the global outrage over Russia's barbarian invasion of Ukraine and the Western countries joining forces against Russia placed Beijing in an awkward position. The United States deepened its partnerships with the EU and the rest of the developed world, including many Asian countries, to impose unprecedented sanctions against Russia. China's international standing was badly damaged by its appearance as a silent partner in Russia's brutal invasion, which went blatantly against Beijing's own principles of state sovereignty and territorial integrity. Facing increasing pressure to distance itself with Russia, Beijing moved toward a fine but uncomfortable line on the fence. The Chinese ambassador to the United States added a caveat to the partnership, "China and Russia's cooperation has no forbidden areas, but it has a bottom line."58 In other words, Beijing became concerned that the "unlimited friendship" could become a liability.

China's power aspirations in the diverse and crowded neighborhood are checked by the presence and influence of the United States and other regional powers. While it becomes difficult for the United States to hold its primacy, it is more difficult for China to overtake the United States anytime soon. Pushing the United States out of Asia so that it would no longer worry about its neighbors counting on American military power, China's ambitions have often exceeded its grasp and unintendedly helped the United States stay in the neighborhood. During the height of China's good neighboring policy, many Asian countries speculated that they would do better by drawing close to China because an economically vibrant and diplomatically modest China became a perfect partner. But China's aggressive claims over the disputed maritime territory motivated its neighbors to realign with the United States. These countries used to ask "what we could get from the Americans in return for their military personnel and basing rights. The new question is, what will we have to give them to get them to stay? And it's all because of China."[59]

Historically, jumping on the bandwagon with a rising power was common due to potentially great gains. The most successful rising powers often attracted a great number of bandwagoners. But this has not happened with China. Surrounding by many worrying countries, China has only one ally in the neighborhood, North Korea, which is more of a liability than an asset. Pakistan is China's close partner but also more of a liability. Japan, South Korea, Vietnam, Australia, and India are all on the spectrum from cool to hostile toward China and are allies or friendly with the United States.

President Trump's failing policy in the region bestowed a huge gift on China. But China failed to take this opportunity to gain trust. Demonstrating a remarkable ability to press its expanded interests, China picked fights even amid COVID-19. Setting up two new administrative districts, China announced the naming of eighty islands, reefs, seamounts, shoals, and ridges in the South China Sea in April 2020. The last time China named the geographical features there was in 1983. Chinese ships repeatedly entered Japan's claimed territorial waters near the Diaoyu/Senkaku islands and harassed ships from Japan and Vietnam in areas they consider their EEZ.

Beijing's earlier success in shifting the geopolitical orientation of the Philippines away from Washington under President Duterte led to the announcement of the termination of the 1999 Philippine-US Visiting Forces Agreement. But Manila reversed course to scrap the Agreement in June 2020 and suspended the decision after President Joe Biden was elected because Beijing continued to maintain a stubborn position on disputed territory in the South China Sea. Pressuring the Philippines to choose between China and the United States, a fleet of about 220 Chinese maritime militia fishing vessels presented at Whitsun Reef within the Philippines's EEZ in March 2021, causing the Philippines to lodge a diplomatic protest. Although most of the vessels left in late April, the Chinese Foreign Ministry spokesman reiterated China's position that "the reef was Chinese territory."[60] Incidents like this one tremendously complicated Duterte's China-friendly approach.

Chinese and Indian troops clashed in a series of tense encounters along the disputed Himalayan border in May 2020, resulting in casualties on both sides, the most serious conflict since 1962. Indian prime minister Narendra Modi had tried for years to maintain good relations with both the United States and China. The border clash erupted with the anti-Chinese sentiment, advocating a sharp foreign policy shift for a robust US relationship because enjoying the best of both worlds was no longer possible. In the transition from nonaligned to strategic autonomy, a growing number of Indian strategists, and increasingly the Modi government, have concluded that India's strategic autonomy could be enhanced by a strategic partnership with the United States.[61] Although India has not aligned with the US, India has sought to deepen security ties with the US and its partners while building its military capacity against China with the assistance from Russia.

Driving the Philippines, Vietnam, and India to lambast its heavy-handed territorial actions, China allowed a series of disparate incidents to congeal into anti-China sentiment in its neighborhood. A leading Chinese scholar has advocated for many years to change nonalliance orthodoxy and establish a system of formal alliances.[62] Although this vision seems far-flung, many countries do not seek China's protection because of increased distrust and fear of Chinese power to their security. As a result of Xi's swaggering position, many countries in China's neighborhood have increasingly hardened their attitudes against a superpower they once considered a potential partner. China's military actions and wolf warrior diplomacy constituted a strategic blunder, sacrificing the propaganda of its contributions to regional stability and weakening its attempts to dilute US influence. China cannot win the rivalry with the United States without winning the support of its neighbors and preempting their balancing motives.

The Durability of Bipolarity

In this case, one observer predicts that the Sino-US standoff "will end only when one side defeats or exhausts the other. As of now, the smart money is on the U.S. side, which has far more wealth and military assets than China does and better prospects for future growth."63 But it is too early to predict the result of the Sino-US rivalry. While it may be a mistake to take an overconfident and bellicose approach toward many countries, China has built a broad-based and dynamic economy that's globally competitive, going far beyond the tottering command economy that defined the Soviet Union in its final years and a lopsided Soviet-style overridingly focusing on the military sector. Taking advantage of a relatively benign external environment when the United States was preoccupied with the wars in Iraq and Afghanistan, the Chinese leadership at the Sixteenth Party Congress in 2002 found an extended period of strategic opportunity to focus on economic development. The precept was validated by the Seventeenth Party Congress in 2007 and the Eighteenth Party Congress in 2012. Facing a more precarious and competitive external environment, Xi has grasped the narrowed window to catch up quickly.

The US trade war and the threat of decoupling were a wake-up call for the vulnerability of high dependency on the US market and technologies. China adopted a strategy different from the United States in the science and technology contest. The United States focused on pioneering basic research. China prioritized applications and focused on *deploying* rather than *developing* cutting-edge science capabilities because advances in science and technology were easy to access in the globalized world. It is much more expensive and riskier to invest in basic research than to obtain something already developed or close to maturity. This strategy helped China get to the end cheaply but could not let China win the science and technology race.64

In response to the US market and technology denials, Xi Jinping announced the domestic and international "Dual Circulation Strategy" (DCS), emphasizing domestic consumption as new economic driver.65 Leveraging nearly 1.4 billion consumers, DCS recalibrated the industrial policy with an emphasis on state-led growth and self-reliance to build upon the development that foreign trade and investment have become less critical to growth. Setting an urgent agenda to lessen China's dependence on the United States, Xi has pushed hard for basic science and technology investment and encouraged Chinese firms to localize key industrial products and systems because "there is no way that China can ask for or rely on buying the key and core technology from foreign countries."66 Using all the levers of industrial policy to support indigenous innovation, China moved rapidly in developing key technology sectors and sharpened their focus on the development of the US-embargoed and -controlled technologies.

To quickly close the technology gaps, China spent 2.5 percent of GDP on R&D during the Thirteenth Five Year Plan of 2016–2020, the second-largest amount globally after the United States, and launched the "Medium and Long-Term Plan for Science and Technology 2021–35" to make China a technological powerhouse. The previous plan for 2005–2020 was the basis for the Made in China 2025 industrial policy, which is barely mentioned anymore due to Western criticism. But the policy has continued apace and advanced in the new plan and worked in concert with China's other industrial policies, including the China Standards 2035 to set global standards for the next generation of technology.

Strengthening the relative integrity and autonomy of the domestic industrial chain, particularly in chokepoint (卡脖子) areas and strategic links,[67] China has become the only country in the world that owned all the industrial categories listed in the UN Industrial Classification, with 39 industrial categories, 191 intermediate categories, and 525 subcategories. The system can independently produce all industrial products from clothing and footwear to aerospace. Some technologies have progressed from "running to follow" (跟跑) to "running parallel" (并跑) and to "running to lead" (领跑).[68] The 2020 Nikkei survey of seventy-four high-tech products and services indicated that Chinese companies expanded their presence for dominance in global high-technology markets with a boost from robust domestic demand. China topped Japan and chased the United States in the number of sectors in which it took top market share.[69] Former Google CEO Eric Schmidt reveals that China is on a trajectory to overtake the United States in the rivalry for AI supremacy. China's edge begins with its big population, which affords an unparalleled pool of talent, the largest domestic market in the world, and a massive volume of data collected by companies and government in a political system that always places security before privacy.[70]

Despite the US decoupling attempts, China as the center of gravity of the world economy, consumer market, and product supplier has remained attractive to American companies and organizations. The NBA, Marriott, and others have chosen to yield to Chinese pressure over seemingly minor statements and advertisements to avoid rocking the boat and damaging their hard-won business gains and supply chain.[71] Seduced by China's growing and a massive pool of savings and liberalized elements of its financial system, Wall Street's most storied firms have embedded themselves more deeply than ever into the country.[72] Although the trade war hastened a trend toward diversification in the production chains, "Made in China" has continued a lucrative option for most investors because of China's enormous market and strong business ecosystem. It is tough for any country to match, at least initially, the high standard already set by China as a manufacturing hub, making the exodus from China cost-intensive.[73]

Profiting from the early success at getting COVID-19 under control, China had a quick economic recovery and was the only major economy to post positive GDP growth of 2.3 percent in 2020. Testifying to its robustness as a manufacturing base, the breadth of goods that it can produce and the skill of its exporters in navigating tough times, China's exports continued to jump in 2021. Policy-makers exploited this strength to tackle structural issues such as financial leverage, internet regulation, and their desire to strengthen the manufacturing base and make technology the main driver of investment.

Politically, China is not an ideologically disillusioned and exhausted power. Xi Jinping has consolidated domestic public support through the overwhelming control of information to shape the thinking of the people. While the news in the West about China is largely about repression, most Chinese do not feel so in daily life, except during the periods of COVID-related lockdown of Chinese cities. Even if one dislikes the regime, every sane Chinese person knows that it is dangerous to challenge the regime. More importantly, there is no available public imaginary of an alternative. The collapse of the regime would mean chaos. Citizens fear this alternative probably even more than they fear the regime itself.[74]

Strengthening the CCP position as a disciplined organization, Xi Jinping has relied on the party masquerading as an elite of more than ninety million members and hundreds of million government and SOE employees with vested interests in the party-state. The party's firm response to potentially existential challenges such as pro-democracy protests in Hong Kong, separatist activities in Xinjiang, and devastating coronavirus has helped solidify the support of the Chinese people. Those who complained about the party's initial coronavirus cover-up reflected more positively on their experience after they saw, through the American example, how much worse it could have been. Xi emerged stronger than ever after China's early success in containing the outbreak.

The University of California survey revealed that the average levels of Chinese trust in the government increased from 8.23 in June 2019, to 8.65 in February 2020, and 8.87 in May 2020 when the government controlled the spread of COVID. Average scores (1 to 5 Likert scale) on the question of whether they prefer living under China's political system as compared to others increased from 3.89 in June 2019 to 4.14 in February 2020, and to 4.28 in May 2020. In contrast, Chinese favorability toward the United States on a scale of 1 to 10 dropped from 5.77 in June 2019 to 4.77 in May 2020. Although the reliability of such surveys could be questioned because the Chinese government exercised extensive control over the information available to its citizens, China's relative success in controlling the coronavirus's spread and the dismal performance of the United States contributed to these results.[75]

The domestic support has given Xi confidence to announce China would never allow any force to separate the CPC from the Chinese people or counterpose the party to the Chinese people; to impose their will on China through bullying; to change China's direction of progress; or to obstruct the Chinese people's efforts to create a better life.[76] Taking the lesson that the Soviet Union collapsed because the ruling communist party wavered its ideals and conceded ground to Western liberal values, Xi leveraged China's emergence as the first major economy to return to growth after COVID-19 to strengthen his authority and doubled down on core authoritarian values to brush aside international concern about the crackdown from Xinjiang to Hong Kong and Taiwan.

Recalling the Western interference that kept China weak and divided during the century of humiliation, Xi has portrayed US policies as an attempt to impede China's rise and reinforced Chinese people's loyalty to the party. The US hostility at a time when Chinese suspicion of the United States is at an all-time high has supercharged Xi's popularity for standing up to US pressures. Celebrating the centenary of the CCP in 2021, Xi Jinping presided over the ceremony of its seventy-two years of untrammeled power.

Although China has overreached in some respects, it has not followed European imperial powers that invested heavily in overseas colonies only to have them rebel or demand their release peacefully; or expended heavily on long-term overseas conflicts with few tangible benefits like the United States did. With its disciplined hierarchy of national security priorities, China's leadership has picked its battles literally and figuratively and not truncated its rise with ruinous wars.[77] China has come to conflict with many of its neighbors. But the United States has not built an encircling Cold War-type alliance in the Indo-Pacific because China is the biggest economic partner for many of the United States' allies and partners in the region.

While China has faced immense challenges, the United States has faced no fewer challenges. Deeply rooted internal divisions hampered America's ability to confront external challenges and fueled a tendency to scapegoat China for many problems that Americans largely inflicted upon themselves. A steady drumbeat of stories appearing daily in Chinese media about mass shootings, police brutality, and urban unrest without parallel in China has made the order and predictability of the Chinese system look much better. As a result of information control and propaganda, many Chinese people have identified American democracy with mismanagement of COVID-19, a high poverty rate, inequality, and concentration of power and wealth in comparatively few hands. It was discordant that the US politicians continued pointing to China as the existential threat to democracy when mobs stormed the US Capitol to halt the constitutional process of affirming the results of the presidential election. Compared with an increasingly misfunctioning and disaggregated US version of democracy, Chinese propaganda pointed to the relative success of China as an indicator of its institutional advantage and readily portrayed the United States as chaotic and weakened.

Such propaganda was most effective when reality provided ample ammunition. Freedom House's annual survey in 2021 revealed that less than 20 percent of the world's population lived in a free country, the smallest proportion since 1995. Nearly 75 percent of the world's population lived in a country that faced a deterioration of democratic freedoms. It admitted that "democracy's defenders sustained heavy new losses in their struggle against authoritarian foes, shifting the international balance in favor of tyranny."[78] The mismanaged US withdrawal from Afghanistan reflected not only the limits of US and Western military and geopolitical power but also the inability to create effective democratic states governed by the rule of law. Afghanistan and Iraq, the two places where the United States intervened most forcefully, continued to suffer from poverty, instability, and violence.

Beijing could never dream of achieving such damage to US democracy and power as the image of the mobs storming the US Capital and the failure in Afghanistan have brought. The difficulties encountered by the third wave of democratization, the color revolutions, and the return of the Taliban as well as the rise of authoritarian and populist neo-authoritarian regimes in Europe, Latin America, and arguably the United States made it harder to sell the superiority and feasibility of liberal democracy to the Chinese people. US secretary of state Antony Blinken, therefore, went defensive when he stated that the United States would not advance democracy through costly military interventions or attempting to overthrow authoritarian regimes by force.[79] For all these reasons, many Chinese, especially the younger generation, felt fully justified in meeting US pressure with confidence and even a sense of defiant triumphalism.[80]

Now, neither side can easily put the other one down and pursue the path of power dominance. The Sino-US rivalry may hardly end in one country's collapse any time soon. While Beijing cannot expect the United States to accept its authoritarian system or replace the US power dominance in the world, neither can Washington alter Beijing's intrinsic values, change China's regime, and stop China's rise. But neither the United States nor China is willing to accept the reality to pursue shared interests. Exaggerating each other's hostility and attempting the impossible mission of building opposing alliance systems, these two powers have defined their rivalry in terms of survival versus collapse, hindering their joint pursuit of shared responsibilities on issues such as climate change, nuclear proliferation, and pandemic prevention.

Too much prosperity is at stake for political leaders in Washington and Beijing to risk a cold war, let alone a hot war. The two countries share the same planet, and their economies are stubbornly interlinked. As the two largest greenhouse emitters, the United States and China have contributed to an environment in which neither could survive if they don't work together to constrain emissions. With the rhetoric of the need for cooperation, each has pointed fingers at the other for noncooperation. Linking climate change to other issues, China has insisted that it cannot be expected to meet the same standards of radical decarbonization as richer countries because its mad dash toward national wealth and global power was still young by comparison with the West. In the United States, Republican politicians, among others, have resisted efforts to greatly reduce emissions because doing so would unfairly cost Americans and give a free ride to the Chinese.[81]

The United States and China are nuclear-armed powers and have a genuine and shared interest in keeping the rivalry within boundaries to avoid an unconstrained struggle leading to escalation and mutual destruction. Although they have declared the principles of avoiding nuclear war, they have not negotiated to avoid an arms race nor established strategic rules and effective mechanisms to manage conflicts at the embryonic stage of bipolarity to avoid the risk of accidental military frictions. As their competition escalates, the need for cooperation has grown. While a duopoly with China and the United States working in tandem is unlikely because of their competitive relationship, a large-scale confrontation is extremely costly. Cooperation between rivals may be uncomfortable but necessary. But the leaders in both countries have not yet found a way to structure and manage constructive and peaceful competition in which each nation does its best to demonstrate which country can meet the demands of their people and deliver more global public goods. The idea that countries could compete ruthlessly and cooperate intensely at the same time may sound like a contradiction. "It is natural for big powers to compete. But it is their capacity for cooperation that is the true test of statecraft, and it will determine whether humanity makes progress on global problems."[82]

From Revolutionary State to Revisionist Stakeholder

The World Order and Globalization

ALTHOUGH CHINESE LEADERS HAVE PAID special attention to the international distribution of power, they have also exploited the world order, which is composed of dominant values, rules, norms, and institutions that define the terms of global governance. Great powers have been the rule-makers who have constructed the order to conform to their values and interests. Weak states are the rule-followers. Emerging powers are often the challengers to alter regnant rules and pursue alternative values. The post–World War II order was constructed under US leadership. The newly founded PRC was excluded. Perceiving it as an instrument of the Western countries to ostracize and contain China, Mao Zedong took a revolutionary posture attempting to overthrow the order. After Deng Xiaoping opened up China to the outside world and launched economic reforms, China joined most of international economic and security institutions within the UN system. Benefiting enormously from the participation for economic growth, China gradually boosted its support to the prevailing rules and norms of the order.

As China rises to the big power status, Xi Jinping has become uneasy with the United States' dominance and has challenged the US-led order as unfair and unreasonable enough to reflect the interests and values of emerging powers like China. Rejecting the concept of the rules-based order defined by the United States, Xi has promoted his own concepts about global governance to better suit China's interests and values, grasped influence at international institutions to infuse China's principles on issues such as human rights and state sovereignty into global discourse, and used China's growing might to contest the liberal norms. Xi's challenge has raised the question of whether China is content to preserve or discontented to overhaul the post–World War II order.

The liberal view believes that current world order is open and non-discriminative, creating conditions for a rising China to advance its expanding economic and political goals. Liberal institutions could accommodate and reform illiberal states into responsible stakeholders because they would generate prosperity and therefore enhance international cooperation. Globalization and growing interdependence have increased the common stakes for China to expand cooperation with other countries. The self-interests impose their constraints on China and help ensure its emergence as a responsible stakeholder.[1]

The alarmists, however, argue that China's values are fundamentally different from that of the United States and its allies. An emerging China is ensconced in virtually every aspect of the liberal order. China has unswervingly objected to the values on which the US-led order has been built upon. At stake is the erosion of liberal international norms and institutions. The preeminent geostrategic challenge of this era is the impact that China's ascendance will have on the US-led international order. Moving quickly and adeptly to fill the vacuum left by the decline of US global leadership, the rise of Chinese power has made the world safer for authoritarian governments.[2]

Xi Jinping has indeed attempted to shape the world order according to the illiberal statist values and align it with China's authoritarian rule and equities. But China is not a revolutionary state. It is a revisionist power. Xi has demanded the reforms of the global governance that reflect the Western values and enhance US dominance. Beijing has only tactically exploited the vacuum left by the Americans and has not stepped into the breach in the way that America emerged at the sunset on the British Empire. China remains a beneficiary of the post–World War II order, has limited national capacities to provide sweeping global public goods, and failed to articulate alternative values universally accepted to reshape the order. A disgruntled and ambitious revisionist power, Beijing's demands have focused primarily on obtaining the position commensurate to its power status and making the world order more reflective of the twenty-first-century balance of power rather than replacing it.[3]

From the Revolutionary State to the Stakeholder

The post–World War II world order has been constructed primarily around the UN Charter system based on both state-centric principles and globalist aspirations. Territorial states are the sole legitimate members of the UN, perpetuating the Westphalian principles of state sovereignty, diplomatic equality, and nonintervention in the domestic jurisdiction. The UN has, however, imposed sweeping restrictions on the use of force by states through a collective security system maintained by the Security Council of five big powers. International treaties adopted by the UN such as the International Covenant on Civil and Political Rights and the Responsibility to Protect have depicted state sovereignty as contingent on fulfilling certain obligations such as not committing atrocities or pursuing weapons of mass destruction.

The functional economic institutions under the UN system, notably the Bretton Woods institutions of the World Bank, the IMF, and the General Agreement on Tariffs and Trade (GATT)/WTO have looked beyond territorially bounded nation-state system. Additional UN functional organizations have been established to regulate the behavior of states in response to emerging threats such as infectious disease, environmental degradation, and transnational crimes. Beyond the UN Charter system, the United States has created and led interstate alliances, such as NATO and Organization for Economic Co-operation and Development (OECD), to defend their collective security and economic interests and advocate the liberal values of democratic states to global dominance against the Soviet Union-led communist rivals.

Regarding the UN system as a tool of imperialist aggression and a place for their political transactions, Mao's China was a revolutionary state, proposed radical reorganization of the UN, and encouraged third world countries to support Indonesia's call for the creation of a new UN in the 1960s.[4] But China could not articulate alternative values and, with the rhetoric of anti-imperialism, expressed a preference for the Westphalian principles embodied in the "Five Principles" of mutual respect for sovereignty and territorial integrity, mutual nonaggression, noninterference in each other's internal affairs, equality and mutual benefit, and peaceful coexistence. China embraced the Westphalian principles for historical and realistic reasons. The historical memories of victimization during the century of humiliation produced a deeply rooted fear among Chinese elites about the possible erosion of sovereignty. Sovereignty principles served China as a relatively weak state to participate in international affairs on an equal footing and manage its domestic affairs free from foreign interference. Sovereignty was a sword for the Chinese government to cut down domestic dissidents and ethnic separatists and a shield to ward off external criticism of its human rights abuse.

China's zealousness over state sovereignty came when many of the originators of that concept began to move away from absolute state sovereignty and embraced transnational norms, such as humanitarian intervention. International organizations and transnational forces stood alongside sovereign states as the players in resolving many borderless problems. Globalization, in which decisions and activities in one part of the world had significant consequences for other parts of the world, created the transnational networks of functional interdependence among once distant corners of the world through trade, investment, and immigration.

Transnational norms were alien to Maoist self-reliance. China joined the UN in 1971 to seek international recognition of PRC sovereignty and regime legitimacy rather than subscribe to the transnational norms. Starting with the forceful position to convey a sense of determination and certitude on sovereignty issues, China gradually changed from minimal, selective, cautiously passive, and skeptical to embracing the UN functional institutions. China picked where it engaged and where it pushed back and joined international regimes it deemed beneficial. Deng Xiaoping placed the priority to participate in international economic institutions. China in 1980 joined the World Bank and the IMF, which "provided unique opportunities for China to learn from the experience of other countries in a professional and politically neutral international setting."[5]

Benefiting from the modern technology, management skills, and production practice in the world, China initially was neither to completely open its economy to market competition nor to insert itself into the international division of labor. It was to pursue import-substitution industrialization. China, however, traded out of import substitution after the entry into the WTO in 2001. Pursuing export-led growth to become a key nodal point in global production chains and the hub of dense global trading networks, China's ample and industrious but relatively cheap labor force helped attract foreign investment and promote exports for strong and relentless economic growth. Making a strategic distinction between the domestic market and the international one, the Chinese state protected and insulated its market while taking advantage of foreign markets and accumulated giant trade surpluses and enormous reserves of foreign currency, which provided the government with huge resources for multiple tasks. Joining the global economic institutions, China arguably became the biggest beneficiary of globalization.[6]

But China was cautious in gaining memberships in international security and human rights regimes. Before the 1970s, China took a very negative attitude toward UN peacekeeping operations (UNPKO), regarding humanitarian intervention as docile special detachments of the international gendarmerie to infringe upon individual countries' sovereignty. After entry into the UN in 1971, China's opposition became more verbal than real as Beijing opted not to participate rather than cast negative votes on authorizing resolutions. In 1981 China for the first time voted for the extension of UNPKO in Cyprus and formally requested membership of the UN Special Committee on Peacekeeping Operations.

China participated with incremental and situation-specific conditions in the UNPKO. The Chinese government in 1989 for the first time dispatched five Chinese military observers to the UN Truce Supervision Organization in the Middle East and twenty Chinese civilians as members of the UN Transitional Assistance Group to help monitor the independence process in Namibia. Establishing and expanding training programs for peacekeepers through the Office of Peacekeeping in China, Beijing dispatched its first combat forces to Mali in 2013 and sent a battalion of combat troops to a peacekeeping mission in South Sudan in 2014. China is the second-largest funder of UNPKO after the United States. Committing eight thousand troops to the UN peacekeeping standby force, roughly 20 percent of the total, China deployed peacekeepers on missions more than all the other permanent members of the Security Council combined. China's contribution to intrusive peacekeeping activities is particularly notable given its long-standing opposition to interference in other nations' domestic affairs.

China also participated in international arms control and nuclear nonproliferation regimes. Before the 1980s, China viewed these regimes as Western and particularly American ploys to constrain China, monopolize nuclear weapons, and solidify the large nuclear powers' advantages. Shifting from dismissal to selective support in the 1990s, Beijing began to gain membership to key treaties and conventions and participate in multilateral negotiations in such forums as the Conference on Disarmament in Geneva. China signed the Comprehensive Test Ban Treaty (CTBT) in 1996, the second country to do so after the United States, and placed itself under international legal constraints of nonproliferation principles.[7] After President Obama declared for the nuclear-weapon-free world and the UNSC endorsed Obama's vision, Hu Jintao welcomed the vision and called for a bolstered arms-control agenda at the UN General Assembly in 2009.[8]

Although China often abstained from votes for sanctions in UNSC, its abstentions have declined significantly. China has supported most of the votes, including the sanctions for North Korea's nuclear programs in 2006. Despite significant economic interests and investments in Libya, Beijing voted in favor of sanctions in 2011. One of the main obstacles to a global climate change agreement at the Copenhagen climate conference in 2009, China signed the Paris Climate Accord in 2016.

Beijing's changing attitudes reflected the perception of Chinese leaders in China's changing position in globalization, which represented a significant threat to state sovereignty when China was relatively weak. Rising as a big power, China could reap the benefits of globalization without undue concern over the loss of sovereignty. China's increasing prominence both allowed and obligated it to take on a flexible attitude toward the issue of sovereignty. With China's rising power status, Chinese leaders realized that participation in these regimes helped demonstrate that China was not an outcast or impediment to international efforts to maintain security. More importantly, these regimes offered tangible benefits for China, not the least of which was the prohibition of Japan, the Koreas, and Taiwan to acquire nuclear weapons. While these treaties constrained China's nuclear programs, Beijing was willing to pay the price to prevent these countries from joining the nuclear club.[9] Additionally, China's participation in activities such as UNPKO could help advance its economic interests, including export markets and resource imports.[10] In this case, Chinese leaders welcomed US deputy secretary of state Robert Zoellick's 2005 invitation to become a "responsible stakeholder" in the international system that enabled its success.

A Revisionist Power

But China is a revisionist stakeholder. Seeing "the post-1945 liberal international order as reflecting the worldview of the victorious white colonial powers that created it,"[11] Chinese leaders, from Deng Xiaoping to Xi Jinping, have never felt easy with American predominance to conform American values and power, which are intrinsically antagonistic to the principles on which the CCP regime is organized and which ostracize China as an outlier for not being a democracy.

To the relief of Chinese leaders, American promotion of liberal values has not produced global peace and prosperity and has often led to disruption and chaos. Chinese media reported that ten years after the Arab Spring in the Middle East, "while these countries threw away their original 'dictators,' they ushered in greater uncertainty and instability and experienced one of the most destructive decades of the modern era."[12] The result of the United States using force to spread democracy, symbolized by the war in Iraq and Afghanistan, was discouraging and devastating, undermining the very support for democracy and generating anti-Americanism. When the United States and its allies tried to use military forces to change the world to their liking, the UN was powerless to stop them. Blaming the United States for the fragmentation and dysfunction of the global order, Beijing warned that "the post–World War II order has quickly become disorder and is in danger to fail. World conflicts and contradictions have approached the new thresholds, leading to unpredictable and turbulent future, causing the world anxiety and leading to a global trust deficit, governance deficit, peace deficit, and development deficit."[13]

The US-led order worked well when American democracy was attractive to the rest of the world and America was willing to defend and pay for it. But American democracy is no longer shining. Many Americans are not willing to pay for the costly global leadership. Bill Clinton was elected president partially because he promised the arrival of a peace dividend after the Cold War to be invested at home. Barack Obama was elected president partially because he promised to pull the US troops from the Middle East and Afghanistan. Focusing on America first (and ultimately America only) and favoring a sovereign normative order over a liberal order, President Trump curtailed US promotion for democracy and cut US global commitments. President Biden has declared the return of US leadership. But the daunting global and domestic challenges have grown more complex. While US influence in the world is much diminished and its creditability lost, a sharply divided American society has made Biden's job harder. Facing the meteoric rise of China, the United States can hardly maintain its dominance in the world.

China has complained that the United States has followed double standards in compliance with the rules of the world order. A Chinese scholar wrote that the United States had played the role of "Leviathan" even at the expense of breaking the very rules it was supposed to uphold.[14] Since World War II, no country has done more than the United States to build international rules to guide the actions of other states. And yet, few have so resisted submitting to rules it hopes to bind others.[15] Although Washington has claimed UNCLOS as part of customary international law for its navigational and other freedoms of operation in the South China Sea, the US Congress has not ratified UNCLOS. Washington has insisted others obey the treaty rules that the United States has refused to accept. Additionally, the rule of prohibiting military force in the absence of UNSC authorization suffered major blows by the US-led NATO intervention in Kosovo in 1999 and the US-led coalition invasion of Iraq in 2003 justified by the doctrine of preemption. For Beijing, the US invasion of Iraq was illegal and foolish and wrecked the Middle East, destroyed the world order, and undermined international law.

If the United States exercises the privilege of hypocrisy and does not comply with the rules that it expects others to comply with, the post–World War II order certainly cannot work. American "exceptionalism" and the Janus-like US attitude toward international rules have set a bad example. Asserting the same great power privilege, China has mimicked US behavior by refusing to participate in and accept the ruling by the International Court of Arbitration over the territorial disputes in the South China Sea. Although China was criticized as a blatant violator of the UN convention obligations, "the US is still miles ahead of China when it comes to ignoring international law and undermining global order."[16]

Expressing China's revisionist demands forcefully by unveiling new initiatives like the AIIB and the BRI and making heterodox interpretations of UNCLOS and the South China Sea Island building campaign, Xi Jinping has vowed to show Chinese characteristics, Chinese style, and Chinese ambition and provide Chinese solutions and Chinese wisdom to the reform of the world order. As Xi's call went viral in Chinese media, the CCP Politburo devoted two collective study sessions in 2015–16 to the subject of global governance. Claiming that "the international community wants to hear China's voice and see China's solutions," Xi urges Chinese foreign policy officials to strengthen four capacities of rule-making, agenda-setting, opinion-shaping, and coordinating.[17]

Xi put forward "Two Guidances" in 2017: China should guide the international community to build a more just and reasonable new world order, and it should guide the international community to safeguard international security. A commentary in the CCP Central Party School held that Xi's "Two Guidances" were profound as they came when the Western-dominated world order was near its end.[18] In the past, Xi had called on China to merely participate in the creation of a new world order. "Xi's call on China to take leadership in improving the world order is significantly above and beyond China's leadership."[19] Foreign Minister Wang Yi used the term "leading goat" (领头羊) to describe China's role in "guiding the reform of the global governance."[20]

Presenting the Chinese vision for the reform of the world order, Xi proposed the Community of Shared Future for Mankind (CSFM) in 2013. The Chinese term (人类命运共同体) was at first translated into English as "the Community of Common Destiny for Mankind." As the term is used widely, the English translation is standardized as the CSFM because the word "destiny" implies a lack of choice along a predetermined trajectory. The phrase was written into the CCP constitution in 2017 and the state constitution in 2018. The Chinese government managed to incorporate this phrase into the resolution on the UN Commission for Social Development in 2017. The phrase was also enshrined by the UN Disarmament Council, the Human Rights Council, and the First Committee of the UN General Assembly.

The CSFM rejects Western values as universal and calls for all sociopolitical systems to be respected as equally valid, i.e., democracies are not a model superior to authoritarianism. All should peacefully coexist and not attempt to transform the others.[21] As Xi said, "Each country is unique with its history, culture and social system, and none is superior to the other." How countries organize themselves internally, along with whatever authoritarian strictures and human rights violations, just is not others' business.[22] Portraying CSFM as a relatively benign slogan that hearkens back to the five principles of peaceful coexistence to tolerate alternative governing systems, Xi's vision "is designed to appeal to those, especially developing world elites, who feel estranged, disaffected or threatened by the prospect of liberal democracy."[23]

Beijing has, therefore, rejected the concept of the "rules-based order" defined by the United States and other Western countries. For Beijing, the only set of legitimate rules is "the basic norms of international relations based on the purposes and principles of the UN Charter at the core and the international order based on international law, instead of the so-called rules formulated by a small number of countries."[24] Demonstrating the revisionist position, China has demanded reforms to carve out more space over which China can exert control as a rule-maker, expand its influence in the power hierarchy, adjust some rules in its favor, and change aspects of the order that it views as undermining its values and interests.[25]

Taking the Commanding Height

Xi's objective to reform the world order is "to position China in the commanding heights of the international competition."[26] For this purpose, Beijing has sent its very best and most talented diplomats to compete and grasp leadership positions in the UN institutions where the United States has dominated due to its predominant economic and political clout. But the US share of the world GDP has come down from about 50 percent at the end of World War II to less than 25 percent in the 2020s. China's share has reached more than 15 percent. Although the global power distribution has taken a fundamental shift, US domination has continued. For example. the United States holds the dominant voting share and veto power in the World Bank and the IMF, both headquartered in Washington, DC, and each always led by an American and a European national, respectively. These institutions could issue loans with a quid pro quo: to implement liberal reforms in line with the lenders' preferences.

The United States has been adept at encouraging and in many cases assisting China's integration into the global order but is not prepared to see China as a contender. The serious geopolitical rivalry has undercut the goal of reforming global governance as the United States clings tenaciously to its privileges. China has, therefore, demanded greater representation and voting shares. China in 2009 demanded RMB to be included in the basket of key international currencies (the dollar, euro, pound, and yen), on which the value of the IMF's Special Drawing Rights is based. The proposal was approved in 2015, paving the way for Beijing to flex its muscle in the global economy. In 2010, China proposed an increase in its voting rights from 3.994 percent to 6.390 percent to become the third-largest share-holding nation in the IMF. The reform was ratified by all other members in 2010 but stuck in the US Congress until December 2015.

Enjoying veto power as a permanent member in the UNSC, Chinese diplomats have held the position of undersecretary-general for the UN Department of Economic and Social Affairs since 2007 and taken the helm in four of fifteen UN specialized agencies since 2015: Food and Agriculture Organization (FAO), International Telecommunication Union (ITU), UN Industrial Development Organization (UNIDP), and International Civil Aviation Organization (ICAO). A Chinese delegation also chairs the Program Coordinating Board of United Nations Program on HIV/AIDS (UNAIDS) in 2020. These are elected posts, which Beijing won with a heavy dose of lobbying among member states.

The job holders in the UN organizations are meant to be politically neutral, but Chinese diplomats have used these positions to advance China's economic and political interests. The ICAO has denied Taiwan's participation as an observer since a Chinese official became secretary-general in 2015. Headed in 2006–17 by Margaret Chan, a Chinese national from Hong Kong, WHO allowed Taiwan to participate as an observer with the title "Chinese Taipei" after Beijing accepted Ma Ying-jeou was elected president in 2008. It suspended Taiwan's observer position after pro-independence president Tsai Ing-wen was elected in 2016. When China can't get one of its nationals into the leadership position, it sought someone who was considered pro-China. During the WHO director-general election in 2017, China supported Tedros Adhanom, former Ethiopian minister of health and minister of foreign affairs. The day after his electoral victory, Tedros reiterated adherence to the "One China" principle, "meaning that WHO would not invite Taiwan for participation without China's approval,"[27] leaving the impression that "WHO officials have acted like good soldiers in China's campaign to cut off Taiwan."[28]

The increase of China's leadership positions in UN agencies has raised concern about Chinese diplomatic muscle-flexing to skew UN agencies in

China's favor. The United States coordinated with its allies and blocked a Chinese official from grabbing the head position of the World Intellectual Property Organization (WIPO) in March 2020. Had China won the position, China would have taken one-third of the leadership positions of all UN specialized agencies.[29]

Outside of the UN system, China has taken initiatives to create Beijing-inspired international institutions, notably the New Development Bank (NDB) of the BRICS countries in 2014, a symbolic gesture to create a sort of IMF clone writ small toward reshaping the Western-dominated international financial architecture. BRICS established a $100 billion currency reserve to lessen dependence on the IMF. The fact that the NDB is headquartered in Shanghai is evidence of the role of China.

China also launched the AIIB in 2015, headquartered in Beijing and headed by a Chinese national. The United States tried to dissuade its allies from joining the AIIB but was caught flat-footed when the UK, France, Germany, Italy, Australia, and South Korea applied as founding members, a powerful testament to China's influence in the rule-making of international development finance. A Chinese scholar claimed that the AIIB represented China's effort to reconstruct the international rules. The Bretton Woods system as an old vehicle was tired and needed reform. The US attempts to delay the reforms caused tensions. China launched the AIIB to help reduce the tension, provide international public goods, and participate in international rule-making.[30]

The G7, comprising the United States and its six closest allies, has long been the leader in international economic affairs. But China is not included and, therefore, has promoted the G20 as an alternative to the G7. China has held BRICS leaders' meetings on the G20 sidelines to coordinate their positions there. In addition, although China has never joined the G77 of developing nations in the UN, Beijing supports the group and has formed G77+China to advance their common interests.

The Statist Value in Offensive

China's revisionist demand has been guided by the sovereignty-centered value to leave ample leeway for states to conduct themselves as they please and push back intrusive liberal values. Economically, the value is expressed in the state-capitalist industrial policy that has blended market mechanisms with state control and directed enormous capital and other resources to state-owned enterprises and state-backed national champions for global competition. China's state-capitalism is designed to benefit from market for mercantilist gain. Treating international economic institutions as the cost-effective delivery boys for market and technology, China has used subsidies to help its companies to dominate global markets and protect its domestic market with tariff and nontariff barriers and tried to have its political independence cake while eating its economic interdependence one too.[31]

On security issues, China's participation in the UNPKOs has emphasized state consent. Acknowledging the responsibility to respond to humanitarian catastrophes in certain circumstances but ensuring their limited application to reduce the instances where it might breach state sovereignty, China has demanded two essential preconditions: endorsement by the UNSC and consent by the government of the host country, the latter of which can only be omitted in the failed state situation. It makes a crucial difference to China's voting behavior if this consent has been obtained.

State sovereignty has been the core principle of the international initiatives inspired by Beijing. Agreeing not to intervene in one another's internal affairs, the SCO is used by member states to shield each other from international criticism regarding their human rights violations. The RCEP, a China-dominated free trade agreement signed in 2020, has allowed members the flexibility to choose commitments they signed up to so that their state sovereignty would be protected. Jealous national rivalry, historic grievances, and mutual suspicion among many member states complicated its negotiation agenda. Dissatisfied with the slow progress, the more progressive countries in the region launched the Trans-Pacific Partnership (TPP) negotiations in 2014 and signed the Comprehensive and Progressive Trans-Pacific Partnership (CPTPP) in 2018.

For many decades, China was on the defensive side of its statist value. But Beijing has become increasingly aggressive. Rejecting the US open and decentralized multistakeholder model to tear down geopolitical barriers, Beijing insisted on the concept of "cyberspace sovereignty" to regulate its cyberspace and patrol online discourse. Building its independent internet with Chinese technology, standards, and infrastructure, China has drawn the world's largest group of internet users away from interconnected commons. Living under

Cyber-totalitarianism

cyber-totalitarianism, Chinese people no longer have the same access to the World Wide Web as those in other countries.

Assuming leadership positions in liberal international institutions such as UNHRC, China has also tried to reshape the norms of international human rights governance in an illiberal direction. Having ratified five of the six core human rights treaties, China was elected as a member state of the UN Commission on Human Rights in 1986 and has remained as a member state in its replacement, the UNHRC, since 2006. While the UN Universal Declaration of Human Rights emphasizes universal civic and political rights, Beijing has claimed that the priority of human rights protection in developing countries is different from the priority in the West. Deconstructing the notion of universal human rights with a concept that economic and social rights are more fundamental than civil and political rights, Beijing insists that the proper balance is to be determined by the state according to national circumstances.[32] *Chinese conception of human rights*

Regularly using its veto in the UNSC to block international interventions to end human rights abuses in authoritarian states, and attacking the Western countries for their records on human rights, China's insistence on development rights is attractive to many developing countries where leaders see the paramount task as the eradication of poverty rather than protection of civil rights. Becoming the leader of a block of countries sympathetic to the statist values, China has often put Western democracies in the voting minority in the UNHRC. China's resolutions passed in UNHRC since its first one in 2017 have treated human rights as primarily the rights of states and did not have any balancing reference to the rights of individuals, the role of civil society, or the mandate of UNHRC to monitor abuses. Taking the individual out of the picture, China framed human rights as purely a matter for states, focusing solely on intergovernmental cooperation. While rights organizations saw these resolutions as tools to make the world a safer place for autocrats, the Chinese government has celebrated the setback to the West's monopoly on human rights discourse and the advance of the so-called "people-centered development for human rights."[33] *insistence on development rights*

China's position was strengthened significantly after the US withdrawal from the UNHRC in 2018. At the forty-fourth UNHRC in July 2020, while twenty-seven countries supported a UK-led joint statement criticizing China's

actions in Xinjiang and Hong Kong, a statement by forty-six countries led by
Belarus dismissed the criticism on Xinjiang. Another statement presented by
Cuba and backed by fifty-three countries defended China's action in Hong
Kong. China was appointed on April 1, 2020, to the influential UNHRC panel
of five nations in charge of picking UN human rights mandate-holders who
investigate, monitor, and report on specific country situations or thematic
issues in the world, and helped vet candidates for critical posts and decide
the appointments.[34]

Standing vigilant on state sovereignty, Xi Jinping has emerged as a champion for statist globalization amid the mounting backlash against liberal globalization, which, by promoting free markets, open borders, and transnational
institutions, not only created a disparity in income distribution and regional
development and the concentration of wealth in a few rich countries and
multilateral corporations, but also challenged traditional beliefs and institutions such as state sovereignty, nationalism, and authoritarianism. Xi Jinping
attended the World Economic Forum in Davos in 2017 and positioned China
as the torchbearer of globalization. But the globalization that China has advocated is different from globalization promoted by Western countries. According to one Chinese scholar, each country must make a choice of globalization
that is good for itself. China has promoted economic globalization supported
by political multipolarity and multiculturalism while West-led globalization
emphasizes political democratization, economic privatization, and universal-
ization of liberal values.[35]

China's statist values gained ground amid COVID-19 because the growing connectedness brought about by liberal globalization made the world
vulnerable to the pandemic. The virus transmitted farther, faster, and deeper
than ever. Lives and livelihoods were destroyed but the government was
powerless to help them. A *Nature* article found that "as the new coronavirus
marches around the globe, countries with escalating outbreaks are eager to
learn whether China's extreme lockdowns were responsible for bringing the
crisis there under control."[36] Many countries, including liberal democracies,
began to enhance the state authorities to fight the borderless virus, including closing national borders, imposing stringent quarantines, and erecting
barriers to the movement of people. National borders became tighter and
protectionism became the norm rather than the exception. America's borders

with Canada and Mexico remained open during World War II but were closed this time.

While China was criticized for its contact-tracing systems that facilitated surveillance of its citizenry, some democratic countries used surveillance technologies to enforce quarantines and track people's contacts with the virus, putting a new twist on the tradeoff among privacy, accountability, and safety. Although the adoption of invasive health surveillance systems could have astounding consequences, including a vast increase in state authority and a host of opportunities for serious abuses, these contact-tracing models became attractive as countries struggled to balance concerns about public health and the economy. Many countries adopted smartphone app-tracking technology for contact tracing among populations and emphasized the collective good over personal freedoms.

Although the United States benefited enormously from having a large open global economy, it followed China to unleash a fresh wave of industrial policy. The Trump administration stepped into the marketplace to slap tariffs on foreign products and enhanced the state's role to rebuild a national economy instead of a global one. Hillary Clinton, a quintessential globalist, urged the incoming Biden administration to adopt "ambitious industrial policies," impose stronger "Buy American" provisions, restore sensitive supply chains, and expand strategic stockpiles of essential goods.[37] The first executive orders issued by President Biden included buy-American provisions and a review of gaps in domestic manufacturing and supply chains dominated by or run through nations unfriendly or unstable. The report released by the White House in June 2021 recommended building a resilient supply chain and increasing the levels of redundancy. One observer commented that "resilient supply chain" is a catchy new term in old-school industrial policy themes and can come across as a call for trade protectionism.[38]

As globalization has intensified economic, informational, technological, and other forms of competition, what used to be a self-regulating economic process is turned into a political instrument for suppressing business competitors in the name of national security. The US government tightened the restrictions by barring US companies from supplying Chinese competitors with products manufactured with American technology. Using industrial policy and exercising intrusive control to selectively support American companies and protect them in the global competition, the United States moved away from a proponent of state-led growth and adopted some elements of the Chinese model of state capitalism instead of China adopting the US model.

Still a Beneficiary

China is a revisionist rather than a revolutionary state because its power ambition has been checked by its self-interests and limited soft and hard power. China has enjoyed rapid catch-up growth and become the world's second-largest economy in a largely liberal economic environment maintained by the US-led world order. Relying on global trade for continued growth, it is not in China's interest to see the development of rival protectionist blocks. Signing and staying in the Paris Climate Change Accord, China shares an interest with other countries in reducing emissions because China's economic growth at all costs has produced the unsustainable pollution of air, water, and soil and the advance of climate change, making itself a victim.

In the security areas, US treaty alliances, troops on the ground, and naval presence in the Western Pacific have maintained regional peace and facilitated flourishing commerce. Residing in a neighborhood with complicated power competition and historical animosities, China must be measured and judicious. "The corollary of the decline of the West is not the rise of Asia. It is the erosion of Asia, at least as an idea, as rivalries within geographic Asia overtake the notion of regional cohesion that once bound these countries together."[39] America's long-standing alliances and its role as guarantor of regional security enabled it to paper over these differences and coax and cajole fractious or recalcitrant Asian countries into certain agreements. With the uncertainty of the US role, old animosities have broken through again.

China has expressed concern over the US alliances with Japan and South Korea. But the alliances are parts of the regional security architecture that has prevented the remilitarization of Japan and protected South Korea from attack by North Korea. Without the US nuclear umbrella, Japan and South Korea would have developed nuclear weapons a long time ago, prompting other countries to develop their nuclear weapons. The prospect of the regional security picture would be a nightmare for China. A Chinese scholar, therefore, admitted that "Chinese policymakers and analysts should not believe their jingoistic rhetoric about the US in decline. Even if it's true, a weak America isn't good news for China."[40] Despite its increasing military strength, China is unable to take over the US security role in the Asia-Pacific because, unlike the United States, it has competing territorial claims with several countries and can hardly play a role of stability. The US role as offshore balancer has helped to maintain stability.

China has launched new multilateral initiatives such as AIIB and BRI to leverage its revisionist power. But these initiatives can resemble that of its many antecedents to languish in obscurity if they do not follow the standards of established institutions and seek integration into the world order. The AIIB has become a successful example of integration but the BRI has failed to do so and may eventually languish.

Founded in June 2015, the AIIB has become the second-largest multilateral development institution in the world after the World Bank. Beijing originally envisioned it as a China-dominated agency. A diverse group of fifty-seven founding members, however, came at a cost to China's intention. While Beijing initially planned to contribute 50 percent of the bank's shares to have absolute veto power over issues that require a simple majority, it scaled back to 26.06 percent to have veto power only on issues that require a supermajority. One of China's most controversial goals, promoting exports to absorb excess capacity, disappeared because it ran the risk of encouraging antidumping lawsuits and undermining the AIIB's legitimacy and credibility. With memberships from many Western countries, the AIIB has responded to the pressure of the active and vocal NGO communities badgering it to impose restrictions on environmental and human rights concerns. Becoming a party to the Agreement for Mutual Enforcement of Debarment Decisions (AMEDD), the AIIB voluntarily recognizes the debarment list of entities and individuals sanctioned under AMEDD. About thirty Chinese companies, mostly SOEs, are on the debarment list of the multilateral development banks.[41]

Modeling the governance structure and standards in line with the practice of the established institutions on the disclosure, procurement, debt sustainability, and oversight mechanism, the AIIB engaged former officials from other multilateral institutions and crafted policies, pledged "lean, clean, and green," and emphasized transparency, accountability, openness, and independence. Additionally, drawing from China's cultural and historical background, the AIIB has adopted a new set of norms and practices with an emphasis on

efficiency and more equal participation of the borrowing countries.[42] Despite
the border clash between China and India, AIIB president Jin Liqun assured in
June 2021 that "bilateral contradictions among member States should not be
dragged into multilateral institutions." He revealed that India was the largest
borrower and accounted for 25 percent of the total loans of AIIB.[43]

The World Bank, IMF, and ADB have, therefore, welcomed and cooper-
ated with the AIIB as a complement to the Bretton Woods institutions to
increase the overall capacity of multilateral development funds. The ADB
announced in May 2015 the first joint financing with the AIIB. The World
Bank signed the first cofinancing framework agreement with the AIIB in
April 2016. As a result, the United States' principal concern, that the AIIB
would undermine existing international lenders and their standards, is mis-
placed. Praising the success of the AIIB, one Singapore scholar suggested that
"a race to the top in corporate governance, and not a race to the bottom, it
does not matter whether America wins, or China wins. Either way, we will
see an improvement in the standards of managing institutions of global
governance."[44] One Japanese scholar agreed that the competition between
America and China in this case produced a better multilateral institution
good for the world.[45]

The key reason that China adapted its positions from its original design is
the participation of many democracies that balanced, influenced, and checked
China's ambitions. China was willing to make the AIIB a multilateral institution also because of the sobering experiences of China's bilateral lending
institutions such as the China Development Bank and the Export-Import
Bank of China. Through these agencies, Beijing became the largest global
provider of development finance. But the attempt to use lending to buy political allegiance and secure imports of natural resources and export markets
became a cropper. It transpired that opaque lending to unstable regimes was
no guarantee of either a commercial or a geopolitical return. The AIIB must
reassure borrowers that it is not just old Chinese lending practices in new
clothes.[46]

But the quality of the governance under Beijing's aegis at the AIIB has not
provided the impetus for the BRI. The Chinese government's strong backing
helped get many projects up and running faster than might have happened
otherwise. Without thorough risk and cost-benefit analysis, many financially

[handwritten marginal notes: "claims ab BRI", "of debt-trap diplomacy?", "mistakes?"]

dubious schemes got the imprimatur of BRI. China's politically motivated investments in excess infrastructure, "zombie" firms, vanity projects, and tens of billions in bad loans were notoriously unproductive. Some critics of the BRI assumed that the failures were intentional, part of "debt-trap diplomacy" to ensnare other countries in debt and seize strategic assets from them. But everyone was a loser in these investments. While the nations in debt could be beholden to Chinese largesse, it was up to the borrowers to decide if they wanted to have the deals at significant long-term costs. Falling victim to Beijing's snare and lending missteps, China has often quietly reined in its ambitions as they faced pressure to reschedule or forgive debts owed by poorer country partners.[47]

Leaders in some developing countries chose Chinese loans because the money did not come with fiscal discipline and Beijing did not observe best governance practices around transparency, labor, and the environment. Relying on nontransparent deals, many BRI projects met the appetites of corrupt leaders. Corruption was a serious problem in China, but even worse in many developing countries. Working with corrupt foreign leaders seeking mutual advantage, the BRI involved Chinese dealmakers and corrupted foreign leaders seeking to advance authoritarian rule. This symbiosis of Chinese-foreign government interests represented a strong asset in China's growing international influence as the world is full of corrupted regimes.[48]

Western countries have been reluctant to join the BRI because it has not met the acceptable standards of openness, fairness, and transparency. Taking a cautious approach, the leaders of all major Western countries skipped the lavish 2017 Forum for International Cooperation in Beijing hosted by Xi. Representatives from EU countries did not sign on the statement prepared by the Chinese government until a series of concerns they had raised were incorporated into the text.[49] As a result, despite the heavy-handed push by President Xi personally, BRI has come off to a slow start. Unprecedented excitement from the Chinese government has often stood in contrast to the reticence and anxiety of Chinese companies and their foreign partners. Relying heavily on lumbering and inefficient SOEs, China has yet to bring international corporations into the initiative. Without adapting and embracing the norms of the prevailing order, the BRI could become a huge white elephant leaving an enormous amount of wasted resources strewn along its path.

The Baggage of Pax-Sinica

China's revisionist ambition is also checked by its inability to articulate universally accepted values to substitute the values underpinning the current world order. The CSFM has drawn heavily from traditional Chinese culture of harmony based upon the hierarchical order in which Chinese civilization was superior and others inferior, instead of promoting freedom and equality. It is, therefore, often confused with the *tianxia* order that is normatively and practically at odds with modern diplomacy. If the tianxia order prevails, all countries along China's margins must show fealty, deference, and allegiance to Beijing in the modern version of the tributary system. It would prevail only in an environment where China is the largest and most powerful state, its civilization superiority is widely acknowledged, and in the absence of a competing paradigm. None of these factors characterize today's world. There are several powerful states, several claims to have superior civilizations of their own, and there are alternative organizing principles for the parts of the totality.[50]

China has limited experience in modern diplomacy as an equal player. For most of its history, China was either an imperial power dominating its neighborhood or a victim of Western imperialism. Thinking of foreign relations in terms of cultural and power superiority or victimization, Chinese leaders have yet been socialized with the modern statecraft to calibrate their interests against those of others on equal footing and through compromise. Claiming to strive for a shared future, Beijing cannot be sure that every country wishes to share the same future with China. With its idiosyncratic mix of canonical Marxist-Leninism, socialism "with Chinese characteristics," nationalism, and sprinkled elements of Confucianism, the CCP's belief system has not helped convince other countries that its leadership would contribute to a better world rather than just a more powerful and autocratic China.

China has targeted primarily authoritarian states and hoped that its preferred norms and values would be more readily accepted by the regimes estranged, disaffected, or threatened by the prospect of liberal democracy. The expansion of Chinese authoritarianism has, therefore, caused concerns in Western countries about China's attempt to reshape the world order drawing from a "macrocosm of its domestic political order" and emphasizing "privileges rather than rights, power rather than law, fealty rather than alliance."[51] The tensions surrounding China's rise, therefore, do not simply result from clashing economic and geopolitical interests but also from the distrust that often afflicts relationships between democratic and authoritarian regimes. Observing the gulf between Beijing's political values and those of the democracies, one analyst worried that "the U.S. democratic system is facing one of the great stress tests of its history without any certainty about the outcome."[52]

But the liberal value of open and participatory politics with restraint in authority remains appealing to many countries. Chinese traditional value is less appealing because of its emphasis on steep power hierarchies. Chinese scholars admit that although China's rise may help expand the influence of its traditional values of benevolence and righteousness, liberalism still wields greater influence than any other ideology. China is short of international discursive power. The traditional Chinese system is not universal and cannot automatically transform into modern discursive power. China might one day overtake the United States in the size of its economy but may never overtake US influence and leadership in the world.[53]

While China's insistence on sovereignty principles looked attractive to some countries where intense interventionism by the United States often ended in chaos and chronic instability, many of China's neighbors have viewed China's power aspiration with wary eyes that its imperial past can produce an undue pressure on its leaders to restore the old Chinese order. Despite Beijing's efforts to assure that China's rise would be peaceful and its leadership benign, China's assertive moves in the territorial disputes with its neighbors were more like hard realism than benevolent suzerainty. Given choices, most countries still would rather navigate a world order where the United States is dominant. A regional *Pax Sinica* is not desirable for China's neighbors.

For all their differences with Washington and periodic resentment of its policies, many countries invested more confidence in the United States than in China because US leadership was underlined by the aspirations of universal values. Despite China's ambition and many successes, it is still the United States, with all its hypocrisy and failures, that captivates audiences in most global dramas. The liberal values that have undergirded US power continue to drive global trends. The global marches in solidarity with Black Americans and oppressed minorities in their own countries loathing the hypocrisy and brutality of many American politicians show that many nations still identify with aspects of America's pluralistic society and values. They asked Americans to live up to American ideals.[54]

China has invested enormous resources for extensive public diplomacy to boost its positive image. Opening more than five hundred Confucius Institutes across the world, China's state media has aggressively expanded the overseas operations to push the Chinese culture and language and tell China's stories to foster an environment more conducive to CCP values and interests. But this mission is almost impossible. Other than the difficulty to convince the world to adopt Chinese as its working language, the CCP rhetoric is hardly resonated with those who object to authoritarianism. China's story cannot have any meaningful effect on mainstream international opinion until the Chinese media and people can criticize their leaders without fear.

Beijing was forced to abandon its Confucius Institute brand after a global backlash and switched to a new look as a "language exchange and cooperation center" in 2020. The image-building backfired because the world's perception of China was shaped more by Chinese narratives and behaviors than by its propaganda. Leadership is not just about taking the titles in UN organizations but also about individuals who can confidently and freely express their opinions. Chinese representatives in international organizations are reluctant to speak off the script and can hardly express their independent views because of fear of getting into trouble at home.[55] No amount of CCP rhetoric in international fora fully makes up for the appeal of how a government treats its people.

Beijing's overreliance on economic prowess reveals the shortage of normative power. When China started economic reform in the early 1980s, Deng Xiaoping convinced the Chinese people that "economic development is the hard truth" to move the country away from the ideological intoxication of Mao's times. But taking it to foreign policy is an oversimplification. Money is only one of the many important tools to achieve and preserve power. Influence does not simply derive from a country's coffers. Money cannot buy loyalty. Economic ties are hardly enough to build strong trust between countries, especially those with conflicting security interests. Building common identity and value is equally important. Beijing's authoritarian system at home and hierarchical perception abroad has not inspired many countries to share its values. Unable to construct shared values, China has changed nothing of substance in the world order. Until China builds a strong and free civil society at home and develops values that appeal universally, it misses one of the core qualifications to shape the world order.

The Strategic Overdraft

China's projected powerful and confident image tends to cover up the reality of serious internal and external challenges. Internally, other than the environment, corruption, and other problems, China's one-child policy has hastened and exacerbated the slowdown in birth rates, leading to the aging crisis. The costs of social security and caring for the elderly are increasing. The level of inequality is also worrying. China stopped publicizing its Gini coefficient is 2014. But Premier Li Keqiang admitted in 2020 that over six hundred million people still live on a monthly income of less than 1,000 yuan (US$140).[56] To reduce social-economic inequality, Xi Jinping has called for "common prosperity" to improve people's sense of gain, happiness, and security. One of the major initiatives is to clamp down on private sectors, disorderly expansion of capital and platform monopolies, and services deemed to have exacerbated inequalities. The stated purpose was to protect the economy from financial instability and data abuse and nail down the party's control and bring the private sector to political heel. But they are hardly compatible with the productivity growth and innovation on which China's lofty economic ambition depended. They reflected more of the political concerns about regime security than social inequality, a reminder of the arbitrary nature of decision-making in Xi's China, which could impede productivity growth and keep China in the fabled middle-income trap.[57]

The most acute internal challenge is the possible succession crisis. Making himself the president for life and thus far refusing to nominate his successor, Xi has ensured that nobody would challenge him at the expense of the process that had seen three peaceful transfers of power. This concentration of power in the hands of one man makes China politically stable for now, but it means uncertainty for the future and possible political turmoil if anything happens to Xi. Xi has now faced the strongman's dilemma: how to set up a successor without creating a rival and how to leave a government able to outlast the leader without making themselves redundant and vulnerable. As Mao, Stalin, and many other dictators have shown, a life-long term in office tends to magnify the worst characteristics of an autocrat: leaving office is perilous. Since the Cold War's end, most governments headed by strongmen collapsed after their rulers departed.[58] The longer Xi remains in charge, the more the political structure will conform to his personality, whims, and network of clients, coming at a cost to China's long-term stability. If Xi clings to power well into old age, the political system will likely calcify into structures of rigid repression, which creates its own set of challenges.[59]

Externally, China's expanding access to foreign markets and technology, and other low-hanging fruit during the decades of catch-up growth, have exhausted. Export-led growth has hit the limits. In response, Xi Jinping has pushed for the internal circulation that relies on the domestic market and technology for continued growth. But China has decimated its natural endowments and imported more food and energy than any other nation, and China's manufacturing sectors have still relied heavily on external markets and technology. It needs unfettered access to global markets, resources, and technology to reach the critical breakthrough. China is instead facing its harshest external environment since the Mao era and shut out by the United States and others in many sectors. Its authoritarian turn and diplomatic provocations have led to comprehensive strategies to hedge against China across the board among Western countries and China's neighbors.

As the structural headwinds of foreign protectionism, resource depletion, and domestic problems take their toll, China is brittle and vulnerable to domestic instability. When China's economy was booming, Presidents Jiang and Hu loosened political controls. Although China has never enjoyed the current level of international reach, economic strength, and military might, Xi has repeatedly warned party members of the potential for a Soviet-style collapse and rushed to tighten the screws on dissent, construct a vast techno-security state to stop any kind of unrest, assert new controls over private business, and vastly strengthen the party's prerogatives and power. Xi is in a hurry because he might have only a short window before China's demographic decline, economic downturn, and domestic upheavals threaten to reduce the historic possibility currently presented to him by China's technological advance, geopolitical gains, and his current hold on power.[60] Xi's sense of insecurity was also expressed in his campaign to promote the cult of personality. Although no obvious challenges or factional opposition was emerging, he has continued to purge or cow any senior leaders who dared to disobey his order, drag his foot and lacked enthusiasm for his course.

China is a fragile rising power, and it is not clear if it could become the first authoritarian regime to avoid the middle-income trap that had kept many emerging economies from entering the club of high-income countries. No large economy has made the transition without liberalizing. Riding the waves of economic globalization, Deng Xiaoping's market-oriented economic reform and political liberalization brought about rapid economic growth. But Xi has maximized ideological and totalitarian control over society and economy. The already dominant position of the party-state has been strengthened further. These policies may eventually come at war with the market efficiency. In a society where nobody under forty has experienced national economic setbacks, the Chinese government warned that "young people cannot take the fast track of national development for grant" and should prepare for "long-term hardship." Individuals should share the responsibility for the hardship.[61] The warning underscored the insecurity of the regime.

After COVID-19 started, Xi Jinping was stung by widespread criticism of his initial handling of the pandemic. The state played by the book to squarely blame local officials, and it fired the party chief in Hubei Province and the mayor of Wuhan, along with some health officials. But Chinese social media were still overwhelmed by messages demanding accountability and transparency. Many Chinese saw the initial cover-up by Wuhan and Hubei officials not just as a bad performance by local officials, but also symptomatic of the weakness of the Chinese system in which bureaucrats feared revealing bad news. The death of Dr. Li Wenliang in Wuhan came to be martyrdom for the cause of free speech. Although democracy was under attack, its basic ideas still inspired Chinese liberal intellectuals. The government's mismanagement provided an opportunity for liberals—such as Tsinghua University professor Xu Zhangrun, private entrepreneur Ren Zhiqiang, and activist Xu Zhiyong—to publicly denounce Xi's autocracy and demand freedom of speech. While the domestic criticisms were rapidly silenced, some foreign organizations filed lawsuits demanding Chinese compensation for their damages because the pandemic started in China. Although it was unlikely that they could make China legally responsible, Chinese leaders were nervous about the scapegoating caused by the geopolitics and strategic rivalries.

COVID-frame game

Zero-covid policy

After the virus was contained, Beijing started to reshape the narrative by blaming foreigners to deflect criticism and shore up its legitimacy. Depicting Beijing as a heroic leader against the pandemic, Chinese propagandists whitewashed China's culpability in the initial cover-up and suppression of early warnings. The failure of Trump's efforts in controlling the spread of the virus in the United States and his blame on China extended the creditability to the Chinese propaganda. While most Western states bungled their initial response, they developed highly effective vaccines to help the population return to normal lives. But China continued pursuing a zero-COVID strategy inside the world's tightest border controls. Some medical professionals, eyeing other countries, suggested China stop pursuing the strategy and learn to live with the virus. Xi was furious and criticized them as becoming "lax and numbed" in fighting the virus.[62]

In response to new surges of COVID in spring 2022, China imposed draconian measures to lockdown several major cities, including the important industrial and trade hubs, Shanghai and Shenzhen. The Shanghai lockdown caused struggles to obtain daily necessities like food and medical care and triggered outrage and rare protests from residents. Despite mounting public frustration, Xi doubled down on the zero-COVID approach because he did not want to take any chance to loosen the totalitarian control leading up to his crowning as ruler for life at the CCP's 20th Congress in the fall of the year. The zero-COVID approach paid heavy economic prices. Shanghai and Shenzhen are China's economic dynamos and accounted for over 20 percent of China's total trade. Overall, cities under lockdown accounted for nearly one-quarter of the total population and over 40 percent of China's economic output. The zero-Covid policy winded an economy which just had been bouncing back from the pandemic.[63]

This development revealed that although the Chinese state was strong in mobilizing public sentiment, ensuring compliance, and constructing infrastructure, it was considerably less capable of optimizing between containment and mitigation measures. Relentlessly reminding citizens of the country's success and showing the superiority of its system compared to liberal democracy made it impossible to contemplate living with COVID-19. The state was also concerned about the lack of capacity in overcrowded and under-resourced public hospitals. Living with COVID-19 requires capabilities that authoritarian governments usually lack: respect for diversity and debate in policy choices and an active citizenry that has the means to check and question the state.[64]

Realizing the formidable and daunting internal and external challenges, a Beijing strategist had long warned about "the risk of strategic overdraft," or making international promises and setting strategic objectives beyond the reach of China's national strength.[65] Another Chinese scholar confirmed that "China does not have the comprehensive national strength to change the global order led by the US and other Western countries."[66] One Chinese scholar went further, saying that China "will never seek to lead the current global system let alone invent, and pay for, a new one to run the world."[67]

With finite resources, China has been reluctant to take on international obligations where Chinese interests are not immediately at stake. Beijing has not matched its rhetoric to mount serious responses to global problems. For example, China as the largest polluter has emitted more carbon from burning fossil fuels than the United States and Europe combined, contributing to a quarter of the world's greenhouse gas emissions. Proposing the principle of "common but differentiated responsibilities," China once pressed the United States and other developed countries to commit financial pledges to poorer nations while China and other developing countries only need to do what they could in the light of their national conditions.[68] Although Xi pledged in September 2020 to achieve carbon neutrality by 2060, China's growth has faced a serious challenge in the struggle to reduce the dependency on coal, steel, cement, aluminum, and petrochemical products.

Portraying itself as leading a massive international aid operation, China's "mask diplomacy" and "vaccine diplomacy" amid COVID-19 were not contributing to the global public goods, which implies for free and for everyone. A good portion of Chinese medical supplies and vaccines were not free. Manufacturing half of the world's medical masks, China hoarded its supply and banned exports after the outbreak and started shipping these supplies only after it contained the spread at home.[69] Playing mask and vaccine diplomacy as leverage to compete with the United States, China's insistence on public gratitude and praise by recipients undercut much of the goodwill, taking the wind out of China's sails. In addition, many recipients rejected Chinese supplies as substandard. Finland's prime minister fired the head of the country's emergency supply agency for spending millions of euros on defective Chinese face masks, which fed distrust of Chinese product safety standards.[70]

China's propaganda catered primarily to the domestic audience and often framed the assistance in ways that highlight the benefit to China. This propaganda perpetuated the perception that China's aid targeted at furthering China's strategic objectives and interests. Bolstering its influence in the countries struggling to secure enough vaccines, China rolled vaccines into its BRI framework and enhanced its position of preferential access to jabs alongside infrastructure and connectivity projects. According to one study in April 2021, of the fifty-six countries to which China pledged vaccines, all but one were participants in BRI.[71] Beijing also used vaccine diplomacy to push back against criticism of its human rights record. Ukraine briefly joined a statement by over forty countries at the UNHRC in June 2021, urging China to allow immediate access for independent observers to Xinjiang, but pulled its name off the list after China warned Kyiv that they would block a planned shipment of vaccines to Ukraine unless it did so.[72]

As a result, some European leaders criticized China for eschewing its aid as the "battle of narratives" and "politics of generosity." Public attention in Africa was riveted by stories of widespread discrimination and racism against African ex-pats in China in general and in Guangzhou in particular, triggering for the first time a group of African ambassadors in Beijing to write a letter to the Chinese foreign minister protesting the way their nationals were treated in China.[73]

Although the pandemic hurt the United States' prestige and compounded concerns about American competence and reliability, China was not able to demonstrate its enlightened, positive leadership; instead it was gripped by nationalist impulses to confront the United States in a rhetorical battle to see who could be more sanctimonious in blaming the other. The aggressiveness and incoherence of narratives from both China and the United States poisoned the environment to tackle the shared challenge. Instead of an opportunity to mitigate their growing tensions, COVID-19 added fuel to the simmering US-China tension and turned the global public health crisis into a battleground of power rivalry, preventing the UNSC from passing a resolution to declare COVID-19 an international security threat. China held the rotating presidency of the UNSC in March 2020 and insisted that the UNSC involvement in

[margin handwritten notes:] politics of generosity

effect of covid on Sino-US relations

COVID-19 was unwarranted mission creep because the matter did not fall within the UNSC's "geopolitical" ambit.[74]

Washington also dragged its feet by demanding that any resolution specify the Chinese origins of the coronavirus. The Chinese blasted Washington for politicizing the outbreak.[75] Estonia, a rotating member of the UNSC, proposed a statement on March 24, expressing growing concern that the unprecedented extent of the COVID-19 outbreak constituted a threat to international peace and security. China rejected the draft because it included a phrase that all countries show "full transparency" in their reporting on the outbreak. China interpreted it as a veiled attack on their lack of transparency in the initial outbreak and blocked the statement to avoid embarrassment.[76]

Beijing's handling of the crisis eroded trust just when it had a chance to win it. Although Western governments were faulted for mismanaging the pandemic or failing to galvanize an international response, China's standing was not much better. All countries advance their interests. It is not wrong that China does so rigorously and vigorously. But China has used the rhetoric of reforming global governance to advance its interests. Touting its gawky "community of shared future for mankind," Beijing has yet to demonstrate the willingness to align and in some cases subordinate China's narrow interests to the greater global good.

Conclusion

The Mandate of Heaven?
China's Quest and Peril

THIS FAMOUS QUOTE—"CHINA is a sleeping lion in Asia. Let China Sleep, for when she wakes, she will shake the world"—has been attributed to Napoleon Bonaparte about three hundred years ago. Whether or not spoken by Napoleon, it sounds increasingly prescient. According to one count, Napoleon wanted to keep China asleep because China's existentialism posed a global threat to other nations, a threat foresaw in its population and potential to global power and recognition when its resources were annexed. So, let China remain unconscious toward its social, political, and economic development; let it remain blinded by its complacency; let China never realize its global potential; let China never become the envy of other nations; let China be enslaved and highly dependent on other nations.[1] But the sleeping lion has awakened in the twenty-first century and roars back to the center of the world stage it occupied through most of human history, and it is retaking the mandate of heaven.

The Quest for Security, Prosperity, and Power

During the time of Napoleon Bonaparte, China's rulers remained blinded by their illusion of *tianxia*, everything under heaven. But their tianxia was soon broken up. China endured a century of subjugation after the defeats in the

[handwritten: Mao's FP full of revolutionary rhetoric]

Opium Wars. In the search for national independence, security, wealth, and power, the CCP established the PRC and declared that Chinese people were standing up. Mao's foreign policy was filled with revolutionary rhetoric. But a deep sense of insecurity pervaded among Chinese leaders as the newly founded People's Republic was besieged by hostile imperialist powers. Fighting wars with both superpowers—the United States and the Soviet Union—to keep the wolves away from the door, Mao maneuvered between the two superpowers. He allied with the Soviet Union against US imperialism but rejected the junior-brother position under the Soviet Union. Asserting China's national interests even at the cost of the Sino-Soviet split, he made an alignment with the United States to reduce Soviet threats. Mao's revolutionary diplomacy was flexible and incongruent with China's power and his strategic visions.

Deng Xiaoping moderated the revolutionary rhetoric and shifted foreign policy priority to create a peaceful and stable external environment so that China could focus on economic development. He emphasized China's integration into the global economy while maintaining an independent policy position. In response to the isolation after the Cold War, Deng formulated low-profile policy guidance to bide for China's time and laid the economic foundation for China's take-off in the twenty-first century. After China's rising power sparked anxieties in many countries, including the complacent and myopic Western countries, Jiang Zemin and Hu Jintao followed the course set by Deng Xiaoping to emphasize China's peaceful intention.

Believing that China's time has finally arrived, Xi Jinping has reset the course of foreign policy to resume big power status and make the Middle Kingdom the envy of other nations. Flexing the muscle to dominate its enlarged periphery as a pathway for global preeminence, China has expanded its security perimeter to push the United States out of its neighborhood and made uncompromising claims in the territorial disputes with its neighbors. China's assertive behavior is widely seen as a litmus test of China's big power aspirations. Translating its wealth into a strong posture to restore its historical centrality, China's growing preponderance and willingness to back up its interests through coercion raised the question of whether China wanted a neo-tributary system, and it has given a nasty foretaste of what the world would be like if Beijing attains global mastery.

[handwritten, right margin: Xi has reset Chinese FP]

The Intended and Unintended Consequences

These transformational leaders have created the domestic ideational environment in which Chinese people don't just dream to be a big power but believe China deserves to be one. Their quest for security, prosperity, and power to rule under heaven has, therefore, gained support from the Chinese people. The collective memories of China's millennial history of greatness have harbored Chinese people and their leaders a strong sense of entitlement for the natural progress of China to the position of dominant power in the region. A sense of "victimization" generated from the memories of humiliation has made it particularly difficult for Chinese leaders to render compromises in conflicts with foreign countries when China becomes powerful. Motivated by the conviction that China has been denied the rightful place, Xi Jinping has focused much of his foreign policy agenda on overcoming the legacy of China's unjust treatment by foreign powers, setting a nineteenth-century agenda for the twenty-first century.

Following the agenda, Xi Jinping is determined to recapture lost territories—Taiwan is now on the top of the list—and secure its peripheral areas critical to the security of the core. Although it was impractical for China to have the region as its exclusive sphere of influence during the twentieth century when China was too weak to exert real influence on the neighborhood, a powerful China in the twenty-first century is determined to maximize its security, reestablish its geopolitical and cultural centrality in the neighborhood.

Framing China's reemergence from the prism of the rise and fall of dynasties and empires, Xi Jinping is confident in the inevitable rise of China and the decline of the United States. Comparing America to China's Ming dynasty, which crumbled in the 1600s under the weight of corruption, insurrections, and Manchu invasions, China is aimed to break through a ring of geopolitical hostility and dominate Asia, like the Manchu armies who swept over the Asian steppes and crushed the Ming rulers.[2] Adding to the tumult, Chinese scholars warned that a decadent America, stretched to the breaking point by its global commitments and weary of its superpower burdens, would give way to the more focused, organized, and motivated up-and-comer, China.[3] Drumming up triumphalism, a clip from state broadcaster China Central Television went viral with this question: "After 5,000 years of trials and tribulations, what kind of battle have the Chinese not been through?"[4]

[handwritten marginalia] Xi has a 19m agenda for the 21st century for winning support from Chinese ppl

[handwritten annotation: historical victim narratives + Sino-centric mentality = patriotism]

The mixture of historical victim narratives and Sino-centric mentality has empowered Chinese nationalism. Xi Jinping's patriotic education campaign has made Chinese nationalism more assertive than affirmative, producing xenophobia toward ruthless and exploitative foreign powers. Relying on assertive nationalism to boast the big power diplomacy is risky. It could lead China to overestimate its strengths and misjudge how far it can push other countries. It could also encourage the tendency to exaggerate the hostility and threats from the evil "others" and put pressure on the government to take proactive or even preemptive actions.[5]

Amid the devastation of World War II, US secretary of state Cordell Hull looked backward at the path to ruin and said that "nationalism ran riot between the last war and this war, defeated all attempts to carry out indispensable measures of international economic and political action, encouraged and facilitated the rise of dictators, and drove the world straight toward the present war."[6] Seething at humiliations inflicted by Western powers and restoring the imperial glory, China's quest for the mandate to rule under heaven has encouraged and facilitated the rise of dictators and combative patriots.

With their authoritarian power, transformational leaders have restructured policy-making institutions to support their foreign policy priorities. Mao Zedong relied upon his lieutenant Zhou Enlai to tightly control and discipline the foreign policy bureaucracy for his revolutionary diplomacy; Deng Xiaoping decentralized policy-making authority to accommodate the increasingly diversified bureaucratic and societal interests for his developmental diplomacy; Xi Jinping has recentralized power to enhance his supreme leadership as the domestic foundation to establish China's big power authority and credibility overseas.[7]

Loyalty is now the critical measure for officials' performance assessment. No one dares to say anything contrary to Xi even if the instructions from him make no sense or are confusing. This development has prevented his colleagues from counseling against the possible mistakes they anticipated or discovered, a vicious circle that may increase the possibility of intended or unintended consequences of foreign operations and actions of no return. For example, a good number of elites had long realized there was a serious problem in China's approach toward the United States. The momentum was, however, so strong that the moderate and more rational voices were difficult to be heard or acted upon at the top level of policy-making. The emerging Sino-US rivalry has essentially become a match of overcoming the internal challenge as much as overwhelming the other side.

Xi's decision-making ability is hindered by the information provided by many stakeholders competing for his limited attention. Given how many policies Xi involves himself in, officials must come up with creative ways to get his attention.[8] With the plethora of increasing actors and interests, although each player represents only a fraction of China's broad national interests, each sees itself as the most important representative of the whole picture. The MFA represents China's strategic interests; the MOC promotes economic interests; the CLD advocates the CCP ideological line; the PLA defends China's sovereignty and overseas interests; the oil companies ensure China's energy security; local governments expand their foreign economic and cultural links; netizens uphold China's dignity; and so on. When this is combined with the bureaucratic instinct of ensuring enough resources for one's agency, conflations of interest can emerge. For example, the PLA is prone to exaggerate the tensions over maritime interests to ensure enough funding for new vessels and aircraft. In doing so, it is likely to find a natural ally in the national oil companies aspiring to explore resources in contested waters.

Heading up many LSGs and consolidating many visible expressions of power could not change the imperfect foreign-policy-making and implementation in a country as vast and complex as China is. The foreign policy process could have flaws in each step: the collection and analysis of information, the selection and summary of policy recommendations, and the decision-making. Xi's top-level design and leadership style of micromanagement has made it more hazardous for Beijing's opaque bureaucratic agencies to provide him with objective information. With a large number of incomplete suggestions, the foreign policy process could become incoherent. The chance of mistakes has increased. So much can go wrong that must be reversed later.

For example, Xi promised China's carbon emissions would peak around 2030 and reach net zero before 2060 at the 2020 United Nations General Assembly. Some local officials, unsure how far to push Xi's promise, aggressively phased out coal-mining operations and abruptly ordered some factories to close temporarily in summer 2021. The factory shutdowns and electrical-power cuts hit global supply chains. Social media lit up with images of cars driving on dark roads and families trapped in stopped elevators. After emergency meetings in September 2021, Xi reversed course and encouraged more coal production.[9]

Personalizing foreign-policy-making, Xi Jinping has minimized the opportunities for his wrong decisions to be corrected—now a top concern is his threat of subjugating Taiwan by force, which has often been compared with Vladimir Putin's miscalculated and badly executed invasion of Ukraine. Making decisions in an information bubble, Putin took Russia into a poorly thought-out war with extremely severe consequences for his country. Overconfident in his own singular understanding of the situation and surrounded by those who cling to the dictator and are afraid to speak the truth to power, Xi's power grab may be as dangerous as Putin's. Operating on the cardinal principle of tyranny—It is better to be feared than loved—Xi has succeeded in denying the Chinese people the truth and stoking aggressive nationalism. The overriding force of personal ambition and nationalistic pressures can shape the calculations of Xi's decision-making in isolation and sycophancy. He may decide to use force whether China is ready or not, but nobody in the Chinese system would tell the truth and stop him.

no one willing to challenge Xi

The Uncertain Future

While Xi Jinping has been successful in shaping the domestic ideational and institutional environment, his big power ambition is ultimately conditioned by China's relative power position, particularly the power balance with the United States. Although China is catching up quickly, the United States remains the most powerful country in the world. As the two largest economies, the Sino-US rivalry determines China's international future. China may dominate the world, make rules, and subordinate others to its rule if it overtakes US power. This scenario cannot be ruled out. China's rise of economic, political, and military power in recent decades has been faster than any other nations in history. Washington has never faced a rival like China, which is competitive in various realms.

More importantly, US power has been in relative decline and its resilience has been seriously tested. The United States produced nearly half the world's GDP after World War II, one-quarter at the end of the Cold War, and only one-seventh in 2021.[10] As the deeply divided society and uncompromising infights have hampered the functional democracy, the overly aggressive and economically unsustainable expansionism abroad after 9/11 has worsened domestic conditions, leading to unrest and issues that are often neglected. The wars in the Middle East have siphoned off trillions of dollars needed to keep its physical infrastructure competitive to those of China and crippled US statecraft by defunding nonmilitary means to advance American interests. The dismal withdrawal from Afghanistan could prelude the inability of the United States to build and marshal alliances and engage in another far-off conflict with China.

But this scenario is not inevitable. People have claimed the decline of the United States for decades but recanted their predictions many times. Although the United States has gone through many dramatic moments and crises after World War II, it has boasted a superior continuity and a formidable ability to overcome critical phases because of the benefit of regularly electing new leaders to correct course. China doesn't have that luxury. If the party fails to keep delivering, it could be gone. One prominent Chinese scholar admits that although the United States' problems are obvious, its strength "lies in its diversity, its culture of innovation, and the resilience of its civil society—and those attributes remain unchanged. Many countries might be frustrated by Washington's hypocrisy, dysfunction, and flagging leadership, but few genuinely wish to see the United States depart from their region and leave behind a power vacuum."[11]

Neither China's undeniable successes nor America's decline is inevitable. China's triumphant claim that the United States is no longer qualified to speak from the position of strength could become a "Sputnik moment," as when America was awakened by the Soviet Union's launch of the first satellite into space and became the first nation to send a man to the moon. The awakening may help reverse America's complacency and make China a full-spectrum peer competitor to a response proportionate to the challenge.[12]

Although the "Sputnik moment" is not guaranteed, China has faced no less internal and external challenges to match the US power anytime soon. By most of the power indicators, the world is only roughly and loosely bipolar. The existence of multiple and independent powers such as the EU, Russia, India, and Japan has further complicated the power balance. Even the most hawkish Chinese scholar had to admit that "the world structure has changed from one superpower, many great powers (一超多强), to two superpowers, many great powers (两超多强)."[13] Other than Russia, China has not won over any other big powers to confront the United States.

Far from the position to dislodge American power even in its neighborhood, hegemony is "unnecessary to secure China's interests and not something to be particularly wished for because pursuing global hegemony would be counterproductive and destabilizing in ways that would not be conducive to China's interests or its security."[14] Juggling the array of internal and external challenges requires nothing short of adroit diplomatic engagement to ameliorate the tensions between China and the United States and continue the self-strengthening before even talking about the goal of overtaking the US global hegemony. It is certainly prudent for officials in Beijing to assure that "China does not want to replace U.S. dominance in the world."[15]

More importantly, China lacks soft power to inspire followers. Xi Jinping describes three big barriers that China must overcome before rising to the center of the world stage: "if you are backward, you will be beaten up (挨打), if you are poor, you will starve (挨饿), if you lose the right to speak (失语), you will be scolded (挨骂)." He told his colleagues that China had overcome the first two barriers but not yet the third one. China must work hard to take back the narratives.[16]

The CCP has derived legitimacy at home primarily from economic development and nationalist credentials. But it cannot overcome the "scolded" problem abroad unless it overcomes its authoritarianism and demonstrates respect for individual rights. China has resented US dominance in the world order and attempted to foist its norms and practices onto those who desired formal relations with the Middle Kingdom. But China has not articulated universally accepted values. Rejecting human rights, freedom, and democracy as universal values, the Chinese traditional tianxia hierarchy cannot substitute the liberal values to reshape the world order.

Although US global leadership has been seriously damaged, China has not developed the capacity to step up and take global leadership. Both the United States and China are distracted by internal and external tensions to provide global leadership. The world is in danger of moving toward the jungle of anarchy, disorder, and power vacuum, where it is everyone for themselves, might make right, the strong do what they can, and the weak suffer what they must. China's failure to provide global leadership at a time of need could result in a Kindleberger Trap in which the failure of the then rising United States to assume Great Britain's function as the lead global stabilizer was a key factor in the global economic chaos that erupted in 1929.[17] A power vacuum could be a more dangerous scenario than hegemony.

danger of power vacuum

Notes

Introduction

1. John A. Hobson, *Imperialism* (London: Allen and Unwin, 1948); Adam Tooze, "Why there is no solution to our age of crisis without China," *New Statesman*, July 21, 2021, https://www.newstatesman.com/international/places/2021/07/why-there-no-solution-our-age-crisis-without-china.

2. John Mearsheimer, *The Tragedy of Great Power Politics* (New York: Norton, 2001); Graham Allison, *Destined for War: Can American and China Escape Thucydides' Trap?* (Boston: Houghton Muffin Harcourt, 2017); Andrew Nathan and Andrew Scobell, *China's Search for Security* (New York: Columbia University Press, 2012); Øystein Tunsjø, *The Return of Bipolarity in World Politics: China, the United States, and Geostructural Realism* (New York City: Columbia University Press, 2018); Thomas J. Christensen, *The China Challenge: Shaping the Choices of a Rising Power* (New York: W.W. Norton, 2016); Kori Schake, "How International Hegemony Changes Hands," *Cato Unbound*, March 5, 2018, https://www.cato-unbound.org/2018/03/05/kori-schake/how-international-hegemony-changes-hands; John Mearsheimer, "The Inevitable Rivalry: America, China, and the Tragedy of Great-Power Politics," *Foreign Affairs*, November/December 2021, https://www.foreignaffairs.com/articles/china/2021-10-19/inevitable-rivalry-cold-war.

3. Robert Jervis, for example, categorically argues that leaders don't matter. Although Presidents Bill Clinton, George W. Bush, and Barrack Obama had different outlooks on the world, their foreign policies demonstrated clear continuities due to common structural incentives. Baohui Zhang argues that President Obama shifted the United States' China policy from a defensive toward an offensive realist posture. The Trump

and Biden administrations continued the approach because of the same realist logic to preserve the US position amid profound power shifts. Robert Jervis, "Do Leaders Matter and How Would We Know?," *Security Studies* 22, no. 2 (2013): 153–79; Baohui Zhang, "From Defensive toward Offensive Realism: Strategic Competition and Continuities in the United States' China Policy," *Journal of Contemporary China* 31, no. 137 (2022).

4. Randall L. Schweller, "Domestic Structure and Preventive War: Are Democracies More Pacific?," *World Politics* 44, no. 2 (1992): 235–69; T. Clifton Morgan and Kenneth N. Bickers, "Domestic Discontent and the External Use of Force," *Journal of Conflict Resolution* 36, no. 1 (1992): 25–52; Douglas Lemke and William Reed, "Regime Types and Status Quo Evaluations: Power Transition Theory and the Democratic Peace," *International Interactions* 22, no. 2 (1996): 143–64; Brett Ashley Leeds, and David R. Davis, "Domestic Political Vulnerability and International Disputes," *Journal of Conflict Resolution* 41, no. 6 (1997): 814–34; Mark Peceny, Caroline C. Beer, and Shannon Sanchez-Terry, "Dictatorial Peace?," *American Political Science Review,* 96.01 (2002); Milan W. Svolik, *The Politics of Authoritarian Rule* (Cambridge: Cambridge University Press, 2012); Knarik Gasparyan, "The Man and the System: How Leadership Changes Affect Foreign Policymaking in Authoritarian States," Eurasian Research and Analysis Institute, November 14, 2014, https://erainstitute.org/the-man-and-the-system-how-leadership-changes-affect-foreign-policymaking-in-authoritarian-states/.

5. Kenneth G. Lieberthal and Micel Oksenberg, *Policy Making in China: Leaders, Structures, and Processes* (Princeton, NJ: Princeton University Press, 1988); Kenneth G. Lieberthal and David M. Lampton, eds., *Bureaucracy, Politics, and Decision Making in Post-Mao China* (Berkeley: University of California Press, 1992); David M. Lampton, *The Making of Chinese Foreign and Security Policy* (Stanford: Stanford University Press, 2001); Kingsley Edney, Stanley Rosen, and Ying Zhu, eds., *Soft Power Chinese Characteristics: China's Campaign for Hearts and Minds* (London: Routledge: 2020); Hoo Tiang Boon, *China's Global Identity: Considering the Responsibilities of Great Power* (Washington, DC: Georgetown University Press, 2018); Ben Wang, ed., *Chinese Visions of World Order, Tianxia, Culture, and World Politics* (Durham, NC: Duke University Press, 2017).

6. Quansheng Zhao, *Interpreting Chinese Foreign Policy: The Micro-Macro Linkage Approach* (Oxford University Press, 1996); Lowell Dittmer, *China's Asia* (Lanham, MD: Rowman & Littlefield Publishers, 2018); Robert G. Sutter, *Foreign Relations of the PRC: Legacies and Constraints of China's International Politics since 1949* (Lanham, MD: Rowman & Littlefield Publishers, 2013); Robert G. Sutter, *Chinese Foreign Relations: Power and Policy since the Cold War* (Lanham, MD: Rowman & Littlefield Publishers, 2016); Alexander Lukin, *China and Russia: The New Rapprochement* (Cambridge, UK: Polity Press, 2018); Amitai Etzioni, *Avoiding War with China: Two Nations, One World* (Charlottesville: University of Virginia Press, 2017); Eric Hyer, *The Pragmatic Dragon: China's Grand Strategy and Boundary Settlements* (Vancouver: UBC Press,

2015); David Shambaugh, *China Goes Global: The Partial Power* (Oxford, UK: Oxford University Press, 2013); Cris Ogden, *China and India: Asia's Emergent Great Powers* (Cambridge, UK: Polity Press, 2017); James Reardon-Anderson, ed., *The Red Star & the Crescent* (Oxford, UK: Oxford University Press, 2018); Deborah Brautigan, *Will Africa Feed China?* (Oxford, UK: Oxford University Press, 2015); Rhys Jenkins, *How China Is Reshaping the Global Economy: Development Impacts in Africa and Latin America* (Oxford, UK: Oxford University Press, 2019); Nicola Horsburgh, *China & Global Nuclear Order: From Engagement to Active Engagement* (Oxford, UK: Oxford University Press, 2015); Gordon G. Chang, *The Great US-China Tech War* (Jackson, TN: Encounter Books, 2020); Robert Ross and Jo Inge Bekkevold, *China in the Era of Xi Jinping* (Washington, DC: Georgetown University Press, 2016).

7. David Chambaugh, *China's Leaders: From Mao to Now* (Cambridge, UK: Polity Press, 2021), 1.

8. Harold Sprout and Margaret Sprout, *The Ecological Perspective on Human Affairs with Special Reference to International Politics* (Princeton, NJ: Princeton, NJ: Princeton University Press, 1965); Robert Jervis, *Perception and Misperception in International Politics* (Princeton, NJ: Princeton University Press 1976); Maryann E. Gallagher and Susan H. Allen, "Presidential Personality: Not Just a Nuisance," *Foreign Policy Analysis* 10, no. 1 (2014): 1–21; Margaret G. Hermann and Thomas Preston, "Presidents, Advisers, and Foreign Policy: The Effects of Leadership Style on Executive Arrangements." *Political Psychology* 15, no. 1 (1994): 75–96; Margaret G. Hermann, "Explaining Foreign Policy Behavior Using the Personal Characteristics of Political Leaders," *International Studies Quarterly* 24, no. 1 (1980): 7–46; Alexander L. George, *Bridging the Gap: Theory and Practice in Foreign Policy* (Washington, DC: United States Institute of Peace Press, 1993).

9. Weixing Hu, "Xi Jinping's 'Major Country Diplomacy': The Role of Leadership in Foreign Policy Transformation," *Journal of Contemporary China* 28, no. 115 (2019).

10. 刘胜向 [Liu Shengxiang], "中国外交周期与外交转型" [China's diplomatic cycles and diplomatic transformation], 现代国际关系 [Contemporary international relations], no. 1 (2010): 49.

11. Joseph Nye Jr., *Presidential Leadership and the Creation of the American Era* (Princeton, NJ: Princeton University Press, 2013); James MacGregor Burns, *Leadership* (New York: Harper & Row, 1978).

12. 谭乃彰 [Tan Naizhang], "毛泽东有关时代问题的理论" [Mao Zedong's theories on the era], *Global Perspective*, February 11, 2008, http://www.mzdbl.cn/gushi/lilun2/shidai.html.

13. Li Zhisui, *The Private Life of Chairman Mao* (New York: Random House, 1994), 118.

14. Kuisong Yang Yafeng Xia, "Vacillating between Revolution and Détente: Mao's Changing Psyche and Policy toward the United States, 1969–1976," *Diplomatic History* 34, no. 2 (April 2010): 395–423.

15. Deng Xiaoping, "The Present Situation and the Tasks Before Us," in *Selected Works of Deng Xiaoping, 1975–1982* (Beijing: Foreign Language Press, 1983), 224–58.

16. Deng Xiaoping, "Opening Speech at the Twelfth National Congress of the Chinese Communist Party," in *Selected Works*, 396.

17. Qingmin Zhang, "Towards an Integrated Theory of Chinese Foreign Policy: Bringing Leadership Personality Back In," *Journal of Contemporary China* 23, no. 89 (September 2014).

18. Frederick C. Teiwes, "Normal Politics with Chinese Characteristics," *China Journal* no. 45 (January 2001): 74.

19. This quote is from Li Shenzhi, former director of the Institute of American Studies at Chinese Academy of Social Science, who accompanied Deng's visit to the US in 1979. Onboard the airplane, he asked Deng, "Why should we attach so much importance to the relationship with the United States?" Deng replied: "Looking back over the past few decades, all countries that have good relations with the United States have become rich." But Chinese official media have never published this quote. The first article that quoted this sentence was "Mourning for Mr. Li Shenzhi" by Li Yu in the self-printed book *Missing Li Shenzhi* [怀念李慎之], compiled and printed by his friend after Li Shenzhi's death in 2003, vol. 2, 393, https://blog.sciencenet.cn/blog-415-398202.html.

20. 黄华 [Huang Hua], 亲历与见闻：黄华回忆录 [Personal experiences: The memoir] (Beijing: World Knowledge Press, 2007), 209.

21. Joseph Torigian, "Elite Politics and Foreign policy in China from Mao to Deng," Brookings Institution, January 22, 2019, https://www.brookings.edu/articles/elite-politics-and-foreign-policy-in-china-from-mao-to-xi/.

22. 陈有为 [Chen Youwei], 天安门事件后中国与美国外交内幕 [Inside story of China's diplomatic relations with the US after the Tiananmen incident] (Taipei: Zhongzheng Books, 1999), 100.

23. 胡鞍钢 [Angang Hu], 中國集體领导体制 [The system of collective leadership in China] (Beijing: China Renmin University Press, 2013).

24. Yun Sun, "China's National Security Decision-Making: Processes and Challenges," Brookings Institution, Center for Northeast Asian Policy Studies, May 2013, http://www.brookings.edu/research/papers/2013/05/chinese-national-security-decision-making-sun.

25. Quansheng Zhao, "Domestic Factors of Chinese Foreign Policy: From Vertical to Horizontal Authoritarianism," Annuals of the American Academy of Political and Social Science, January 1992, https://journals.sagepub.com/doi/abs/10.1177/0002716292519001012.

26. "Xi Vows Peaceful Development While Not Waiving Legitimate Rights," Xinhua, January 29, 2013, http://en.people.cn/90785/8113230.html.

27. Sangkuk Lee, "An Institutional Analysis of Xi Jinping's Centralization of Power," *Journal of Contemporary China* 26, no. 105 (2017); Nimrod Baranovitch, "A Strong

Leader for a Time of Crisis: Xi Jinping's Strongman Politics as a Collective Response to Regime Weakness," *Journal of Contemporary China* 30, no. 128 (March 2021).

28. Minxin Pei, "Rewriting the Rules of the Chinese Party-State: Xi's Progress in Reinvigorating the CCP," *China Leadership Monitor*, June 1, 2019, https://www.prcleader.org/peiclm60?utm_campaign=0e8d2bf3-7669-4cb1-b447-cc162ffdffd7&utm_source=so.

29. Phillip Charlier, "Xi Jinping Awkwardly Takes Praise for His 'Toilet Revolution' Policy," *Taiwan English News*, March 9, 2021, https://taiwanenglishnews.com/xi-jinping-awkwardly-takes-praise-for-his-toilet-revolution-policy/; Amber Wang, "Xi Jinping Tells China's Writers and Artists to 'Practice Morality and Decency,'" *South China Morning Post*, December 15, 2021, https://www.scmp.com/news/china/politics/article/3159720/xi-jinping-tells-chinas-writers-and-artists-practise-morality.

30. Josh Chin, "Xi Jinping's Leadership Style: Micromanagement That Leaves Underlings Scrambling," *Wall Street Journal*, December 15, 2021, https://www.wsj.com/articles/xi-jinpings-leadership-style-micromanagement-that-leaves-underlings-scrambling-11639582426

31. Zhimin Lin, "Xi Jinping's 'Major Country Diplomacy': The Impacts of China's Growing Capacity," *Journal of Contemporary China* 28, no. 115 (2019).

32. Andrew J. Nathan and Boshu Zhang, "A Shared Future for Mankind: Rhetoric and Reality in Chinese Foreign Policy under Xi Jinping," *Journal of Contemporary China* 31, no. 133 (January 2022).

33. Neil Thomas, "China Overtakes America in Presidential Diplomacy," *Interpreter*, June 9, 2021, https://www.lowyinstitute.org/the-interpreter/china-overtakes-america-presidential-diplomacy.

34. "习近平抗疫"云外交"彰显大国担当" [Xi Jinping's 'cloud diplomacy' in the fight against the pandemic demonstrates the responsibility of a major power], Xinhua, December 29, 2021, https://china.chinadaily.com.cn/a/202112/29/WS61cc08b73107be4979ffa72.html.

35. Yi Wang, "The Backward Will Be Beaten: Historical Lesson, Security, and Nationalism in China," *Journal of Contemporary China* 26, no. 129 (November 2020).

36. Graham T. Allison, *Essence of Decision: Explaining the Cuban Missile Crisis* (Boston: Little, Brown, 1971); Graham T. Allison and Morton H. Halperin, 'Bureaucratic Politics: a Paradigm and Some Policy Implications,' in *Theory and Policy in International Relations*, ed. Raymond Tanter and Richard H. Ullman (Princeton, NJ: Princeton University Press, 1972), 40–79; Klaus Brummer And Thies Cameron, "The Contested Selection of National Role Conceptions." *Foreign Policy Analysis* 11 (2014): 1–21.

Chapter I

1. 毛泽东 [Mao Zedong], "美帝国主义是纸老虎" [American imperialists are paper tigers],毛泽东选集 [Selected works of Mao Zedong] (People's Press, 1977), 5:289–92.

2. Colin D. Campbell and Gordon C. Tullock, "Hyperinflation in China, 1937–49," *Journal of Political Economy* 62, no. 3 (1954): 237.

3. Vladimir Dedjier, *The Battle Stalin Lost: Memoirs of Yugoslavia, 1948–1953* (New York: Viking Press, 1971), 68.

4. 朱钟立 [Zhu Zhongli], "王稼祥外交生涯宗忆" [Reminiscence of Wang Jiaxiang's diplomatic career], Diplomatic History Research Office of the Chinese Ministry of Foreign Affairs, 当代中国使节外交生涯 [Contemporary Chinese ambassadors' diplomatic careers] (Beijing: World Knowledge Press, 1995), 16–17.

5. 刘晓 [Liu Xiao], 出使苏联八年 [Eight years as ambassador to the Soviet Union] (Beijing: Chinese Communist Party History Publishing House, 1986), 4–5.

6. Alfred D. Low, *The Sino-Soviet Confrontation Since Mao Zedong: Dispute, Detonate, or Conflict* (New York: Columbia University Press, 1987), 3.

7. He Di, "The Most Respected Enemy: Mao Zedong's Perception of the United States," in *Toward a History of Communist Foreign Relations: 1920s–1960s*, ed. Michale H. Hunt and Niu Jun (Washington, DC: Woodrow Wilson International Center for Scholars, 1989), 28.

8. Zi Zhongyun, "The Clash of Ideas: Ideology and Sino-US Relations," *Journal of Contemporary China* 6, no. 16 (fall 1997): 545.

9. 周恩来一九四六年谈判文选 [Selected works of Zhou Enlai's negotiations in 1946] (Beijing: Central Literature Press, 1996), 92–93.

10. Yu-ming Shaw, "John Leighton Stuart and U.S.-Chinese Communist Rapprochement in 1949: Was There Another 'Lost Chance in China?,'" *China Quarterly* no. 89 (March 1982): 74–96.

11. Mao Zedong, "Cast Away Illusions, Prepare for Struggle," *Selected Works of Mao Zedong*, vol. 4 (Beijing: Foreign Language Press, 1969), 425–32.

12. Liu Ji, "Making the Right Choices in Twenty‑First Century Sino‑American Relations," *Journal of Contemporary China* 7, no. 17 (Spring 1998): 92.

13. Thomas Christensen, *Useful Adversaries: Grand Strategy, Domestic Mobilization, and Sino-American Conflict, 1947–1958* (Princeton, NJ: Princeton University Press, 1996), 138–40.

14. 陶文钊 [Tao Wenzhao], 中美关系史, *1949–1972* [The history of Sino-US relations, 1949–1972] (Shanghai: Shanghai People's Press, 1999), 11.

15. 毛泽东 [Mao Zedong], "在中国共产党七届二中全会上的报告, 1949年3月5日," [Report to the Second Plenum of the CCP Seventh Central Committee, March 5, 1949], 毛泽东选集 [Selected works of Mao Zedong] (Beijing: People's Press), vol. 4, 1325.

16. Chen Jian, *China's Road to the Korean War: The Making of Sino-American Confrontation* (New York: Columbia University Press, 1994), 38–43.

17. 师哲 [Shi Zhe], "跟随毛主席访问苏联" [With Chairman Mao on a visit to the Soviet Union], 人物 [Persons], May 1988, 8–10.

18. Mao Zedong, "On the People's Democratic Dictatorship," in *Selected Works*, 4:415.

19. 朱钟丽 [Zhu Zhongli], "王稼祥外交生涯" [Diplomatic career of Wang Jiaxiang], in *Diplomatic History Research Office of Chinese Ministry of Foreign Affairs*, 当代中国外交使节外交生涯 [Ambassadors' diplomatic lives of contemporary China] (Beijing: World Knowledge Press, 1995), 1–33.

20. 周恩来 [Zhou Enlai], "中苏条约签订后的国际形势与外交任务" [International situation and diplomatic tasks after the signing of the Sino-Soviet treaty], 周恩来文选 [Selected diplomatic papers of Zhou Enlai] (Beijing: Central Literatures Press, 1990), 11–17.

21. 毛泽东在中央人民政府政务院第六次会议的讲话 [Mao Zedong's address to the sixth session of the Central People's Government Council], April 1, 1950, 建国以来毛泽东文稿 [Mao Zedong manuscripts since the founding of the PRC] (Beijing: Central Literatures Press, 1987), vol. 1, 291.

22. Rosemary Foot, *The Wrong War: American Policy and the Dimensions of the Korean Conflict, 1950–1953* (Ithaca, NY: Cornell University Press, 1985), 101; Tang Tsou, *America's Failure in China, 1941–1950* (Chicago: University of Chicago Press, 1963), 555–56.

23. Nikita Khrushchev, *Khrushchev Remembers* (Boston: Little, Brown, 1970), 367–69.

24. He Di, "Most Respected Enemy," 35.

25. Zhihua Shen and Yafeng Xia, *Mao and the Sino-Soviet Partnership, 1945–1959, a New History* (Lanham, MD: Lexington Books, 2015), 70–71.

26. 沈志华 [Shen Zhihua], 最后的天朝], 毛泽东], 金日成与中朝关系 [The last dynasty: Mao Zedong, Kim Il-sung, and Sino-North Korean relations] (Hong Kong: Chinese University Press, 2018), 205.

27. John Lewis Gaddis, "Korea in American Politics, Strategy and Diplomacy, 1945–1950," in *The Origins of the Cold War in Asia*, ed. Yonosuke Nagai and Akira Iriye (New York: Columbia University Press, 1977), 281.

28. Myung Hyun Cho, *Korea and the Major Powers* (Seoul, Korea: Research Center for Peace and Unification of Korea, 1989), 192.

29. James I. Matray, "Dean Acheson's Press Club Speech Reexamined," *Journal of Conflict Studies* 22, no. 1 (Spring 2002): 28.

30. Alexander L. George and Richard Smoke, *Deterrence in American Foreign Policy: Theory and Practice* (New York: Columbia University Press, 1959), 164.

31. He Di, "Most Respected Enemy," 35.

32. 毛泽东曾三次召见邓华：面授朝鲜作战机宜 [Mao Zedong summoned Deng Hua three times: face-to-face teaching on Korean War strategy], *PLA Daily*, January 20, 2014, http://history.sina.com.cn/bk/jgcqs/2014-01-20/113280605.shtml.

33. 薄一波 [Bo Yibo], 若干重大事件的决策与回顾 [Memoir about the decisions on some major issues] (CCP Central Party School Press, 1997), vol. 1, 43.

34. 齐德学 [Qi Dexue], "关于抗美援朝战争的几个问题" [Some issues about the war of resisting American and assisting Korea], 中共党史研究 [CCP party history studies], no. 1 (1998): 75–76.

35. John Wilson Lewis and Xue Litai, *China Builds the Bomb* (Stanford, CA: Stanford University Press, 1988), 8.

36. Son Daekwon, "Domestic Instability as a Key Factor Shaping China's Decision to Enter the Korean War," *China Journal* no. 83 (January 2020), https://www.journals.uchicago.edu/doi/full/10.1086/705539.

37. 军事科学院军事历史研究部 [Military history research department of the Chinese Military Academy], 中国人民志愿军抗美援朝战史 [Battle history of Chinese people's volunteers in the war of resisting America and assisting Korea] (Beijing: Military Science Press, 1992), 9–11.

38. 周恩来 [Zhou Enlai], "抗美援朝保卫和平" [Resisting America, assisting Korea, and defending peace], 周恩来外交文选 [Selected diplomatic works of Zhou Enlai] (Beijing: Central Literatures Press, 1990), 31.

39. Chinese Ministry of Foreign Affairs, *Diplomacy of Contemporary China* (Hong Kong: New Horizon Press, 1990), 46.

40. 军事科学院军事历史研究部 [Military history research department of the Chinese Military Academy], 中国人民志愿军抗美援朝战史 [Battle history of Chinese people's volunteers in the war of resisting America and assisting Korea], 3.

41. 师哲[Shi Zhe], 在历史巨人身边, 师哲回忆录 [With the historical giants: Shi Zhe memoirs] (Beijing: Central Literatures Press, 1992), 495–99.

42. 李健 [Li Jian], 钓鱼台国事风云 [The wind and cloud of state affairs in Tiaoyutai] (Taiyuan: Taiyai Literatures Press, 1995), vol. 2, 538–39.

43. Harry Truman, *Years of Trial and Hope* (Garden City, NY: Doubleday & Co., 1956), 378–80.

44. US Senate Committees on Armed Services and Foreign Relations, *Military Situation in the Far East* (Washington, DC: US Government Printing Office (1951), 731–32.

45. Zhihua Shen and Yafeng Xia, *Mao and the Sino-Soviet Partnership, 1945–1959* (Lanham, MD: Lexington Book, 2015), 82.

46. Chen Zhimin, "Nationalism, Internationalism and Chinese Foreign Policy," *Journal of Contemporary China* 14, no. 42 (2005).

47. Tang Tsou, *America's Failure in China*, 589.

48. Harry S. Truman, "Statement on Formosa," January 5, 1950, USC US-China Institute, https://china.usc.edu/harry-s-truman-%E2%80%9Cstatement-formosa%E2%80%9D-january-5-1950.

49. Lindsay Hughes, "China, the United States and the Taiwan Factor," *Future Directions International*, April 4, 2019, https://www.futuredirections.org.au/publication/china-the-united-states-and-the-taiwan-factor/.

50. "周恩來總理發表聲明反對美国武裝干涉朝鮮" [Premier Zhou Enlai issued a statement against US armed intervention in North Korea], 新华月报 [Xinhua monthly] 2, no. 3 (July 1950): 525.

51. He Di, "The Evolution of the People's Republic of China's Policy toward the Offshore Islands," in *The Great Powers in East Asia: 1953–1960*, ed. Warren I. Cohen and Akira Iriye (New York: Columbia University Press, 1990), 223.

52. Dwight D. Eisenhower, *Mandate for Change, 1953–1956* (Garden City, NY: Doubleday, 1963), 459.

53. 外交部研究室 [Research office of Chinese Ministry of Foreign Affairs], 中美关系文件汇编 [Collected literature on Sino-US relations] (Beijing: World Knowledge Press, 1960), 2250–51.

54. 贾庆国 [Jia Qingguo], 未实现的和解], 中美关系的隔阂与危机 [Unrealized compromise, the barriers and crises in the Sino-US relations] (Beijing: Cultural and Art Press, 1998), 115–28.

55. Thomas. E. Stolper, *China, Taiwan, and the Offshore Islands* (Armonk, NY: M. E. Sharpe, 1985), 118.

56. Charlie Savage, "Risk of Nuclear War Over Taiwan in 1958 Said to Be Greater Than Publicly Known," *New York Times*, May 22, 2021, https://www.nytimes .com/2021/05/22/us/politics/nuclear-war-risk-1958-us-china.html.

57. Dwight D. Eisenhower, *Waging Peace, 1956–1961* (Garden City, NY: Doubleday, 1965), 300.

58. 吴冷西 [Wu Lengxi], "武仗与文仗" [Armed war versus words war), 许世铨 [Xu Shiquan], 台海风云录 [The winds and cloud cross the Taiwan Strait] (Beijing: Huayi Press, 1998), 68.

59. 李健 [Li Jian], 钓鱼台国事风云 [The wind and cloud of state affairs in Tiaoyutai], 2:637.

60. 童小鹏 [Tong Xiaopeng], "为了台湾早日回归祖国" [Making Taiwan return to the Motherland as soon as possible), 许世铨 [Xu Shiquan], 台海风云录 [The winds and cloud cross the Taiwan Strait], 93.

61. 叶飞 [Ye Fei], "毛主席指挥炮击金门" [The bombardment of Jingmen commanded by Chairman Mao], 许世铨 [Xu Shiquan], 台海风云录 [The winds and cloud cross the Taiwan Strait], 19.

62. 雷英夫 [Lei Yingfu], 炮击金门内幕 [The inside story of the bombardment of Jingmen], 许世铨 [Xu Shiquan], 台海风云录 [The winds and cloud cross the Taiwan Strait], 30–31.

63. Harrison E. Salisbury, *The New Emperors: China in the Era of Mao and Deng* (New York: Avon Books, 1992), 155.

64. Morton H. Halperin, *Sino-Soviet Relations and Armed Control* (Cambridge, MA: Harvard University Press, 1967), 44.

65. 余湛 [Yu Zhan], "一次不寻常的使命: 忆周总理最后一次访问苏联" [An unusual mission: Premier Zhou's last visit to the Soviet Union], in Diplomatic

Research Office of the Foreign Ministry, 新中国外交风云：中国外交官回忆录 [Diplomatic winds and clouds of new China: Memoirs of the Chinese diplomats] (Beijing: World Knowledge Press, 1994), 18.

66. Nikita Khrushchev, *Khrushchev Remembers: The Last Testament* (Little, Brown, 1974), 276–78.

67. 吴冷西 [Wu Lengxi], 十年论战 [Ten Years of Polemics] (Beijing: Central Party School Press, 1999), 191–92.

68. Zhihua Shen and Yafeng Xia, "The Great Leap Forward, the People's Commune and the Sino-Soviet Split," *Journal of Contemporary China* 20, no. 72 (November 2011).

69. Chen Zhimin, "Nationalism, Internationalism and Chinese Foreign Policy," *Journal of Contemporary China* 14, no. 42 (2005).

70. Allen W. Whiting, *The Chinese Calculus of Deterrence, India and Indochina* (Ann Arbor: University of Michigan Press, 1975), 132.

71. 余湛 [Yu Zhan], "一次不寻常的使命: 忆周总理最后一次访问苏联" [An unusual mission: Premier Zhou's last visit to the Soviet Union], 18–19.

72. "列宁主义万岁" [Long live Leninism], 红旗 [Red flag], April 6, 1960, 1–21.

73. Yafeng Xia, "Wang Jiaxiang: New China's First Ambassador and the First Director of the International Liaison Department of the CCP," *American Journal of Chinese Studies* 16 (October 2009): 501–19.

74. Chinese Ministry of Foreign Affairs, *Diplomacy of Contemporary China* (Hong Kong: New Horizon Press, 1990), 157.

75. John Gottings, *Survey of the Sino-Soviet Dispute: A Commentary and Extracts from the Recent Polemics, 1963–1967* (London: Oxford University Press, 1968), 254——70.

76. Peter Van Ness, *Revolution and Chinese Foreign Policy* (Berkeley: University of California Press, 1970), 77–200.

77. 林彪 [Lin Biao], "人民战争胜利万岁" [Long Live the Victory of the People's War], *People's Daily,* September 3, 1965, 3.

78. Editorial, "痛击苏修混蛋们的疯狂挑衅" [Hit back hard at the rabid provocation of the filthy Soviet revisionist swine], *People's Daily*, January 27, 1967, 1.

79. Peter Jones and Sian Kevill, *China and the Soviet Union, 1949–84* (New York: Facts on File Publications, 1985), 73–110.

80. "The Crux of the Sino-Soviet Boundary Question (1)," *Beijing Review*, July 28, 1981, 12; "The Crux of the Sino-Soviet Boundary Question (2)," *Beijing Review*, September 14, 1981, 21–23.

81. This story was revealed by Mao in 1964 when he told a delegation of the Japanese Socialist Party that there were too many places occupied by the Soviet Union, and that the Kuriles should be returned to Japan and Outer Mongolia to the PRC. Low, *Sino-Soviet Confrontation Since Mao Zedong*, 78.

82. 李健 [Li Jian], 钓鱼台国事风云 [Looking at the wind and cloud of diplomatic events from Tiaoyutai] (Taiyuan: Taiyai Literatures Press, 1995), vol. 1, 270–277.

83. "Letter of the Central Committee of the CCP on February 29, 1964, to the Central Committee of CPSU," *Beijing Review*, May 8, 1964, 12–18.

84. Neville Maxwell, "Why the Russians lifted the Blockade at Bear Island," *Foreign Affairs* 57, no. 1 (Fall 1978): 138–45.

85. Akira Iriye, *Across the Pacific: An Inner History of American-East Asian Relations* (Chicago: Imprint Publications, 1992), 308–9.

86. Richard Nixon, *No More Vietnams* (New York: Arbor House, 1985), 29.

87. Franz Schurmann, *The Logic of World Power: An Inquiry into the Origins, Currents, and Contradictions of World Politics* (New York: Pantheon Books, 1974), 460.

88. 薄一波 [Bo Yibo], 若干重大事件的决策与回顾 [Memoir about the decisions on some major issues] (CCP Central Party School Press, 1997), vol. 2, 1192–1219.

89. Covell Meyskens, *Mao's Third Front: The Militarization of Cold War China* (Cambridge: Cambridge University Press, 2020).

90. Editorial, "全世界人民动员起来], 援助南越人们打败美国侵略者" [The people of the world should be mobilized to assist the Vietnam people to defeat the American invaders], *People's Daily*, March 25, 1965, 1.

91. 王贤根 [Wang Xiangeng], 抗美援越实录 [The records of the war of resisting the America and assisting Korea] (Beijing: International Cultural Press, 1990), 158.

92. 邓立峰 [Deng Lifeng], 建国后军事行动全录 [Complete records of military actions since the founding of the PRC] (Taiyuan: Shanxi People's Press, 1994), 329–31.

93. Dong Wang, "Grand Strategy, Power Politics, and China's Policy Toward the United States in the 1960s," *Diplomatic History* 41, no. 2 (April 2017): 265–87.

94. 毛泽东 [Mao Zedong], "中间地带有两个" [There are two intermediate zone], 毛泽东外交文选 [The selected works of Mao Zedong on diplomacy] (Central Literature Press, 1994), 487.

95. 李海闻 [Li Haiwen], "冷眼向洋看世界：国际政治家毛泽东" [Looking the world through cool eyes: Mao Zedong in international politics], in 侯树栋 [Hou Shudong], ed., 一代巨人毛泽东 [A giant of the generation: Mao Zedong] (Beijing: China Youth Press, 1993), 271.

96. 徐金洲 [Xu Jinzhou], "1969年开始的全军临战状态何时结束" [When did the situation of ready for battle end], 当代中国史研究 [The study of contemporary Chinese history] 23, no. 1 (2016): 113–22.

97. 熊向辉 [Xiong Xianghui], "打开中美关系的前奏: 1969年四位老帅对国际形势的研究与建议" [The prelude of the opening-up of Sino-US relationship: Four veteran marshals' study of international situation and their proposals in 1969], 新中国外交风云 [Diplomacy of new China] (Beijing: World Knowledge Press, 1996), vol. 4, 7–34.

98. Shibusawa Masahide, *Japan and the Asian Pacific Region* (New York: St. Martin's Press, 1984), 27.

99. Kuisong Yang Yafeng Xia, "Vacillating between Revolution and Détente: Mao's Changing Psyche and Policy toward the United States, 1969–1976,"

Diplomatic History 34, no. 2 (April 1, 2010): 395–423, https://doi-org.du.idm.oclc.org/10.1111/j.1467-7709.2009.00853.x.

100. Michael Lumbers, "'Staying Out of This Chinese Muddle': The Johnson Administration's Response to the Cultural Revolution," *Diplomatic History* 31, no. 2 (April 2007): 285, and Lumbers, *Piercing the Bamboo Curtain: Tentative Bridge-Building to China during the Johnson Years* (Manchester: Manchester University Press, 2008), 155.

101. 陈峰 [Cheng Feng], 中美较量大写真 [the China-US competition] (Beijing: China Renshi Press, 1996), vol. 1, 264–75.

102. Henry Kissinger, *White House Years* (Boston: Little, Brown, 1979), 755.

103. Richard H. Solomon, "The China Factor in America's Foreign Relations," in *The China Factor, Sino-American Relations & The Global Scene*, ed. Richard, H. Solomon (Englewood Cliffs, NJ: Prentice-Hall, 1981), 2.

104. 魏史言 [Wei Shiyan], "尼克松总统访华" [The visit to China by President Nixon], in Diplomatic History Research Office, the Ministry of Foreign Affairs, 新中国外交风云 [Diplomatic winds and clouds of new China], 69–85.

105. Kissinger, *White House Years*, 765.

106. Richard Nixon, *Memoirs of Richard Nixon*, vol. 1 (New York: Warner Books, 1978), 502–11.

107. Hongqian Zhu, "China and the Triangular Relationship," in *The Chinese View of the World*, ed. Yufan Hao and Guocang Huan (New York: Pantheon Books, 1989), 37.

108. Joint Communiqué of the People's Republic of China and the United States of America (February 28, 1972), Embassy of the People's Republic of China, http://www.china-embassy.org/eng/zmgx/doc/ctc/t36255.htm.

109. Kuisong Yang Yafeng Xia, "Vacillating between Revolution and Détente: Mao's Changing Psyche and Policy toward the United States, 1969–1976," *Diplomatic History* 34, no. 2 (April 1, 2010): 395–423.

110. David Nickles, ed., *Foreign Relations of the United States, 1969–1976*, vol. 18, China, 1973–1976, Document 12, Memorandum of Conversation, Beijing, February 17–18, 1973, 11:30 p.m.–1:20 a.m. (United States Government Printing Office, 2007), https://history.state.gov/historicaldocuments/frus1969-76v18/d12.

111. Shibusawa Masahide, *Japan and the Asian Pacific Region* (New York: St. Martin's Press, 1984), 62.

112. Roger Buckley, *US-Japan Alliance Diplomacy, 1945–1990* (Cambridge: Cambridge University Press, 1992), 131.

113. Roger Buckley, *US-Japan Alliance Diplomacy, 1945–1990* (New York: Cambridge University Press, 1992), 131.

114. 陆维昭 [Lu Weizhao], "田中访华于中日邦交正常化" [The visit to China by Tanaka and normalization of the Sino-Japanese relations], in Diplomatic History Research Office, the Ministry of Foreign Affairs, 新中国外交风云 [Diplomatic winds and clouds of new China], 134.

115. R. K. Jain, *China and Japan, 1949–1980* (Oxford, UK: Martin Robertson, 1981), 217.

116. Yinan He, "History, Chinese Nationalism and the Emerging Sino-Japanese conflict," *Journal of Contemporary China* 16, no. 50 (February 2007).

117. Danald W. Klein, "China and the Second World," in Samuel Kim, *China and the World, New Directions in Chinese Foreign Policy* (Boulder, CO: Westview Press, 1989), 131.

Chapter 2

1. 赵可金 [Zhao Kejing], "中国的外交新思维与外交理论的发展" [China's diplomatic new thinking and the development of diplomatic theory], 复旦国际关系评论 [Fudan review of international relations], no. 8 (2009): 210.

2. 谷牧 [Gu Mu], "谷牧回忆改革开放年代," [Gu Mu recalls the era of reform and opening up], 北京日报 [Beijing daily], December 25, 2008, http://cpc.people.com.cn/GB/85037/8580895.html.

3. Ezra F. Vogel, *Deng Xiaoping and the Transformation of China* (Cambridge, MA: Harvard University Press, 2011), 2–3, 312.

4. Henry Kissinger, *Years of Upheaval* (Boston: Little, Brown, 1982), 54.

5. John W. Garver, "The Reagan Administration's Southeast Asian Policy," in *US-Asian Relations: The National Security Paradox,* ed. James C. Hsiung (New York: Praeger, 1983), 96.

6. Lowell Dittmer, *Sino-Soviet Normalization and Its International Implications, 1945–1990* (Seattle: University of Washington Press, 1992), 209.

7. "Huang Hua's Report on the World Situation," *Issues and Studies* 14, no. 1 (January 1978): 110–11.

8. Michael Oksenberg, "China Policy for the 1980s," *Foreign Policy* 59, no. 2 (Winter 1980–81): 318.

9. Zbigniew Brezinski, *Power and Principle: Memoirs of the National Security Adviser, 1977–1981* (New York: Farrar Straus & Giroux, 1983), chapter 6.

10. Huang Hua, *Huang Hua Memoirs* (Beijing Foreign Language Press, 2008), 347.

11. Ezra F. Vogel, *Deng Xiaoping and the Transformation of China* (Cambridge, MA: Harvard University Press, 2011), 332.

12. Harry Harding, *A Fragile Relationship, The United States and China since 1972* (Washington, DC: Brookings Institution, 1992), 95–99.

13. Harding, *Fragile Relationship,* 107–8.

14. Anne Gilks, *The Breakdown of the Sino-Vietnamese Alliance, 1970–1979,* China Research Monograph, 39 (Berkeley: Institute of East Asian Studies, University of California, 1992), 40.

15. Yu Gang, "The Situation in Kampuchea after Eight Years of Vietnamese Aggression," in International Security Council Conference Proceedings, *The Balance of Power in Asia* (New York: International Council, 1987), 107.

16. John W. Garver, *China's Quest: The History of the Foreign Relations of the People's Republic of China* (New York: Oxford University Press, 2016), 386.

17. 云随 [Yun Sui], 国际风云中的中国外交官 [Chinese diplomats in the international winds and clouds], 北京 [Beijing], 世界知识出版社 [World Knowledge Press, 1992], 85–112.

18. 邓礼峰 [Deng Lifeng], 建国后军事行动全录 [Full record of military operations after the founding of the PRC] (Taiyuan: Shanxi People's Press, 1994), 415–23.

19. 郑德荣 [Zheng Derong], 新中国纪事 [New China chronicle] (Changchun: Northeast Normal University Press, 1986), 657.

20. Zbigniew Brezinski, *Power and Principle: Memoirs of the National Security Adviser, 1977–1981* (New York: Farrar, Straus, Giroux, 1983), 409–10.

21. Min Chen, *The Strategic Triangle and Regional Conflicts: Lessons from the Indochina Wars* (Boulder, CO: Lynn Rienner Publishers, 1992), 184.

22. 郑德荣 [Zheng Derong], 新中国纪事 [New China chronicle], 654.

23. Sharon Sloan Fiffer, *Imagining America: Paul Thai's Journey from the Killing Fields of Cambodia to Freedom in the USA* (New York: Paragon House, 1991).

24. Lowell Dittmer, *Sino-Soviet Normalization and its International Implications, 1945-1990* (Seattle, WA.: University of Washington Press, 1992), 215.

25. Harlan W. Jencks, "China's 'Punitive' War on Vietnam: A Military Assessment," *Asian Survey* 19, no. 8 (August 1979): 801–15.

26. 刘连第 [Liu Liandi], 汪大为 [Wang Dawei], 中美关系的轨迹 [The trajectory of Sino-US relations] (Beijing: Current Affairs Press, 1994), 6.

27. John W. Garver, *China's Quest: The History of the Foreign Relations of the People's Republic of China* (New York: Oxford University Press, 2016), 420

28. Charles E. Ziegler, *Foreign Policy and East Asia: Learning and Adaptation in the Gorbachev Era* (Cambridge: Cambridge University Press, 1993), 62.

29. Peter Jones and Sian Kevill, *China and the Soviet Union, 1949–1984* (New York: Facts on File Publications, 1985), 176–177.

30. 钱其琛 [Qian Qichen], 外交十记 [Ten notes on diplomacy] (Beijing: World Knowledge Press, 2003), 4.

31. 钱其琛 [Qian Qichen], "结束过去], 开辟未来], 回忆邓小平同志关于实现中苏关系正常化的战略决策" [End the past and open up the future, recalling comrade Deng Xiaoping's strategic decision to normalize Sino-Soviet relation], *People's Daily*, February 20, 1998, 5.

32. Hu Yaobang, "Create a New Situation in All Fields of Socialist Modernization," in *The Twelfth National Congress of the CPC, September 1982* (Beijing: Foreign Language Press, 1982), 59.

33. 郑启荣 [Zheng Qirong], 改革开放以来的中国外交 1978–2008 [Chinese diplomacy since the reform and open-up, 1979–2008] (Beijing: World Knowledge Press, 2008), 56–57.

34. Chi Su, "Sino-Soviet Relations of the 1980s: From Confrontation to Conciliation," in *China and the World, New Directions in Chinese Foreign Relations*, ed. Samuel Kim (Boulder, CO: Westview Press, 1989), 112.

35. Guo-cang Huan, *Sino-Soviet Relations to the Year 2000: Implications for US Interests* (Washington, DC: Atlantic Council of the United States, 1986), 8.

36. 郑启荣 [Zheng Qirong], 改革开放以来的中国外交 *1978–2008* [Chinese diplomacy since the reform and open-up, 1979–2008], 56–58.

37. John W. Garver, "Arms Sales, the Taiwan Question, and Sino-US relations," *Orbis* 26, no. 4 (Winter 1983): 999–1104; James C. Hsiung, "Reagan's China Policy and the Sino-Soviet Détente," *Asian Affairs* 11, no. 2 (Summer 1984): 1–11.

38. Robert Legvold, "Sino-Soviet Relations: The American Factor," in *China, the United States, and the Soviet Union: Tripolarity and Policy Making in the Cold War World*, ed. Robert S. Ross (Armonk, NY: M. E. Sharpe, 1993), 71.

39. 曲星 [Qu Xin], 中国外交50年 [50 years of Chinese diplomacy] (Nanjing: Jiangsu People' Press, 2000), 449.

40. 陈之骅 [Cheng Zhiye], 勃列日涅夫时期的苏联 [The Soviet Union under Brezhnev] (Beijing: China Social Science Press, 1998), 76.

41. 唐秀泽 [Tang Xiuzhe], "戈尔巴乔夫答记者问 [Gorbachev answers correspondent], 瞭望周刊 [Liaowang weekly], January 11, 1988, 4.

42. Chi Su, "Sino-Soviet Relations of the 1980s," 123.

43. Ziegler, *Foreign Policy and East Asia*, 63.

44. Harry Harding, *China and Northeast Asia, The Political Dimension* (Lanham, MD: University Press of America, 1988), 24.

45. 钱其琛 [Qian Qichen], 外交十记 [Ten notes on diplomacy], 36.

46. John W. Garver, "The 'New Type' of Sino-Soviet Relations," *Asian Survey* 29, no. 12 (December 1989): 1136–52.

47. Jimmy Carter, *Keeping Faith: Memoirs of a President* (New York: Bantam Books, 1982), 202–3.

48. President Jimmy Carter personally told the story several times when the author attended the conferences in the Carter Center in Atlanta, Georgia. The most recent time was President Carter's keynote speech at the conference to celebrate the fortieth anniversary of normalization of Sino-US relations in January 2019.

49. 邓小平 [Deng Xiaoping], 邓小平文选 [Selected works of Deng Xiaoping] (Beijing: People's Press, 1993), 321.

50. Jia Qingguo, "Learning to Live with the Hegemon: Evolution of China's Policy toward the US since the End of the Cold War," *Journal of Contemporary China* 14, no. 44 (2005): 395.

51. 沈骥如 [Shen Jiru], 中国不当不先生 [China does not want to be Mr. No] (Beijing: China Today Press, 1998), 62.

52. 贾庆国 [Jia Qingguo], 汤炜 [Tang Wei], 棘手的合作], 中美关系的现状与前瞻 [Difficult cooperation, the current situation and the prospect of Sino-US relations] (Beijing: Culture and Arts Press, 1998), 92–94.

53. Rone Tempest, "China Asks US Apology, Damages for Search of Ship," *Las Angeles Times*, September 6, 1993, https://www.latimes.com/archives/la-xpm-1993-09-06-mn-32214-story.html.

54. 刘连第 (Liu Liandi), 汪大为 (Wang Dawei), 中美关系的轨迹 (The trajectory of Sino-US relations), 北京 (Beijing): 时事出版社 (Current Affairs Press, 1994), 470.

55. 倪世雄 [Ni Shixiong], 一个中国学者眼中的中美建交30周年 [The 30th anniversary of the establishment of Sino-US diplomatic relations in the eyes of a Chinese scholar] (Shanghai: Fudan University Press, 2009), 117.

56. Joseph Fewsmith, "China and the WTO: The Politics Behind the Agreement," National Bureau of Asian Research, November 1999, https://www.iatp.org/sites/default/files/China_and_the_WTO_The_Politics_Behind_the_Agre.htm.

57. 吴莼思 [Wu Chunsi], 倪世雄 [Ni Shixiong], "美国对外战略调整与中美关系: 小布什政府对华政策走向 学术研讨会综述" [US foreign strategic adjustment and Sino-US relations: The trend of the Bush administration's China policy], 国际观察 [International Outlook], no. 4 (2001): 63–64.

58. James A. Kelly, US-China Relations, Testimony before the Senate Foreign Relations Committee, Washington, DC, September 11, 2003, https://2001-2009.state.gov/p/eap/rls/rm/2003/24004.htm.

59. Robert Sutter, "Bush Administration Policy Toward Beijing and Taipei," *Journal of Contemporary China* 12, no. 36 (August 2003): 478–79.

60. Wang Jisi, "China's Search for Stability with America," *Foreign Affairs* 84, no. 5 (September/October 2005): 39.

61. "十六大特别报道], 一起走过十三年" [The 16th Party Congress Special Report: Walk Through 13 Years Together], 瞭望周刊 [Outlook Weekly], no. 44 (November 4, 2002, 31.

62. Wu Baiyi, "The Chinese Security Concept and Its Historical Evolution," *Journal of Contemporary China* 10, no. 27 (May 2001): 279–89.

63. Wang Jisi, "Reflecting on China," *American Interest* 1, no. 4 (Summer 2006): 75.

64. Hillary Clinton, "'We Are Ready to Listen' to Asia," Asia Society, February 13, 2009, https://asiasociety.org/new-york/hillary-clinton-we-are-ready-listen-asia.

65. You Ji and Jia Qingguo, "China's Re-emergence and Its Foreign Policy Strategy," in *China Review, 1998*, ed. Joseph Y. S. Cheng (Hong Kong: Chinese University Press, 1998), 128.

66. 陈有为 [Chen Youwei], 天安门事件后中国与美国外交内幕 [The inside stories of diplomacy between China and the US after the Tiananmen incident] (Hong Kong: Zhongzheng Publishing House, 1999), 200–211.

67. 阎学通 [Yan Xuetong], 中国崛起：国际环境评估 [The rise of China: An evaluation of the international environment] (Tianjin: Tianjin Renmin Chuban She, 1998), 234–36.

68. 田培曾 [Tian Peizeng], 改革开放以来的中国外交 [Chinese diplomacy since the reform and opening up] (Beijing: World Knowledge Press, 1993), 6–7.

69. Allen Carlson, "Constructing the Dragon's Scales: China's Approaches to Territorial Sovereignty and Boarder Relations," in *Chinese Foreign Policy: Pragmatism and Strategic Behavior*, ed. Suisheng Zhao (Armonk, NY: M. E. Sharpe, 2004), 276–96.

70. 谢一新 [Xie Yixing], 中国当代外交史 [History of contemporary Chinese diplomacy] (Beijing: China Youth Press, 1996), 430.

71. "中俄联合公报" [Sino-Russian joint communiqué], *People's Daily*, December 13, 1999, 1.

72. World Bank, *Global Economic Prospects and Developing Countries, 1998/99: Beyond Financial Crisis* (Washington, DC: World Bank, 1999), 34.

73. You Ji, "China and North Korea: A Fragile Relationship of Strategic Convenience," *Journal of Contemporary China* 10, no. 28 (August 2001): 396.

74. Suisheng Zhao, "Management of Rival Relations Across the Taiwan Strait: 1979–1991," *Issues and Studies* 29, no. 4 (April 1993): 77–78.

75. Hugo Restall, "China's Bid for Asian Hegemony," *Far Eastern Economic Review*, May 2007, http://viet-studies.com/kinhte/China_asian_hegemony_FEER.pdf

76. Charles Hutzler, "Hu's Up, Bush Down at Pacific Rim Summit," Associated Press, September 8, 2007, https://oklahoman.com/article/3120485/hus-up-bush-down-at-pacific-rim-summit.

77. John Burton, Victor Mallet, and Richard McGregor, "A New Sphere of Influence: How Trade Clout Is Winning China Allies Yet Stoking Distrust," *Financial Times*, December 9, 2005, http://news.ft.com/cms/s/2276a164-6859-11da-bfce-0000779e2340.html.

78. Robert Sutter, *China's Rise in Asia: Promises and Perils* (Lanham, MD: Rowman & Little Field Publishers, 2005), 10.

79. 庞大鹏 [Pang Dapeng], "中国对外战略中的上海合作组织" [Shanghai Cooperation Organization in China's external strategy], 世界知识 [World Knowledge], October 21, 2020, http://www.gjjmxh.com/gjjmxh/Article/ShowArticle.asp?ArticleID=4859.

80. Jian Xu, "Comparing Security Concepts of China and the USA," in *China-US Relations Transformed: Perspective and Strategic Interactions*, ed. Suisheng Zhao (London: Routledge, 2008), 77.

81. 林珉璟 [Lin Mianjin], 刘江永 [Liu Jiangyong], "上海合作组织的形成及其动因" [The formation and motivation of the Shanghai Cooperation Organization] 国际政治科学 [International Political Science], no. 1 (2009): 7.

82. Shi Yinghong, "China and the North Korean Nuclear Problem: Diplomatic Initiatives, Strategic Complexities, and Relevance of Security Multilateralism," in

China Turns to Multilateralism: Foreign Policy and Regional Security, ed. Guoguang Wu and Helen Lansdowne (London: Routledge, 2008), 93.

83. 朱锋 [Zhu Feng], "六方会谈与朝鲜弃核：多边主义 为什么能发挥作用" [The Six-Party Talks and denuclearization in North Korea: Why multilateralism can play a role], 国际政治研究 [International politics studies], no. 4 (2007): 157–73.

84. Jayshreeand Beina Xu, "The Six Party Talks on North Korea's Nuclear Program," Council on Foreign Relations, September 30, 2013, https://www.cfr.org/backgrounder/six-party-talks-north-koreas-nuclear-program.

85. "The Statement by the Ministry of Foreign Affairs of the People's Republic of China on a Nuclear Test Conducted by the Democratic People's Republic of Korea," October 9, 2006, https://www.armscontrol.org/factsheets/6partytalks.

86. 林利民 [Lin Limin], 程亚克 [Chen Yake], "试析"六方会谈"各方在朝核问题上的地缘政治博弈" [The geopolitical game played by each party on North Korean nuclear issue in the Six-Party Talk], 中国与国际关系学刊 [Journal of China and international relations], no. 2 (2017): 17–29.

87. Christopher Twomey, "Explaining Chinese Foreign Policy Toward North Korea: Navigating between the Scylla and Charybdis of Proliferation and Instability," *Journal of Contemporary China* 17, no. 56 (August 2008): 411–19.

88. "N. Korea Loudly Declares Its Withdrawal from Six-Party Talks," *The Hankyoreh*, April 14, 2009, http://english.hani.co.kr/arti/english_edition/e_north korea/349869.html.

89. 林利民 [Lin Limin], 程亚克 [Chen Yake], "试析"六方会谈"各方在朝核问题上的地缘政治博弈" [The geopolitical game played by each party on North Korean nuclear issue in the Six-Party Talk], 27.

90. Jong Kun Choi, "The Cheonan and Uncertainty over the Six Party Talks," *East Asian Forum*, May 19, 2010, http://www.eastasiaforum.org/2010/05/19/the-cheonan-and-uncertainty-over-the-six-party-talks/.

91. Bonnie Glaser and Liang Wang, "The North Korea Nuclear Crisis," in *China and the United States, Cooperation and Competition in Northeast Asia*, ed. Suisheng Zhao (New York, NY: Palgrave/Macmillan, 2008,) 162.

92. Yan Xuetong, "The Rise of China and Its Power Status," *Chinese Journal of International Politics* 1, no. 1 (2006): 12.

93. Zheng Bijian, "China's Peaceful Rise and New Role of Asia," *China Forum*, Autumn 2005, 3.

94. Liu Jiafei, "Sino-US Relations and building a Harmonious World," *Journal of Contemporary China* 18, no. 60 (June 2009): 479; Lun Tan, "China's Dream of Harmonious Existence," *China Daily*, November 11, 2005, 4.

95. James Miles, "China and the West, A Time for Muscle-Flexing," *The Economist*, March 19, 2009, https://www.economist.com/briefing/2009/03/19/a-time-for-muscle-flexing.

96. Sephanie Kleine-Ablbrandt and Andrew Small, "China's New Dictatorship Diplomacy," *Foreign Affairs*, January/February 2008, 38–39.

97. 刘海斌 [Liu Haibin], "评析中国责任论" [On the argument of China responsibility], 潘中齐 [Pan Zhongqi], ed., 国际责任与大国战略 [International responsibility and great power strategy] (Shanghai: Shanghai People's Press, 2008), 95.

98. Robert J. Samuelson, "The danger behind China's 'Me First' Worldview," *Washington Post*, February 15, 2010, A17; John Garnaut, "Battle for Shanghai Takes Centre Stage in Hu's Strategy," *Sydney Morning Herald*, February 1, 2010, https://www.smh.com.au/business/battle-for-shanghai-takes-centre-stage-in-hus-strategy-20100131-n6je.html; Orville Schell, "China Reluctant to Lead," *YaleGlobal*, March 11, 2009, https://yaleglobal.yale.edu/content/china-reluctant-lead; Stephanie T. Kleine-Ahlbrandt, "Beijing, Global Free-Rider," *Foreign Policy*, November 12, 2009, http://www.foreignpolicy.com/articles/2009/11/12/beijing_global_free_rider.

99. 郭震远 [Guo Zhenyuan], "21世纪第二个十年中国的国际地位和作用" [China's international status and role in the second decade of the 21st century], 中国评论 [China review], no. 137 (March 2010): 11.

100. "重大理论创新:瞭望载文阐述胡锦涛时代观五大主张" [Important theoretical innovation: *Outlook Weekly* on Hu Jintao's five viewpoints of the time], *RenminNet*, November 24, 2009, http://politics.people.com.cn/GB/1024/10438064.html.

101. Wen Jiabao, "Our Historical Tasks at the Primary Stage of Socialism and Several Issues Concerning China's Foreign Policy," *People's Daily*, February 27, 2007, http://www.bjreview.com/document/txt/2007-03/12/content_58927.htm.

Chapter 3

1. Wu Xinbo, "Four Contradictions Constraining China's Foreign Policy Behavior," *Journal of Contemporary China* 10, no. 27 (May 2001): 293–302.

2. Weixing Hu, "Xi Jinping 'Big Power Diplomacy' and China's Central National Security Commission (CNSC)," *Journal of Contemporary China* 25, no. 98 (2016).

3. "Chinese Premier's Speech at World Economic Forum Annual Meeting 2009," Xinhua, January 28, 2009, http://news.xinhuanet.com/english/2009-01/29/content_10731877.htm.

4. "China Opens Top Economic Work Meeting with Focus on Stable Growth," Xinhua, December 9, 2008, http://www.xinhuanet.com/fortune/08zygzhy/.

5. Suisheng Zhao, "The China Model: Can It Replace the Western Model of Modernization?," *Journal of Contemporary China* 19, no. 65 (June 2010).

6. John Garnaut, "China's Money Mandarins Take the Hard Line," *Sydney Morning Herald*, April 20, 2009], https://www.smh.com.au/business/chinas-money-mandarins-take-the-hard-line-20090419-abes.html.

7. Suisheng Zhao, "Whither the China Model: Revisiting the Debate," *Journal of Contemporary China* 26, no. 103 (2017).

8. 刘云山 [Liu Yunshan], "中国制度无比优越" [The Chinese system is incomparably superior], Xinhua, October 5, 2008, http://www.chinanews.co/news/gb/china/2008/10/200810060925.shtml.

9. Fan Gang, "the Roots of China's Rapid Recovery," *Project Syndicate*, January 31, 2010, http://www.project-syndicate.org/commentary/gang11.

10. 潘维 [Pan Wei], "国际关系咏叹调" [An aria of international relations], *New Legalists*, September 17, 2009, http://www.xinfajia.net/content/view/6751.page.

11. The National Defence Law (Revised Draft) promulgated in October 2020 officially listed the defense of "national development interests" together with the defense of "national sovereignty, unity, territorial integrity, and security" as the duty of the military and one of the conditions for war.

12. Justin Blum, "Shareholders Vote in Favor of Unocal Acquisition," *Washington Post*, August 11, 2005, http://www.washingtonpost.com/wp-dyn/content/article/2005/08/10/AR2005081000986.html.

13. Myra Saefong and Simon Kennedy, "Rio Tinto Rejects Chinalco Deal, to Sell Stock," *Wall Street Journal*, June 5, 2009, http://www.marketwatch.com/story/rio-tinto-hints-195-bln-chinalco-deal-may-fail.

14. 张维维 [Zhang Weiwei], "次贷危机还求中国买债券,美国稍复苏就忘恩负义" [Asking China to buy bonds during the subprime mortgage crisis, the US becomes ungrateful soon after recovery], *Guanchanet,* November 21, 2019, https://k.sina.cn/article_1887344341_707e96d502700hysh.html?from=news&subch=0news.

15. 任仲平 [Ren Zhongping], "筑就民族复兴的"中国梦" [Building the "Chinese Dream" of national rejuvenation], *People's Daily*, April 1, 2012, 1.

16. 朱炳元 [Zhu Binyuan], "实现"两个一百年"奋斗目标的内在逻辑" [The internal logic of achieving the "two centenaries" goals) 红旗文稿 [The Red Flag Manuscripts], March 9, 2018, http://theory.people.com.cn/n1/2018/0309/c40531-29858071.html.

17. 石毓智 [Shi Mingzhi], "中国梦区别于美国梦的七大特征" [Seven characteristics that distinguish the Chinese dream from the American dream], *People's Forum*, May 28, 2013, https://opinion.huanqiu.com/article/9CaKrnJAFzV.

18. 费士廷 [Fei Shiting], 尹航 [Ying Hang], 李宣良 [Li Xuanliang], "党中央、中央军委领导推进国防和军队建设七十年纪实" [The CPC Central Committee and the Central Military Commission led the advancement of national defense and army building for 70 years], *PLA Daily*, September 9, 2019, http://www.mod.gov.cn/topnews/2019-09/29/content_4851649.htm.

19. "党的十八大以来习近平主席和中央军委推进强军兴军纪实" [Since the 18th National Congress of the Communist Party of China, Chairman Xi Jinping and the Central Military Commission have promoted the development of the army], Xinhua, February 29, 2016, http://fms.news.cn/swf/2016_qmtt/2_29_2016_sgqm/index.html.

20. Edward Wong, "Chinese Colonel's Hard-Line Views Seep into the Mainstream," *New York Times*, October 3, 2015, http://www.nytimes.com/2015/10/03/world/asia/chinese-colonels-hard-line-views-seep-into-the-mainstream.html?partner=rss&emc=rss&_r=0.

21. Liu Mingfu, "The World Is Too Important to Be Left to America: A Chinese bestseller Charting a Path for Global Dominance Appears in English for the First Time," *The Atlantic*, Jun 4, 2015, http://www.theatlantic.com/international/archive/2015/06/china-dream-liu-mingfu-power/394748/.

22. It increased 10.75 percent in 2013, 12.22 percent in 2014, 9.7 percent in 2015, 7.6 percent in 2016, 7.2 percent in 2017, 8.1 percent in 2018, and 7.5 percent in 2019. Maintaining 6.6 percent increase in 2020 when COVID-19 disrupted China's economic growth, it increased to 6.8 percent in 2021 and to 7.1 in 2022. Military budget of China, Wikipedia, https://en.wikipedia.org/wiki/Military_budget_of_China.

23. "习近平在省部级主要领导干部学习贯彻党的十九届五中全会精神专题研讨班开班式上发表重要讲话" [Xi Jinping delivered an important speech at the opening ceremony of the seminar on learning and implementing the spirit of the Fifth Plenary Session of the Nineteenth Central Committee of the Party], Xinhua, January 12, 2021, http://cn.chinadaily.com.cn/a/202101/12/WS5ffce6d1a3101e7ce973a3f9.html.

24. "为什么说现在是百年未有之大变局" [Why this is a big change unseen in a century], *CCP Members*, August 29, 2019, http://www.12371.cn/2019/08/29/ARTI1567071473915983.shtml.

25. 何亚非 [He Yafei], "百年未有之大变局和大挑战" [Big changes and challenges unseen in a century], *China Focus*, April 29, 2019, http://cn.chinausfocus.com/m/show.php?id=39006; 王文 [Wang Wen], "在风险挑战中推动中国之治" [Promote China's governance amid risks and challenges], *Changjiang Daily*, November 22, 2019, http://cjrb.cjn.cn/html/2019-11/22/content_156394.htm.

26. 李杰 [Li Jie], "深刻理解把握世界"百年未有之大变局" [Deeply understand and grasp the world's big changes unseen in a century], *Xuexi Daily*, September 3, 2018, http://www.qstheory.cn/llwx/2018-09/03/c_1123369881.htm; 金灿荣 [Jing Canrong], "第四次工业革命主要是中美竞争], 且中国胜算更大" [The fourth industrial revolution is mainly about Sino-US competition, China has greater chance of winning], *Leadership Science Forum*, no. 7 (2019), 来源：雪球App], 作者：资管网], [https://xueqiu.com/3619239198/130340358) https://www.guancha.cn/JinCanRong/2019_07_29_511347.shtml; 华生 [Hua Sheng] "百年未有之大变局的认识与应对" [Understanding and coping with the great changes unseen in a century], *Sina Finance*, September 21, 2019, https://finance.sina.com.cn/hy/hyjz/2019-09-21/doc-iicezzrq7468145.shtml; 朱锋 [Zhu Feng], 近期学界关于"百年未有之大变局"研究综述 [A summary of recent academic research on major changes unseen in a century], *Aisixiang*, March 12, 2019, http://www.aisixiang.com/data/120385.html.

27. 张维为 [Zhang Weiwei], "中国崛起集四次工业革命为一体,突破中心" [The rise of China integrates the four industrial revolutions], Fudan University China Development Center, November 26, 2019, http://www.cifu.fudan.edu.cn/24/91/c12233a205969/page.htm; 杨虎涛 [Yang Hutao], "新基建的新意义" [The significance of the new construction], *Red Flag Manuscripts*, no. 10 (2020), http://www.qstheory.cn/dukan/hqwg/2020-05/20/c_1126005242.htm.

28. 高飞 [Gao Fei], "大变局与中国外交的选择" [Great changes and China's diplomatic choice], 国际问题研究 [International issue studies], no. 6 (2019), http://www.ciis.org.cn/gyzz/2019-12/18/content_41001919.htm.

29. 刘建飞 [Liu Jiafei], 领导干部如何认识世界百年未有之大变局" [How do leading cadres understand the great changes in the world unseen in a century?], China party and government cadre forum, October 2010, https://www.ccps.gov.cn/zl/ldl/201910/t20191022_135071.shtml.

30. 习近平 [Xi Jinping], "让命运共同体意识在周边国家落地生根" [Let the concept of the community of common destination take root among China's peripheral countries], Xinhua, October 25, 2013, http://news.xinhuanet.com/politics/2013-10/25/c_117878944.htm.

31. "外交部长王毅就中国外交政策和对外关系回答中外记者提问" [Foreign Minister Wang Yi meets the press], March 8, 2014, Ministry of Foreign Affairs, PRC, http://www.fmprc.gov.cn/mfa_chn/wjb_602314/wjbz_602318/xghds/t1135388.shtml.

32. "习近平出席中央外事工作会议并发表重要讲话" [Xi Jinping attended the Central Foreign Affairs Work Conference and made an important speech], Xinhua, November 29, 2014, http://news.xinhuanet.com/politics/2014-11/29/c_1113457723.htm.

33. 张广昭 [Zhang Guangzhao], 陈振凯 [Cheng Zhengkai], "习近平内政外交新思路" [New thoughts of Xi Jinping's internal affairs and diplomacy], *People's Daily, Overseas Edition*, April 5, 2013, 1.

34. Pang Zhongying, "From Tao Guang Yang Hui to Xin Xing: China's Complex Foreign Policy Transformation and Southeast Asia," ISEAS, Yusof Ishak Institute, 2020, https://bookshop.iseas.edu.sg/publication/2437a.

35. 赵可金 [Zhao Kejin], "中国外交70年：历史逻辑与基本经验" [Chinese diplomacy in 70 years: Historical logic and basic experiences], 东北亚论坛 [Northeast Asia Forum], no. 6 (2019): 3–20.

36. Jian Zhang, "China's New Foreign Policy under Xi Jinping: Towards 'Peaceful Rise 2.0'?," *Global Change, Peace & Security*, 2015, http://dx.doi.org/10.1080/14781158.2015.993958.

37. 王子晖 [Wang Zhihui], "斗争！习近平这篇讲话大有深意" [Fighting! Xi Jinping's speech is deeply meaningful], Xinhua, September 4, 2019, http://www.xinhuanet.com/politics/leaders/xijinping/index.htm.

38. "中国驻法大使：我们现在外交风格变了,你们要适应" [Chinese ambassador to France: Our diplomatic style has changed, you must adapt], 观察者 [Guancha], June 16, 2021, https://www.wenxuecity.com/news/2021/06/16/10649308.html.

39. Shi Jiangtao, "Why China's Fiercest Wolf Warrior in Sweden Was Just Fighting the Good Fight," *South China Morning Post*, October 12, 2021, https://www.scmp.com/news/china/diplomacy/article/3152102/why-chinas-fiercest-wolf-warrior-sweden-was-just-fighting-good.

40. Jonathan Swan, "Top Chinese Official Disowns US Military Lab Coronavirus Conspiracy," *Axios*, March 22, 2020, https://www.axios.com/china-coronavirus-ambassador-cui-tiankai-1b0404e8-026d-4b7d-8290-98076f95df14.html.

41. "State Councilor and Foreign Minister Wang Yi Meets the Press," PRC Ministry of Foreign Affairs, May 24, 2020, https://www.fmprc.gov.cn/mfa_eng/zxxx_662805/t1782262.shtml.

42. Editorial, "West Feels Challenged by China's New 'Wolf Warrior' Diplomacy," *Global Times*, April 16, 2020, https://www.globaltimes.cn/content/1185776.shtml.

43. "Xi Jinping's Report at the 19th CPC National Congress," Xinhua, October 18, 2017, http://news.xinhuanet.com/english/special/2017-11/03/c_136725942.htm.

44. "习近平在莫斯科国际关系学院的演讲" [Xi Jinping spoke at Moscow International Relations College], *People's Daily*, March 24, 2013, http://politics.people.com.cn/n/2013/0324/c1024-20892661.html.

45. "习近平在比利时布鲁日欧洲学院的演讲" [Xi Jinping spoke at Brussel's European College], *People's Daily*, April 2, 2014, 2.

46. "习近平在北京大学师生座谈会上的讲话" [Xi Jinping spoke to the faculty and students in Beijing University], Xinhua, May 4, 2014, http://www.gov.cn/xinwen/2014-05/05/content_2671258.htm.

47. Eric X. Li, "The Life of the Party: The Post-Democratic Future Begins in China," *Foreign Affairs* 92, no. 1 (2013), https://www.jstor.org/stable/41721002?refreqid=excelsior%3A2b9779718ea7ff8bb3ce0d72d109b1fa&seq=1#metadata_info_tab_contents.

48. Adam O'Neal, "Coronavirus and the Chernobyl Analogy," *Wall Street Journal*, May 22, 2020, https://www.wsj.com/articles/coronavirus-and-the-chernobyl-analogy-11590167999.

49. Anne Applebaum, "The Rest of the World Is Laughing at Trump: The President Created a Leadership Vacuum. China Intends to Fill It," *The Atlantic*, May 3, 2020, https://www.theatlantic.com/ideas/archive/2020/05/time-americans-are-doing-nothing/611056/.

50. Kareem Fahim and Karen DeYoung, "China has made big vaccine promises. When they come up short, nations struggle," *Washington Post*, April 7, 2021, https://www.washingtonpost.com/world/middle_east/china-sinovac-turkey-coronavirus-vaccine/2021/04/06/f87bc1bc-93cd-11eb-aadc-af78701a30ca_story.html

51. 习近平 [Xi Jinping], "在中央政治局常委会会议研究应对新型冠状病毒肺炎疫情工作时的讲话" [Speech at the Politburo Standing Committee on the response to the coronavirus], *Qiushi*, February 15, 2020, http://www.gov.cn/xinwen/2020-02/15/content_5479271.htm.

52. 国务院新闻办公室 [The State Council Information Office], 抗击新冠肺炎疫情的中国行动 [Fighting Covid-19 China in action], June 2020, http://www.gov.cn/zhengce/2020-06/07/content_5517737.htm.

53. 郝身永 [Hao Shengyong], "抗"疫"背后的中国之治 [China's governance behind the success of combating the virus], *Dongfangnet*, April 8, 2020, http://pinglun.eastday.com/p/20200408/u1ai20467098.html; 郭凯 [Guo Kai], 金信烨 [Jing Xinye], "疫情防控阻击战彰显中国制度优势" [The epidemic prevention highlighted the Chinese system advantage], *Peoplenet*, April 7, 2020, http://dangjian.people.com.cn/n1/2020/0407/c117092-31663979.html.

54. 范勇鹏 [Fan Yongpeng], "中央集权只适用于极端状态？这种观点忽略了一个问题," [The centralization of power only applies to extreme conditions? This view ignores a problem], *Guangcha-net*, April 7, 2010, https://www.guancha.cn/FanYongPeng/2020_04_07_545745.shtml.

55. 吴心伯 [Wu Xinbo], 疫情加速世界后霸权时代到来 [COVID-19 has accelerated the advent of post-hegemony era] 参考消息 [Reference News], June 16, 2020, http://www.cankaoxiaoxi.com/china/20200616/2412828.shtml.

56. 王勇 [Wang Yong], "疫情下的中美关系与国际大变局" [The Sino-US relations and global great changes under the pandemic], *Pangoal,* April 16, 2020, https://ishare.ifeng.com/c/s/v002gWw9LSxl9U-_xlbAYfxgjdOsRPZf3Nj6mIAR3GLLM2JY__.

57. Li Jingtian, "Building on the Bottom Line," *China Daily*, July 1, 2013, http://www.chinadaily.com.cn/cndy/2013-07/01/content_16694116.htm.

58. 胡鞍钢 [Hu Angang], 郑云峰 [Zhen Yunfeng], 高宇宇 [Gao Yuyu], "对中美综合国力的评估" [Assessing comprehensive national strength of China and the US], 清华大学学报 [Journal of Qinghua University] 1 (2015): 26–39.

59. The White House, "Statement by the President to the US-China Strategic and Economic Dialogue," July 8, 2014, http://www.whitehouse.gov/the-press-office/2014/07/08/statement-president-us-china-strategic-and-economic-dialogue.

60. Suisheng Zhao, "Shaping the Regional Context of China's Rise: How the Obama Administration Brought Back Hedge in Its Engagement with China," *Journal of Contemporary China* 21, no. 75 (2012).

61. H. R. McMaster, "How China Sees the World—And How We Should See China," *The Atlantic*, May 2020, https://www.theatlantic.com/magazine/archive/2020/05/mcmaster-china-strategy/609088/.

62. 社论 [Editorial], "对于贸易战], 中国不想打、不怕打" [Regarding the trade war, China does not want to fight, is not afraid to fight], Xinhua, March 24, 2018, http://www.xinhuanet.com/world/2018-03/24/c_129836600.htm.

63. 辛识平 [Xin Shiping], "崇美、跪美的软骨病 [The soft bone disease of worshiping America and kneeling to America must should be cured], Xinhua, December 16, 2020, http://www.xinhuanet.com/2020-12/16/c_1126869721.htm.

64. 王缉思 [Wang Jisi], "新冠疫情下的中美关系" [Sino-US relations during the novel coronovirus pandemic], *Aisixiang*, April 8, 2020, http://www.aisixiang.com/data/120783.html.

65. Editorial, "Anti-Dumping on Aussie Wine Not 'Trade War,' but Canberra Urged to 'Grow Up' or Face More Pain," *Global Times*, November 27, 2020, accessed May 1, 2021, https://www.globaltimes.cn/content/1208273.shtml.

66. "How It Happened: Transcript of the US-China Opening Remarks in Alaska," *Nikkei Asia*, March 19, 2021, https://asia.nikkei.com/Politics/International-relations/US-China-tensions/How-it-happened-Transcript-of-the-US-China-opening-remarks-in-Alaska.

67. Yan Xuetong, "Becoming Strong: The New Chinese Foreign Policy," *Foreign Affairs*, July/August 2021, https://www.foreignaffairs.com/articles/united-states/2021-06-22/becoming-strong.

68. Catherine Wong, "US-China Relations: Beijing Takes Pointers from Mao in Protracted Power Struggle with US," *South China Morning Post*, August 2, 2021, https://www.scmp.com/news/china/diplomacy/article/3143505/us-china-relations-beijing-takes-pointers-mao-protracted-power.

69. Ministry of the PRC, "Wang Yi Meets with US Special Presidential Envoy for Climate John Kerry via Video Link at Request," September 1, 2021, https://www.fmprc.gov.cn/mfa_eng/zxxx_662805/t1904000.shtml.

70. 祁怀高 [Qi Huaigao], 石源华 [Shi Yuanhua], "中国的周边安全挑战与大周边外交战略" [China's Peripheral security challenges and enlarged periphery diplomatic strategy] 世界政治与经济 [World economics and politics], no. 3 (2013): 25.

71. 陈向阳 [Cheng Xiangyang], "中国推进"大周边战略"正当时" [It is time for China to advance the enlarged periphery strategy], *Fisnet*, January 16, 2015, http://comment.cfisnet.com/2015/0116/1300445.html.

72. Rory Medcalf, "China's Premature Power Play Goes Very Wrong," *National Interest*, June 3, 2014, http://nationalinterest.org/feature/chinas-premature-power-play-goes-very-wrong-10587.

73. Suisheng Zhao, "China's Belt-Road Initiative as the Signature of President Xi Jinping Diplomacy: Easier Said Than Done," *Journal of Contemporary China* 29, no. 123 (May 2020).

74. John Hemmings, "Reconstructing Order: The Geopolitical Risks in China's Digital Silk Road," *Asia Policy*, January 15, 2020, https://www.nbr.org/publication/reconstructing-order-the-geopolitical-risks-in-chinas-digital-silk-road/.

75. 余燕芳 [Yu Yanfang], "国内关于发展中大国研究的历程], 评估与展望" [The process, evaluation, and prospect of the studies of developing big powers in China] 国际问题研究参考 [References of international studies], no. 7 (2019): 50–51.

76. John Hawksworth, Hannah Audino, and Rob Clarry, "The Long View: How Will the Global Economic Order Change by 2050," Pwc Economics & Policy Services,

February 2017, https://www.pwc.com.au/government/pwc-the-world-in-2050-full-report-feb-2017.pdf.

77. 萧劲光 [Xiao Jingguang], 萧劲光回忆录 [Memoir of Xiao Jingguang] (Beijing: PLA Press, 1989), 2.

78. 刘霏 [Liu Fei], "改革开放以来中国的海洋战略思想" [China's maritime strategic thinking since the reform and opening up], 社科纵横 [Social science review] 27, no. 4 (April 2012): 39–44; 刘中民 [Liu Zhongmin], 世界海洋政治与中国海洋发展战略 [World maritime politics and China's maritime development strategy] (Beijing: Current Affairs Press, 2009), 392, 384.

79. "Hu Jintao's Report at the 18th Party Congress," Xinhua, November 17, 2012, http://news.xinhuanet.com/english/special/18cpcnc/2012-11/17/c_131981259.htm.

80. 习近平 [Xi Jinping], "进一步关心海洋认识海洋经略海洋 推动海洋强国建设不断取得新成就" [Further care about the oceans, understand the oceans and manage the oceans, building a maritime power and make new achievements], Xinhua, July 31, 2013, http://www.xinhuanet.com//politics/2013-07/31/c_116762285.htm.

81. 国务院新闻办公室 [PRC state council information office], 中国的军事战略 [China's military strategy], May 2015, http://www.mod.gov.cn/affair/2015-05/26/content_4588132.htm.

82. 国务院新闻办公室 [PRC state council information office], 新时代的中国国防 [China's national defense in the new era], July 2019, http://www.mod.gov.cn/regulatory/2019-07/24/content_4846424.htm.

83. Office of Secretary of Defense, Military and Security Development involving the People's Republic of China, 2020, *Annual Report to the Congress*, https://media.defense.gov/2020/Sep/01/2002488689/-1/-1/1/2020-DOD-CHINA-MILITARY-POWER-REPORT-FINAL.PDF.

84. 习近平出席庆祝人民海军成立70周年海上阅兵活动 [Xi Jinping attends the maritime parade celebrating the 70th anniversary of the founding of the People's Navy], Xinhua, April 23, 2019, http://www.xinhuanet.com/politics/leaders/2019-04/23/c_1124406339.htm.

85. Richard E. Caroll, "China has Almost Breached the First Island Containment Chain," *International Policy Digest*, March 17, 2020, https://intpolicydigest.org/2020/03/17/china-has-almost-breached-the-first-island-containment-chain/.

86. Chen-yuan Tung, "An Assessment of China's Taiwan Policy under the Third Leadership, *Asian Survey* 45, no. 3 (May/June 2005): 352.

87. "习近平总书记会见萧万长一行" [General Secretary Xi Jinping meets with Siew Wanchang and his party], Xinhua, October 6, 2013, http://www.gwytb.gov.cn/wyly/201310/t20131007_4979072.htm.

88. 李秘 [Li Mi], "习近平国家统一思想初探" [An exploration of Xi Jinping National University thoughts], Taiwan.cn, August 16, 2016, http://www.taiwan.cn/plzhx/zhjzhl/zhjlw/201608/t20160816_11539031.htm.

89. Foreign Ministry Spokesperson Wang Wenbin's Regular Press Conference on September 21, 2020, PRC Ministry of Foreign Affairs, https://www.fmprc.gov.cn/mfa_eng/xwfw_665399/s2510_665401/2511_665403/t1816753.shtml.

90. 说透了！"武统"台湾什么时候开始？解放军专家权威解读 [That's it! When did the "Wu Tong" Taiwan begin? Authoritative interpretation of PLA experts], Taiwan.cn, April 15, 2020, http://www.taiwan.cn/plzhx/plyzl/202004/t20200415_12265753.htm.

91. Yang Sheng and Xu Keyue, "Two Sessions Release Clearer Signals for Promoting Reunification with Taiwan," *Global Times*, March 9, 2021, https://www.globaltimes.cn/page/202103/1217765.shtml.

92. 王海运 [Wang Hairun], 我主张尽快将武力统台提上日程 [I advocate putting military unification with Taiwan on the agenda as soon as possible], *Headline Today*, July 6, 2020, https://www.toutiao.com/i6846310697643704845/.

93. 王洪光 [Wang Hongguang], "大陆如何在战争中统一台湾" [How the mainland united with Taiwan by war], *Huanqiunet*, April 10, 2015, http://mil.huanqiu.com/observation/2015-04/6141845.html.

94. "The Dragon's New Teeth, A Rare Look Inside the world's Biggest Military Expansion," *The Economist*, April 7, 2012, http://www.economist.com/node/21552193.

95. "Japan asked U.S. to change its position on neutrality over Senkakus in 1970s," *Japan Times*, May 3, 2021, https://www.japantimes.co.jp/news/2021/05/03/national/japan-us-neutrality-senkakus/

96. Robert D. Eldridge, "The dangerously flawed U.S. Senkakus policy," *Japan Times*, April 12, 2021, https://www.japantimes.co.jp/opinion/2021/04/12/commentary/japan-commentary/senkakus-u-s-china/).

97. 张香山 [Zhang Xiangshan], "中日复交谈判回顾" [Recollection of Sino-Japanese Normalization Negotiation], 日本研究 [Japan Studies], 1, 1998, at http://www.china.com.cn/chinese/HIAW/143113.htm.

98. 侯杰 [Hou Jie], "邓小平谈钓鱼岛归属问题：先搁置它二三十年" [Deng Xiaoping on sovereignty over the Diaoyu Islands: Shelve the problem for two-three decades], *Sohu History*, August 15, 2014, https://history.sohu.com/20140815/n403477003.shtml.

99. Suisheng Zhao, "Beijing's Japan Dilemma: Balancing Nationalism, Legitimacy, and Economic Opportunity," in *Uneasy Partnerships: China's Engagement with Japan, the Koreas, and Russia in the Era of Reform*, ed. Thomas Fingar (Stanford, CA: Stanford University Press, 2017), 82.

100. Suisheng Zhao, "China's Difficult Relations with Japan: Pragmatism, Superficial Friendship, and Historical Memories," *Asian Journal of Contemporary Politics* 1, no. 4 (December 2016).

101. Junya Hashimoto, "Government Drew Up Multiple Plans for Senkaku Use," *Yomiuri Shimbun*, September 13, 2012, http://www.yomiuri.co.jp/dy/national/T120912004075.htm.

102. 钟声 [Zhongsheng], "日本], 不要自讨没趣" [Japan, don't be boring], *People's Daily*, July 18, 2013, http://world.people.com.cn/n/2013/0718/c14549-22232913.html.

103. "四点共识是中日间意外突破" [Four point consensus is an unintended breakthrough], *Global Times*, November 8, 2014, http://opinion.huanqiu.com/edito rial/2014-11/5195641.html?referer=huanqiu.

104. Fravel, M Taylor, "China's Strategy in the South China Sea," *Contemporary Southeast Asia* 33, no. 3 (2011): 297.

105. 祁怀高 [Qi Huaigao], "中美在西太平洋的海权博弈及影响" [The impacts of Sino-US competition in the West Pacific], 武汉大学学报 [Wuhan university journal] 72, no. 3 (2019), http://www.iis.fudan.edu.cn/a3/96/c6852a172950/page.htm.

106. Dai Bingguo [戴秉国], "The South China Sea Arbitration Is a Piece of Wasted Paper" [南海仲裁结果是一张废纸], *Caixin*, July 6, 2016, http://international.caixin .com/2016-07-06/100962838.html.

107. "White Paper on South China Sea," *People's Daily*, July 13, 2016, http://www .chinadailyasia.com/chinafocus/2016-07/13/content_15462174_10.html.

108. Wang Yi [王毅], "仲裁庭背后的政治操作必将大白于天" [The political maneuvers behind the arbitration must be opposed], Xinhua, July 26, 2016, http:// www.chinanews.com/gn/2016/07-26/7952408.shtml.

109. Graham Allison, "Of Course China, Like All Great Powers, Will Ignore an International Legal Verdict," *The Diplomat*, July 11, 2016, http://thediplomat.com/2016/07/ of-course-china-like-all-great-powers-will-ignore-an-international-legal-verdict/.

110. Suisheng Zhao, "China and the South China Sea Arbitration: Geopolitics versus International Law," *Journal of Contemporary China* 27, no. 109 (2018): 1–15.

111. Hong Thao Nguyen, "How to Make China Comply with the Tribunal Award," *Maritime Awareness Project*, http://maritimeawarenessproject.org/2016/08/10/ how-to-make-china-comply-with-the-tribunal-award/.

112. "Wang Yi Meets with Secretary of State John Kerry of the US," *Chinese Foreign Ministry*, July 26, 2016, http://www.fmprc.gov.cn/mfa_eng/zxxx_662805/ t1384980.shtml.

113. Martin Petty and Neil Jerome Morales, "Philippines Duterte Says No Concern about China's Militarization, Made Isles," Reuters, December 29, 2016, http://www .reuters.com/article/us-philippines-duterte-southchinasea-idUSKBN14I0JL.

114. Ben Blanchard, "China berates visiting New Zealand defense minister over South China Sea stance," *Reuters*, October 11, 2016, http://www.reuters.com/article/ us-china-security-idUSKCN12B0C8

Chapter 4

1. John Fairbank, "China's Foreign Policy in Historical Perspective," *Foreign Affairs* 47, no. 3 (April 1969): 449.

2. Michel Foucault, "Film and Popular Memory: An Interview with Michel Foucault," *Edinburgh Magazine,* no. 2 (1977): 22.

3. George Orwell, *Nineteen Eighty-Four* (Signet Classics, 1961), 162.

4. 高翔 [Gao Xiang], "推动新时代中国史学繁荣发展" [Striving for the flourishing and development of history studies in China], *People's Daily*, January 15, 2019, 5.

5. Haiyang Yu, "Glorious Memories of Imperial China and the Rise of Chinese Populist Nationalism," *Journal of Contemporary China* 23, no. 90 (2014): 1183.

6. Yi Wang, "The Backward Will Be Beaten: Historical Lesson, Security, and Nationalism in China," *Journal of Contemporary China*, 26:129, (November 2020): 982.

7. Stephen R. Platt, "'Great State' Review: Rising and Setting in the East," *Wall Street Journal*, May 1, 2020, https://www.wsj.com/articles/great-state-review-rising -and-setting-in-the-east-11588370242.

8. Lien-sheng Yang, "Historical Notes on the Chinese World Order," in *The Chinese World Order*, ed. John K. Fairbank (Cambridge, MA: Harvard University Press, 1968), 20.

9. Benjamin I. Schwartz, *The World of Thought in Ancient China* (Cambridge, MA: Belknap Press of Harvard University Press, 1985).

10. Mark Mancall, "The Persistence of Tradition in Chinese Foreign Policy," in *The Foreign Policy of China*, ed. King C. Chen (South Orange, NJ: Seton Hall University Press, 1972), 31–32.

11. Suisheng Zhao, "Rethinking the Chinese World Order: the Imperial Cycle and the Rise of China," *Journal of Contemporary China*, vol. 24, no. 96 (November 2015): 963.

12. James Harrison, *Modern Chinese Nationalism* (New York: Hunter College of the City University of New York, 1969), 2.

13. Lucian W. Pye, *Asian Power and Politics: The Cultural Dimensions of Authority* (Cambridge, MA: Harvard University Press, 1985), 41.

14. John K. Fairbank and Shu-yu Teng, "On the Ch'ing Tributary System," *Harvard Journal of Asiatic Studies* 6, no. 4 (1941): 135–48.

15. King C. Chen, "Traditional Chinese Foreign Relations," in Chen, *Foreign Policy of China*, 9.

16. 钦定大清会典 [The Collected Statutes of the Great Qing], 卷五十六 [vol. 56], 主客清司 [host and guest], 宾礼 [ceremony], 朝贡 [tributary], 宾馆 [guest accommodation], 马馆[horse housing], 1644–1911, https://ctext.org/wiki .pl?if=gb&res=209451&remap=gb.

17. Mark Mancall, "The Persistence of Tradition in Chinese Foreign Policy," *Annals of the American Academy of Political and Social Science* 349 (1963): 30.

18. "习近平在德国科尔伯基金会的演讲" [Xi Jinping speech at the Korber Foundation, Germany], Xinhua, March 28, 2014, http://www.gov.cn/xinwen/2014-03/29/ content_2649512.htm.

19. Editorial, "为了更美好的世界—习近平的天下情怀" [For a better world— Xi Jinping's tianxia feeling], 人民日报 [People's daily], July 1, 2021, 1.

20. 郭伟华 [Guo Weihua], "甲午战争缘何让'天朝礼治体系'彻底坍塌" [How did the Sino-Japanese war collapse the etiquette system of the heavenly dynasty], *Chinanews*, June 9, 2014, http://www.chinanews.com/mil/2014/06-09/6260301.shtml.

21. 赵汀阳 [Zhao Tingyang], 天下体制：世界制度哲学导论 [The all-under-heaven system: A philosophy for the world system] (Nanjing: Jiangsu Education Press, 2005).

22. Tingyang Zhao, "A Political World Philosophy in Terms of All-Under-Heaven (Tian-xia)," *Diogenes*, no. 56 (2009): 5–18.

23. Tingyang Zhao, "The 'China Dream' in Question," *Economic and Political Studies* 2, no. 1 (2014): 128.

24. Allen Carlson, "Moving Beyond Sovereignty? A Brief Consideration of Recent Changes in China's Approach to International Order and the Emergence of the Tianxia Concept," Journal of *Contemporary China* 20, no. 68 (2011): 89.

25. Tingyang Zhao, "Rethinking Empire from a Chinese Concept 'All-under-heaven,'" *Social Identities* 12, no. 1 (January 2006): 29–41.

26. Ban Wang, "Tianxia: Imperial Ambition or Cosmopolitanism?," *Asia Dialogue*, October 5, 2016, https://cpianalysis.org/2016/10/05/tianxia-imperial-ambition-or-cosmopolitanism/.

27. Qin Yaqing, "Chinese School of International Relations Theory," in *China Orders the World: Normative Soft Power and Foreign Policy*, ed. William A. Callanhan and Elena Barabantseva (Washington, DC: Woodrow Wilson Center Press, 2011), 42–43.

28. 张启雄 [Chang Chi-hsiung], "近代东亚国际体系的崩解与再生" [The collapse and rebirth of modern East Asian international system], *Chinese Social Science News*, no. 613 (June 27, 2014), http://ex.cssn.cn/djch/djch_djchhg/guojishijiaoxi-adeguojitixibianqian/201406/t20140627_1230778.shtml.

29. 阎学通 [Yan Xuetong], 徐进 [Xu Jing], [etc.], 王霸天下思想及启迪 [The thoughts of world leadership and implications] (Beijing: World Knowledge Press, 2009), 73–82.

30. Yan Xuetong, "How China Can Defeat America," *New York Times*, November 20, 2011, http://www.nytimes.com/2011/11/21/opinion/how-china-can-defeat-america.html?pagewanted=all&_r=0; "The Winner of China–US Conflict Rides on National Leadership," *East Asia Forum*, April 2, 2019, https://www.eastasiaforum.org/2019/04/02/the-winner-of-china-us-conflict-rides-on-national-leadership/.

31. 辛旗 [Xin Qi], "在弘扬中华文化：探讨王道理念], 构建和谐世界—王道思想的当代意义研讨会上的致辞" [Remarks at the Symposium on royal ethics and construction of harmonious world—royal ethics and its contemporary significance], *Chinanews*, April 22, 2011, http://www.chinanews.com/tw/2011/04-22/2992337.shtml.

32. Tiewa Liu, "Chinese Strategic Culture and the Use of Force: Moral and Political Perspectives," *Journal of Contemporary China* 23, no. 87 (2014): 562.

33. 毛泽东[Mao Zedong], "论持久战" [On protracted war], 毛泽东选集 [Selected Works of Mao Zedong] (Beijing: People's Publishing House, 1962), vol. 2, 437.

34. Zhang Junbo and Yao Yunzhu, "Traditional Chinese Military Thinking: A Comparative Perspective," *Journal of Contemporary China* 5, no. 12 (1996): 209–21.

35. 熊光清 [Xiong Guangqing], "东亚国家未反省战争 崇尚武力风习阴魂不散" [East Asian countries have not reflected wars: Militancy ethos lingers], *Global Times*, April 1, 2013, http://www.chinanews.com/mil/2013/04-01/4692110.shtml.

36. Haiyang Yu, "Glorious Memories of Imperial China and the Rise of Chinese Populist Nationalism," *Journal of Contemporary China* 23, no. 90 (2014): 1183.

37. Martin Jacques, *When China Rules the World: The End of the Western World and the Birth of a New Global Order* (New York: Penguin Press, 2009).

38. David C. Kang, *East Asia before the West: Five Centuries of Trade and Tribute* (New York, Columbia University Press, 2010); David C. Kang, *China Rising: Peace, Power, and Order in East Asia* (New York: Columbia University Press, 2007).

39. Brantly Womack, "Traditional China and the Globalization of International Relations Thinking"; and James C. Hsiung, "A Re-Appraisal of Abrahamic Values and Neorealist IR Theory: From a Confucian-Asian Perspective"; both in *China and International Relations, the Chinese View and the Contribution of Wang Gungwu*, ed. Heng Yongnian (London: Routledge, 2010), 117–133 (Womack), 17–37 (Hsiung).

40. Claude A. Buss, *Asia in the Modern World: A History of China, Japan, South and Southeast Asia* (London: Collier-Macmillan Limited, 1964), 34–35.

41. Howard French, *Everything Under the Heavens: How the Past Helps Shape China's Push for Global Power* (New York: Penguin Random House, 2017).

42. Odd Arne Westad, *Restless Empire: China and the World since 1750* (New York: Basic Books, 2012), 9–10; William T. Rowe, "Violence in Ming-Qing China: An Overview," *Crime, Histoire & Sociétés/Crime, History & Societies* 18, no. 2 (2014): 85–98.

43. Kevin Rudd, "How Ancient Chinese Thought Applies Today," *World Post*, February 4, 2015, http://www.huffingtonpost.com/kevin-rudd/chinese-strategic -thoughts_b_6417754.html?clear.

44. Timothy Brook, *Great State: China and the World* (London: Profile Books, 2019).

45. Peter Perdue, "The Tenacious Tributary System," *Journal of Contemporary China* 24, no. 96 (2015).

46. 范文澜 [Fan Wenlan], "中国历史上的民族融合与斗争" [The struggles and amalgamations among nationalities in Chinese history], 历史研究 [Studies of history], no. 1 (1980): 7.

47. 孙扎民 [Sun Zamin], "处理历史上民族关系的几个重要准则" [Some important norms concerning research on the relations among nationalities in Chinese history], 历史研究 [Studies of history], no. 5 (1980): 40–43.

48. Alastair Iain Johnston, *Cultural Realism: Strategic Culture and Grand Strategy in Chinese History* (Princeton, NJ: Princeton University Press, 1995).

49. Andrew Scobell, *China's Use of Military Force* (Cambridge: Cambridge University Press, 2003).

50. Christopher A. Ford, "Realpolitik with Chinese Characteristics: Chinese Strategic Culture and the Modern Communist Party-State," in *Strategic Asia 2016–17*, ed. Michael Wills, Ashley J. Tellis, and Alison Szalwinski (Seattle, WA: The National Bureau of Asian Research, November 2016), https://www.nbr.org/publication/realpolitik-with-chinese-characteristics-chinese-strategic-culture-and-the-modern-communist-party-state/.

51. William A. Callahan, "Introduction: Tradition, Modernity, and Foreign Policy in China," in *China Orders the World: Normative Soft Power and Foreign Policy*, ed. William A. Callahan and Elena Barabantseva (Washington, DC: Woodrow Wilson Center Press, 2011), 6; Howard French, *Everything Under the Heavens: How the Past Helps Shape China's Push for Global Power* (New York: Penguin Random House, 2017).

52. Peter Perdue, "The Tenacious Tributary System," *Journal of Contemporary China* 24, no. 96 (2015).

53. Fei-ling Wang, *The China Order: Centralia, World Empire, and the Nature of Chinese Power* (Albany, NY: SUNY Press, 2017), 39–71, 99–133.

54. June Teufel Dreyer, "The 'Tianxia Trope': Will China Change the International System?," *Journal of Contemporary China* 24, no. 96 (2015).

55. Prapin Manomaivibool, "Viewing Sino-Siamese Tributary Relations via the Two Courts' Letters of the 1780s," paper presented at the 11th Beijing Forum, The Harmony of Civilization and Prosperity for All, November 7–9, 2014.

56. Ji-Young Lee, *China's Hegemony: Four Hundred Years of East Asian Domination* (New York: Columbia University Press, 2017).

57. 魏志江 [Wei Zhijiang]], 论东亚传统国际安全体系与所谓华夷次序 [Traditional East Asian international security system and the so-called Chinese-barbarian order], paper presented at the 11th Beijing Forum, The Harmony of Civilization and Prosperity for All, November 7–9, 2014, http://www.xueshutianxia.com/conference/detail/3004650002542172.html.

58. 卢汉超 [Lu Hanchao]. "中国从来就是一个开放的国家吗—再论西方'唱盛中国'" [Has China always been an open country?: Think about the praise of China by the West again], 清华大学学报：哲社版 [Tsinghua University journal: Philosophy and social science edition], no. 3 (2012), http://site.douban.com/125457/widget/notes/4971340/note/270982522/.

59. 周群 [Zhou Qun], "牢牢把握清史研究话语权" [Firmly grasp the right to the discourse of the history of the Qing dynasty], *People's Daily*, January 14, 2019, http://opinion.people.com.cn/n1/2019/0114/c1003-30524940.html.

60. Dittmer and Kim, "Conclusion," in *China's Quest for National Identity*, ed. Lowell Dittmer and Samuel S. Kim (Ithaca, NY: Cornell University Press, 1994), 249.

61. 张启雄 [Chang Chi-hsiung], "近代东亚国际体系的崩解与再生" [The collapse and rebirth of modern East Asian international system], *Chinese Social Science News*, no. 613 (June 27, 2014), http://ex.cssn.cn/djch/djch_djchhg/guojishijiaoxiadeguojitixibianqian/201406/t20140627_1230778.shtml.

62. Benjamin I. Schwartz, "The Chinese Perception of World Order, Past and Present," in Fairbank, *Chinese World Order*, 284.

63. Zhang Yongjin, *China in the International System, 1918–20: The Middle Kingdom at the Periphery* (New York: St. Martin's Press, 1991), 16.

64. James Legge, *The Chinese Classics*, vol. 5, *The Ch'un Ts'ew with the Tso Chuen* (London: Henry Frowned, 1872, reprinted by Hong Kong University Press, 1961), 52.

65. Alvin Y. So and Stephen W. K. Chiu, *East Asia and the World Economy* (Thousand Oaks, CA: Sage Publications, 1995), 34.

66. T. R. Banister, *A History of the External Trade of China, 1834–1881* (Shanghai: Inspector General of Chinese Customs, 1931), 99.

67. Hsin-Pao Chang, *Commissioner Lin and the Opium War* (Cambridge, MA: Harvard University Press, 1964), 10.

68. Peter Ward Fay, *The Opium War, 1840–1842* (Chapel Hill: University of North Carolina Press, 1975), 17.

69. John King Fairbank, *The United States and China* (Cambridge, MA: Harvard University Press, 1983), 161–62.

70. So and Chiu, *East Asia and the World Economy*, 38.

71. Compilation Group for the History of Modern China Series, *The Opium War* (Beijing: Foreign Language Press, 1976), 19.

72. Miles Maochun Yu, "Did China Have a Chance to Win the Opium War?," *Military History in the News*, July 3, 2018, https://www.hoover.org/research/did-china-have-chance-win-opium-war.

73. 胡绳 [Hu Sheng], 从鸦片战争到五四运动 [From the Opium War to the May-Fourth Movement] (Beijing: Renmin Chuban She, 1980).

74. 蒋廷黻 [Jiang Tingfu], 近代中国外交史料辑 [the collection of modern Chinese diplomacy] (Beijing: Dongfang Publishing House, 2014), vol. 1, 270–73.

75. Richard Baum, "The Second Opium War and the Sacking of the Summer Palace," *Great Courses Daily*, February 23, 2021, https://www.thegreatcoursesdaily.com/the-second-opium-war-and-the-sacking-of-the-summer-palace/.

76. Liah Greenfeld, "Roots of Japan-China Rivalry," *Japan Times*, September 27, 2012, http://www.japantimes.co.jp/print/eo20120927a1.html.

77. Yong Deng, "Escaping the Periphery: China's National Identity in World Politics," in *China's International Relations in the 21st Century*, ed. Weixing Hu, Gerald Chan, and Daojiong Zha (Lanham, MD: University Press of America, 2000), 46.

78. Michael Yahuda, "The Changing Face of Chinese Nationalism: The Dimension of Statehood," in *Asian Nationalism*, ed. Michael Leifer (London: Routledge, 2000), 26.

79. Arthur Cotterell, *East Asia: From Chinese Predominance to the Rise of the Pacific Rim* (New York: Oxford University Press, 1993), 113.

80. US State Department, *Foreign Relations of the United States, 1899* (Washington, DC: US Government Printing Office, 1901), 132–33.

81. US State Department, *Foreign Relations of the United States, 1900* (Washington, DC: US Government Printing Office, 1902), 299.

82. 钟述和 [Zhong Shuhe], 走向世界 [Strive toward the world] (Beijing: Chinese Books, 1985), 78.

83. Joseph W. Esherick, "China and the World: From Tribute to Treaties," in *China's Rise in Historical Perspective*, ed. Brantly Womack (Lanham, MD: Bowman & Littlefield Publishers, 2010), 27.

84. Lane J. Jarris, *Peking Gazette* (Leiden, NL: Brill, 2018), 309–23.

85. Ye Jiajia, "Coronavirus and the Boxer War of 1900: Do They Have Something in Common," *Bitter Winter*, June 7, 2020, https://bitterwinter.org/coronavirus-and-the-boxer-war-of-1900-do-they-have-something-in-common/.

86. Yi Wang, "The Backward Will Be Beaten: Historical Lesson, Security, and Nationalism in China," *Journal of Contemporary China* 26, no. 129 (November 2020).

87. 张启雄 [Chang Chi-hsiung], "近代东亚国际体系的崩解与再生" [The collapse and rebirth of modern East Asian international system].

88. Deng Xiaoping, *Build Socialism with Chinese Characteristics* (Beijing: Foreign Languages Press, 1985), 61.

89. 沈骥如 [Shen Jiru], 中国不当不先生 [China does not want to be Mr. No] (Beijing: China Today Press, 1998), 385.

90. 邓小平 [Deng Xiaoping], 坚持四项基本原则 [Insisting the four cardinal principle], 邓小平文选 [Selected works of Deng Xiaoping], vol. 2 (Beijing: People's Press, 1983), 158.

91. Suisheng Zhao, A Nation-State by Construction (Stanford, CA: Stanford University Press, 2004), 250–61.

92. 刘建飞 [Liu Jianfei], 大博弈：中国的太极与美国的拳击 [The great game: China's taiji versus America's boxing] (Hangzhou: Zejiang People's Press, 2005), 268–69.

93. 赵丽球 [Zhao Liqiu], 李志臣 [Li Zhichen], "写在习近平考察曲阜五周年之际" [Written on the occasion of the fifth anniversary of Xi Jinping's inspection of Qufu], *China News*, November 25, 2018, http://www.chinanews.com/gn/2018/11-25/8685028.shtml.

94. H. R. McMaster, "How China Sees the World—And How We Should See China," *The Atlantic*, May 2020, https://www.theatlantic.com/magazine/archive/2020/05/mcmaster-china-strategy/609088/.

95. Jojje Olsson, "The Real Reasons Behind Chinese Expansionism," *Taiwan Sentinel*, July 25, 2017, https://sentinel.tw/real-reasons-behind-chinese-expansionism/.

96. Mao Zedong, "On New Democracy," in *Selected Works of Mao Tse-tung*, vol. 2 (Beijing: Foreign Language Press, 1967), 350–54.

97. Matt Schiavenza, "When Margaret Thatcher Came to China," *The Atlantic*, April 9, 2012, https://www.theatlantic.com/china/archive/2013/04/when-margaret-thatcher-came-to-china/274796/.

98. Xi Jinping, "Speech at a Ceremony Marking the Centenary of the Communist Party of China," Xinhua, July 1, 2021, http://www.xinhuanet.com/english/special/2021-07/01/c_1310038244.htm.

99. 民族意识觉醒—义和团反帝爱国运动 [The awakening of national consciousness—the Boxer movement against imperialism], Xinhua, November 13, 2018, http://www.xinhuanet.com/politics/2018-11/13/c_1123707133.htm.

100. Li Jiaming, "Every Move to Stigmatize China Evokes our Historical Memory," *Global Time,* April 19, 2020, https://www.globaltimes.cn/content/1186037.shtml.

101. Zamir Ahmed Awan, "China Can No Longer Be Coerced by Any Country," *People's Daily Online*, April 15, 2020, https://www.chinadaily.com.cn/a/202004/15/WS5e967846a3105d50a3d1659b.html.

102. Editorial, "West's Pandemic Falsehoods Debunked," *Global Times*, April 16, 2020, https://www.globaltimes.cn/content/1185819.shtml.

103. 胡锡进 [Hu Xijing], 方方日记在美国出版], 公众对她的态度会变得更快 [Fang Fang's diary is published in the United States, and the public's attitude toward her will quickly become worse faster], *Global Times*, April 9, 2020, https://china.huanqiu.com/article/3xktVL9JRkI.

104. 吴稼祥 [Wu Jiaxiang], 中国为轴], 世界为轮—重构全球体系的新天下国际战略 [China is the axis, the world is the wheel—A new world international strategy to reconstruct the global system], *Aisixiang*, September 26, 2014, http://www.aisixiang.com/data/78336-2.html.

105. Michael Hunt, "Chinese Foreign Relations in Historical Perspective," in *China's Foreign Relations in the 1980s*, ed. Harry Harding (New Haven, CT: Yale University Press, 1984), 7.

106. "习近平出席2022年世界经济论坛视频会议并发表演讲" [Xi Jinping attends 2022 World Economic Forum video conference and delivers a speech], Xinhua, January 17, 2022, http://www.gov.cn/xinwen/2022-01/17/content_5668929.htm.

Chapter 5

1. Erica Strecker Downs and Philip C. Saunders, "Legitimacy and the Limits of Nationalism: China and the Diaoyu Island," *International Security* 23, no. 3 (Winter 1989–99); Allen Whiting, "Chinese Nationalism and Foreign Policy After Deng," *China Quarterly* 142 (1995); Yinan He, "History, Chinese Nationalism and the Emerging Sino-Japanese Conflict," *Journal of Contemporary China* 16, no. 50 (2007); Suisheng Zhao, *A Nation-State by Construction: Dynamics of Modern Chinese Nationalism* (Stanford, CA: Stanford University Press, 2004).

2. Peter Gries, *China's New Nationalism* (Berkeley, CA: University of California Press, 2004), 12, 134; Richard Bernstein and Ross H. Munro, "The Coming Conflict with America," *Foreign Affairs* 76, no. 2 (1997): 19; Christopher Hughes, "Reclassifying Chinese Nationalism: The *Geopolitik* Turn," *Journal of Contemporary China* 20, no. 70 (2011): 602–18; Suisheng Zhao, "Foreign Policy Implications of Chinese

Nationalism Revisited: The Strident Turn," *Journal of Contemporary China* 22, no. 82 (2013).

3. Steven I. Levine, "Perception and Ideology in Chinese Foreign Policy," in *Chinese Foreign Policy: Theory and Practice*, ed. Thomas W. Robinson and David Shambaught (Oxford, UK: Clarendon Press, 1994), 37–38.

4. Lau Siu-kai, "The Hong Kong Policy of the People's Republic of China: 1949–1997," *Journal of Contemporary China* 9, no. 23 (March 2000).

5. Andrew Scobell, "Soldiers, Statesmen, Strategic Culture and China's 1950 Intervention in Korea," *Journal of Contemporary China* 8, no. 22 (November 1999).

6. Mao Zedong, "On the People's Democratic Dictatorship," in *Selected Works of Mao Zedong*, vol. 4 (Beijing: Foreign Language Press, 1969), 417.

7. Hugo Restall, "China's Bid for Asian Hegemony," *Far Eastern Economic Review*, May 2007, http://viet-studies.com/kinhte/China_asian_hegemony_FEER.pdf.

8. This part draws on the author's book, Suisheng Zhao, *A Nation-State by Construction, Dynamics of Modern Chinese Nationalism* (Stanford, CA: Stanford University Press, 2004).

9. 汤应武 [Tang Yingwu], *1976 年以来的中国* [China since 1976] (Beijing: Economic Daily Press, 1997), 329.

10. 中共北京市委宣传部 [The propaganda department of the CCP Beijing municipal committee], 国家教委基础教育司 [The basic education department of the State Education Commission], 国情教育读本 [The readers of national essence education] (Beijing: Military Translation Press, 1991), 50–51.

11. Suisheng Zhao, "A State-Led Nationalism: The Patriotic Education Campaign in Post-Tiananmen China," *Communist and Post-Communist Studies* 31, no. 3 (1998).

12. Jia Qingguo, "From Self-Imposed Isolation to Global Cooperation: The Evolution of Chinese Foreign Policy since the 1980s," *Politik und Gesellschaft, International Politics and Society*, no. 2 (1999): 169.

13. Yan Xuetong, 中国国家利益分析 [Analysis of China's national interests] (Tianjin, China: Tianjin Renmin Chuban She, 1996).

14. "首轮中美经济对话:除上月球外主要问题均已谈" [The first round of China-US economic dialogue: All subjects are covered except landing on the moon], *China News Agency*, July 28, 2009, http://www.chinanews.com.cn/gn/news/2009/07-29/1794984.shtml.

15. Feiling Wang, ""Preservation, Prosperity and Power: What Motivates China's Foreign Policy," *Journal of Contemporary China* 14, no. 45 (November 2005).

16. Feiling Wang, "Preservation, Prosperity and Power," 678–79.

17. Susan V. Lawrence, "China—The Say No Club," *Far Eastern Economic Review*, January 13, 2000, 16.

18. 肖功秦 [Xiao Gongxin], "中国民族主义的历史与前景" [The history and prospect of Chinese nationalism], 战略与管理 [Strategy and management], no. 2 (1996): 59.

19. Ian Seckington, "Nationalism, Ideology and China's 'Fourth Generation' Leadership," *Journal of Contemporary China* 14, no. 42 (2005): 28.

20. Wu Xinbo, *Managing Crisis and Sustaining Peace between China and the United States* (Washington, D.C.: United States Institute of Peace, 2003), 10–13.

21. Peter Hay Gries and Kaiping Feng, "Culture Clash? Apologies East and West," *Journal of Contemporary China* 11, no. 30 (2002): 173–78.

22. Yue-him Tam, "Who Engineered the Anti-Japanese Protest in 2005," *Macalester International* 18, no. 25 (Spring 2007), https://core.ac.uk/download/pdf/46721784.pdf.

23. Suisheng Zhao, "China's Pragmatic Nationalism: Is It Manageable?," *Washington Quarterly* 29, no. 1 (Winter 2005–06) (http://www.twq.com/06winter/docs/06winter _zhao.pdf).

24. Yun Su, "Chinese Public Opinion: Shaping China's Foreign Policy, or Shaped by It?," *Brookings East Asia Commentary*, December 13, 2011, https://www.brookings.edu/opinions/chinese-public-opinion-shaping-chinas-foreign-policy-or-shaped-by-it/.

25. Chen Zimin, "Nationalism, Internationalism and Chinese Foreign Policy," *Journal of Contemporary China* 14, no. 42 (2005): 51–52.

26. Suisheng Zhao, "Foreign Policy Implications of Chinese Nationalism Revisited: The Strident Turn," *Journal of Contemporary China* 22, no. 82 (July 2013).

27. Christopher Hughes, "Reclassifying Chinese Nationalism: The *Geopolitik* Turn," *Journal of Contemporary China* 20, no. 70 (2011): 602, 618.

28. 宋小军 [Song Xiaojun], 王晓东 [Wang Xiaodong], Huang Jisu [黄际苏], 宋强 [Song Qiang], 中国不高兴 [China is not happy] (Nanjing: Jiangsu People's Press, 2009).

29. 戴旭 [Dai Xu], C形包围—内忧外患下的中国突围 [C-shape encircle, China's breakthrough with the internal concerns and external dangers] (Beijing: Wenhui Press, 2009).

30. 刘明福 [Liu Mingfu], 中国梦 [The China dream] (Beijing: Friendship Publishing Company, 2010).

31. Luo Yuan, "China Won't 'Abandon' War Option," China.org.cn, May 10, 2012, http://www.china.org.cn/opinion/2012-05/10/content_25350539.htm.

32. Editorial, "Don't Take Peaceful Approach for Granted," *Global Times*, October 25, 2011, http://www.globaltimes.cn/NEWS/tabid/99/ID/680694/Dont-take-peaceful-approach-for-granted.aspx.

33. Ou Yang Ray, "Political Process and Widespread Protests in China: The 2010 Labour Protest," *Journal of Contemporary China* 24, no. 91 (January 2015); Yang Zhong, Wonjae Hwang, "Pollution, Institutions and Street Protest in Urban China," *Journal of Contemporary China* 25, no. 98 (March 2016).

34. Thomas J. Christensen, "The Advantages of an Assertive China: Responding to Beijing's Abrasive Diplomacy," *Foreign Affairs* 90, no. 2 (2011), http://www.foreignaffairs.com/articles/67477/thomas-j-christensen/the-advantages-of-an-assertive-china.

35. Mimi Lau, "Class Ideology: China's Education Chiefs Order Schools to Roll Out Patriotic Campaign on New Media," *South China Morning Post*, February 10, 2016, http://www.scmp.com/news/china/policies-politics/article/1911336/class-ideology-chinas-education-chiefs-order-schools.

36. "Xi Urges China's Youth to Embrace Nationalism on Key Anniversary," *Bloomberg News*, April 29, 2019, https://www.bloomberg.com/news/articles/2019-04-30/xi-urges-china-s-youth-to-embrace-nationalism-on-key-anniversary.

37. "Top Party Leadership Highlights Patriotic Education," *China Daily*, September 25, 2019, https://www.chinadaily.com.cn/a/201909/25/WS5d8a7e4ca310cf3e3556d425.html.

38. 中共中央组织部 中共中央宣传部关于在广大知识分子中深入开展"弘扬爱国奋斗精神、建功立业新时代"活动的通知 [Notice of the CPC Central Committee Organization Department and Propaganda Department on the in-depth development of the "promoting the spirit of patriotic struggle and building a new era" among the intellectuals], Xinhua, July 31, 2018, https://app.peopleapp.com/Api/600/DetailApi/shareArticle?type=0&article_id=2073565.

39. David Bandurski, "Parsing the 'Public Opinion Struggle,'" *China Media Project*, September 24, 2013, http://chinamediaproject.org/2013/09/24/parsing-chinas-public-opinion-struggle/.

40. 成其圣 [Cheng Qisheng], "意识形态工作一刻也不能放松和削弱" [Can never relax ideological works], *Qiushi*, no. 17 (September 1, 2013), http://theory.people.com.cn/n/2013/1202/c49150-23715228.html.

41. "大学老师], 请不要这样讲谈论中国 致高校哲学社会科学老师的一封公开信" [University teachers, please don't talk about China like that: An open letter to teachers of philosophy and social sciences," *Liaoning Daily*, November 13, 2014, https://www.guancha.cn/LiaoNingRiBao/2014_11_14_286323.shtml.

42. "习近平对高校党建工作做出重要指示" [Xi Jinping important instructions on the party building in higher learning], *People's Daily*, December 30, 2014, 1.

43. 中共中央办公厅、国务院办公厅 [General offices of the CCP Central Committee and the State Council], "关于进一步加强和改进新形势下高校宣传思想工作的意见" [The opinion concerning further strengthening and improving propaganda and ideology work in higher education under new circumstances], Xinhua, January 19, 2015, http://www.xinhuanet.com/politics/2015-01/19/c_1114051345.htm.

44. Hualing Fu, "The July 9th (709) Crackdown on Human Rights Lawyers: Legal Advocacy in an Authoritarian State," *Journal of Contemporary China* 27, no. 112 (July 2018)>

45. Andrew Browne, "Nationalism Gives Xi a Boost, but Comes with Risk, Power Parade Rallies the Masses, but Sets Up New Tensions," *Wall Street Journal*, September 8, 2015, https://www.wsj.com/articles/nationalism-gives-xi-a-boost-but-comes-with-risk-1441703668.

46. "首都各界隆重纪念全民族抗战爆发七十七周年 习近平发表重要讲话" [Commemorating the 77th anniversary of the outbreak of the national war of resistance, Xi Jinping delivers an important speech], July 7, 2014, Xinhua, http://www.xinhuanet.com//politics/2014-07/07/c_1111491529.htm.

47. "China Stresses Nationalism in Second World War 70th Anniversary Propaganda Push," Reuters, July 6, 2015, http://www.scmp.com/news/china/society/article/1833346/china-prepares-huge-wave-propaganda-70th-anniversary-second-world.

48. Rana Mitter, *China's Good War: How World War II Is Shaping a New Nationalism* (New York: Belknap Press, 2020), 21–25.

49. Commentary, "To enjoy the Chinese film Wolf Warrior II, shed your biases," Xinhua, August 16, 2017, http://news.xinhuanet.com/english/2017-08/16/c_136530175.htm.

50. "庆祝中华人民共和国成立70周年大会隆重举行" [Celebrating the 70th anniversary of the founding of the People's Republic of China], Xinhua, October 1, 2019, http://www.gov.cn/xinwen/2019-10/01/content_5435777.htm.

51. Edward Cunningham, Tony Saich, and Jesse Turiel, *Understanding CCP Resilience: Surveying Chinese Public Opinion through Time*, Ash Center for Democratic Governance and Innovation, Harvard Kennedy School, July 2020, https://ash.harvard.edu/files/ash/files/final_policy_brief_7.6.2020.pdf.

52. Liza Lin, "Xi's China Crafts Campaign to Boost Youth Patriotism," *Wall Street Journal*, December 30, 2020, https://www.wsj.com/articles/xi-china-campaign-youth-patriotism-propaganda-11609343255?mod=hp_lead_pos10.

53. Tania Branigan, "China's 'Great Firewall' Creator Pelted with Shoes," *The Guardian*, May 20, 2011, https://www.theguardian.com/world/2011/may/20/china-great-firewall-creator-pelted-shoes.

54. 公安部 [The Ministry of Public Security], "将在重点网站和互联网企业设网安警务室" [Setting internet security stations in key websites and internet enterprises], Xinhua, August 4, 2015, http://politics.people.com.cn/n/2015/0804/c1001-27410883.html.

55. Sarah Cook, "Five Predictions for Chinese Censorship in the Year of the Sheep," *Foreign Policy*, February 19, 2015, http://foreignpolicy.com/2015/02/19/five-predictions-for-chinese-censorship-in-the-year-of-the-sheep/.

56. Yaqiu Wang, "In China, the 'Great Firewall' Is Changing a Generation," *Politico*, September 1, 2020, https://www.politico.com/news/magazine/2020/09/01/china-great-firewall-generation-405385.

57. Kecheng Fang and Maria Repnikova, "Demystifying 'Little Pink': The Creation and Evolution of a Gendered Label for Nationalistic Activists in China," *New Media & Society* 20, no. 6 (2017): 2162–85; Anthony Tao, "China's Little Pink Are Not Who You Think," *SupChina*, November 15, 2017, https://supchina.com/2017/11/15/chinas-little-pink-are-not-who-you-think/; Lotus Ruan, "The New Face of Chinese

Nationalism," *Foreign Affairs*, August 25, 2016, https://foreignpolicy.com/2016/08/25/the-new-face-of-chinese-nationalism/.

58. Chris Buckley, "China's Combative Nationalists See a World Turning Their Way," *New York Times*, December 14, 2020, https://www.nytimes.com/2020/12/14/world/asia/china-nationalists-covid.html.

59. Yang Zhong and Wonjae Hwang, "Why Do Chinese Democrats Tend to Be More Nationalistic? Explaining Popular Nationalism in Urban China," *Journal of Contemporary China* 29, no. 121 (January 2020).

60. Jessica Chen Weiss, "How Hawkish Is the Chinese Public? Another Look at "Rising Nationalism" and Chinese Foreign Policy," *Journal of Contemporary China* 28, no. 119 (September 2019).

61. Haifeng Huang, "How Information Bubble Drives the Chinese Public's Views of China's Global Standing and Fuels Grassroots Nationalism," China Data Lab, the 21st Century China Center, University of California, San Diego, December 2020, http://chinadatalab.ucsd.edu/viz-blog/how-information-bubble-drives-the-chinese-publics-views-of-chinas-global-standing-and-fuels-grassroots-nationalism/?s=03.

62. Zheping Huang, "'Fangirls' Defend China from Hong Kong Protesters and the World," *Bloomberg News*, December 9, 2019, https://www.bloomberg.com/news/articles/2019-12-09/-fangirls-defend-china-from-hong-kong-protesters-and-the-world.

63. Yifu Dong, "Chinese Citizens around the World Are Shamefully Siding with Beijing against Hong Kong," *Washington Post*, August 30, 2019, https://www.washingtonpost.com/opinions/2019/08/30/chinese-citizens-around-world-are-shamefully-siding-with-beijing-against-hong-kong/.

64. Kristin Huang, "China's Nationalism Might Work at Home, but It's Causing Upset on the World Stage," *South China Morning Post*, April 26, 2020, https://www.scmp.com/news/china/diplomacy/article/3081546/chinas-nationalism-might-work-home-its-causing-upset-world.

65. Yaqiu Wang, "'Great Firewall' Is Changing a Generation."

66. Chris Buckley, China's Combative Nationalists See a World Turning Their Way," *New York Times*, December 14, 2020, https://www.nytimes.com/2020/12/14/world/asia/china-nationalists-covid.html.

67. Huang Lanlan, "'Invaders United Kingdom 1900': Chinese Cartoonist Wuheqilin Mocks G7 Meeting with New Illustration," *Global Times*, May 7, 2021, https://www.globaltimes.cn/page/202105/1222868.shtml.

68. Sarah Zheng, "US Leads World in Pandemic Failure: Chinese Report Takes Aim at American Coronavirus Response," *South China Morning Post*, August 9, 2021, https://www.scmp.com/news/china/diplomacy/article/3144400/us-leads-world-pandemic-failure-chinese-report-takes-aim?module=perpetual_scroll&pgtype=article&campaign=3144400.

69. "If Zhang Wenhong Does Not Dare to Speak, What Will We Lose?," iNews, August 24, 2021, https://inf.news/en/news/e32906291456e4f89743703f6be9103a.html.

70. Donald Low, "Beijing's Insistence on Zero-Covid Strategy Challenges Long-Held Assumptions about China," *South China Morning Post*, October 22, 2021, https://www.scmp.com/week-asia/opinion/article/3153262/beijings-insistence-zero-covid-strategy-challenges-long-held.

71. "外交部副部长乐玉成, 战狼外交是"中国威胁论的又一翻版" [Vice foreign minister Le Yucheng, wolf warriors diplomacy is another version of China threat theory], PRC Ministry of Foreign Affairs, December 5, 2020, https://www.fmprc.gov.cn/web/wjbxw_673019/t1838078.shtml.

72. Andrew Browne, "Xi Jinping's Words of Warning Echo China's Youthful Nationalism," *Bloomberg News*, July 3, 2021, https://www.bloomberg.com/news/newsletters/2021-07-03/xi-s-words-of-warning-echo-china-s-youth-new-economy-saturday.

Chapter 6

1. 中国中共文献研究会 [China central literature research society],周恩来与马克思主义中国化 [Zhou Enlai and the Chinese Marxism] (Heilongjiang People's Publishing House, 2012), 468.

2. 周恩来 [Zhou Enlai], "外交队伍是文装解放军" [Diplomatic troops are PLA with civilian clothes], Zhou Enlai Memorial Net, November 30, 2020, http://zhouenlai.people.cn/n1/2018/1130/c409117-30434781.html.

3. David M. Lampton, "China's Foreign and National Security Policy-Making Process: Is It Changing and Does It Matter?," in David M. Lampton, *The Making of Chinese Foreign and Security Policy* (Stanford, CA: Stanford University Press, 20010, 12.

4. Zhoa Kejin and Gao Xin, "Pursuing the Chinese Dream: Institutional Changes of Chinese Diplomacy under President Xi Jinping," *China Quarterly of International Strategic Studies* 1, no. 1 (2015): 39.

5. Kenneth G. Lieberthal, "Introduction: The Fragmented Authoritarianism Model and Its Limitations," in *Bureaucracy, Politics, and Decision Making in Post-Mao China*, ed. Kenneth G. Lieberthal and David M. Lampton (Berkeley, CA: University of California Press, 1992), 1–32.

6. Michel C. Oksenberg, "Policy Making under Mao Tse-tung, 1949–1968," *Comparative Politics* 3, no. 3 (1971): 324.

7. 中央财经领导小组的变迁 [Evolution of the central finance and economic leadership small group], 人民网 [Peoplesnet], June 25, 2014, http://politics.people.com.cn/n/2014/0625/c1001-25199975.html.

8. Taeho Kim, "Leading Small Group: Managing All Under Heaven," in *China's Leadership in the 21st Century: The Rise of the Fourth Generation*, ed. David M. Finkelstein and Maryanne Kivlehan (Armonk, NY: M. E. Sharpe, 2003), 127–28.

9. Suisheng Zhao, "The Structure of Authority and Decision-Making: A Theoretical Framework," in *Decision-Making in Deng's China: Perspective from Insiders*, ed. Carol Lee Hamrin and Suisheng Zhao (Armonk, NY: M. E. Sharpe, 1995), 233–46.

10. 若拙 [Rouzhuo], 中国外交系统人事盘点 [Inventory of China's foreign affairs sector], 上观新闻 [Shangguan Observer], September 24, 2014, https://web.shobserver.com/news/detail?id=433.

11. Guoguang Wu, "The Emergence of the Central Office of Foreign Affairs: From Leadership Politics to Greater Diplomacy," China Leadership Monitor, September 1, 2021, https://www.prcleader.org/wu-1.

12. Yun Sun, "China's National Security Decision-Making: Processes and Challenges," Brookings Institution, Center for Northeast Asian Policy Studies, May 2013, http://www.brookings.edu/research/papers/2013/05/chinese-national-security-decision-making-sun.

13. Weixing Hu, "Xi Jinping 'Big Power Diplomacy' and China's Central National Security Commission (CNSC)," Journal of Contemporary China 25, no. 98 (March 2016).

14. David, M. Lampton, "Xi Jinping and the National Security Commission: Policy Coordination and Political Power," Journal of Contemporary China 24, no. 95 (September 2015).

15. "十九届中央国安委首会], 习近平压实责任" [the First meeting of the central national security commission, President Xi pushed for taking responsibilities], Xinhua, April 18, 2018, http://politics.people.com.cn/n1/2018/0418/c1001-29935332.html.

16. Samantha Hoffman And Peter Mattis, "Managing the Power Within: China's State Security Commission," War On the Rocks, July 18, 2016, http://warontherocks.com/2016/07/managing-the-power-within-chinas-state-security-commission/.

17. "习近平主持召开中央外事工作委员会第一次会议" [Xi Jinping hosts the first meeting of the Central Foreign Affairs Commission], Xinhua, May 15, 2018, http://www.gov.cn/xinwen/2018-05/15/content_5291161.htm.

18. "习近平在周边外交工作座谈会上发表重要讲话" [President Xi made an important speech at the Central Work Conference on Peripheral Diplomacy], Xinhua, October 25, 2013, http://www.xinhuanet.com/politics/2013-10/25/c_117878897.htm.

19. "习近平, 努力开创中国特色大国外交新局面" [Xi Jinping urges breaking new ground in major country diplomacy with Chinese characteristics], Xinhua, June 23, 2018, http://www.xinhuanet.com/politics/2018-06/23/c_1123025806.htm.

20. Yen-Chiang Chang and Xiuhua Li, "The Disappearance of the State Oceanic Administration in China?—Current Developments," Marine Policy 107 (2019): 1–2.

21. Yu Jie and Lucy Ridout, "Who Decides China's Foreign Policy? The Role of Central Government, Provincial-Level Authorities and State-Owned Enterprises," Briefing Paper, Chatham House, November 2021, file:///C:/Users/suisheng.zhao/Desktop/Documents/chinaForeingPolicy/forpolimaking/who-decides-chinas-foreign-policy-jie-et-al.pdf.pdf.

22. George Yang, "Mechanism of Foreign Policy-Making and Implementation in the Ministry of Foreign Affairs," in Hamrin and Zhao, Decision-Making in Deng's China, 91–100.

23. Lu Ning, *The Dynamics of Foreign Policy Decision Making in China* (Boulder, CO: Westview Press, 1997), 20.

24. Jing Sun, "Growing Diplomacy, Retreating Diplomats: How Chinese Foreign Ministry Has Been Marginalized in Foreign Policymaking," *Journal of Contemporary China* 26, no. 105 (May 2017).

25. 习近平接见2017年度驻外使节工作会议与会使节并发表重要讲话 [Xi Jinping met with the 2017 meeting of chinese diplomatic envoys and made important speech], Xinhua, December 28, 2017, http://www.xinhuanet.com/politics/leaders/2017-12/28/c_1122181743.htm; "习近平对中国外交人员提四点要求" [Xi Jinping made four requirements for Chinese diplomats], Xinhua, December 28, 2017, http://www.chinanews.com/gn/2017/12-28/8411832.shtml.

26. Markus Herrmann and Sabine Mokry, "China Races to Catch Up on Foreign Affairs Spending," *The Diplomat*, August 9, 2018, https://thediplomat.com/2018/08/china-races-to-catch-up-on-foreign-affairs-spending/.

27. David Shambaugh, "China's Quiet Diplomacy: The International Department of the Chinese Communist Party," *China, An International Journal* 5, no. 1 (March 2017): 26–54.

28. 中共中央对外联络部官网 [The CCP Central Committee international liaison department introduction official website], http://www.idcpc.org.cn/zlbjj/wbjj/.

29. "传播中国方案, 讲好中共故事—专访中共中央对外联络部部长宋涛" [Spread China's solution and tell the CCP story—interview of the CCP CLD minister Song Tao], *China News Week*, October 21, 2016, http://www.idcpc.org.cn/bzhd/mtzf/201912/t20191216_107362.html.

30. Neil Thomas, "Proselytizing Power: The Party Wants the World to Learn from Its Experiences," *MacroPolo*, January 22, 2020, https://macropolo.org/international-liaison-department-ccp/.

31. 宋涛 [Song Tao], "建立新型政党关系 建设更加美好世界" [Establishing the new type of political party relations and building a better world], January 4, 2018, CLD official website, https://www.idcpc.org.cn/bzhd/smwz/201912/t20191216_107283.html.

32. "2017年中国共产党与世界政党高层对话会" [The CCP in Dialogue with World Political Parties High-Level Meeting in 2017], People.com, December 3, 2017, http://cpc.people.com.cn/GB/67481/415498/index.html.

33. "中国共产党与世界政党高层对话会非洲专题会为中非交流合作注入强劲动力" [The African special subject conference of the CCP in Dialogue with World Political Parties High-Level Meeting have motivated the exchange and cooperation between China and Africa], *China African Forum*, July 23, 2018, https://www.fmprc.gov.cn/zflt/chn/zxxx/t1578642.htm.

34. Yew Lun Tian, "China's Xi Takes Dig at US in Speech to Political Parties around World," Reuters, July 6, 2021, https://www.reuters.com/world/china/chinas-xi-takes-dig-us-speech-political-parties-around-2021-07-06/.

35. "Keynote Address by Xi Jinping at CPC and World Political Parties Summit," Xinhua, July 7, 2021, http://www.xinhuanet.com/english/2021-07/07/c_1310048196 .htm.

36. Clyde Yicheng Wang, "Changing Strategies and Mixed Agendas: China's External Propaganda and Its Organizational Structure," *Journal of Contemporary China* 32, no. 142 (July 2023).

37. "Xinhua: The World's Biggest Propaganda Agency," Reporters Without Borders, September 30, 2005, https://rsf.org/en/reports/xinhua-worlds-biggest-propaganda -agency.

38. Mao Zedong, "Introducing the Communist, October 4, 1939," *Selected Works of Mao Tse-tung*, vol. 2, https://www.marxists.org/reference/archive/mao/selected-works/ volume-2/mswv2_20.htm.

39. 冯海波 [Feng Haibo], "十八大以来习近平总书记对统一战线理论的丰 富和发展" [Enrichment and development of the United Front theories by General Secretary Xi Jinping after the 18th Party Congress], Jinchu United Front, January 5, 2018, http://www.zytzb.gov.cn/tzb2010/wxwb/201801/243f42014b5f4f2bad384e47d2 2f23cc.shtml.

40. 康琪雪 [Kang Qicue], "部委撤并10天后], 部长转任" [Ten days after the merge of the ministries and commissions], *New Beijing News*, April 2, 2018, http:// www.bjd.com.cn/sd/mrq/201804/02/t20180402_11083557.html.

41. "China's Overseas United Front Work and Implications for United States, US China Economic and Security Review Commission," US-China Economic and Security Review Commission, August 24, 2018, https://www.uscc.gov/research/ chinas-overseas-united-front-work-background-and-implications-united-states; Alex Joske, "The Party Speaks for You: Foreign Interference and the Chinese Communist Party's United Front System," Australian Strategic Policy Institute, June 9, 2020, https://s3-ap-southeast-2.amazonaws.com/ad-aspi/2020-06/The%20 party%20speaks%20for%20you_0.pdf?gFHuXyYMR0XuDQOs.6JSmrdyk7Mr alcN.

42. Information Office of the State Council, the People's Republic of China, *China's National Defense in 1998*, September 1998, https://jamestown.org/wp-content/ uploads/2016/07/China%E2%80%99s-National-Defense-in-1998.pdf?x87069.

43. Franz-Stefan Gady, "Why the West Should Not Underestimate China-Russia Military Ties," *Stratfor*, February 13, 2019, https://worldview.stratfor.com/article/ why-west-should-not-underestimate-china-russia-military-ties.

44. Shaio H. Zerba, "China's Libya Evacuation Operation: A New Diplomatic Imperative—Overseas Citizen Protection," *Journal of Contemporary China* 23, no. 90 (November 2014).

45. Jean-Pierre Cabestan, "China's Military Base in Djibouti: A Microcosm of China's Growing Competition with the United States and New Bipolarity," *Journal of Contemporary China* 29, no. 125 (September 2020).

46. Jing-dong Yuan, "China's Pragmatic Approach to Nonproliferation Policy in the Post–Cold War Era," in *Chinese Foreign Policy, Pragmatism and Strategic Behavior*, ed. Suisheng Zhao (Armonk, NY: M. E. Sharpe, 2004), 151–78.

47. Jing Sun, "Growing Diplomacy, Retreating Diplomats: How Chinese Foreign Ministry Has Been Marginalized in Foreign Policymaking," *Journal of Contemporary China* 26, no. 105 (May 2017).

48. Yawei Liu and Justine Zheng Ren, "An Emerging Consensus on the US Threat: The United States According to PLA Officers," *Journal of Contemporary China* 23, no. 86 (March 2014).

49. You Ji, "The PLA and Diplomacy: Unraveling Some Myths about Civil Military Interaction in Chinese Foreign Policy-Making," *Journal of Contemporary China* 23, no. 86 (March 2014).

50. Joseph Kahn, "Chinese General Threatens Use of A-Bombs If US Intrudes," *New York Times*, July 15, 2005, https://www.nytimes.com/2005/07/15/washington/world/chinese-general-threatens-use-of-abombs-if-us-intrudes.html.

51. Personal interview with General Zhu Chenghu when he visited Denver in May 2015.

52. You Ji, "PLA and Diplomacy."

53. 社论 [Editorial], "确保人民军队绝对忠诚于党和人民" [Ensure that the People's Army is absolutely loyal to the party and the people], *People's Daily*, July 31, 2020, http://www.chinanews.com/mil/2020/07-31/9252607.shtml.

54. Liu Zhen, "Xi Jinping Shakes Up China's Military Leadership . . . What Changes at the Top Mean for World's Biggest Armed Forces," *South China Morning Post*, October 26, 2017, https://www.scmp.com/news/china/diplomacy-defence/article/2116856/what-changes-top-mean-chinas-military.

55. 李宣良 [Li Xuanliang], "全军外事工作会议召开：军事外交要抓好服务大局和行动协同" [PLA foreign affairs work conference held: Military diplomacy must serve the overall situation and coordinate actions], Xinhua, January 31, 2015, https://www.thepaper.cn/newsDetail_forward_1299697.

56. Kenneth Allen, Phillip C. Saunders, and John Chen, "Chinese Military Diplomacy, 2003–2016: Trends and Implications," *China Strategic Perspectives*, No. 11, National Defense University Press, July 2017, http://www.dmrsc.com/DocumentUS/INSSreportChinaPerspectives.pdf.

57. 朱书缘 [Zhu Shuyuan], "习近平为何特别强调"新型智库建设" [Why has Xi Jinping stressed the construction of think tanks], *Cpcnews.com*, October 29, 2014, http://theory.people.com.cn/n/2014/1029/c148980-25928251.html.

58. PRC State Council Official Website, Chinese Academy of Social Sciences, http://www.gov.cn/english/2005-12/02/content_116009.htm.

59. Pascal Abb, "China's Foreign Policy Think Tanks: Institutional Evolution and Changing Roles," *Journal of Contemporary China* 24, no. 93 (May 2015).

60. Pascal Abb, "China's Foreign Policy Think Tanks."

61. Wen-Hsuan Tsai and Liao Xingmiu, "Concentrating Power to Accomplish Big Things: The CCP's *Pishi* System and Operation in Contemporary China," *Journal of Contemporary China* 26, no. 104 (March 2017).

62. Xue Li, "The Problems with China's Foreign Policy Bureaucracy," *The Diplomat,* April 17, 2015, https://thediplomat.com/2015/04/the-problems-with-chinas-foreign-policy-bureaucracy/.

63. James G. McGann, *Think Tanks: The New Knowledge and Policy Brokers in Asia* (Washington, DC: Brookings Institution, 2019), 4.

64. Zhu Xufeng, "The Influence of Think-Tanks in the Chinese Policy Process: Different Ways and Mechanisms," *Asian Survey* 49 (2009): 333–57.

65. Jianwei Wang, "Chinese Media and Foreign Policy," *Journal of Contemporary China* 23, no. 86 (March 2014).

66. Peter T. Y. Cheung and James T. H. Tang, "The External Relations of China's Provinces," in *The Making of Chinese Foreign and Security Policy*, ed. David Lampton (Stanford, CA: Stanford University Press, 2001), 91–120.

67. Mingjiang Li, "Local Liberalism: China's Provincial Approaches to Relations with Southeast Asia," *Journal of Contemporary China* 23, no. 86 (March 2014).

68. Yu Jie and Lucy Ridout, "Who Decides China's Foreign Policy? The Role of Central Government, Provincial-Level Authorities and State-Owned Enterprises," Briefing Paper, Chatham House, November 2021, https://www.chathamhouse.org/2021/11/who-decides-chinas-foreign-policy.

69. Amanda Coletta, "Canada's 'Two Michaels' Back Home after More Than 1,000 Days Imprisoned in China As Huawei's Meng Cuts Deal with US," *Washington Post*, September 25, 2021, https://www.washingtonpost.com/world/2021/09/24/canada-two-michaels-china-huawei/.

Chapter 7

1. Wang Jisi, "International Relations Theory and Study of Chinese Foreign Policy: A Chinese Perspective," in *Chinese Foreign Policy: Theory and Practice*, ed. Thomas W. Robinson and David Shambaugh (Oxford, UK: Clarendon Press, 1995), 489.

2. Hal Brands and John Lewis Gaddis, "The New Cold War: America, China, and the Echoes of History," *Foreign Affairs*, November/December 2021, https://www.foreignaffairs.com/articles/united-states/2021-10-19/new-cold-war.

3. Jonathan D. Pollack, "China and the Global Strategic Balance," in *China's Foreign Relations in the 1980s*, ed. Harry Harding (New Haven, CT: Yale University Press, 1984), 147–48.

4. "Chairman Mao's Theory of the Differentiation of the Three Worlds Is a Major Contribution to Marxism-Leninism," in *Beijing Review*, no. 45 (November 4, 1977): 29–33.

5. Lowell Dittmer, *Sino-Soviet Normalization and Its International Implications, 1945–1990* (Seattle: University of Washington Press, 1992), 151.

6. Robert A. Scalapino, "Relations Between the Nations of the Pacific Quadrille: Stability and Fluctuation in East Asian Politics," in *Japan and the Pacific Quadrille: The Major Powers in East Asia*, ed. Herbert J. Ellison (Boulder, CO: Westview Press, 1987), 12.

7. Donald Zagoria, "The Soviet Union's Eastern Problem," in *Northeast Asian Security after Vietnam*, ed. Martin E. Weinstein (Urbana: University of Illinois Press, 1982), 91–92.

8. John W. Garver, *Foreign Relations of the People's Republic of China* (Englewood Cliffs, NJ: Prentice Hall, 1993), 32–33.

9. Robert S. Ross, "Conclusion: Tripolarity and Policy Making," in *China, the United States, and the Soviet Union: Tripolarity and Policy Making in the Cold War World*, ed. Robert S. Ross (Armonk, NY: M. E. Sharpe, 1993), 182.

10. 陈启懋[Chen Qimao], "世界体系从两极到多极发展研究" [A study of the development of the world system from bipolarity to multipolarity], 国际问题研究 [International studies], no.4 (1990): 1–6; 宋一鸣 [Song Yimin], "世界形势变化的新问题" [The New problems associated with the changing world situation], *Outlook Weekly*, no. 36 (1990): 39–42; 王光 [Wang Guang], "西方想要什么样的新世界秩序" [What new world order does the west want?) *Outlook Weekly*, no. 37 (1990): 38–43; and 黄丁伟 [Huang Dingwi], 王玉林 [Wang Yulin], "迅速变化的世界形势" [The rapidly changing world situation], 现代国际关系 [Contemporary international relations], no. 3 (1990,): 1–8.

11. Suisheng Zhao, "China's Perception of International System and Foreign Policy Adjustment after the Tiananmen Incident," in *Chinese Foreign Policy: Pragmatism and Strategic Behavior*, ed. Suisheng Zhao (Armonk, NY: M. E. Sharpe, 2004), 142.

12. Qian Qichen, "Adhering to Independent Foreign Policy," *Beijing Review* 34, no. 52 (Dec. 30, 1991–Jan.5, 1992): 7; "Chinese Foreign Minister Qian Qichen Press Conference," *Beijing Review* 35, no. 14 (April 6–12, 1992): 15.

13. 冯立东 [Feng Lidong], "访谈国际问题研究所所长杨成绪" [Interview with Yang Chengxu, director of international studies institute], *Bimonthly Talk*, January 10, 1995, 67.

14. Suisheng Zhao, " China's Perception of International System," 141–44.

15. 习蜀光 [Xi Shuguang], 世界新格局 [the new structure of the world] (Chengdu: Sichuan People's Press, 1992), 230.

16. Brantly Womack, "Asymmetry Theory and China's Concept of Multipolarity," *Journal of Contemporary China* 13, no. 39 (May 2004).

17. Chen Xiaogong, "The World in Transition," *Beijing Review* 35, no. 5–6 (Feb. 3–16. 1992): 13–14.

18. Xiaoxiong Yi, "Chinese Foreign Policy in Transition: Understanding China's Peaceful Development," *Journal of East Asian Studies* 19, no. 1 (Spring/Summer 2005): 91–92.

19. Suisheng Zhao, "Chinese Foreign Policy under Hu Jintao: The Struggle between *taoguang yanghui* and Diplomatic Activism," *Hague Journal of Diplomacy* 5, no. 3 (October 2010): 367–69.

20. Wang Jisi, "China's Search for Stability with America," *Foreign Affairs* 84, no. 5 (September/October 2005): 40, 46.

21. Zbigniew Brzezinski, "The Group of Two That Could Change the World," *Financial Times*, January 13, 2019, https://www.ft.com/content/d99369b8-e178-11dd-afa0-0000779fd2ac; Fred Bergsten, "The Case for the US-China G-2, Peterson Perspectives," Person Institute for International Economics, July 8, 2008, https://www.piie.com/experts/peterson-perspectives/case-us-china-g-2.

22. Hugh White, *The China Choice: Why America Should Share Power* (Oxford: Oxford University Press, 2013).

23. An Gang, "Rejecting the G2: China's Rise Should Not Be Accompanied by Hegemony," *Beijing Review* 40 (October 2013), http://www.bjreview.com/print/txt/2013-09/29/content_570346.htm.

24. Raul Pedrozo, "Close Encounter at Sea: The USNS Impeccable Incident," *Naval War College Review* 62, no. 3 (Summer 2009): 100–111.

25. Cary Huang, "PLA Ramped Up China's stand on US-Korea Drill: Beijing Rhetoric Evolves from Neutral to Shrill Saber-Rattling," *South China Morning Post*, August 6, 2010, http://www.scmp.com/portal/site/SCMP/menuitem.2af62ecb329d3d7733492d9253a0a0a0/?vgnextoid=8018423df234a210VgnVCM100000360a0a0aRCRD&ss=China&s=News.

26. Li Xiaokun and Wu Jiao, "Warning Issued over Arms Sales to Taiwan," *China Daily*, January 8, 2010, http://www.chinadaily.com.cn/china/2010-01/08/content_9284287.htm.

27. Suisheng Zhao, "Shaping the Regional Context of China's Rise: How the Obama Administration Brought Back Hedge in Its Engagement with China," *Journal of Contemporary China* 21, no. 75 (May 2012).

28. "N.K. Commits 221 Provocations since 1953," *Korean Herald*, January 5, 2011, http://www.koreaherald.com/national/Detail.jsp?newsMLId=20110105000563.

29. Suisheng Zhao and Xiong Qi, "Hedging and Geostrategic Balance of East Asian Countries toward China," *Journal of Contemporary China* 25, no. 100 (2016).

30. Suisheng Zhao, "A New Model of Big Power Relations? China-US Strategic Rivalry and Balance of Power in the Asia-Pacific," *Journal of Contemporary China* 24, no. 93 (May 2015).

31. Elizabeth Economy and Adam Segal, "The G-2 Mirage," *Foreign Affairs*, May/June 2009, https://www.foreignaffairs.com/articles/east-asia/2009-05-01/g-2-mirage.

32. Jonas Parello-Plesner, "The G 2: No Good for China and for World Governance," *East Asia Forum*, May 23, 2009, https://www.eastasiaforum.org/2009/05/23/the-g-2-no-good-for-china-and-for-world-governance/.

33. "Wen Rejects Allegation of China, US Monopolizing World Affairs in Future," *Xinhua*, May 21, 2009, https://www.chinadaily.com.cn/china/2009-05/21/content_7920906.htm.

34. Minxin Pei, "Why China Won't Rule the World," *Newsweek*, December 7, 2009, http://www.newsweek.com/id/225627.

35. Zbigniew Brzezinski, *The Grand Chessboard: American Primacy and Its Geostrategic Imperatives* (New York: Basic Books, 1998), 54.

36. No author, "President Xi wraps up visit to Russia," *Xinhua*, March 24, 2013, http://europe.chinadaily.com.cn/china/2013-03/24/content_16340736.htm.

37. Editor, "Xi and Putin, Best Friends Forever?," *Foreign Affairs*, June 6, 2019, https://foreignpolicy.com/2019/06/06/xi-and-putin-best-friends-forever/.

38. "Wang Yi Speaks on the Phone with Russian Foreign Minister Sergey Lavrov," Chinese Ministry of Foreign Affairs, July 18, 2020, http://www.china-embassy.org/eng/zgyw/t1799273.htm.

39. "China-Russia Ties Deepen While US and Allies Flail," *Global Times*, March 21, 2021, https://www.globaltimes.cn/page/202103/1219002.shtml.

40. Shan Jie and Yang Sheng, "China, Russia Reaffirm Mutual Support on Core Interests, Sovereignty," *Global Times*, July 8, 2020, https://www.globaltimes.cn/content/1193952.shtml.

41. "Russian and Chinese Ambassadors: Respecting People's Democratic Rights," *National Interests*, November 26, 2021, https://nationalinterest.org/feature/russian-and-chinese-ambassadors-respecting-people%E2%80%99s-democratic-rights-197165?mc_cid=f06d85fd82&mc_eid=9df4945e7a.

42. Eduardo Baptista, "Why Russia's Vladivostok Celebration Promoted Backlash in China," *South China Morning Post*, July 2, 2020, https://www.scmp.com/news/china/diplomacy/article/3091611/why-russias-vladivostok-celebration-prompted-nationalist.

43. Robert Sutter, "How the United States Influences Russia-China Relations," National Bureau of Asian Research, February 27, 2018, http://www.nbr.org/research/activity.aspx?id=848.

44. Daniel R. Coasts, *Statement for the Record, Worldwide Threat Assessment by the US Intelligence Community to Senator Select Committee on Intelligence*, May 11, 2017, https://www.dni.gov/files/documents/Newsroom/Testimonies/SSCI%20Unclassified%20SFR%20-%20Final.pdf.

45. Neil Thompson, "The Dragon and the Lion: How China Will Win Big from Trump's Scrapping of Iran Deal," *Informed Comment*, October 5,/2018, https://www.juancole.com/2018/05/dragon-trumps-scrapping.html.

46. Ali Dadpay, "A Perspective on China-Iran Relations," *The Atlantic*, May 7, 2020, https://www.atlanticcouncil.org/blogs/iransource/how-the-coronavirus-is-cementing-irans-tilt-towards-china/.

47. Saad Ali-Qahtani, "Will the Sino-Iranian Agreement Serve the Ambitious Geopolitical Interests of China?," Carnegie Endowment for International Peace, August 2021, https://carnegieendowment.org/sada/85122.

48. Michael R. Pompeo, Secretary of State, "Communist China and the Free World's Future," US State Department, July 23, 2020, https://www.state.gov/communist-china-and-the-free-worlds-future/.

49. "Remarks by President Biden Before the 76th Session of the United Nations General Assembly," White House, September 21,2021, https://www.whitehouse.gov/briefing-room/speeches-remarks/2021/09/21/remarks-by-president-biden-before-the-76th-session-of-the-united-nations-general-assembly/.

50. Press Briefing by Press Secretary Jen Psaki and National Security Advisor Jake Sullivan, White House, March 12, 2021, https://www.whitehouse.gov/briefing-room/press-briefings/2021/03/12/press-briefing-by-press-secretary-jen-psaki-march-12-2021/.

51. 钟声 [Zhong Sheng], "冷战思维当休矣" [The Cold War mentality should stop], *People's Daily*, July 10, 2020, http://theory.people.com.cn/n1/2020/0710/c40531-31778024.html; Editorial, "China Urges US to Discard Cold War Mentality," Xinhua, July 21,2020, http://www.xinhuanet.com/english/2020-07/21/c_139227316.htm.

52. "Xi Jinping's Speech at the Virtual Davos Agenda Event," *CGTN*, January 26, 2021, accessed May 1, 2021, https://news.cgtn.com/news/2021-01-25/Full-text-Xi-Jinping-s-speech-at-the-virtual-Davos-Agenda-event-Xln4hwjO2Q/index.html.

53. Laura Zhou, "US' China Strategy Has No Bottom Line, Beijing's Former Washington Envoy Says," *South China Morning Post*, December 21, 2021, https://www.scmp.com/news/china/diplomacy/article/3160586/us-china-strategy-has-no-bottom-line-beijings-former.

54. Michael Beckley, "How Fear of China is Forging a New World Order," *Foreign Affairs*, March/April 2022, https://www.foreignaffairs.com/articles/2021-02-14/china-new-world-order-enemies-my-enemy?utm_source=religionbulletin&utm_medium=email&utm_campaign=CFRAcademicBulletin24Feb2022&utm_term=AcademicBulletin.

55. Chas W. Freeman Jr., "The Struggle with China Is Not a Replay of the Cold War," Remarks to the Asia American Forum, September 25, 2020, https://chasfreeman.net/the-struggle-with-china-is-not-a-replay-of-the-cold-war/.

56. Kerry A. Dolan, "Forbes 35th Annual World Billionaires List: Facts and Figures2021," *Forbes*, April 6, 2021, https://www.forbes.com/sites/kerryadolan/2021/04/06/forbes-35th-annual-worlds-billionaires-list-facts-and-figures-2021/?sh=3385e89d5e58.

57. 徐焰 [Xu Yan], "国防投入增加背后的历史巨变" [Magnificent historical change behind the increase in defense input], *Global Times*, March 30, 2017, http://opinion.huanqiu.com/1152/2017-03/10400006.html.

58. "China Envoy Says Xi-Putin Friendship Actually Does Have a Limit," *Bloomberg News*, March 24, 2022, https://www.bloomberg.com/news/articles/2022-03-24/china-envoy-says-xi-putin-friendship-actually-does-have-a-limit.

59. David F. Gordon, "A Trade Opportunity Washington Shouldn't Pass Up," *Washington Post,* November 10, 2011, http://www.washingtonpost.com/opinions/a-trade-opportunity-washington-shouldnt-pass-up/2011/11/10/gIQA1K3t9M_story.html?sub=AR.

60. Steven Stashwich, "Chinese Militia Vessels Departing Contested South China Sea Reef," *The Diplomat,* April 15, 2021, https://thediplomat.com/2021/04/chinese-militia-vessels-departing-contested-south-china-sea-reef/.

61. Jeff M. Smith, "Strategic Autonomy and US-India Relations," *War on the Rocks,* November 6, 2020, https://warontherocks.com/2020/11/strategic-autonomy-and-u-s-indian-relations/.

62. Yan Xuetong, "Alliances Can Present Greater Conflicts between China, United States," *Global Times,* March 31, 2016, accessed May 11, 2021, https://www.globaltimes.cn/page/201603/976746.shtml.

63. Michael Beckley, "How Fear of China is Forging a New World Order," *Foreign Affairs,* March/April 2022, https://www.foreignaffairs.com/articles/2021-02-14/china-new-world-order-enemies-my-enemy?utm_source=religionbulletin&utm_medium=email&utm_campaign=CFRAcademicBulletin24Feb2022&utm_term=AcademicBulletin.

64. Jordan Schneider, "China Talk: China's True Tech Ambitions," *Lawfare,* October 16, 2020, https://www.lawfareblog.com/chinatalk-chinas-true-tech-ambitions.

65. "习近平在省部级主要领导干部学习贯彻党的十九届五中全会精神专题研讨班开班式上发表重要讲话" [Jinping delivered an important speech at the opening ceremony of the seminar on learning and implementing the spirit of the Fifth Plenary Session of the Nineteenth Central Committee of the party], Xinhua, January 12, 2021, http://cn.chinadaily.com.cn/a/202101/12/WS5ffce6d1a3101e7ce973a3f9.html.

66. "习近平在中国科学院第十九次院士大会、中国工程院第十四次院士大会上的讲话" [Xi speech at the China academy of sciences], Xinhua, May 28, 2018, http://www.xinhuanet.com/politics/2018-05/28/c_1122901308.htm.

67. 李晓华 [Li Xiaohua], "推进产业链现代化要坚持独立自主和开发合作相促进" [The modernization of the industrial chain must adhere to the promotion of independence and development cooperation], *Guangmin Daily,* April 10, 2020, 11.

68. "我国是全世界唯一拥有全部工业门类的国家" [China is the only country in the world with all industrial categories], Xinhua, September 20, 2019, http://www.xinhuanet.com/politics/2019-09/20/c_1125020250.htm.

69. Staff writers, "Chinese Tech Companies Topple Japan, Chase US in Market Share," *Nikkei,* August 12, 2020, https://asia.nikkei.com/Business/China-tech/Chinese-tech-companies-topple-Japan-chase-US-in-market-share.

70. Eric Schmidt and Graham Allison, "Is China Winning the AI Race?," *Project Syndicate,* August 4, 2020, https://www.project-syndicate.org/commentary/china-versus-america-ai-race-pandemic-by-eric-schmidt-and-graham-allison-2020-08.

71. David Moschella And Robert D. Atkinson, "Competing with China: A Strategic Framework," Information Technology & Innovation Foundation, August 31, 2020, https://itif.org/publications/2020/08/31/competing-china-strategic-framework.

72. Thomas Hale, Harriet Agnew, Michael Mackenzie, and Demetri Sevastopulo, "Wall Street's New Love Affair with China," *Financial Times*, May 28, 2021, https://www.ft.com/content/d5e09db3-549e-4a0b-8dbf-e499d0606df4.

73. Amrita Jash, "Will Covid-19 Cost China Its 'World's Factory' Title?," *PacNet*, October 6, 2020, https://mailchi.mp/pacforum/pacnet-55-will-covid19-cost-china-its-worlds-factory-title-1170474?e=19e05c85a8.

74. Andrew J. Nathan, Bruce J. Dickson, David Gitter, Heike Holbig, and Drew Thompson, "Party Watch Annual Report 2020: Covid-19 and Chinese Communist Party Resilience," Center for Advanced China, January 25, 2021, https://www.ccpwatch.org/single-post/party-watch-annual-report-2020-covid-19-and-chinese-communist-party-resilience.

75. China Data Lab, UC San Diego," Pandemic Sees Increase in Chinese Support for Regime, Decrease in Views Towards the US," China Data Lab, July 2020, http://chinadatalab.ucsd.edu/viz-blog/pandemic-sees-increase-in-chinese-support-for-regime-decrease-in-views-towards-us/.

76. 习近平 [Xi Jinping], "在纪念中国人民抗日战争暨世界反法西斯战争胜利75周年座谈会上的讲话" [Speech at the symposium to commemorate the 75th Anniversary Of The Victory of the Chinese people's anti-Japanese war and the world antifascist war], Xinhua, September 3, 2020, http://cpc.people.com.cn/n1/2020/0904/c64094-31848723.html.

77. Andrew Erickson, "Make China Great Again: Xi's Truly Grand Strategy," *War on the Rocks*, October 30, 2019, https://warontherocks.com/2019/10/make-china-great-again-xis-truly-grand-strategy/.

78. Sarah Repucci and Amy Slipowitz, "Freedom in the World 2021: Democracy Under Siege," Freedom House, https://freedomhouse.org/report/freedom-world/2021/democracy-under-siege.

79. Secretary of State Antony Blinken, "A Foreign Policy for American People," US State Department, March 3, 2021, https://www.state.gov/a-foreign-policy-for-the-american-people/.

80. Wang Jisi, "The Plot against China? How Beijing Sees the New Washington Consensus," *Foreign Affairs*, July/August 2021, https://www.foreignaffairs.com/articles/united-states/2021-06-22/plot-against-china.

81. Howard W. French, "The US and China Are Both Failing the Global Leadership Test," *World Politics Review*, July 21, 2021, https://www.worldpoliticsreview.com/articles/29821/on-the-coronavirus-china-and-the-u-s-are-failing-the-leadership-test.

82. Lee Hisen Loong, "The Endangered Asian Century, America, China, and the Perils of Confrontation," *Foreign Affairs*, June 4, 2020, https://www.foreignaffairs.com/articles/asia/2020-06-04/lee-hsien-loong-endangered-asian-century.

Chapter 8

1. G. John Ikenberry, "The Rise of China and the Future of the West," *Foreign Affairs*, January/February 2008, https://www.foreignaffairs.com/articles/asia/2008-01-01/rise-china-and-future-west.

2. Nadège Rolland, "China's Vision for a New World Order," *NBR Special Report*, no. 83 January 27, 2020, https://www.nbr.org/wp-content/uploads/pdfs/publications/sr83_chinasvision_jan2020.pdf; Graham Allison, "The Thucydides Trap: Are the US and China Headed for War?," *The Atlantic*, September 24, 2015, http://www.theatlantic.com/international/archive/2015/09/united-states-china-war-thucydides-trap/406756/; Kevin D. Williamson, "Pandemic: The First Great Crisis of the Post-American Era," *National Review*, March 29, 2020, https://www.nationalreview.com/2020/03/coronavirus-pandemic-first-great-crisis-post-american-era/; Kurt M. Campbell and Rush Doshi, "The Coronavirus Could Reshape Global Order. China Is Maneuvering for International Leadership as the United States Falters," *Foreign Affairs*, March 18, 2020, https://www.foreignaffairs.com/articles/china/2020-03-18/coronavirus-could-reshape-global-order.

3. Paul Heer, "Understanding US-China Strategic Competition," *National Interest*, October 20, 2020, https://nationalinterest.org/feature/understanding-us-china-strategic-competition-171014.

4. 刘宏松 [Liu Hongsong], "中国参与全球治理70年: 迈向新形势下的再引领" [70 years of China's participation in global governance: Re-leading in the new situation], 国际观察 [International Outlook], no. 5 (2019), http://www.cssn.cn/gjgxx/201910/t20191016_5015006.shtml.

5. Pieter Bottelier, "China and the World Bank: How a Partnership Was Built," *Journal of Contemporary China* 16, no. 51 (2007): 341.

6. Yeling Tan, "How the WTO Changed China: The Mixed Legacy of Economic Engagement," *Foreign Affairs*, February 16, 2021, https://www.foreignaffairs.com/articles/china/2021-02-16/how-wto-changed-china.

7. Jing-dong Yuan, "The Evolution of China's Nonproliferation Policy Since the 1990s: Progress, Problems, and Prospects," *Journal of Contemporary China* 11, no. 31 (May 2002): 209–34.

8. Hu Jintao, "Unite as One and Work for a Bright Future," statement at the General Debate of the 64th session of the UN General Assembly, September 23, 2009, https://gadebate.un.org/sites/default/files/gastatements/64/64_CN_en.pdf.

9. Jing Chen, "Explaining the Change in China's Attitude toward UN Peacekeeping: A Norm Change Perspective," *Journal of Contemporary China* 18, no. 58 (2009).

10. Sunghee Cho, "China's Participation in UN Peacekeeping Operations since the 2000s," *Journal of Contemporary China* 28, no. 117 (2018).

11. Kevin Rudd, "The Coronavirus and Xi Jinping's Worldview," *Project Syndicate*, February 8, 2020, https://www.project-syndicate.org/commentary/coronavirus-will-not-change-xi-jinping-china-governance-by-kevin-rudd-2020-02.

12. Huang Peizhao, Jing Yue, and Li Xiao, "Ten Years since Arab Spring, the US Leaves a Mess, Ruin in Middle East with Interference, Imposing 'Western Democracy,'" *Global Times*, December 16, 2020, https://www.globaltimes.cn/content/1210160 .shtml.

13. 寒竹 [Han Zhu], "国际秩序与世界秩序的博弈与中国的位置" [The game between international order and world order and China's position], China Research Center, Fudan University, November 26, 2019, http://www.cifu.fudan.edu.cn/24/91/ c12233a205969/page.htm; 周新民 [Zhou Xinmin], "大变局时代呼唤世界政治领袖" [The era of great changes calls for world political leaders], *Military Net*, June 9, 2020, https://club.6parkbbs.com/military/index.php?app=forum&act=threadview &tid=15782581.

14. Eric X. Li, "The Middle Kingdom and the Coming World Disorder," *World Post*, a Partnership of the Huffington Post and Berggruen Institute on Governance, February 4, 2014, http://feedly.com/k/1e3JeDm.

15. Stewart Patrick, "World Order: What, Exactly, are the Rules?," *Washington Quarterly* 39, no. 1 (2016): 16, 18.

16. Jared McKinney and Nicholas Butts, "3 Myths about China and the South Sea Tribunal Verdict," *National Interest*, July 14, 2016, http://nationalinterest.org/ feature/3-myths-about-china-the-south-sea-tribunal-verdict-16968.

17. "Chinese President Xi Jinping's 2016 New Year Message," Ministry of Foreign Affairs of the People's Republic of China, December 31, 2015, http://www.fmprc.gov. cn/mfa_eng/wjdt_665385/zyjh_665391/t1331985.shtml; 习近平 [Xi Jinping], "加强合作推动全球治理体系变革 共同促进人类和平与发展崇高事业" [Strengthening cooperation to push for the reform of global governance system, advance human peace and development], Xinhua, September 28, 2016, http://news.xinhuanet.com/ politics/2016-09/28/c_1119641652.htm.

18. "习近平首提"两个引导"有深意" [It is profound that Xi Jinping stated the Two Guides for the first time], *Learning China*, February 21, 2017, accessed January 11, 2018, http://www.ccln.gov.cn/hotnews/230779.shtml.

19. Wenshan Jia, "China: Shifting from a Participant to a Leader of the New World Order," *China Plus*, March 1, 2017, accessed January 11, 2018, http://chinaplus.cri .cn/opinion/opedblog/23/20170301/871.html?from=groupmessage&isappinstalled=0.

20. "王毅谈2021年中国外交工作重点" [Wang Yi on the priorities of Chinese diplomatic works], *China Daily*, January 4, 2020, https://language.chinadaily.com .cn/a/202101/04/WS5ff27c44a31024adobaa03fc_1.html.

21. Xiang Bo, "China Keywords: Community with Shared Future for Mankind," Xinhua, January 24, 2018, http://www.xinhuanet.com/english/2018-01/24/c_1369 21370htm.

22. "Xi Jinping's Speech at the Virtual Davos Agenda Event," *CGTN*, January 26, 2021, https://news.cgtn.com/news/2021-01-25/Full-text-Xi-Jinping-s-speech-at-the -virtual-Davos-Agenda-event-Xln4hwjO2Q/index.html.

23. Nadège Rolland, "Testimony before the US-China Economic and Security Review Commission, A 'China Model'? Beijing's Promotion of Alternative Global Norms and Standard," National Bureau for Asian Research, April 8, 2020, https://www.nbr.org/publication/a-china-model-beijings-promotion-of-alternative-global-norms-and-standards/.

24. "Yang Jiechi Speaks with US Secretary of State Antony Blinken on the Phone at Request," Ministry of Foreign Affairs of the PRC, June 11, 2021, https://www.fmprc.gov.cn/mfa_eng/zxxx_662805/t1883497.shtml.

25. Suisheng Zhao, "A Revisionist Stakeholder: China and the Post–World War II World Order," *Journal of Contemporary China* 27, no. 113 (2018).

26. 习近平 [Xi Jinping], "推动全球治理体制更加公正更加合理" [Pushing for a more just and reasonable global governance], Xinhua, October 13, 2015, http://news.xinhuanet.com/politics/2015-10/13/c_1116812159.htm.

27. Yanzhong Huang, "Tedros, Taiwan, and Trump: What They Tell Us about China's Growing Clout in Global Health," *Council on Foreign Relations*, June 7, 2017, https://www.cfr.org/blog/tedros-taiwan-and-trump-what-they-tell-us-about-chinas-growing-clout-global-health.

28. John Pomfret, "Taiwan Must Participate in the WHO. Global Health Is Too Important to Play Politics," *Washington Post*, April 14, 2020, https://www.washingtonpost.com/opinions/2020/04/14/taiwan-must-join-who-global-health-is-too-important-play-politics.

29. Mary Hui, "The US Is Relieved That Singapore Beat Out China's Nominee as the New UN IP Agency Head," *Quartz*, March 4, 2020, https://qz.com/1809325/to-us-relief-singapore-beats-china-as-new-un-ip-agency-head/.

30. 王义桅 [Wang Yiwei], "中国在一带一路中的三大担当与使命" [China's three responsibilities and missions in the one belt one road], Xinhua, July 11, 2015, http://news.xinhuanet.com/world/2015-07/11/c_128009555.htm.

31. Samuel Kim, "Mainland China and New World Order," *Issues & Studies* 27, no. 11 (November 1991): 17.

32. 张军 [Zhang Jun], "在发展进程中促进和保护人权" [Promote and protect human rights in the process of development], 外交 [Foreign affairs journal], no. 130 (winter 2018): 8.

33. Editorial, "UN Human Rights Council Passes China's Resolution Calling for People-Centered Development for Human Rights," *Global Times*, July 13, 2021, https://www.globaltimes.cn/page/202107/1228502.shtml.

34. "Sophie, Richardson, "China's Influence on the Global Human Rights System," Human Rights Watch, September 14, 2020, https://www.hrw.org/news/2020/09/14/chinas-influence-global-human-rights-system.

35. 黄仁伟 [Huang Renwei], 从全球化、逆全球化到有选择的全球化 [From globalization and antiglobalization to selective globalization], 探索与争鸣杂志 [Exploration and contention], March 21, 2017, https://www.yicai.com/news/5251702.html.

36. David Cyranoski, "What China's Coronavirus Response Can Teach the Rest of the World," *Nature*, March 7, 2020, https://www.nature.com/articles/d41586-020-00741-x.

37. Hillary Clinton, "A National Security Reckoning: How Washington Should Think about Power," *Foreign Affairs*, November December 2020, https://www.foreignaffairs.com/articles/united-states/2020-10-09/hillary-clinton-national-security-reckoning?utm_medium=newsletters&utm_source=pre_release&utm_campaign=&utm_content=20201009&utm_term=PressCFR%2C%20Members%2C%20and%20Staff.

38. Marc L. Busch, "Tariffs Won't Make Critical US Supply Chains More Resilient," *The Hill*, June 12, 2021, https://thehill.com/opinion/international/557929-tariffs-wont-make-critical-us-supply-chains-more-resilient.

39. Philip Bowring, "China's Delusions of Regional Hegemony," *Financial Times*, August 10, 2015, http://www.ft.com/intl/cms/s/0/b8b90350-3f46-11e5-b98b-87c7270955cf.html?siteedition=intl#axzz3iTRPbCpz.

40. Zha Daojiong, "China Must See Past Its Own Hype of an America in Decline," *South China Morning Post*, June 18, 2014, http://www.scmp.com/comment/article/1535623/china-must-see-past-its-own-hype-america-decline?page=all.

41. Asian Infrastructure Investment Bank, "Policy on Prohibited Practices," May 2016, https://www.aiib.org/en/policies-strategies/operational-policies/prohibited-practices.html.

42. Wei Liang, "China's Institutional Statecraft Under Xi Jinping: Has the AIIB Served China's Interest?," *Journal of Contemporary China* 30, no. 128 (March 2021).

43. Zichen Wang, "Jin Liqun, President of AIIB, speaks on AIIB, India, Belt & Road, Coal Financing, Bretton Woods, etc." *Pekingnology*, June 20, 2021, https://pekingnology.substack.com/p/jin-liqun-president-of-aiib-speaks.

44. Kishore Mahbubani, "Helping China's Doves," *New York Times*, July 17, 2014, http://www.nytimes.com/2014/07/18/opinion/helping-chinas-doves.html.

45. Terada Takashi, "Japan and Geo-Economic Regionalism in Asia: The Rise of TPP and AIIB," *EAI Issue Briefing*, February 03, 20162018http://www.eai.or.kr/type/panelView.asp?bytag=p&catcode=+&code=eng_report&idx=14501&page=1.

46. Alan Beattie, "Europeans in the AIIB: A Sign Of Chinese Weakness," *Financial Times*, March 26, 2015, https://www.ft.com/content/6d8798d0-2ae6-34a0-9760-96ca119edda9.

47. Deborah Brautigam, "The Chinese 'Debt Trap' Is a Myth," *The Atlantic*, February 6, 2021, https://www.theatlantic.com/international/archive/2021/02/china-debt-trap-diplomacy/617953/.

48. Robert Sutter, "Watch China's Unconventional Levers of Power in World Affairs," *Japan Times*, January 8, 2020, https://www.japantimes.co.jp/opinion/2020/07/08/commentary/world-commentary/watch-chinas-unconventional-levers-power-world-affairs/.

49. Tom Phillips, "EU Backs Away from Trade Statement in Blow to China's 'Modern Silk Road' Plan," *The Guardian*, May 15, 2017, https://www.theguardian.com/world/2017/may/15/eu-china-summit-bejing-xi-jinping-belt-and-road.

50. June Teufel Dreyer, "The Tianxia Trope: Will China Change the International Order?," *Journal of Contemporary China* 24, no. 96 (November 2015).

51. Kori Schake, "How International Hegemony Changes Hands," *Cato Unbound*, March 5, 2018, https://www.cato-unbound.org/2018/03/05/kori-schake/how-international-hegemony-changes-hands.

52. Frederick Kempe, "Who China's Xi Jinping Really Wants to Win the 2020 US Election," CNBC, June 27, 2020, accessed June 27, 2020, https://www.cnbc.com/2020/06/27/op-ed-china-gains-political-influence-in-strategic-outpost-kiribati.html.

53. Yan Xuetong, "The Winner of China–US Conflict Rides on National Leadership," East Asia Forum, April 2, 2019, https://www.eastasiaforum.org/2019/04/02/the-winner-of-china-us-conflict-rides-on-national-leadership/; 王义桅 [Wang Yiwei], "打造国际话语体系的困境与路径" [Predicament and pathway in devising an international discursive system], *Aisixiang*, August 4, 2015, http://www.aisixiang.com/data/91024.html; 薛力 [Xue Li], "中国崛起的标志: 国力还是影响力" (Indicator of China's rise: National strength or influence?], Xinhua, July 27, 2015, http://www.gd.xinhuanet.com/newscenter/2015-07/27/c_1116050936.htm.

54. Robert Daly, "Why George Floyd protests Do Not Mark the Death of US Soft Power, Despite China's Glee," *South China Morning Post*, June 10, 2020, https://www.scmp.com/comment/opinion/article/3088054/why-george-floyd-protests-do-not-mark-death-us-soft-power-despite.

55. Elizabeth M. Lynch, "Do Human Rights Restrictions at Home Undermine China's Role At the UN?," *China Law and Policy*, March 30, 2020, https://chinalawandpolicy.com/2020/03/30/do-human-rights-restrictions-at-home-undermine-chinas-role-at-the-un/.

56. Zhou Xin, "Is China Rich or Poor? Nation's Wealth Debate Muddied by Conflicting Government Data," *South China Morning Post*, May 29, 2020, https://www.scmp.com/economy/china-economy/article/3086678/china-rich-or-poor-nations-wealth-debate-muddied-conflicting.

57. George Magnus, "Why a China-Centered Future Is Still Uncertain," *New Statesman*, August 10, 2021, https://www.newstatesman.com/world/asia/2021/08/why-china-centered-future-still-uncertain.

58. Max Sisher, "Behind Kazakhstan Unrest, the Strongman's Dilemma," *New York Times*, January 7, 2022, https://www.nytimes.com/2022/01/07/world/asia/kazakhstan-protests-strongmen.html.

59. Jude Blanchette and Richard McGregor, "China's Looming Succession Crisis, What Will Happen When Xi Is Gone?," *Foreign Affairs*, July 20, 2021, https://www.foreignaffairs.com/articles/china/2021-07-20/chinas-looming-succession-crisis.

60. Frederick Kempe, "Chinese Communist Party at Age 100 Confronts Growing," CNBC, June 26, 2021, https://www.cnbc.com/2021/06/26/op-ed-chinese-communist -party-at-age-100-confronts-growing-contradictions.html.

61. 中央政法委 [Central political and law commission], "做好艰苦奋斗的长 期准备 不要涨价就骂娘" [Make long-term preparations for hard work], *Tacent News*, June 1, 2020, https://xw.qq.com/cmsid/20190601A0HLM600?from=groupm essage&isappinstalled=0.

62. Josh Chin, "Xi Jinping's Leadership Style: Micromanagement That Leaves Underlings Scrambling," *Washington Post*, December 15, 2021, https://www.wsj.com/ articles/xi-jinpings-leadership-style-micromanagement-that-leaves-underlings-scram bling-11639582426.

63. Min-Hua Chiang, "China Paying a Price for Xi's Zero-COVID-19 Policy," The Heri- tage Foundation, May 13, 2022, https://www.heritage.org/asia/commentary/china-paying -price-xis-zero-covid-19-policy?mkt_tok=ODI0LU1IVCozMDQAAAGEctl1VD _SBaU7gsUV-19wr5MYxuZb_gdOTTMDcAEi1jAbRZv7f01Ygedrw_kppBcuEW MgoA4787t2fe87naPFV8mVxLFWF5z2HHht_s10CBgjbNA.

64. Donald Low, "Beijing's Insistence on Zero-Covid Strategy Challenges Long- Held Assumptions about China," *South China Morning Post*, October 22, 2021, https://www.scmp.com/week-asia/opinion/article/3153262/beijings-insistence-zero -covid-strategy-challenges-long-held.

65. Shi Yinhong, "Amid Western uncertainties, China mustn't spread too thin," *Global Times*, 26 October 2016, http://www.globaltimes.cn/content/1013884 .shtml.

66. 杨为东 [Yang Weidong], "国际关系失序化与中国的战略思考" [Strate- gic thoughts on the disorder of international relations and China], 现代国际关系 [Contemporary International Relations], no. 6 (2017): 7.

67. Eric X. Li, "The Middle Kingdom and the Coming World Disorder," *World Post*, February 4, 2014, http://feedly.com/k/1e3JeDm.

68. "Foreign Minister: Communication with Other Developing Countries at Co- penhagen Summit," Xinhua, December 18, 2009.

69. Keith Bradsher and Liz Alderman, "The World Needs Masks. China Makes Them, but Has Been Hoarding Them," *New York Times*, March 13, 2020, https:// www.nytimes.com/2020/03/13/business/masks-china-coronavirus.html.

70. Reuters staff, "Finland's Emergency Supply Agency Head Quits over Face Mask Scandal," Reuters, April 10, 2020, https://www.reuters.com/article/health-coronavirus -finland-facemasks/finlands-emergency-supply-agency-head-quits-over-face-mask -scandal-idUSL5N2BY1UY.

71. Samantha Kiernanand Serena, Tohmeand Kailey Shanks, and Basia Rosen- baum, "Politics of Vaccine Donation and Diplomacy: Is a Friend in Need a Friend Indeed?," Think Global Health, April 8, 2021, https://www.thinkglobalhealth.org/ article/politics-vaccine-donation-and-diplomacy.

72. Jamey Keaten, "Diplomats Say China Puts Squeeze on Ukraine," AP, June 25, 2021, https://apnews.com/article/united-nations-china-europe-ukraine-health -a0a5ae8f735b92e39c623e453529cbb9.

73. Reuters staff, "African Ambassadors Complain to China over 'Discrimination' in Guangzhou," Reuters, April 11, 2020, https://www.reuters.com/article/us-health -coronavirus-africa/african-ambassadors-complain-to-china-over-discrimination-in -guangzhou-idUSKCN21T0T7.

74. "Press Conference by Security Council President on Work Program for March," United Nations, March 2, 2020, https://www.un.org/press/en/2020/200302_SC.doc .htm.

75. Josh Lederman, "US Insisting That the UN Call-Out Chinese Origins of Coronavirus," NBS News, March 25, 2020, https://www.nbcnews.com/politics/ national-security/u-s-insisting-u-n-call-out-chinese-origins-coronavirus-n1169111.

76. Stewart M. Patrick, "As COVID-19 Runs Rampant, the UN Security Council Must Act," *World Politics Review*, March 30, 2020, https://www.worldpoliticsreview .com/articles/28640/as-covid-19-runs-rampant-the-u-n-security-council-must-act.

Conclusion

1. Amos Olumatoye, "How Napoleon Bonaparte Predicted the Rise of China in the 19th Century," *History Ville*, October 31, 2020, https://www.thehistoryville.com/ napoleon-bonaparte-let-china-sleep/.

2. Chris Buckley, "China's Combative Nationalists See a World Turning Their Way," *New York Times*, December 14, 2020, https://www.nytimes.com/2020/12/14/world/ asia/china-nationalists-covid.html.

3. Yang Sheng and Liu Caiyu, "American Losing Faith amid Washington Failure," *Global Times*, June 9, 2020, https://www.globaltimes.cn/content/1190981.shtml.

4. "Chinese State Media Touts '5,000 Years of trials and Tribulations,' Gearing Up for a Long Trade War," CNBC, May 14, 2019, https://www.cnbc.com/2019/05/14/ chinese-media-pushes-propaganda-campaign-as-trade-war-fight-escalates.html.

5. Suisheng Zhao, "The US-China Rivalry in the Emerging Bipolar World: Hostility, Realignment, and Power Balance," *Journal of Contemporary China* 31, no. 134 (2022).

6. David Frum, "The Coronavirus Is Demonstrating the Value of Globalization," *The Atlantic*, March 27, 2020, https://www.theatlantic.com/ideas/archive/2020/03/ dont-abandon-globalizationmake-it-better/608872/.

7. 赵可金 [Zhao Kejin], 李海涛[Li Haitao], "大国外交的权威基础——中国共产党的外交领导力研究" [The authoritative foundation of great power diplomacy- the study of the diplomatic leadership of the Communist Party of China], 东北亚论坛 [Northeast Asian Forum], no. 3 (2021): 10–13.

8. Josh Chin, "Xi Jinping's Leadership Style: Micromanagement That Leaves Underlings Scrambling," *Washington Post*, December 15, 2021, https://www.wsj.com/

articles/xi-jinpings-leadership-style-micromanagement-that-leaves-underlings-scram
bling-11639582426.

9. Josh Chin, "Xi Jinping's Leadership Style: Micromanagement That Leaves Underlings Scrambling," *Washington Post*, December 15, 2021, https://www.wsj .com/articles/xi-jinpings-leadership-style-micromanagement-that-leaves-underlings -scrambling-11639582426.

10. Graham Allison, "Grave New World," *Foreign Policy*, January 15, 2021, https:// foreignpolicy.com/2021/01/15/biden-10-challenges-foreign-policy-economy-united -states-china/.

11. Wang Jisi, "The Plot against China? How Beijing Sees the New Washington Consensus," *Foreign Affairs*, July/August 2021, https://www.foreignaffairs.com/articles/ united-states/2021-06-22/plot-against-china.

12. Fraham Allison, "The Geopolitical Olympics: Could China Win Gold?," *National Interest*, July 29, 2021, https://nationalinterest.org/feature/ geopolitical-olympics-could-china-win-gold-190761?page=0%2C1.

13. 金灿荣 [Jin Canrong], "展望未来十年国际格局'两超多强'与'双文明冲突'" [Looking forward to the next ten years, the international pattern of 'two superpowers, multiple powers' and 'dual civilization conflicts'], *South China Urbanity*, September 29, 2019, http://www.sinotf.com/GB/Person/134/2017-09-29/4NMDAwMDI3NjE4Nw .html.

14. Paul Heer, "Understanding US-China Strategic Competition," *National Interest*, October 20, 2020, https://nationalinterest.org/feature/ understanding-us-china-strategic-competition-171014.

15. Fu Ying, "Cooperative Competition Is Possible between China and the United States," *New York Times*, November 24, 2020, https://www.nytimes.com/2020/11/24/ opinion/china-us-biden.html.

16. 习近平 [Xi Jinping], 在全国党校工作会议上的讲话 [Speech at the national CCP school work conference], 求是 [Qiushi], May 1, 2015, http://cpc.people.com .cn/n1/2016/0501/c64094-28317481.html.

17. Carla Freeman, "Reading Kindleberger in Beijing: Xi Jinping's China as a Provider of Global Public Goods," *British Journal of Politics and International Relations*, September 2020, https://doi.org/10.1177/1369148120941401.

Index